THE STAGES OF
SOCIAL RESEARCH

THE STAGES OF
SOCIAL RESEARCH

DAVID CAPLOVITZ

The City University of New York

A Wiley-Interscience Publication

JOHN WILEY & SONS

New York   Chichester   Brisbane   Toronto   Singapore

Library of Congress Cataloging in Publication Data:

Caplovitz, David.
        The stages of social research.

        "A Wiley-Interscience publication."

        Includes index.
        1. Sociology—Research.   2. Social sciences—Research.
3. Proposal writing in the social sciences.   4. Report
writing.   I. Title.

HM48.C36   1983   300'.72   83-6466
ISBN 0-471-08781-5

Printed in the United States of America

10 9 8 7 6 5 4 3 2 1

To Paul F. Lazarsfeld,
The man who showed us the way

PREFACE

This book is the outgrowth of more than 30 years in the research business. In 1950, as a fledgling graduate student at Columbia University, I took a job in the machine room of the Bureau of Applied Social Research, working at a counter sorter for 90 cents an hour. The next year I was promoted to coder, and I soon began work as an interviewer on a number of Bureau studies. I remained at the Bureau for 12 years, achieving the status of study director. In 1962 I left the Bureau and Columbia for two years to join the National Opinion Research Center and the Sociology Department at the University of Chicago. In 1964 I returned to Columbia and the Bureau of Applied Social Research where I was an associate professor of sociology, a director of training, and a study director. In 1971 I joined the City University of New York's Graduate School where, over the next 10 years, I directed three major research projects. In all, I have been the director of a dozen studies and I have published eight books based on my research projects.

I present this brief review of my research career to establish an important fact: this book was written by an experienced researcher. It is organized in terms of the stages of a large-scale research project. Its four sections correspond to the four stages of the research process. As I point out in the first section, it is impossible to do large-scale social research without money. Therefore, a critical research task is writing a proposal that will generate the research money. Part 1 of this book deals with proposal writing. Once the research money is raised, the researcher must go out and collect the data for the study. Part 2 of this book deals with data collection, more specifically, the collection of data through survey research. Inasmuch as the questionnaire is the essential research tool of survey research, this section is limited to the development and use of questionnaires. Once the data have been collected, the researcher must analyze them to generate findings. Part 3 of this book deals with data analysis. Once the researcher has analyzed the data, he or she must write a research report; Part 4 deals with report writing. Data collection and data analysis are themes that are covered in all methods textbooks, but proposal writing and report writing are themes unique to this book. I am prepared to write about these topics because, as a researcher for 30 years, I have written numerous proposals and research reports.

Because this textbook grew out of my own experience in the research business, it is a highly personal document, perhaps the only textbook in which the first person singular figures prominently. At least five of the chapters are based on my own work. Two of the chapters in Part 1 are based on proposals that I wrote. One of the chapters in Part 2, Data Collection, is based on an unpublished paper I wrote for Paul F. Lazarsfeld in 1959 on the role of qualitative data in a quantitative study. Part of Chapter 6 is a history of a questionnaire that I wrote for Lazarsfeld in the late 1950s. And the chapter on contextual analysis in Part 3 is based on another unpublished paper I wrote for Lazarsfeld in 1956.

As these examples make clear, Paul F. Lazarsfeld had a profound influence on my research career. I learned much about research working for him on his *Academic Mind* project. This was an exhilarating experience. That study was based on two-stage sampling, first of colleges and then of teachers within colleges. This research design made possible contextual analysis, that is, showing how professors who comprised the sample were influenced by the groups to which they belonged. I was put in charge of the contextual analysis and, under Paul's tutelage, in 1956 I wrote the first paper ever written on contextual analysis. Since there was no pressure from Paul or anyone else to have it published, the origin of contextual analysis is credited to others. I was in the middle of my graduate school career when I worked for Paul, but he had a way of treating us all as colleagues rather than students and I matured quickly as a researcher under him. As Paul wrote drafts of the chapters of the book that emerged from this project, he would give us copies to read and criticize. Some of my headiest experiences as a graduate student occurred at the staff meetings he called to discuss his chapters. On these occasions, I would tell him what I thought was wrong with his chapters and how he might improve them. He took such criticism in an extremely graceful way and he made us all feel that we had important roles to play in the writing of his book.

Paul's style of research gave rise to the phrase "the Columbia tradition of research," and I am a student of that tradition. The Columbia tradition emphasized tabular analysis over regression analysis. Many of us got our Ph.D.s at Columbia with only a glimmering of the workings of regression analysis and other high-powered statistical procedures. All Bureau studies were based on large samples and Paul knew that percentage differences of 10 points or more would be statistically significant, so we never bothered to compute tests of significance. The absence of such tests and measures of correlation, which we never bothered to compute either, were marks of the Columbia tradition. Paul believed in ad hoc index construction rather than factor analysis. We all learned to evaluate indicators and throw them to-gether into indices, a procedure that is reviewed in Chapter 9 of this book. Paul also believed that laymen could not understand tables (he preferred bar charts) and he taught us to introduce our tables by stating their message and then summarizing the message after presenting the table. Paul was the guardian of clear writing about data. He himself wrote most lucidly and his books are testimonials to clear writing. Those of us who learned research from him also came to write clearly about data and I consider such clarity the hallmark of the Columbia tradition associated with Lazarsfeld.

Paul believed that the case method was the best way to instruct people in research. He had us keep histories of the questionnaires we developed, a technique that inspired Chapter 6 of this book. He also had us write histories of our research projects and our analyses of the data. His goal, never realized, was to generate casebooks based on these histories, which would teach people how to do research. This commitment to the case method is evidenced in Chapters 2 through 7 and Chapter 9 of this book and it influences other chapters as well. Paul Lazarsfeld influenced several genera-tions of sociologists and I am proud to be one of them. It is a great pleasure to dedicate this book to him.

DAVID CAPLOVITZ

New York
August 1983

ACKNOWLEDGMENTS

Several people have made enormous contributions to this book and it is a pleasure to acknowledge them. My most heartfelt thanks go to Robert K. Merton, who graciously allowed me to use many examples of his editorial work in Chapter 16 dealing with the art of writing. Mark Gallops did a superb job writing the chapter on regression analysis (Chapter 12), and I am extremely grateful to him. My good friend Sam Sieber contributed an unpublished paper dealing with qualitative data in survey research which is used in Chapter 7 as well as a history of a questionnaire which appears in Chapter 6. Patricia Nash kindly allowed me to use her history of a questionnaire in the same chapter. And three people gave me permission to use their proposals to illustrate good proposals, Allan D. Heskin, Henry M. Levin, and Theresa Rogers. My thanks go to each of them. A book that covers many topics, some of which are quite complex, is bound to contain errors and responsibility for these errors rests solely with me.

D.C.

CONTENTS

PART ONE

Proposal Writing

Proposal writing is a critical research task, yet it is never covered in textbooks on research methods. One reason for this omission is that many writers of these textbooks have never written proposals—indeed, they have never done research. Another reason may be that proposal writing is viewed as a creative act, one that does not lend itself to principles that can be conveyed to the novice. I am convinced that principles of good proposal writing do exist and can be taught. And I feel that the best way to learn about proposal writing is the case method. Following a discussion of some principles of proposal writing in Chapter 1, I present cases of winning proposals in Chapters 2 and 3 and a case of a losing proposal in Chapter 4. A reading of these proposals should provide some instruction in proposal writing.

1

Some Principles of Proposal Writing

Funded research in social science invites considerable cynicism and confusion. In some circles soliciting money for research is considered to be selling out to the establishment that controls research funds: since the ruling class will give money only to research that legitimizes its power, anyone who does funded research is serving the interests of the ruling class. This is the radical critique of funded research. At the other extreme is the conservative view: pure research is the domain of the lone scholar who has no need for large sums of money to pursue the truth. Money would only corrupt the lone scholar by distracting from the pursuit of unpopular but essential truths.

These critiques of funded research are voiced by those at the margin of social science disciplines. The people at the center of the disciplines, those who push back the frontiers of knowledge through their research, fully understand that funded research is essential to scientific enterprise. They know that most research projects are extremely costly in terms of time and money. To do serious research in any discipline—anthropology, sociology, psychology, political science, or economics—one must have money to pay for data collection and to buy time from other duties such as teaching. Moreover, many research projects require a team of people to carry them out and however much people might be motivated by the joy of discovery, they need money to live. Whatever one's politics, it is increasingly essential to have money to carry out research in the physical sciences and the social sciences today.

The radical critique of funded research is contradicted by government-sponsored research that has questioned cherished values and beliefs of the dominant culture. For example, the National Institute on Drug Abuse funded research on marijuana use in Jamaica that showed that marijuana was not only not harmful to its users but actually helpful to them, research that has contributed much to the movement to decriminalize marijuana. Consider as well government-sponsored research bearing on the recent movement in the United States for workers to take over plants that corporations want to shut down. Workers thus become owners, following the Yugo-slavian model of self-management. Several government agencies have sponsored research on worker-owned plants designed to find out how successful this experiment is and how to make it more successful.

Another topic of concern to some radicals is how class-conscious the working class is, for, according to Marx, the working class will move to change the social structure only if it is conscious of its self-interests. Research on the class-consciousness of workers has been going on for some time with government grants and foundation grants, as a by-product of studies of the morale of assemblyline workers and the connection between mental health and the economy. As these examples suggest, it is always possible to package a research interest in terms that broaden its appeal and make it seem less controversial. Instead of focusing on class-consciousness, one would discuss the problem of workers' morale and the conditions that affect it, which would inevitably shed light on class-consciousness.

An extremely popular research style in the social sciences is survey research. Surveys have been conducted in a wide range of areas: voting behavior, juvenile delinquency, mass communications, drug abuse, religious behavior, marriage and the family, and so on. Many surveys have incorporated the panel design and have been extended over months and years. The typical survey invovles a fairly large sample, often several thousand cases. Interviewing costs have risen sharply in the past decade and it now costs anywhere from $50 to $100 per case in national surveys. Interviewing costs alone for a major survey can run from $100,000 to $150,000 or more. Clearly no social scientist can conduct a survey without major funding. In sum, if social scientists are to push back the frontiers of knowledge through research, they must get outside funding. And the manner in which this is done is through submitting a research proposal to a funding agency. Anyone who would be a worthy social scientist must learn how to write a proposal. The purpose of Part 1 of this book is to provide some pointers on proposal writing. I do not pretend to know everything about good proposal writing, but I hope that by making this topic explicit in a methods textbook, the attention of the profession can be directed to the principles of proposal writing. In turn, as more proposal writers take the trouble to formalize the principles of this activity, the art of proposal writing can be transmitted to each new generation of social researchers.

TYPES OF PROPOSALS

Research proposals tend to fall into two basic types defined by the source of the research idea. One source of research ideas is *theory*; the other source is some practical *problem* in the world. The theoretically oriented proposal identifies some hypothesis that bears on a theory that must be tested. The theory will be either confirmed or sharply modified depending on the outcome of the test of the new hypothesis. Theoretically oriented proposals are less common in sociology than in psychology, which has many more empirically verified theories. These two types of proposal, the theoretically oriented and the problem oriented, are very different and have different organizational schemes.

The theoretically oriented proposal usually stems from some idea that occurs to the researcher that challenges or elaborates on some widely held theory. For example, there has been a vast tradition of research in psychology dealing with subliminal perception. Among these experiments have been those that have tested reaction time to "dirty" words. This research has found that subjects take longer to recognize dirty than nondirty words. One interpretation of these results is that people tend to reject unpleasant words rather than recognize them. According to this theory, people correctly perceived the dirty word on some unconscious level and then engaged in a process of denying what they read so that the conscious mind would not learn that what was read was a dirty word. Note that this theory assumes subconscious perception and a mechanism of suppression of the unpleasant. Someone might read about these experiments and their interpretation and come up with a totally different interpretation. For example, it might occur to one that word recognition is dependent on familiarity with the word. Since dirty words are seen in print much less frequently than nondirty words, most people are unfamiliar with the printed version of dirty words. Thus, a counterhypothesis would be that the reason dirty words take longer to recognize is that they are less familiar. The person would then design an experiment to test this idea, perhaps utilizing four classes of words ranging from those widely known to those that are rare. The reaction time of words in these four classes would be compared with the reaction time to dirty words. This is theoretically oriented research.

Another example is a study dealing with the right and left hemispheres of the brain that I would like to do to test a theory of mine. Since thinking (left hemisphere) is silent speech, how do late talkers (those who do not talk until age 3) think? My answer: they learn to think with their right hemisphere; that is, they think in pictures. These late talkers grow up to have right-hemisphere brains, meaning they are more intuitive, more creative, more artistic, and the like, than left hemisphere people. I want to test this hypothesis by studying age of speech among children and relating this to the children's artistic talents. Obviously, this is a theoretically oriented study.

Problem-oriented proposals are of a different order. The originating idea stems from some concern or puzzlement about something in the real world, such as unemployment, inflation, drug abuse, alcoholism, divorce, single parents, poverty, welfare families, teenage mothers, juvenile delinquency, debt entanglement, communal living, child abuse, spouse abuse, pollution. The researcher's goal in doing such a study is to learn as much as possible about the problem: how widespread it is, the kinds of people that are affected by it, its apparent causes and consequences. Whereas in theoretically oriented research it is appropriate to specify hypotheses, hypotheses are not really relevant to problem-oriented research. There are no theories of these problems that need to be tested. Unfortunately, many of the proposals for such studies do list hypotheses, but these tend to be stilted and awkward since they are not based on an underlying theory.

In writing a proposal for a problem study, the researcher would be better advised to list questions that the research is designed to answer rather than hypotheses. For example:

1. Are men more likely to have this problem than women?
2. Are poor people more likely to have the problem than rich people?
3. Does the problem have implications for physical and mental health?
4. What are the economic, social, and psychological costs of the problem?

What is interesting about such questions is that they apply to every one of the problems listed above and they probably apply to all problem-oriented studies. Whatever the problem, the researcher wants to know its extent, the characteristics of the people who have the problem, the costs of the problem, and so forth.

The structure of the proposal is somewhat different for the theoretically oriented study than it is for the problem-oriented one. In the theory proposal there is little need to justify the research since it bears on a known theory. But in the problem-oriented study, the researcher must do a selling job. After all, each researcher is competing against a number of other problem-oriented proposals. In the discussion of proposals that follows I am concerned primarily with the problem-oriented proposal, largely because most funding sources are problem oriented.

SOURCES OF RESEARCH FUNDS

There are two basic sources of research funds, private foundations and the federal government; industry may become a more important source in the future. Private foundations tend to give out much smaller sums than the federal government and most expensive research, like surveys, usually is funded by the federal government. Almost all the federal granting agencies have proposal forms that must be used in applying. These forms specify the various topics that must be covered in the proposal. Foundations do not generally have specific application forms. Proposals submitted to federal agencies are evaluated by peer review committees, generally of nine or ten members who are almost exclusively academics. For these various reasons, proposals submitted to the government tend to be much longer than those submitted to foundations. They generally range from 20 to 50 pages, although some run to more than 100 pages. The five proposals that I wrote that resulted in major funding ranged from 20 to 40 pages in length. Proposals should not be too long and those who write 70- and 100-page proposals are making a mistake. If nothing else, they are imposing on the members of the review committee.

Contracts Versus Grants

Government research money is given out under two different arrangements, contracts and grants. In contract research, the researchers enter into a legal contract with the funding agency. The basic difference between contracts and grants concerns the origin of the research idea. Frequently the funding agency wants a piece of research done. For example, all the agencies that sponsor action programs need research to evaluate the programs. When the agency wants to learn something, it will prepare a document specifying the kind of study wanted and inviting research firms to submit proposals for such a study. This document is known as an RFP, a Request for a Proposal. The RFP might be sent to hundreds of research firms, resulting in dozens of proposals. The funding agency staff evaluates these proposals and chooses one. It then enters a contract with the research firm that will carry out the study. Contract research is generally limited to profit-making firms, whereas academic research is funded under the grant system. When the idea for the research stems from the researcher, he or she writes a proposal and submits it to a funding agency for possible sponsorship. The funding agency, if it approves, issues a grant to the researcher.

The rules regulating contracts are different from the rules regulating grants. All research instruments developed for contract research, including questionnaires, must be approved by the Office of Management and Budget, and this can lead to considerable problems for the researcher, who often must defend questions from the OMB critics. A contract specifies the completion of the research report by a certain date; if it is not completed in time, the government can, in principle, sue the research firm. The recipient of a grant, in contrast, does not have to show any instruments to the OMB and is not held to a completion date. Unfortunately, all too many grant recipients do not live up to their promises and do not produce a final report by the prescribed date, and sometimes they never produce one. They cannot be sued. In this chapter, I have in mind the kind of proposal written for a grant rather than a contract proposal written in responses to an RFP.

Government Agencies

Numerous branches of the federal government sponsor research, from the Agriculture Department, to the Commerce Department, to the Energy Department, to the Departments of Education and of Health and Human Resources, formerly Health, Education and Welfare. These various government departments tend to be interested in problem-oriented research. The one government agency clearly prepared to sponsor theoretically oriented research is the National Science Foundation, which has a division dealing with sociology. The government agencies most likely to sponsor social research are located in the Public Health Service. Within this superagency are the National Institute of Mental Health, the National Institute on Drug Abuse, the National Institute on Alcohol Abuse and Alcoholism, the National Institute on Aging, and the National Institute of Child Health and Human Development. These agencies support the large bulk of social science research in the United States.

THE INGREDIENTS OF A PROPOSAL

As noted, each agency generally has a specific form that must be used in preparing the application for a grant. The form used by the National Institute of Mental Health—which includes agencies dealing with sex, discrimination and minority groups, the economy and occupations, aging and children—is typical. The first page requires the name and address of the principal investigator, the name and address of the sponsoring institution, and the signature of the projects and grants officer of the institution. The second page requires the names and social security numbers of all the professional personnel on the project and an abstract of the proposed research. The third and fourth pages deal with the budget. Pages 5 and as many pages as are necessary are for the biographical sketches of the professional personnel, beginning with the principal investigator (the government's term for the grantee). The biographical sketches are then followed by the heart of the proposal, the section entitled Research Plan and Supporting Data. This section must be organized according to NIMH's specifications as follows:

   A. Research plan
      1. Specific aims
      2. Methods of procedure
      3. Significance of this research
      4. Facilities available
   B. Supporting data
      1. Previous work done on proposed research
      2. Results obtained by others
      3. Pertinent literature references

It is the quality of the Research Plan and Supporting Data section that determines whether a grant will be awarded. This section of the proposal generally runs from 15 to 40 pages.

The first item in the outline refers to the specific aims of the research. It is here that the researcher must do a good selling job pointing out why it is terribly important to do research on this problem. In this section the researcher specifies the topics that will be covered in the research and what is to be learned from it. It is in this section that the types of questions to be answered are listed.

The second topic in the outline is Methods of Procedure. Here the researcher must list research plans. A researcher proposing to do a survey must say something about the sampling plan and the size of the sample. If a questionnaire is to be used, the topics that will be covered in it should be specified, and sample questions might be helpful. Plans for analyzing the data must be presented. Analytical techniques, such as factor analysis, regression analysis, path analysis, or whatever, must be described. The purpose here is to persuade the members of the review committee that the principal investigator is knowledgeable in the methods of data analysis, especially modern, sophisticated methods. A researcher planning to do a panel study would be well advised to demonstrate an awareness of the latest developments in panel analysis. In evaluating proposals, the members of the review committee give as much importance to the methods section as to the specific aims section.

The third topic under the research plan is Significance of the Research. As NIMH puts it: "What is the potential importance of the proposed work? Discuss any novel ideas or contributions which the project offers. Make clear the health-related implications of the research." This section tends to overlap considerably with the Specific Aims section.

The last topic in the research plan, Facilities Available, is more appropriate to biomedical research than to social research. Here the proposal writer would mention the laboratories in which the research will be done and the space that the sponsoring institution is ready to provide for this research. For social research proposals there are no laboratories, but availability of computer facilities is equally important. The Facilities Available section of the proposal is quite short, often not more than a paragraph or two.

Part II of the proposal according to the NIMH guideline, deals with Supporting Data. Here the proposal writer must list the previous research that has been done on the subject, report the results obtained by others, and provide a bibliography on the subject. The Review of the Literature section is very important and reviewers tend to pay close attention to it. The length of this section depends on how much work has been done in the problem area under discussion. For example, divorce is a topic that has generated considerable research, but inflation is a problem that has been studied only by economists, not by sociologists, psychologists, or anthropologists. Juvenile delinquency and minority groups and drug abuse are also topics that have been heavily researched, but spouse abuse and communal living and debt entanglement are relatively new problems and hence there is not an extensive literature on these topics. The researcher who is writing a proposal on a topic that has been heavily researched is obligated to carry out an extensive review of the literature; if this review is not substantial, the proposal will likely be rejected. Reviewing the literature can be a time-consuming process; fortunately, computer-generated annotated bibliographies are now available on virtually any topic. These greatly simplify the process of reviewing the literature.

Not only is an extensive review of the literature necessary, but the principal investigator who can cite his or her own research in the bibliography has a distinct advantage in possibly being considered an expert on the problem under study. Of course, the person writing a first proposal is at a corresponding disadvantage. Given the emphasis that some reviewers place on the review of the literature, the chances of getting funded are perhaps somewhat greater if the problem that has been chosen for study is a relatively new one that has not been researched in the past. In 1966 I was able to get a substantial grant to do a study of the problem of debt entanglement, in part, I think, because this was a relatively new problem. In any event, when the problem chosen for study is relatively new, preparing the supporting data section of the proposal is greatly simplified.

SOME STRATEGIES FOR PROPOSAL WRITING

Members of review committees tend to be from different disciplines, a mixture of sociologists, psychologists, anthropologists, and perhaps political scientists. The methods of research tend to vary from discipline to discipline. Sociologists and psychologists are accustomed to doing quantitative research but political scientists and anthropologists are likely to have a bias in favor of qualitative research. This mixture of the review committees is one reason why the principal investigator planning a survey should make plans to include qualitative data in the research design. The proposal may note that before the survey is carried out, depth interviews will be done with a small sample of respondents. Stressing qualitative as well as quantitative methods not only improves the chances of getting funded, but it is also likely to improve the research product. Many quantitative studies are greatly enriched by qualitative data (Chapter 7 deals with this topic in some detail).

Another strategy that I have found useful is to break up the problem under study into several different but related studies and point out how each study will enhance our knowledge of the problem. If this strategy is employed, then separate budgets can be developed for each component. Although this strategy may not increase the chances of getting funded, it has several important advantages for the principal investigator once the study is funded. For one thing, funds can be shifted from one study to another if needed. This flexibility in the budget is frequently of great help in managing the project. Another advantage is that one can live up to the terms of the grant and still produce fewer than the initially promised number of reports. If, for example, the proposal specifies three separate studies on the problem and only two are completed, no one is likely to fault the researcher. In the study of debt entanglement that I did in 1966, I pointed out in the proposal that we would interview approximately 1500 debtors in default in four cities. But in addition to this survey, I said we would do a qualitative study of collection lawyers and a quantitative study of industry's experience with garnishment orders, a legal device for collecting debts. The proposal specified separate budgets for the collection lawyer study and the industry survey. In fact, almost all the research was devoted to the survey of default debtors and it was this study that led to the book *Consumers in Trouble: A Study of Debtors in Default.** We did not study collection lawyers. A survey of industry's experience with garnishment orders was carried out but it was documented only in the doctoral thesis of one of the research associates on this project and it was never written up as a separate report for the client. But the client was so pleased with the report he received on debtors in default that he did not seem to mind the missing report. Of course, not all topics lend themselves to substudies, but where it is appropriate the proposal writer might well consider this strategy.

Another tactic that ought to be given serious consideration by the proposal writer is the use of consultants. The NIMH budget page has a line for consultants and it is fairly common for proposal writers to list one or two consultants for their project at a cost generally ranging from $1000 to $3000 per year. If the proposal writer knows some experts in the proposed area of study, why not consider soliciting them as consultants? The consultant's vita becomes one of the biographical sketches included with the proposal, and having well-known experts as consultants probably enhances the appeal of the proposal in the eyes of the reviewers.

SELLING YOUR RESEARCH IDEA

As noted, a problem-oriented proposal must persuade the reviewers that the problem to be studied is an extremely important one. The proposal writer must be so convincing that the reviewers are made to feel that they will be doing irreparable harm if they do not fund the study. This selling job is a matter of "packaging" the proposal. The packaging of the proposal is carried out in the opening paragraphs of the first section on specific aims. These opening paragraphs can present either an exciting or a fairly routine and even dull package for the proposal. The more exciting the package, the greater the chances that the proposal will be funded.

*New York: Free Press, 1974.

To illustrate this idea of packaging, I will draw on some of my own proposals and one of a colleague. One of my proposals was for a study of youngsters—preteens—experimenting with drugs. It began as follows:

> This proposal sets forth plans for a longitudinal study of pre-teens, ten to twelve year olds in a high risk community, in order to learn about the processes that ensnare some youngsters into the world of drug use and abuse and permit others to escape the hazards of drugs. Experimentation with drugs is very much a youth phenomenon, as countless studies have documented, and the sad fact is that exposure to drugs takes place at an ever earlier age. Today many children as young as eight, nine, ten or eleven are exposed to and experiment with drugs.

The selling point in this proposal was the very young age at which youngsters in a high-risk community are exposed to drugs. Later in this proposal this age theme came up again:

> As noted, this research studies a critical stage in the socialization process of youngsters growing up in a community where there is a high risk of drug abuse. The 10 to 12 year old period is when the primary agency of socialization shifts from the family to the peer group. In the middle class, the primacy of the family may extend into the early teens, but in low income communities, the young quickly become absorbed into peer cultures and even from the age of eight or nine peer influence tends to predominate over familial influence in the shaping of the value-orientations, attitudes and personalities of the young.

As noted earlier, a very important section of a proposal is the review of the literature, which usually takes up quite a bit of space. But in this proposal for a study of preteens and drug abuse, the review of the literature was carried out in three paragraphs and only two studies were cited; in spite of the vast array of drug research, hardly anyone had studied drug use among preteens. The very fact that virtually no research had been done in this area became a major selling point for the proposal.

The next proposal, which was submitted to the National Science Foundation, also dealt with a seldom researched problem. It was called "Debt Entanglement and Personal Bankruptcy: A Major Problem and a Potential Solution."

> One of the most pressing problems undermining the mental health of millions of Americans has received scant attention from social scientists and policy makers alike and that is the problem of debt entanglement. This problem is the direct result of a major change that has taken place in our economy since World War II. Within the span of a generation, America has been transformed from a cash to a credit society. Whereas debt was once frowned upon as the mark of the imprudent man, today debt is part of the American way of life. The growth of consumer credit has truly been explosive. In 1955, outstanding consumer installment debt amounted to 29 billion dollars. This figure does not include mortgage and such noninstallment debt as charge accounts and debts for

professional services such as medical bills. By 1965 outstanding installment debt had climbed to 66 billion and by 1975 it had more than doubled again reaching 150 billion. It took only five years for the figure to double again. By the end of 1980 outstanding installment debt had soared to 305 billion. This comes to more than $5000 in installment debt for every American family.

By encouraging consumption, consumer credit has been a great boon to the economy and it is largely responsible for the postwar affluence. At the same time, it has given rise to a new, pervasive and serious social problem: debt entanglement. Each year, more than seven million workers have their wages garnisheed to meet their unpaid debts. Extrapolating from this figure to those who cannot be garnisheed because they are federal employees or because they live in a state where garnishment is prohibited or because they are on welfare or are unemployed or self-employed or who have not yet been garnisheed although they are deep in debt, it is safe to conclude that anywhere from 15 to 20 million Americans are deeply entangled in debt. The research of the principal investigator of this proposal has shown that debt entanglement wreaks havoc with the lives of default debtors. It tends to undermine their jobs, their health and their marriages. More than half of a sample of default debtors said that their health had been adversely affected by their debt problem, an equal number reported that their marriages had suffered and a substantial minority lost their jobs because of their debts.

Not all Americans are equally vulnerable to the problem of debt entanglement. Previous research has shown that the working class and the poor as distinct from the middle class are especially prone to this problem and minority groups, the blacks and the hispanic speaking, are much more likely to suffer from debt entanglement than the whites. A solution to the problem of debt entanglement would do much to improve the lives of these minorities and enhance their chances of succeeding in society.

In sum, debt entanglement is a major social problem undermining the mental health of millions of people and yet, oddly enough, this problem is largely unrecognized. A popular course in sociology is entitled "social problems" and there are hundreds of social problems textbooks. They have chapters dealing with crime, divorce, unemployment, drug addiction, alcoholism, juvenile delinquency and mental illness, but none of these textbooks deal with debt entanglement. And in spite of the millions affected and the great harm done to their lives, we have yet to hear a public outcry over indebtedness. There is no war on debt entanglement. One aim of the proposed research is to increase public consciousness of this problem and direct attention to the need to find solutions to it.

Ironically, there is a "cure" for this debilitating social problem of debt entanglement: bankruptcy. Almost two hundred years before debt entanglement became so pervasive as to constitute a social problem, the founding fathers provided constitutional authority for a national bankruptcy law. In 1800 the first bankruptcy act was passed by Congress which permitted businesses to go into bankruptcy and in 1871, Congress passed a statute that permitted all debtors, including individuals, to declare bankruptcy and in 1898 a revised bankruptcy law was enacted that existed until September of 1979 when a new bankruptcy law was enacted. The new bankruptcy law is much more liberal than the old one. In many business circles it is being criticized as being a stimulus to bankruptcy.

In spite of this longstanding cure that came into existence well in advance of the problem, only a tiny fraction of those entrapped in debt take advantage of this remedy. In the late sixties and early seventies, personal bankruptcies numbered about 168,000 a year. In 1975, under the pressures of the recession, personal bankruptcies soared to 250,000. But even so this constitutes less than 2 per cent of those eligible for this remedy. In the years after 1975 personal bankruptcies declined to under 200,000 but under the most recent recession of 1980, personal bankruptcies have again soared to 250,000. The critics of the new bankruptcy law blame it for the high rate in 1980 but it is much more likely that the economy is at fault, just as the economy caused the very high bankruptcy rate in 1975.

A major purpose of the proposed research is to find out why the bankruptcy law has not been more successful. More specifically, we intend to learn why some of those afflicted with debt entanglement do file for bankruptcy while many others, similarly afflicted, do not. Such a study is particularly appropriate at this time, a year or so after the enactment of the new law. We will be in a position to evaluate the new law and learn how its provisions have influenced the decision of debtors to file for bankruptcy. At the same time the research will increase our knowledge of the problem of debt entanglement, that is, the processes through which some people find themselves hopelessly entrapped in debt.

As this text indicates, this proposal was packaged around the discovery of a new social problem, one that affected millions of people and had dire social consequences: debt entanglement. Part and parcel of this new social problem is a mystery: there is a solution to the problem but almost no one is taking the cure. Why? The review of the literature for this proposal dealt almost exclusively with the potential solution, personal bankruptcy. A handful of empirical studies of bankruptcy had been carried out which showed the social characteristics of people who declare bankruptcy and a somewhat larger literature existed on the legal aspects of bankruptcy. But the only work on debt entanglement was my earlier study of debtors in default.

Still a third example of persuasive packaging is provided by the proposal I wrote in 1974 for a study of the impact of inflation and recession on American families that was submitted to NIMH:

The United States is now undergoing its most severe economic crisis since the Great Depression of the thirties. We are currently experiencing a staggering rate of inflation well into double digits (at this writing, pressing 15 percent a year). At the same time, contrary to all economic theory, we are experiencing a severe recession, as the unemployment rate has risen above 7 percent and the Gross National Product has steadily declined, sure symptoms of a recession that might well mushroom into full-scale depression. This double bind of rampant inflation and recession has given rise to a new coinage by economists, "stagflation" or even more dramatically, "slumpflation."

Just as the Great Depression was a worldwide phenomenon, so the current rampant inflation is devastating all the major countries of the world. In Britain the inflation rate is beyond 16 percent; in Japan it is over 25 percent, a rate comparable to that of Italy; in Greece the inflation rate is 34 percent and in Israel it is even higher. Only Canada, Sweden, and West Germany have managed to keep their inflation rates well below 15 percent.

Economists have diagnosed the current inflation as both "demand-pull" inflation in which consumer demand far exceeds the supply of goods and services
(too much money chasing too few goods) and as "cost-push" inflation in which
rising costs of labor push prices ever higher. The general consensus is that both
of these forces are now at work, reinforcing each other in an ever upward spiral
of prices. Underlying these inflationary pressures are decidedly new features
of the world economy such as the energy crisis and the general scarcity of
essential resources. The consensus among most scholars is that the current
inflation, with or without recession, is a long-range phenomenon not likely to
recede in the near future. In fact, we may be on the verge of a new society, one
in which inflation is endemic to our way of life. In a variety of circles, the alarm
has been raised that hyperinflation can lead to the downfall of our democratic
society. President Ford has identified inflation as "public enemy number 1"
and the conservative Arthur Burns, Chairman of the Federal Reserve, recently
observed, "if long continued, inflation at anything like the present rate would
threaten the very foundations of our society." The highly prestigious journal
Skeptic, published by the Forum of Contemporary History, recently devoted a
special issue to inflation. The lead editorial of this issue warns that inflation
can sap our freedom and bring down our democratic society, in much the way
that Uruguay in the past decade has been transformed from a thriving democracy to a bankrupt dictatorship under the pressure of inflation. To quote from
this editorial:

> "As stiff as inflation's toll has been up to now, it is nothing compared to the
> cost which confronts us at the end of the road. Unless we check inflation, it
> will cost us our freedom. And if that sounds too apocalyptic, consider the
> ways in which inflation already has chipped away at freedoms we have
> taken for granted. Our options in the marketplace are more limited than they
> used to be . . . Our freedom of movement is circumscribed by the rising
> costs of operating a car . . . Our freedom to locate where we choose is
> limited by soaring rents and real estate prices . . . Our freedom to make
> plans of every imaginable sort, from having a baby to taking a vacation, has
> been diminished by inflation . . . Inflation has narrowed our choices and
> options. In the end it threatens to eliminate them entirely."*

Hovering over this period of rampant inflation is the specter of Weimar
Germany in which the finances of whole classes of the population were wiped
out by hyperinflation and the way was paved for the rise of Naziism.

Whether these apocalyptic events ever come to pass it is clear that rampant
inflation now joined by a dangerous recession has already had a dramatic
impact on the way of life of many Americans.

To dramatize the problem under study, the proposal points out that rampant inflation is a new phenomenon, heralding a new kind of society in
which rampant inflation will be a permanent feature. "The consensus
among most scholars is that the current inflation . . . is a long range
phenomenon not likely to recede in the near future." Eight years later, this
statement appears to be all too true as inflation is still the number one
economic problem. The packaging not only stressed a new phenomenon
causing considerable hardship but it also highlighted the threat of inflation
to our fundamental values, our freedoms and our democratic way of life.

Skeptic, Special Issue Number 3, October 1974, p. 5.

The quote from *Skeptic* drove this point home. With such trappings, the proposal calls attention to a very important problem well worth studying.

A final example of expert proposal packaging is provided by the work of a friend and former colleague, Dr. Theresa Rogers. In 1976 Dr. Rogers became interested in the lay support groups that have evolved around major illnesses; generally they are made up of people who have had the illness and who are ready to help people now facing it. Dr. Rogers discovered a brilliant way to package her proposal. She linked her research problem to the essential mission of the medical profession as follows:

> In recent decades medicine has been rightfully credited with giant scientific advances and the development of life-extending techniques. To cite only one example, the extraordinary strides in surgery have made it possible for many patients confronting life shortening and incurable conditions to not only live, but to be capable of active, productive lives. Advances in cardiac, abdominal and breast surgery are among the present day triumphs of medicine which give patients hope and the opportunity to continue life.

> These very advances, however, have called sharp attention to a new and little understood class of problems, namely, how patients adapt to a permanent health condition and at the same time maximize their capability to live a full life as worker, spouse, parent and citizen. The patient, for example, who has had breast surgery or the one who has had an ileostomy confronts a wide range of social, psychological and physical problems that strain the capacity of traditional medical facilities.

> More generally, the same may be said for the increasing number of patients with chronic conditions that must be managed for the rest of their lives. It is well known that health facilities are far better organized to care for the patient with an acute, curable, short-term condition than for the one confronting a long-term, incurable condition which only episodically takes on the characteristics of acute illness.

> It is in the context of enduring health problems that a new voluntary patient resource has begun to multiply rapidly. This resource is the lay or mutual support group composed of members who have a particular health problem and who seek to help others facing the same problem. These groups now number several thousand and exist to help patients and their families adapt to health conditions or impairments. Nearly all seventeen World Health Organization disease categories are now represented by some type of self-help organization.

> These new organizations have been described in various health publications and have been given wide coverage by the popular media, but they have been little studied. In particular, we don't know whether these mutual aid groups have any effect on recovery. The proposed research seeks to answer this question as well as others.

The critical message of the packaging is found in the second paragraph. Here Dr. Rogers links the problem she wants to study to the very successes of modern medicine. The miracles of modern medicine are now keeping alive people who where destined to die. But this very success of modern medicine has given rise to a new problem, one that modern medicine is ill equipped to handle: the social, psychological, and physical adjustment to the health problem, what might be called the problem of adjusting to health. And it is in this context that the self-help groups that Dr. Rogers wants to study may play a substantial role. And, as in my proposals cited earlier, Dr. Rogers stresses the fact that there has been little research on what she wants to study, that her research deals with a new phenomenon.

As these examples of proposal packaging indicate, the strategy is to stress the uniqueness of the proposed research, to point out how it touches on a major, important social problem, and to note how the research will contribute to solving the problem by answering important questions.

In this chapter some of the strategies for writing good proposals have been reviewed. There are other topics that could be included in a chapter on proposal writing. For example, we could consider the politics of proposals: the relationships that evolve between those who submit proposals and the funding agencies and the members of their review committees. For all the emphasis on free competition of ideas carried out in complete impartiality, the fact is that who you know plays a role in the world of proposal funding. All too often the members of the review committee know the researchers who have submitted proposals and they allow their personal relationships with the researchers to influence their decisions regarding the merits of the proposal. I once competed with another New York city university for funds to initiate a drug research center. The National Institute on Drug Abuse issued an RFP for a university-based drug research center. They were prepared to fund four or five of these around the country. I was able to read the proposal submitted by the other New York institution, and I know that it was inferior to our proposal. Yet the director of the institute at the other university was a close friend of several members of the review committee. His institution received the grant, and since NIDA was not prepared to fund more than one research center in the same city, we were turned down. Well-known professors have little difficulty getting research grants regardless of the quality of their proposals. But we should not lose sight of the other side of the coin. The fact is that good proposals submitted by unknowns do get funded. And the beginner should take heart. Submitting proposals that eventually lead to funding is a sure way to dramatically improve one's career. Research grants mean being released from teaching duties, they mean having full-time secretaries, and, most important, they mean added income in the form of summer salaries. And of course they mean doing research and getting published.

2

Four Winning Proposals

The case method is a time-honored tradition of instruction. Applying it to the art of proposal writing means examining cases of successful proposals in the hope that principles of good proposal writing will emerge. To carry out this task, I contacted a government agency that has played a major role in the past several decades in funding research proposals by sociologists. The agency is a branch of the National Institute of Mental Health known until recently as The Center for the Study of Metropolitan Problems under the directorship of the sociologist Elliot Liebow. I asked Dr. Liebow for a sample of outstanding proposals that his center had funded and he sent me 16 examples. They ranged in length from 12 to 77 pages, with the average being 31 pages. The first 10 or so pages of these proposals are taken up with the title page listing the sponsoring institution, a second page that contains the names of the research personnel and an abstract of the proposal, three budget pages, and anywhere from three to eight pages of biographical sketches of key personnel. The rest of the proposal is devoted to a description of the research plan, the relevant literature, and the research methods.

For this chapter I have chosen a sample of three of these proposals to which I have added the proposal by Theresa Rogers referred to in the previous chapter. All of these proposals as well as all but one of the others in the Liebow sample were generated by problems rather than by theory.

The first proposal is an extremely short one prepared by Angus Campbell of the Survey Research Center at the University of Michigan in 1969. This proposal requests funds for additional analysis of data already collected dealing with the race riots that swept many cities during the 1960s. The proposal telescopes the introductory section dealing with objectives, background (meaning review of literature), and specific aims, a section that ordinarily takes many pages to complete and devotes a mere paragraph to the Methods of Procedure, another usually long section. The Campbell proposal is a prime example of brevity in proposal writing and proof that a very short proposal can succeed.

========

Ecological Bases of Racial Experiences and Attitudes

ANGUS CAMPBELL

RESEARCH PLAN

A. Introduction and Specific Aims

The Survey Research Center has in hand an extensive collection of information obtained in 1968 by personal interview with samples of whites and blacks living in 15 of America's largest cities. This material was collected at the instigation of the Kerner Commission and with the financial support of The Ford Foundation. A preliminary report of descriptive data from the study was issued by the Kerner Commission on July 31, 1968 and a more comprehensive manuscript is now being completed for commercial publication at the end of 1969.

Because of the interests of the Kerner Commission the study was designed to make possible independent representation of whites and blacks in each of the 15 cities in the sample. Approximately 200 persons of each race were interviewed in each of the 15 cities, having been selected by probability methods to represent all persons of their race between the ages of 16 and 69 living within the boundaries of their city. Suburban white samples were also interviewed for two of the cities. The interviews themselves covered an extensive range of information, requiring over an hour on the average with the white respondents and close to an hour and a half with the black. It is apparent that the analysis potentialities of this incomparable collection of data will be only partially realized in the publications now in process.

B. Methods of Procedure

Our method of analysis involves use of multiple classification analysis, with both ecological units and individual attributes as predictors, in order to determine both gross and net effects of the ecological variables on a wide range of experiences and attitudes included in the questionnaire. This will be done separately for the black and white samples to allow comparisons across race. Covariance analysis will be employed to uncover relationships (for example, between reports of experience with discrimination and attitudes bearing on riots and rioting) that vary from one city to another. Insofar as "city" is a useful predictor variable, we will use multivariate methods to determine the patterning of cities across all variables and the characteristics of cities that are most closely linked (and therefore help to explain) this patterning. Similar methods will be employed with lower level ecological units, such as tracts.

Target samples of approximately 200 Negroes and 200 whites were drawn from each city. Due to variations in the success of estimates needed for sampling and in response rates, actual sample sizes varied. We will later consider effects of these variations and show that they have little, if any, influence on the results.

Our data allow for a detailed analysis of the extent to which "city" and other ecological units are an important factor, similar to age, sex, education, and so forth, in accounting for systematic variations in black and white attitudes and experiences in America. At one extreme it might be (and has been) argued that some cities are much more successful than others in meeting the needs of their populations. At the other extreme, it is possible that urban problems, and especially urban racial problems, are so general, massive, and intractable that they afflict all cities to much the same degree. The former argument was heard strongly immediately after the Newark riot in July, 1967, which seemed to occur in a city which reached the extreme in extent of urban problems of health, unemployment, poverty, poor housing, lack of black participation in government, etc. Just 10 days later a serious riot began in Detroit, reputed to be a high-wage, home-owning city with a progressive and energetic administration. This naturally called into question the extent to which apparent differences among cities were of real importance with regard to racial problems. Our data allow us to determine whether cities do differ greatly in the satisfactions of their populations with city services, in beliefs about race and racial issues, and in hostilities of a racial nature.

Our most general concern is not with any particular city, but with "city" as an explanatory variable. We will be interested in which attitudes and beliefs vary in important ways among cities, and which are uniform across cities. For the former, we will explore the extent to which the differences are due to "accidental" variations in demographic composition (e.g., age structure), as against the extent to which differences seem to reside in more intrinsic (or at least unexplainable) city characteristics. For all attitudes we will be especially interested in the difference between the black and white populations. While our main concern will be with city as a general factor, we will provide descriptive information on individual cities, and attempt to discover why some have had special success or lack of success. Finally, we will look at the extent to which "city" seems to play an indirect role in *other* relationships. For example, does the *link between* general dissatisfaction and willingness to riot vary across cities.

The original grant from The Ford Foundation, which was largely expended on the very heavy field costs of the survey, was exhausted in preparing the reports mentioned above and the analysis of the data will shortly come to a standstill. This state of affairs impresses us as unfortunate in the extreme, not so much because of the personal frustration of the principal investigators as for the significant social loss which will be suffered if the opportunities offered by this collection are allowed to languish. The time is past when large collections of data can be thought to be the personal plaything of individual researchers; they are assembled at significant social cost and if intelligently generated they have great potential social value. It required a national crisis to provide the financing for the particular data set with which we are concerned; the crisis remains and it appears to us intolerable that these data should not be thoroughly mined to provide the greatest possible illumination they can give of the confrontation between whites and blacks in the cities.

We are proposing herewith a year-and-a-half program of research and training based on the data of the 15 city study. On the research side we expect the major emphasis to be on the analysis of the geographical and ecological distribution of racial characteristics. This begins with the comparison of the 15 individual cities of the sample, an undertaking which can only be begun in the work now being completed. Preliminary investigation of city as an independent variable indicates that it is important in explaining variation in the data, and that this importance is not simply a function of differences among cities in their demographic composition. Moreover, we know the specific addresses of all of our black and white respondents and are able to group them by block, census tract, amount of segregation, distance from riot area, and other geographical divisions. Our capacity to compare such ecological units within individual cities is limited because of sample size, but grouping of comparable units across cities, using city as a control, offers opportunities which have not previously been available.

On the training side we propose to make this program a vehicle for the direct involvement of black and white scholars in the analysis of these racial data. We propose a mixed team to be composed of two persons of postdoctoral level, one part-time and the other full-time, and two doctoral students, half-time during the academic year and full-time during the summer. It would be our expectation that these individuals would develop their own analytical interests and would publish their findings in the usual channels. The student members of the team would presumably develop their doctoral dissertations from the data with which they would be working. It is our ultimate hope that following this period of analysis it would be possible to repeat the 1968 study in order to assess changes during the intervening period. The present proposal is in no way dependent on that eventuality, however, and should be considered entirely on the basis of its own merits.

C. Significance

Most of the attempts by social scientists to explain the outbreak of violence in the cities has depended on the analysis of individual data. We have had a number of descriptions of the rioter or the riot-prone person. Typically these studies have been done within a single city (Watts, Detroit) and no consideration of city variables was possible. Fifteen cities is not a very large sample of cities, of course, but it is by long odds the largest sample of cities with comparable data which has ever been available for this type of analysis. We already know at this point that city differences contribute a significant part of the variance we see between cities in the characteristics of the racial confrontation. Our purpose is to describe and understand better the role of cities and other ecological and community units in relation to race-related experiences and attitudes.

━━━━━━━━━━━━

The successful packaging of this proposal is provided by the third paragraph where Campbell explains that the original grant was used up before the data could be fully analyzed. As Campbell says,

> This state of affairs impresses us as unfortunate in the extreme, not so much because of the personal frustration of the principal investigators as for the significant social loss which will be suffered if the opportunities offered by this collection are allowed to languish. The time is past when large collections of data can be thought to be the personal plaything of individual researchers; they are assembled at considerable social cost and if intelligently generated, they have great potential social value. It required a national crisis to provide the financing for the particular data set with which we are concerned; the crisis remains and it appears to us intolerable that these data should not be thoroughly mined to provide the greatest possible illumination they can give of the confrontation between whites and blacks in the cities.

Such a strong statement makes it hard for a granting agency to refuse the request for funds.

The next proposal, by Allan D. Heskin, a professor of Urban Planning at the University of California, Los Angeles, is an excellent example of staking out entirely new territory for research, a field in which no one ever did any research.

Tenant Consciousness

ALLAN D. HESKIN

RESEARCH PLAN

A. Introduction

Being a tenant is not part of the American Dream. Tenants are, in an essential way, the unpropertied in a society in which private property is central. Some see their continued existence as a constant contradiction in American life. Periodically, tenants, reacting to their position in society, have acted collectively in their own behalf. Sometimes this action has been violent and other times it has taken the form of orderly political processes. Some observers of both the past and recent history of tenant collective action are claiming an increasingly important role in our society for a tenant social movement. However, we know very little about the status of tenants. We know little about how tenants adjust to their particular position in American society or the extent to which they see themselves in a collective sense.

1. OBJECTIVES

The primary objectives of this study are (1) gaining an understanding of the extent to which tenants have a collective identity and solidarity in achieving collective goals and (2) examining the factors that contribute to this level of collective consciousness.

To accomplish these ends this proposal sets forth a study design directed at identifying and measuring "tenant consciousness" and the factors that contribute to or inhibit its existence. A scale of tenant consciousness will be constructed and variables which affect the level of tenant consciousness will be derived. Because this study is the first of its kind, the scale and variables, initially drawn from the literature, will be grounded in the experience of specially selected groups of tenant activists, organizers and tenants. These groups will be selected with the assistance of tenant organizations. The scale, criteria and variables will then be incorporated in a survey instrument. This instrument will be administered by telephone to a random sample of 1,500 Los Angeles County tenants and a random sample of 500 Santa Monica tenants. Santa Monica has been the scene of the most intensive tenant activism in this region.

Social scientists have studied the impact of age, class, race and sex on individuals' self-identity and quality of life. We hope to contribute an understanding of the impact of individuals' relationship to private property, i.e., tenant status, to this body of knowledge. We also hope to contribute to a broader understanding of social movements— what is at their base and the factors that lead individuals to seek or reject collective action.

2. BACKGROUND

A. THE POSITION OF TENANTS IN AMERICAN SOCIETY.   Every American is supposed to own their (*sic*) own home. From the very beginning of this country the assumption has been that a burgeoning affluence would erase the categories of landlord and tenant. The first settlers came here seeking the freedom and independence that landowner-ship necessarily confers in an agricultural economy. They built a society that had the ownership of property at its center. People who did not own land could not vote nor could they hold office. It was not unitl 1860 that tenants received the right to vote in federal elections, and it should be noted that, even today, many tenants continue to be ineligible to vote in bond, property tax, and special district elections.

Tenants were characterized as second class citizens early in our history. The movement to give suffrage to tenants spread throughout the states before the federal rule was changed. In the 1820s and 30s the constitutions of Massachusetts, New York and Virginia were amended in tenants' favor. The list of those opposed to the change in these states is impressive. Among them were John Adams, Daniel Webster, James Madison, James Monroe and John Marshall. Clinton Rossiter reports on their opposi-tion:

> They were, for the most part, libertarians who took pride in the "great subdivision of the soil" among the American people and were devoted to the cause of a yeoman republic. But they could not abandon a fundamental teaching of their fathers: that *men without property lack the independence, interest, judgment, and virtue to be participating citizens of a free republic*. They clung tenaciously, like the good conservatives they were, to the inherited doctrine of the *"stake-in-society,"* which affirms that officeholding voting should be the concern of those only who have *"a common interest with, and attachment to the community."* Their chief concern, of course, was the rapidly growing urban mass, which they insisted on identifying with "the mobs of Paris and London." (emphasis added)

Despite the fears of many of our founding fathers, tenants became a significant social group in our society. In the 1840s, the first deliberately planned rental units— "tenements"—were built in New York City. By the 1890s nearly two-thirds of the residents of our major metropolitan areas were tenants. This overwhelming number of tenants did not, however, reduce the importance of landownership in American life. With industrialization and urbanization the drive for agricultural land was transformed into the desire to own urban land and especially into a passion for homeownership. In the expansionist period of our history tenants could escape oppressive conditions by claiming the free land to the west. At the turn of the century this escape was increasingly accomplished by the upwardly mobile who sought homeownership and a move to the suburbs.

The 20th century has seen the playing out of the pattern set in the late 19th century. By 1950, 55 percent of the population in the standard metropolitan areas owned their own homes. In 1976 this percentage had risen to 64.7 percent. The substantial increase in homeownership was aided by a continuous policy of the federal govern-ment favoring homeownership. The federal intervention began with President Hoover, who in 1931 artfully located the place of homeowners and tenants in the American psyche:

> To possess one's own home is the hope and ambition of almost every individual in our country, whether he lives in hotel, apartment or tenement . . . Those

immortal ballads, Home Sweet Home, My Old Kentucky Home, and The Little Gray Home in the West, were not written about tenements or apartments . . . they never sing songs about a pile of rent receipts.

Even with this extraordinary rise in homeownership, the unsung tenant remains in the majority among important segments of our society. In the central cities tenants made up 50.5 percent of the population of 1976. In the states of New York and Hawaii tenants are in the majority. In California, the third most populous tenant state, the percentage of tenants in the population grew from 37.1 percent in 1960 to 45 percent in 1970. In the Los Angeles–Long Beach SMSA tenants make up 51.7 percent of the population. Los Angeles, itself, is 61.7 percent tenants and smaller cities such as Santa Monica, which is 80.2 percent tenants, have even larger tenant majorities.

Tenants are predominant among lower income people. A 1976 study of California's population indicated that tenants were in the majority in all income groups up to $10,000 annual income. Among the total of families with up to $15,000 income per year, 51.5 percent are tenants. It is important, however, not to overemphasize the low income tenant for this study also indicated that 26.4 percent of tenants had annual incomes in excess of $20,000.

B. History of Tenant Collective Action

The history of tenant collective action is not well documented. Charles Beard gives us only the slightest view of the period in which tenants obtained the vote. He reports that the movement began in the new states—"In none of them was there an upper class of wealth and power comparable to that represented by the great landlords or rich merchants of the original thirteen colonies"—and was aided by the substantial immigration of industrial workers who were forming trade unions and labor parties in the growing industrial cities.

.　.　.

The war on poverty brought organizers and lawyers to the tenant movement, and the lawyers, in particular, brought major reforms to landlord–tenant law. For example, the National Housing Law Project, formed in 1968, joined NTO's effort in Washington and supported the efforts of the many neighborhood legal services programs throughout the country. Major reforms of this period were the warranty of habitability and the protection against retaliatory eviction. These laws allowed tenants to withhold rent if a landlord fails to maintain the leased property, and protect a tenant against eviction for complaining about the condition of the property and demanding repair. All the major states and many smaller ones now have these reforms.

The student efforts brought rent strikes and rent control drives to college towns such as Cambridge, Berkeley, Ann Arbor and Madison. These efforts had mixed results, but they did create a group of people trained and involved with housing issues who still play a major role in helping to further define the role of tenants in American society.

State-wide tenant organizations also emerged in the early 1970s in Massachusetts and New Jersey. New Jersey's organization has served as a model which other states have followed. Founded in 1972 following the end of the Nixon rent freeze, it has been successful in winning an extraordinary number of battles in the courts and state legislature, and has helped bring rent control to 26 cities in the state. It has also led to the formation of Shelterforce, a collective, which puts out a national tenant newspaper by the same name. The newspaper reports on tenant activity around the country and expresses tenants' opinions on a broad array of housing and national policy questions.

C. Tenant Collective Action in California

Even though California has the third highest proportion of tenant units population among the states, it has not historically been a major scene of tenant organizing. Although there were episodes during difficult years, especially in the college towns, little has been sustained. The California tenant was thought of by aspiring tenant organizers to be too individualistic and too mobile to be organized. In addition, housing conditions have been seen as relatively good, particularly in light of the mild California winter, and urban settlement in the state too spread out and tenant densities too low for collective action.

California, however, has seen a substantial increase in tenant activity over the past few years, and an explosion in tenant activity over the past few months. A number of factors have led to the dramatic rise in activity. The 1970s have seen a substantial drop in vacancy rates, an unusually rapid rate in rent increases, and an extraordinary rise in the price of houses. The year 1978 brought Proposition 13, known as the property-owners' revolt, which in turn has generated a tenant revolt of unheard of proportions.

1. PRESSURES ON CALIFORNIA TENANTS

The 1970 vacancy rates in the Los Angeles area were around 5 percent, thought by many to be a critical level indicative of a housing shortage. Since 1970, this rate has been steadily dropping. The current Los Angeles vacancy rate is said to be 2.6 percent, and the Santa Monica vacancy rate is at an extraordinary low 1.4 percent.

It is an unwritten rule in the real estate business that rents increase at a rate less than that of the Consumer Price Index. However, during the 1970s rents have been steadily increasing at a rate approaching that of the Index. And, in 1977, the rate of increase in rents was nearly 13 percent—well above the Index figure. This figure is even more significant when it is considered that around 30 percent of tenants received no rent increases at all during this period.

While rents were climbing rapidly, house prices jumped at an extraordinary rate. In the seven county Los Angeles–Long Beach–San Diego area, prices rose at an annual rate of 23 percent in the period from December 1977 to April 1978 and at the rate of 30 percent per year in the six months previous to that. The average price of a house in Santa Monica rose from $95,000 in March 1977 to $125,000 in December of the same year. It is not unusual in the area to find a nearly 300 percent increase in value since 1970.

These figures are particularly important to tenants. The *Los Angeles Times* reported that an analyst estimated that each time the price of the least expensive home is increased in price by $1,000, about 100,000 Californians are priced out of the market. With the present median price for all houses in California at $63,000, the analyst estimated that three-fourths or more of the State's families are unable to break into the homeownership market for the first time. Many families who might, with sacrifice, make the monthly payments do not have the savings necessary to make the down payment. With homeownership so central to the American image of success and security, one has to wonder what impact this is having on the many young tenant families entering the home buying phase of their lives.

D. Tenant Movement as Social Movement?

At this point, no one knows the depth of the tenant awakening. This could be another episode that will pass or it could be significant advancement of a building tenant movement. Even before the activists in California, there were those who saw what was happening across the country as an increasingly important social movement. The accuracy of this observation will depend on both the size of the latent collectivity of tenants and the ability of that collectivity to mobilize. No one knows the potential of tenants to organize. If the potential is there and it is realized, no one knows how significant a change in our society it will bring.

One of the possible paths for a tenant movement to take is toward unionization in the model of labor unions. The relatively new national and even newer state tenant organizations indicate a move in this direction. Chester Hartman has written that such tenant unions could work a profound change not only in the landlord–tenant relationship, but in the entire system of local and national housing policy. These reforms could be far reaching.

If being a tenant or having tenant support became a significant advantage when running for office, the security of tenure protection against arbitrary eviction, now present only in New Jersey, could sweep the country. Beyond this, it is not difficult to conceive of a law that would require the sharing of equity build-up between landlords and tenants. The questions posed by state and national tax structures which now favor homeownership would have to be examined, and tenants might press for the right to deduct property taxes just as people now deduct sales tax. At all levels of government, actions could be reviewed for their impact on the tenant population.

. . .

Leaders of California's new tenants' movement see this confrontation between propertied and non-propertied interests emerging in the state. To capture the essence of the situation they have begun to speak to what they call "tenant consciousness." If such a consciousness is emerging among a substantial number of tenants, this would be a new development in the tenant movement. Without the development of tenant consciousness the tenant movement is not likely to develop into either a reform or radical social movement. Without the sense of shared identity, interests and goals inherent in a common consciousness, sustained, effective, collective action is not likely.

E. Tenant Consciousness Literature

1. OVERVIEW

We know very little about how tenants see themselves. Do they claim full citizenship like those tenants who spoke before the Santa Monica City Council? Or, do they accept the characterization made by those of our founding fathers who opposed giving tenants the vote? How do they see themselves in relation to landlords or homeowners? Do they see themselves as consumers or do they see themselves as either oppressed or rightfully subjugated to the powers of private property? Are they attached to the communities in which they live or do they see themselves as transients? Do they feel the pressure of reduced opportunity, particularly in relation to future homeownership? Are they beginning to suffer the anomie that can result from a "breakdown in the relation between goals and legitimate avenues of access to them." Do they feel that their homes and stability are being threatened? Is the pressure building in the fashion described by the tenant who spoke of Watts before the Santa Monica City Council? Have they had bad experiences with landlords and how have they reacted? If they did attempt to act in their own defense did it tend to radicalize them? What is the propensity of tenants to act in their own behalf either individually, in groups or as a "class for itself." Do they sense a change in their status in society and the attitudes of tenants about these questions?

The answer to these and related questions requires an exploration of the nature and level of tenant consciousness. The term is used in the literature to indicate a tenant collective identity and solidarity in achieving collective tenant goals. However, while there have been many studies of tenants and many studies of consciousness, there appear to be no studies of tenant consciousness. The most common studies of tenants examine moving patterns and attitudes about the quality of one's housing and neighborhood. There are other relevant studies which, for example, examine the control of tenants by landlords through the landlord–tenant relationship in low income neighborhoods, the complaints and actions in particular landlord–tenant disputes, or the level of tenants' knowledge of their rights and their sense of justice in landlord–tenant disputes. These studies, however, are too partial to create the complete picture necessary to address the level and nature of tenant consciousness.

Studies that deal with the question of consciousness often use tenants as their subjects. However, although there are occasional references to the impact of housing tenure, they do not focus on the subjects' tenant status, but rather center on their race, the fact that they are welfare recipients or members of the working class. The last category is, perhaps, the most common.

The studies that followed the 1960s revolts indicated that housing, meaning tenants' housing, was a major source of black discontent. What part did the participants' tenant status play in black readiness to participate in the revolts? An Oakland, California Police Department Study that disclosed that landlord–tenant disputes are second only to family disputes as the setting for assault and homicide led to the creation of a crisis intervention unit for landlord–tenant conflicts.

2. CONCEPTUAL FRAMEWORK

Because there are no apparent studies of tenant consciousness, we have looked to the working class consciousness studies for a model. Among these studies, the most appropriate conceptual framework for this study appears in the work of John Leggett. In a study of working class individuals in Detroit, he constructed a working class consciousness scale and tested his subjects against this scale based on a number of variables. Leggett's study was conducted in the early 1960s. The primary finding of the study was that black workers have a significantly high level of working class consciousness while white workers had little such consciousness. Using a Marxist concept of radical or revolutionary consciousness, he predicted an open revolt by the black workers.Unfortunately, the events of the mid-1960s seem to give credence to his method and findings.

We propose to adopt Leggett's strategy in this study. A tenant consciousness scale will be constructed and variables which we hypothesize to affect the level of such consciousness will be selected.

A. TENANT CONSCIOUSNESS SCALE.   The scale criteria employed by Leggett seem a particularly appropriate guide to the construction of the scale in this study. He employed four criteria: class verbalization, skepticism about the system, militancy and egalitarianism.

To measure verbalization Leggett employed questions about political preference. Such questions would seem appropriate here. We would direct our question at attitudes toward rent control, or security of tenure and preferences given to the candidate with tenant status versus that given to landlords or homeowners or to candidates who support pro-tenant reform versus those neutral or against such reform.

To measure skepticism Leggett employed questions relating to who benefits in a business boom. A similar criterion can be constructed with questions regarding the current inflation in rents. Some tenant might see the problem as one of supply and demand while others might doubt the full action of the market, seeing manipulation by speculators.

To measure militancy Leggett, interestingly, used a series of questions regarding action his working-class tenants would take against their landlords. The most extreme of Leggett's actions was picketing one's landlord. We would employ a similar series of questions with the addition of some regarding broader collective political action including forming tenant unions or mounting electoral drives. At the extreme, we would ask who agrees with the Santa Monica tenant who felt a Watts situation was possible.

To measure egalitarianism Leggett asked a direct question about people's attitudes about the proper distribution of wealth. In this study, we would ask questions about private property instead of egalitarianism. Some tenants might be openly hostile to the central place of private property. Others might accept its place in society but feel a balance should be drawn because of the responsibility that comes with ownership. Still others might accept the dominance of private property.

The results of this line of questions would result in a five step scale. The highest or radical level of consciousness would be expected to be typified by a rejection of the central role of private property. Whether this rejection goes so far as to question the place of home ownership will be an important finding of this study. The next highest step might be referred to as consumer consciousness. The consumers would accept the role of private property but seek greater equity or balance between landlord and tenant interests. Tenants with either radical or consumer consciousness would also be expected to be militant, skeptical and have tenant preferences. In many ways, this distinction between radical and consumer is similar to the distinction made in the working-class literature between radical and labor union consciousness.

The next step of the scale would include those who would verbalize tenant identity but would not likely engage in collective tenant action. Still lower on the scale would be those who indicate little or no tenant identity, who, for example, would not see tenant status or positions on tenant issues as significant in voting preferences. At the lowest extreme of tenant consciousness would be those tenants who identify primarily with private property interests. These tenants would fully accept a dominant role for private property and would vote for propertied candidates because they "have a stake in the community." Sub-scales within these steps may become evident with analysis of the data.

B. Specific Aims. The specific aims of this study are:

1. To understand the extent to which tenants have tenant consciousness and the factors that affect the level of this consciousness;

2. To construct a tenant consciousness scale by learning about tenants' political preferences, their understanding of the economic system that determines their rents, their propensity for collective action, and their attitudes toward private property;

3. To determine the importance of tenant status in self-identity in relation to other primary characteristics such as age, class, race, and sex;

4. To determine and test the impact on tenant consciousness of tenants' sense of economic mobility or permanency as tenants, tenants' sense of isolation and/or participation in the collective opportunities of their community, tenants' level of attachment to their apartment and community, tenants' relationships with their landlords, and tenants' experience with landlord–tenant disputes.

C. Methods of Procedure

The study will proceed in two phases. In the first phase a group of tenant activists and organizers and a group of tenants will be interviewed to ensure that the scale and variables are grounded in the experience of people who are the subject of the study. In phase two of the study the survey instrument incorporating the scale criteria and variables will be pre-tested, and then administered by telephone to random samples of tenants from Los Angeles County and Santa Monica. The Santa Monica sample was chosen because that city has been the scene of the most intense tenant activism in the region.

1. PHASE ONE

Because this study is the first of its kind, we have had to employ the apparently analogous working-class literature to form our conceptual framework. To ensure the applicability of this literature and the suitability of our framework we plan to also ground our efforts in the experience of a group of specially selected tenant activists, organizers and a specifically selected group of tenants.

A. INTERVIEWS OF ACTIVISTS AND ORGANIZERS. To do this, a group of 20 tenant activists and organizers will be selected with the assistance of the California Housing and Action Information Network, the statewide tenant organization in California. The selection will be made on the basis of the individual's years and depth of experience and their representativeness of activists and organizers. Particular attention will be paid to selecting individuals who have worked with a number of racial groups along with people of varying ages and income levels.

The interviews of those selected will be conducted in person. They will be loosely structured along lines indicated in the literature and will be exploratory in nature. The primary focus of the interviews will be to determine, as fully as possible, the subjects' meaning of the term tenant consciousness. In addition, questions will be asked about the indicators that organizers use to determine whether tenants have such consciousness, the factors they believe contribute to or inhibit its formulation and the elements that they have found necessary to transform consciousness into collective action.

B. INTERVIEWS OF TENANTS. Following the analysis of these data, a sample of 20 tenants will be selected to test the consistency and reliability of the scale of consciousness and the significance of the variables. These tenants will be identified and selected with the assistance of tenant organizers from the Santa Monica Fair Housing Alliance. Among this group will be individuals that the organizers believe have varying levels of tenant consciousness. Again, an attempt will be made to have representatives of a cross section of racial, sex, age and income groups. The tenants will also be interviewed in person and the interviews will be loosely structured along lines indicated by our framework and the interviews of the activists and organizers.

The interviews of the activists, organizers and tenants should be particularly important for the development of the language employed in the questionnaire. The semantic nuances will have to be carefully noted and incorporated in the survey instrument. These interviews should lead to greater sophistication in our conceptual framework. Elements of the scale or the variables which we will test may be modified.

2. PHASE TWO

The second phase of this study will consist of pre-testing the questionnaire, selecting sample populations, administration of the survey instrument and data analysis. This phase of the study will be completed with the assistance of the Institute for Social Science Research (ISSR). Of particular assistance in this study will be the Survey Research Center (SRC), an integral part of ISSR. It serves the U.C.L.A. faculty and others engaged in social research.

These excerpts represent less than half the research plan in Heskin's proposal. Much of the history of tenancy, the tenant's movement, and developments in that movement in California are not quoted here. Still the excerpt makes clear the author's knowledge of his subject and in the absence of any literature on the topic, his decision to draw upon a related concept, working-class consciousness. His review of that literature provides him with a framework for measuring his concept of "tenant consciousness."

Heskin prepared an addendum to his proposal in which he answered questions raised by the site visitors. One question dealt with the genesis of the application, and Heskin's reply identifies him as an expert in the subject:

> The Principal Investigator has a ten year history of interest in the problems of tenants. This interest began when he was a legal services attorney in Oakland, California. During the time he served as a neighborhood lawyer, he interviewed and assisted in excess of 1000 people, many of whom had tenant problems. The frustration and powerlessness experienced by the tenants with whom he had contact led him to become involved in tenant organizing and initiate a law suit which resulted in a California Supreme Court decision protecting California tenants against retaliatory eviction. Following his Legal Service work and doctoral studies in urban planning, the Principal Investigator joined the staff of the National Housing Law Project. He was responsible for research and development in the area of landlord–tenant relations.

As this proposal makes clear, it helps considerably if the proposal writer is expert in his chosen area of research.

The next proposal also deals with a topic on which there has been little or no research, companies that have been taken over and are now run by their workers. The author, Dr. Henry M. Levin of the Center for Economic Studies, calls them Producer Cooperatives.

Producer Cooperatives—Urban Work and Mental Health

HENRY M. LEVIN

RESEARCH PLAN

A. Introduction

1. OBJECTIVE

The overall objective of this study is to ascertain the potential of the producer cooperative mode of enterprise for increasing employment and improving working conditions in metropolitan areas. Major factors affecting the mental health of metropolitan populations appear to include the lack of availability of jobs and the adverse nature of working conditions in many urban work settings. Producer cooperatives seem to have the potential to improve the retention of urban employment through the transfer of firms (that might otherwise close) to their existing employees. They also have characteristics that suggest some unique advantages for promoting the establishment of new enterprises and jobs that might not arise under other forms of organization. Finally, the democratic aspects of both ownership and worker participation characterized by producer cooperatives can be used to improve the quality of working life of both cooperative participants and of employees in other types of enterprises such as public, urban bureaucracies that are able to adopt successfully some of the beneficial organizational aspects of producer cooperatives. The aim of this research is to estimate the potential impacts that producer cooperatives can have on increasing employment and job satisfaction in urban areas and to suggest the public policy directions and consequences for promoting the formation of producer cooperatives to satisfy these goals.

2. BACKGROUND

The area of work has long been a focus of study as a source of mental stress. There are two broad dimensions of the work activity that have been scrutinized with respect to their effects on mental well-being and on psychophysiological factors that have been implicated in the incidence of other diseases: (1) factors relating to employment and employment security and (2) factors relating to the quality of the work experience itself. The important work of Brenner suggests a link between the level of economic activity and the incidences of such conditions in the population as heart disease mortality, alcohol consumption and associated illnesses, and more general indications of mental well-being. What is particularly interesting is that it is the short run fluctuations reflecting changes in the general employment situation that seem to be most closely associated with these adverse mental states. Thus improving employment security and employment appear to be important areas of focus for designing ways of enhancing mental and physical welfare as well as other social conditions.

The second area of concern has been the nature of the work experience itself and its impact on the mental health status of the worker. From the time of the onset of the industrial revolution there has been concern with the effect of the work organization on the mental condition of the worker. Indeed, two centuries ago Adam Smith in his celebrated *Wealth of Nations* (1776) refers to the effects of the division of labor emerging from the new industrial order:

> In the progress of the division of labor, the employment of the far greater part of those who have labor, that is, of the great body of the people, come to be confined to a few very simple operations, frequently to one or two ... He ... generally becomes as stupid and ignorant as it is possible for a human creature to become . . . .

In more recent years the relation between the organization of work and mental well-being of the worker has been explored empirically, biographically in worker interviews, and in summaries by government bodies.

In general, there is a great deal of evidence that much work is dulling to both the mind and the spirit. Moreover, recent increases in the educational attainments of the labor force may contribute to an even greater mismatch between the conditions of work faced by individuals and their personal and vocational needs. Accordingly, there is some concern that the problems emanating from the workplace because of the nature of existing jobs will become even more serious as those persons entering the workforce possess educational attainments that exceed by a wide margin the necessary educational requirements.

Both of these issues are especially important in urban areas because their severity tends to be greater in the metropolitan context. For example, unemployment rates in the large cities generally tend to exceed those of the nation or the states in which cities are situated.* Further the concentrations of high unemployment groups such as nonwhites and relatively disadvantaged populations tend to be considerably greater in cities than in other areas. Moreover, employment expansion has been relatively slow in cities in contrast with surrounding areas, and in some regions of the country the cities' employment base in manufacturing has actually declined.

The quality of working life is also a very serious problem in the urban areas. Increasingly, it is the less attractive and marginal industries that are left in the cities while the more prosperous and expanding enterprises have sought the suburban fringe. The marginality of such businesses has meant that the available funds for improving the welfare of the workers and their working conditions is less likely to be found or even to be a high priority as survival outweighs other considerations. Moreover, the large cities are becoming increasingly an area of concentration for large, urban, public bureaucracies that provide welfare services for older, impoverished, and disadvantaged populations. Vast public systems for providing health, education, public safety, and welfare, services have represented a relatively large and increasing component of the city's economy. And in many respects these urban, public bureaucracies have been indicted as very detrimental environments in which to work.

In recent years both the employment problem and the quality of working life problem have been addressed by government and by industry. With the highest rates of unemployment in the industrialized world, the federal government has attempted to use

*See U.S. Department of Labor, *Geographic Profile of Employment and Unemployment, 1972*, Bureau of Labor Statistics, Report 421, Government Printing Office, Washington, D.C., Tables 3 and 6.

fiscal and monetary policies as well as limited public programs to alleviate unemployment. But such policies have been found to have limited effects because public employment programs require enormous expenditure levels in order to provide enough jobs for the unemployed and fiscal and monetary policies are limited by their inability to increase employment without increasing already high levels of price level inflation. Even the once-pronounced view that employment difficulties will disappear as we move out of the bottom of the recession has been challenged by top government economists. For example, Arthur Burns, the Chairman of the Federal Reserve Board, announced in December 1975 that the problems of unemployment seem to be structural rather than due strictly to deficiencies in aggregate economic activity. He expressed particular concern with the lack of improvement in the employment rate despite some of the highest rates of inflation experienced in two decades.

The fact that so much of the unemployment problem seems to be structural or emanating from specific and localized labor market situations and that federal fiscal and monetary policy cannot be relied upon to alleviate the condition, especially in the urban areas, means that very specific approaches to increasing or protecting employment must be formulated. That is, even effective federal policies to decrease unemployment must be supplemented by local strategies that address the specific structural obstacles to enhancing employment levels.

Improving the quality of working life is also a problem which must be explored primarily in terms of "local" changes in work organization rather than in terms of national and aggregate effects. Different work situations are characterized by different problems and issues, although there may also be some commonality across workplaces. A fairly large number of work experiments for improving the quality of working life and increasing worker productivity have been attempted, and the results have been quite inconclusive. But what is important is that almost all of these changes have been management-initiated with the decisions made on the basis of management criteria. In some cases, workers have been consulted, but the basic changes have been at the initiative and along the lines of management concerns. Thus a very important area has remained largely unexplored, the changes in organization that workers might make if given the opportunity to improve their own work situations.

3. A STRATEGY FOR ADDRESSING THESE ISSUES

There is no magic solution for problems as complex and deeply rooted as those of unemployment and the quality of working life in urban areas. The interdependence of these problems with the overall social, political, economic, and cultural context which defines our society suggests that basic changes in that large set of institutions must accompany the radical solution of such issues as these. Yet, we believe that there are some promising directions that might be pursued in order to effect a partial solution to the concerns of urban unemployment and work, and that such directions may suggest a more general strategy for addressing various aspects of the problem in the future.

A particular form of enterprise, the producer cooperative, may have a potential role to play in achieving these goals for specific urban sub-populations, industries, and products or services. Producer cooperatives refer to organizations that satisfy two criteria: (1) they are owned by their employees, and (2) they are managed and operated in a democratic fashion through direct and representative participation of employees in virtually all aspects of their activities. A multitude of arrangements exist to satisfy these two criteria, but the employee ownership and control through democratic means are the crucial dimensions of this mode of productive organization.

In recent years there has been a rising interest in producer cooperatives around the world. In the U.S. this has mainly taken the form of substantial numbers of small retail service cooperatives in the major urban areas of the nation such as bookstores, auto repair firms, food outlets, nursery schools, and so on. These have been started primarily by relatively young persons who were unable to find satisfying employment in their fields. There do exist a few larger producer cooperatives in the U.S., most notably the plywood firms in the Pacific Northwest and an asbestos mine in Vermont as well as some agricultural examples.

In contrast to the United States, many countries have a much stronger cooperative tradition. For example, Britain, France, and Spain all have well-known and highly effective producer cooperatives. In Britain, the Triumph motorcycle is now produced by a workers' cooperative, an endeavor with sales estimated at about $30 million a year. In northern Spain there is an entire cooperative movement with over 13,000 workers and sales of about $350 million. The cooperative firms produce products as diverse as home appliances, selenium rectifiers, semi-conductors, factory construction, hydraulic presses, etc. One of the cooperative factories is the largest producer of refrigerators in Spain, and the cooperative movement has its own schools, financial institutions, and research and development center.

This proposal arises out of the present work on industrial democracy that is being carried out by the principal investigator and his colleagues in the Center for Economic Studies. For the last three years the Center has been engaged in a study on "The Educational Requirements for Industrial Democracy" for the National Institute of Education. A major focus of that activity is the analysis of different forms of work organization and prospective changes in work enterprises. Among the various forms of work enterprise that have been reviewed for the study, the producer cooperative mode has come under special scrutiny because of its increasing importance in generating employment and improving working life in other societies as well as its implications for democratic modes of work organization. The principal investigator and his colleagues have visited large producer cooperatives in several European countries as well as several smaller service cooperatives in the San Francisco area. In all of these cases, financial analysis of records and plans, organizational analysis of work arrangements and decision structures, and worker interviews of attitudes were used to provide preliminary information on the potential usefulness and work satisfaction. These preliminary analyses have suggested that producer cooperatives might have significant promise for addressing these problems in urban areas where the employment situation and working conditions are adverse. The more thorough inquiries and their placement in a public policy and urban setting are beyond the resources and the scope of the NIE study, but they represent a natural extension of our previous work into the proposed area of inquiry.

. . .

B. Specific Objectives

The specific objectives of the proposed research are:

1. To explore the history, legal, financial, and technical aspects relating to the establishment and operation of producer cooperatives;

2. To estimate the potential impacts of producer cooperatives for retaining jobs in urban areas through the transfer of firms (that might otherwise close) to their employees;

3. To estimate the potential of producer cooperatives for creating new jobs in urban areas by type of economic activity and among particular population groups;

4. To ascertain which aspects of producer cooperatives tend to improve or reduce worker satisfaction relative to other modes of organization;

5. To determine which of the aspects of producer cooperatives that increase worker satisfaction might be transferred to other urban work settings such as the urban, public bureaucracies; and,

6. To suggest the public policy requirements for and consequences of promoting producer cooperatives as part of the overall policy mix for addressing problems of metropolitan unemployment and adverse working conditions.

C. Methods of Procedure

The research design is composed of four components. These include: (1) History and organizational aspects of producer cooperatives; (2) Employment potential of producer cooperatives; (3) Comparison of particular producer cooperatives with other enterprises; and (4) Policy implications of producer cooperatives in the urban setting. The lack of a research tradition or a readily available data base on producer cooperatives means that much of the work that we propose will be addressed to basic data gathering and analytic formulation rather than more refined statistical and econometric analyses.

1. History and Organizational Aspects of Producer Cooperatives

The fact that there exists a long history of producer cooperatives suggests that logically we should begin by reviewing that history as well as contemporary experience with producer cooperatives. In particular, it is important to know under what circumstances producer cooperatives were formed, and what were the reasons for their success or failure. It has been suggested by Blumberg that ". . . they have always been plagued with chronic shortages of capital, stemming from their inadequate resources, and the hostile milieu in which they operated makes borrowing from the capital market quite difficult." Shirom also draws this conclusion, but he adds that the lack of a cohesive association or agency that could provide technical assistance and expertise for newly formed cooperatives was also a cause for failure. Interestingly, neither of these reasons suggests an intrinsic weakness of the producer cooperative form of enterprise, and both could be overcome by relatively inexpensive forms of governmental assistance.

But, there are also other obstacles that are external to the firm which include the cultural backgrounds and experiences of members in traditional work enterprises and thus their adaptability in functioning as members of a cooperative as well as government regulations that may have acted to promote or retard the development and viability of producer cooperatives. The historical review will address four questions: (a) Under what conditions did producer cooperatives arise? (b) Where did they arise, how were they organized, and what products or services did they produce? (c) What was their overall experience with respect to both the internal organization of the enterprise and its viability? and (d) What were the ostensible reasons for survival or failure? It is our expectation that this historical review will establish some general patterns that suggest the conditions under which producer cooperatives might represent a useful response to urban problems of employment and adverse working conditions.

.   .   .

2. EMPLOYMENT POTENTIAL OF PRODUCER COOPERATIVES

One of the principal foci of this research is to explore the employment potential of producer cooperatives in urban areas. This will be carried out in two phases, one dealing with job retention and the other with job creation. First, the role of producer cooperatives in retaining employment or saving jobs in urban areas will be studied. This will require an attempt to learn the reasons that firms abandon the city and the conditions under which such firms could be transformed into viable producer cooperatives through sale to their workers. Of course, the latter can be effected through long-term commercial or government loans, but what is more important is to find out what portion of enterprise-closures can be salvaged through this form of enterprise.

In principle, not all firms that abandon the city represent candidates for such a transformation. For example, those firms that are not economically viable would not be salvageable nor would those firms that wished to relocate outside of the city or the region and would not welcome competition from their old employees. But, the two groups of firms that would represent potential transfers to their employees as producer cooperatives would appear to be a substantial number. These include firms that are presently viable that must be sold or abandoned and those that are not viable in their present form but could be successful as producer cooperatives.

In the first case, some firms must be sold for personal reasons such as the retirement or death of a principal owner. Other firms must be sold to satisfy various legal edicts or to rationalize the plans and needs of a larger parent entity. For example, bankruptcy of Omega-Alpha of Dallas forced the sale of the Okonite division in Passaic, New Jersey, a major supplier of insulated wire and cable with 1900 employees. Okonite had gone through three changes in ownership over the past decade (two forced by antitrust rulings) even though it had an established record of profitability. The Economic Development Administration of the U.S. Department of Commerce provided a loan to the employees of the firms to purchase the firm from Omega-Alpha to save their jobs. A less successful example is that of the Rheingold Brewing Company in Brooklyn. Rheingold was an old established regional brewery that was acquired by the multinational PepsiCo in 1973 as part of a deal where the latter firm had to purchase a larger group of companies including Rheingold in order to get distribution rights for its soft drinks in Puerto Rico. Continued operation of the Brooklyn brewery did not coincide with the parent corporation's long range plans and PepsiCo decided to close the facility in 1974. Announcement of the pending closure brought protest from the 1600 employees who believed the firm was still economically viable. A new owner was found for the brewery, Chock Full O'Nuts, saving 1300 local jobs.

In addition to the case where viable firms must be sold or closed, there are instances where firms are not viable in their present form because of some peculiarities that could be modified under new ownership. For example, the well-known Railway Express Agency went bankrupt in 1975 with a potential loss of several thousand jobs, most of them in metropolitan areas. According to the analysis of their unions, the REA could be made viable, and the unions attempted to purchase the assets of the firm to maintain jobs. Unfortunately, the massive loans that were required were not forthcoming. More recently, in San Francisco, the most famous baker of a well-known local specialty, sourdough bread, was forced to close because of a liability judgment from a driver accident that exceeded its insurance coverage. In this case, if the one hundred or so employees of Larraburu Bakers had been able to purchase its highly specialized ovens and other equipment, they would have been able to maintain both production of their well-known product and their jobs.

Thus, in the case where firms face closure even though they are viable or could be made viable, it is possible to satisfy the necessary conditions for saving jobs through the transformation of such firms to producer cooperatives. But, the sufficient conditions for such a transformation are more stringent. They require that the employees be committed to the firm and the product or at least to local employment. This condition is likely to be satisfied when the average seniority in the firm is high and when there is a large element of craft specialization in the labor force, factors that especially characterized the Meriden Triumph Motorcycle Works where over 800 jobs were saved. Accordingly, it is the necessary conditions of viability or potential viability and the sufficient conditions of a potentially committed labor force which determine the population of firms where jobs could be retained through conversion to a producer cooperative.

We will attempt to obtain more detailed local data for a sample of cities. Many large cities like New York, Philadelphia, and San Francisco maintain departments of economic development that attempt to monitor the closure of firms and loss of jobs. We intend to contact the 25 largest cities in the country in order to ascertain the types of data that they collect on this issue. Based upon their responses, we will select those cities that seem to have the most appropriate information for a thorough analysis. From these results we will attempt to summarize the number of jobs that could have been salvaged for particular cities through the producer cooperative strategy. In addition some estimates will be made for the major urban areas on the basis of various assumptions about extrapolating the results of the initial sample. These estimates will be constructed with caution, and reasonable assumptions will be used in order to bound the results.

3. COMPARISON OF PRODUCER COOPERATIVES WITH OTHER ENTERPRISES

The third component of the proposed research will focus on a comparison of producer cooperatives with other forms of enterprise in order to assess overall differences in characteristics, structure, and employee experiences. The analysis will take two forms, a comparison of organizational features based upon the literature search and survey from the first component of the project and a comparison of a few enterprises in much greater depth through a field evaluation.

The literature search and survey of existing producer cooperatives that was set out in the first part of the research plan will be used as a basis for constructing a profile of producer cooperatives according to a useful taxonomy. While the precise classification scheme will be formulated on the basis of the salient dimensions that emerge in the search and survey, the particular dimensions of interest include the following:

1. Nature of products and services.
2. Size in terms of personnel and sales.
3. Remuneration levels and structures.
4. Demographic characteristics of personnel—sex, age, education, training, work experience.
5. Amounts and sources of capital.
6. Division of labor.
7. Decision processes with respect to hiring, firing, job assignment, pay, and so on.
8. Structure and process of governance.
9. Form and distribution of ownership.

On each of these dimensions we will describe the characteristics reflected in the data base as well as their distribution among the sampled, producer cooperatives. In addition, we will compare these characteristics with those of enterprises more generally as well as those with the same products. These comparison data will be taken from the reports of the U.S. Census of Business as well as other census documents and statistical reports from the Department of Commerce and Labor.

4. POLICY IMPLICATIONS

The final component of the research will summarize the results in a policy framework. It will attempt to answer four questions. First, what is the potential role of the urban producer cooperative in addressing problems of unemployment and adverse working conditions? Second, what aspects of producer cooperatives might be transferable in some form to other urban work organizations, in particular the public bureaucracies, to improve the quality of working life in those organizations? Third, what are the sources of political support or opposition for producer cooperatives in urban areas? Fourth, what types of government policies would be required to expand urban employment through producer cooperatives? The purpose of this segment of the research will be to suggest the consequences and public policy aspects of urban producer cooperatives for increasing employment and improving working conditions with their implications for improving the mental health status of the urban populations that would be impacted.

─────────────

This excerpt also provides less than half of the original research plan as spelled out in the proposal. Yet it makes clear the case for studying the new organizational form, the "Producer Cooperative."

The fourth example of a winning proposal is the one written by Theresa Rogers for a study of lay support groups.

─────────────

Impact of Lay Groups on Recovery and Functioning

THERESA F. ROGERS

Introduction

In recent decades medicine has been rightfully credited with giant scientific advances and the development of life-extending techniques. To cite only one example, the extraordinary strides in surgery have made it possible for many patients confronting life-shortening and incurable conditions to not only live, but to be capable of active, productive lives. Advances in cardiac, abdominal, and breast surgery are among the present day triumphs of medicine which give patients hope and the opportunity to continue life.

These very advances, however, have called sharp attention to a new and little understood class of problems, namely, how patients adapt to a permanent health condition and at the same time maximize their capability to live a full life as worker, spouse, parent, and citizen. The patient, for example, who has had breast surgery or the one who has had an ileostomy confronts a wide range of social, psychological, and physical problems that strain the capacity of traditional medical facilities.

More generally, the same may be said for the increasing number of patients with chronic conditions that must be managed for the rest of their lives. It is well known that health facilities are far better organized to care for the patient with an acute, curable, short-term condition than for the one confronting a long-term, incurable condition which only episodically takes on the characteristics of acute illness.

It is in the context of enduring health problems that a new voluntary patient resource has begun to multiply rapidly. This resource is the lay or mutual support group composed of members who have a particular health problem and who seek to help others facing this same problem. These groups now number several thousand and exist to help patients and their families adapt to health conditions or impairments. Nearly all seventeen World Health Organization disease categories are now represented by some type of self-help organization.

These new organizations have been described in various health publications and have been given wide coverage by the popular media, but they have been little studied. In particular, we don't know whether these mutual aid groups have any effect on recovery. The proposed research seeks to answer this question, as well as others.

The study is directed specifically to three volunteer groups—Reach To Recovery for the patient who has had breast surgery, The United Ostomy Association for the ileostomy, colostomy, and ileal-bladder patients, and the International Association of Laryngectomies for the patient who has had a laryngectomy. All are engaged in rehabilitative work, but represent alternative empirical models for accomplishing the task they set for themselves.

In sum, one overriding interest underlies the proposed study. Although considerable research has been undertaken to help the dying patient, relatively little has been designed to better understand how to help patients live. The steady increase in chronic illness, the limited time, resources, and expertise of professional health services, and the lack of information about how patients cope with continuing health problems make it imperative that we identify the capabilities and limitations of a potential but unstudied community resource, namely, the mutual support group.

Objective

The goal of the proposed research is to assess the impact of lay or mutual support groups on the rehabilitation of patients who have experienced dramatic surgical intervention—breast surgery, an ostomy, or a laryngectomy. While some specific physical and social problems of recuperation may differ among these three types of patients, each must learn to adapt to a permanent condition rather than overcome a temporary one. (The rationale for choosing these types of patients is spelled out after the objective of the proposed research has been set forth.)

The research focuses on mutual support groups at the point in the patient's treatment when he or she* is beginning to plan and to resume usual daily activities such as self-care, work, socializing with friends, and the like. The study asks what effect do mutual support groups have on this process and more particularly, how helpful are they? What these groups actually represent is an expansion of the health care team

---

*For ease of readership, the masculine gender will be used in the text which follows, but the study is, of course, concerned with both men and women adapting to a health condition or impairment.

concept and the crucial question is are they in fact an effective component, more so than, say, the physician and nurse working without their assistance?

The study will also provide as a byproduct a host of information about patients and their recovery experiences which should help to improve the fit between the needs of patients and the delivery of health services. Thus, the implications of the research may be said to extend to any patient confronting a chronic condition.

The kinds of descriptive information the study will provide merit brief discussion before we explain how we propose to measure the success of mutual support groups. To begin, the lack of research about patients and mutual support groups is so considerable that at a recent conference, "Self-Help and Health" (June 8, 1976, New York City) both professionals and members of various groups stated that there are no data on even the demographics of patients reached. We don't know, for example, whether the population served by various groups is young or old, more likely to be married or single, well or poorly educated, largely from upper income groups or from all income groups, essentially whites or members of various racial/ethnic minorities, etc.

Further, despite general information on the purposes of mutual support groups, no attempt has been made to delineate what they try to do to help a person adapt to his condition so that he may achieve maximum recovery. From a review of the literature and preliminary interviewing of members of selected groups we know that there can be at least five components in the rehabilitation efforts of mutual support groups. These are: (1) provide social-emotional support and encouragement; (2) convey information about stages of the recovery process; (3) teach and assist a person in self-care and physical therapy, such as exercises, if these are prescribed; (4) talk with the person, his spouse, and children about any concerns they may have; and (5) help the person optimize his ability to live a full life, including for example, dating, playing tennis, swimming, and resuming whatever work role he chooses. These efforts may be carried out by participation (e.g., in self-care), by serving as a role model or as a referral source (e.g., to another volunteer, a physician, a nurse) or with the aid of written materials. Groups function somewhat differently and need not carry out all five components specified here.

Finally, we do not know what the problems are that patients face. Are the problems mainly physical, moving their body or adapting to an appliance, or are they more social, such as gaining the confidence and courage to begin visiting friends and going places, or are they more emotional such as sadness, irritability, laughing and crying suddenly for no apparent reason? And, what problems, if any, recur six months later and what resources does the patient have for meeting these needs?

Data to begin to answer these questions and to profile patients will result from the proposed research which takes as its major task assessing the efforts of mutual support groups.

MEASURING PATIENT REHABILITATION

Using a quasi-experimental research design, the study will seek to evaluate the role mutual support groups play in a patient's recovery. Thus, the key dependent variable is patient recovery or rehabilitation and we will be concerned with the effect of support groups on this outcome variable.

At first glance, rehabilitation may seem to be a fairly straightforward concept and one for which indicators can readily be developed. However, measuring role performance and functioning requires attention to two analytically distinct dimensions. The first is behavioral or objective and focuses on the resumption of roles—which roles, how many roles, and to what extent they may be fulfilled. The second is subjective and empha-sizes the extent of social-psychological well being patients are experiencing such as their feelings about life, their self-image, and their perceived health status.The devel-opment of measures of rehabilitation is essential for evaluating health services, whether professional or lay, but work along these lines has only just begun.

To arrive at appropriate and sensitive indicators of these two components of the dependent variable will require careful work. Our plan is to review the instruments and scales already developed to measure performance of daily activities and sickness-related dysfunctions* and to interview selected physicians, nurses, and social workers as well as representatives of support groups. We include "lay specialists" or support group members because their personal experience with rehabilitation combined with their efforts to help others may make them particularly acute observers of what rehabilitation really entails.

The study design includes an advisory board composed of physicians, a nurse or social worker, and one or two representatives of support groups and we expect this group of experts to be of assistance in the development of indicators of the dependent variable.

Distinguishing between subjective and objective measures of recovery suggests a four-fold typology of patients which may be schematically presented as follows:

Role Behavior

	+	−
Subjective + Appraisal of Well Being −	I	II
	III	IV

Type I patient is positive in his subjective appraisal and is actively fulfilling customary roles.

Type II patient is positive in appraising his well being, but has defined a more limited life style for himself as a result of his health condition.

Type III patient is negative in self-appraisal, but manages to actively fulfill customary roles.

Type IV patient is negative in self-appraisal and is only minimally fulfilling roles.

This typology serves a heuristic purpose. While it is conceivable that mutual support groups aid each of the four types of patients in the classification above, we hypothesize that they are most likely to have an impact on patients represented by Types II and III. Our reasoning is that patients with some positive strength— attitudinal or behavioral— may find that another person who knows the problems of adaptation *first hand* is helpful. Correlatively, this may be the kind of patient the volunteer prefers. Knowing the difficulties and barriers to adjustment he may be especially sensitive to "cues" from this type of patient which give him leads to being useful. In the best of circumstances, what is then created is a productive feedback loop with both the patient and the volunteer learning.

The Type I patient may have little need for a mutual support group. This may be the patient who has a close family, a good relationship with his physician, and who experiences a kind of euphoria post-surgery. He has accepted the necessity of the operation, seen and read about the appliance, and finds surgery relieves him from a painful and debilitating condition. The fact that he knows others have overcome the mechanics of adjustment is sufficient to motivate him and he requires only limited help (e.g., while hospitalized).

The Type IV patient is undoubtedly the most difficult and may well require intensive professional help of various kinds before he can turn to the supplementary assistance available through a mutual support group.

In sum, these hypothetical types suggest that the result of support group experience may be multi-faceted.

· · ·

Background

Within the field of health, mutual support groups can best be understood in relation to the current interest in "Self care, consumer performance of activities traditionally performed by providers." Technological advances have made routine kidney dialysis possible without active medical intervention; throat cultures, urine testing and other procedures can now be performed by patients themselves or lay parties acting in their behalf. Breast self-examination and insulin injection have been practiced for some time. In each instance, the consumer functions as the extension of the physician in monitoring and managing the disease process. Viewed somewhat differently, these are examples of "consumer-intensive" services for the consumer plays a central role in actually producing the service.

The self-help or mutual support group is another manifestation of the consumer as active participant in health care. These groups now number many thousands and they are a potential resource for almost every health problem and human crisis from alcoholism to widowhood. Two types of organizations have been identified: those that promote research, disseminate information or raise funds and those which provide direct services and social-psychological support to patients. These latter groups—the focus of the proposed research—have been defined by Katz and Bender as:

> Voluntary small group structures for mutual aid in the accomplishment of a specific purpose. They are usually formed by peers who have come together for mutual assistance in satisfying a common need, overcoming a common handicap or life disrupting problem, and bringing about desired social and/or personal change. The initiators and members of such groups perceive that their needs are not or cannot be met by or through existing social institutions.

A recent review of the literature cited over 200 references in professional journals to these organizations. To date, however, the literature has been essentially descriptive and somewhat anecdotal; specific organizations have been portrayed, including their history, occasionally the characteristics of members, a typical meeting, and the role of the professional in relation to them. Groups dealing with mental health problems have received considerable attention in this descriptive literature. Case study methods have most frequently been employed, and where quantitative data are presented, they have usually not been systematically collected. Subjective measures of effectiveness (incentive for joining, satisfaction with membership, etc.) have been used almost exclusively.

Specific Aims

The specific aims of the proposed study are directed to the need for health-related and demographic information about the individual adapting to a health condition and the role mutual support groups may play in this process.

Four research questions frame the study's aims. (1) Do patients who receive the services of a support group demonstrate benefits which are different from patients with the same condition who do not have the services of such a group? (2) Which patients are reached by a support group and which are not? (3) What are the unmet needs of patients who undergo either breast surgery, an ostomy, or a laryngectomy? (4) What are the strengths and limitations of support groups from the perspective of patients, professionals, and volunteers themselves?

The specific aims are:

1. to develop objective and subjective measures of recovery from three kinds of major surgery;
2. to compare the recovery, subjective and objective, of patients with the same condition who are participants and non-participants in the support group relevant to their condition;
3. to profile the patient population reached and not reached by a support group;
4. to delineate the services offered by different groups;
5. to specify the unmet needs of patients;
6. to inquire into the perceived effectiveness of the support groups being studied from the perspective of patients, professionals, and leaders of these groups.

The analysis will compare participants and non-participants in particular support groups in order to learn how successful they may be in facilitating patient recovery from either breast surgery, an ostomy, or a laryngectomy. In the main, the analysis of these data will be quantitative. Supplementary qualitative data obtained from informant interviews with selected physicians, nurses, and social workers and with leaders of each of the groups under study will also be analyzed to better understand the capabilities and limitations of these groups. The outcome of the proposed research is an answer to the critical question: Are mutual support groups an asset in patient recovery, and if so, for which types of patients with what needs?

This proposal, like the others presented here, has been sharply truncated. The review of the literature had several more pages, and a section on data collection has been omitted, as has a section on data analysis.

These sample proposals are quoted primarily to show how research ideas are presented and justified and how the researchers propose to study them. In each instance the research idea represents a departure into an area that has seen relatively little previous research. Such proposals are probably easier to write and justify. There have been so many studies of such topics as social class, juvenile delinquency, and job satisfaction that someone proposing to do research in such traditional areas would not only have a large literature to review but would be hard put to justify still another study.

3

The Inflation Proposal

In the spring of 1978 a new journal, *Grants Magazine: The Journal of Sponsored Research and Other Programs*, appeared. The publisher was Plenum Press, which a few years earlier had published *The Grants Book*, by Virginia White. This extremely successful book sold many thousands of copies, inspiring Plenum Press to introduce *Grants Magazine* with White as its editor. Prior to accepting this position, White was the projects and grants officer at the Graduate School of the City University of New York and after I submitted various proposals to her office, she and I became friends. In discussing the forthcoming journal, I suggested that in each issue White publish a winning proposal with commentary by the proposal writer. This suggestion led to a permanent feature in the journal, "The Grants Clinic." White chose as the first winning proposal to appear in the magazine (in Volume 1, Number 2, June 1978) my proposal to study the impact of inflation and recession on families. This chapter presents the inflation proposal as it appeared in *Grants Magazine*. Everything in the proposal except the biographical sketches of the research personnel appeared in the magazine including the title page and the budget pages. The proposal was followed by my commentary on the history of the proposal and a commentary by someone on the *Grants Magazine* staff. These commentaries are presented in this chapter as well. Apart from the content of the proposal, this example (pages 46–49) gives the reader some idea of what a complete proposal looks like.

Form Approved
Budget Bureau No. 68-R0249

DEPARTMENT OF HEALTH, EDUCATION, AND WELFARE PUBLIC HEALTH SERVICE	LEAVE BLANK	
	TYPE	PROGRAM	NUMBER
	REVIEW GROUP	FORMERLY
GRANT APPLICATION	COUNCIL *(Month, Year)*	DATE RECEIVED

TO BE COMPLETED BY PRINCIPAL INVESTIGATOR *(Items 1 through 7 and 15A)*

,1. TITLE OF PROPOSAL *(Do not exceed 53 typewriter spaces)*
The Impact of Inflation-Recession on Families in Cities

2. PRINCIPAL INVESTIGATOR	3. DATES OF ENTIRE PROPOSED PROJECT PERIOD *(This application)*	
2A. NAME *(Last, First, Initial)* Caplovitz, David	FROM September 1, 1975	THROUGH August 31, 1977
2B. TITLE OF POSITION Associate Professor of Sociology	**4.** TOTAL DIRECT COSTS REQUESTED FOR PERIOD IN ITEM 3 $303,062	**5.** DIRECT COSTS REQUESTED FOR FIRST 12-MONTH PERIOD $151,077

2C. MAILING ADDRESS *(Street, City, State, Zip Code)*
Graduate School and University Center
of the City University of New York
33 West 42nd Street
New York, New York 10036

6. PERFORMANCE SITE(S) *(See Instructions)*

Graduate School and University Center
of the City University of New York
33 West 42nd Street
New York, New York 10036

2D. DEGREE Ph.D.	**2E. SOCIAL SECURITY NO.** 046-20-6588

2F. TELEPHONE DATA | Area Code 212 | TELEPHONE NUMBER AND EXTENSION 790-4635

2G. DEPARTMENT, SERVICE, LABORATORY OR EQUIVALENT *(See Instructions)*
Ph.D. Program in Sociology

,2H. MAJOR SUBDIVISION *(See Instructions)*
Graduate School of City University of N.Y.

7. Research Involving Human Subjects *(See Instructions)* A.☐ NO B.☐ YES Approved: C.☒ YES – Pending Review Date	**8.** Inventions *(Renewal Applicants Only - See Instructions)* A.☐ NO B.☐ YES – Not previously reported C.☐ YES – Previously reported

TO BE COMPLETED BY RESPONSIBLE ADMINISTRATIVE AUTHORITY *(Items 8 through 13 and 15B)*

9. APPLICANT ORGANIZATION(S) *(See Instructions)*
Graduate School and University Center
of the City University of New York
33 West 42nd Street
New York, New York 10036 Jointly with
The Research Foundation of the City
University of New York IRS# 13-1988190 N.
1411 Broadway
New York, New York 10018

11. TYPE OF ORGANIZATION *(Check applicable item)*
☐ FEDERAL   ☐ STATE   ☒ LOCAL   ☐ OTHER *(Specify)*

12. NAME, TITLE, ADDRESS, AND TELEPHONE NUMBER OF OFFICIAL IN BUSINESS OFFICE WHO SHOULD ALSO BE NOTIFIED IF AN AWARD IS MADE
Mr. Paul Segall, Controller
Research Foundation of the City University
of New York
1411 Broadway, New York, N.Y. 10018
Telephone Number (212) 354-2228

10. NAME, TITLE, AND TELEPHONE NUMBER OF OFFICIAL(S) SIGNING FOR APPLICANT ORGANIZATION(S)
Miss Virginia P. White, Director
Sponsored Research and Program Funding
Graduate School and University Center
The City University of New York
33 West 42 St., New York, N.Y. 10036
Telephone Number (s) (212) 790-4683

13. IDENTIFY ORGANIZATIONAL COMPONENT TO RECEIVE CREDIT FOR INSTITUTIONAL GRANT PURPOSES *(See Instructions)*
The Graduate School and University Center
of the City University of New York

14. ENTITY NUMBER *(Formerly PHS Account Number)*
73-2337

15. CERTIFICATION AND ACCEPTANCE. We, the undersigned, certify that the statements herein are true and complete to the best of our knowledge and accept, as to any grant awarded, the obligation to comply with Public Health Service terms and conditions in effect at the time of the award.

SIGNATURES (Signatures required on original copy only. Use ink, "Per" signatures not acceptable)	A. SIGNATURE OF PERSON NAMED IN ITEM 2A	DATE
	B. SIGNATURE(S) OF PERSON(S) NAMED IN ITEM 10	DATE Jan. 20, 1975

NIH 398 (FORMERLY PHS 398
Rev. 1/73

Page 1

DEPARTMENT OF HEALTH, EDUCATION, AND WELFARE	LEAVE BLANK
PUBLIC HEALTH SERVICE	PROJECT NUMBER
RESEARCH OBJECTIVES	

NAME AND ADDRESS OF APPLICANT ORGANIZATION
Graduate School and University Center of the City University of New York
33 West 42nd Street, New York, New York 10036

NAME, SOCIAL SECURITY NUMBER, OFFICIAL TITLE, AND DEPARTMENT OF **ALL PROFESSIONAL PERSONNEL ENGAGED ON PROJECT**, BEGINNING WITH PRINCIPAL INVESTIGATOR
David Caplovitz, Principal Investigator, Professor of Sociology, Graduate School
  and University Center of the City University of New York, S.S. No. 046-20-6588
William Kornblum, Assistant Professor of Sociology, Graduate School and University
  Center of the City University of New York, S.S. No. 096-32-0307
Roger Alcaly, Assistant Professor of Economics, John Jay College of Criminal Justice
  of the City University of New York, S.S. No. 127-30-2335
Sam D. Sieber, Senior Research Associate, Columbia University, S.S. No. 459-44-4955

TITLE OF PROJECT
The Impact of Inflation-Recession on Families in American Cities

USE THIS SPACE TO ABSTRACT YOUR PROPOSED RESEARCH. OUTLINE OBJECTIVES AND METHODS. UNDERSCORE THE **KEY WORD** (NOT TO EXCEED 10) IN YOUR ABSTRACT.

The proposed research will investigate the impact of stagflation (inflation-recession)
on American families. Through a detailed survey of 2500 households sampled from five
American cities with varying unemployment rates, through repeated depth interviews with
100 families and through economic analyses of official statistics on inflation and
unemployment in major cities and the economy as a whole, we plan to find out the
types of families that are suffering most from stagflation and how families are
adjusting to these severe economic conditions. Specifically, we shall examine the
strategies families employ in their efforts to maintain a balance between their income
and their standard of living. The various ways in which families attempt to raise
their income (e.g. having a secondary wage earner enter the labor force) and the
various ways in which families attempt to reduce their standard of living will be
systematically studied. We shall also examine the impact of inflation on the structure
of families, the relationship between husband and wife, the mental health of family
members and the basic value-orientations of the chief wage earner, such as commitment
to materialism and the work ethic.

LEAVE BLANK

DETAILED BUDGET FOR FIRST 12-MONTH PERIOD

	FROM	THROUGH
	Sept. 1, 1975	Aug. 31, 1976

DESCRIPTION *(Itemize)*		TIME OR EFFORT %/HRS.	AMOUNT REQUESTED *(Omit cents)*		
PERSONNEL			SALARY	FRINGE BENEFITS	TOTAL
NAME	TITLE OF POSITION				
David Caplovitz	PRINCIPAL INVESTIGATOR	20%	$ 5,800	$ 1,566	$ 7,366
2/9 Summer		100%	6,444	1,289	7,733
William Kornblum	Project Director	33%	7,000	1,890	8,890
2/9 Summer		100%	4,666	933	5,599
Roger Alcaly	Project Director	33%	7,000	1,890	8,890
2/9 Summer		100%	4,666	933	5,599
Two and ½ Full-time Graduate					
Research Assistants at $10,000 per year each.....		100%	25,000	5,000	30,000
Secretary		50%	5,000	1,000	6,000
Fringe Benefit Rate					
27% during academic year					
20% during summer and non-faculty personnel					
Total			$65,576	$14,501	$80,077

CONSULTANT COSTS____ Dr. Sam Sieber 20-22 days. 3,000

EQUIPMENT _____

SUPPLIES _____ 1,000

TRAVEL	DOMESTIC	2,000
	FOREIGN	

PATIENT COSTS *(See instructions)*

ALTERATIONS AND RENOVATIONS

OTHER EXPENSES *(Itemize)*____ 2500 interviews at $52 per interview
_____ First year share of this cost 65,000

TOTAL DIRECT COST *(Enter on Page 1, Item 5)* ━━━━━━━━━━━━━━━━━━━▶ $151,077

INDIRECT COST *(See Instructions)*	53% __ % S&W* ____ % TDC*	DATE OF DHEW AGREEMENT: October 17, 1972	☐ WAIVED ☐ UNDER NEGOTIATION WITH:
	*IF THIS IS A SPECIAL RATE *(e.g. off-site)*, SO INDICATE.		

BUDGET ESTIMATES FOR ALL YEARS OF SUPPORT REQUESTED FROM PUBLIC HEALTH SERVICE
DIRECT COSTS ONLY (Omit Cents)

DESCRIPTION		1ST PERIOD (SAME AS DETAILED F	ADDITIONAL YEARS SUPPORT REQUESTED (This application only)					
			2ND YEAR	3RD YEAR	4TH YEAR	5TH YEAR	6TH YEAR	7TH YEAR
PERSONNEL COSTS		$ 80,077	$82,985					
CONSULTANT COSTS (Include fees, travel, etc.)		3,000	2,000					
EQUIPMENT		---	---					
SUPPLIES		1,000	1,000					
TRAVEL	DOMESTIC	2,000	2,000					
	FOREIGN							
PATIENT COSTS		---	---					
ALTERATIONS AND RENOVATIONS		---	---					
OTHER EXPENSES *		$ 65,000	65,000					
TOTAL DIRECT COSTS		$151,077	$151,985					

TOTAL FOR ENTIRE PROPOSED PROJECT PERIOD (Enter on Page 1, Item 4) ⟶ $ 303,062

REMARKS: Justify all costs for the first year for which the need may not be obvious. For future years, justify equipment costs, as well as any significant increases in any other category. If a recurring annual increase in personnel costs is requested, give percentage. (Use continuation page if needed.)

*Since the interviewing for the household survey will be done toward the end of the first year, the total cost of these interviews, $130,000, has been divided equally between the first and second years.

THE IMPACT OF INFLATION—RECESSION ON FAMILIES IN CITIES*

Introduction

The United States is now undergoing its most severe economic crisis since the Great Depression of the thirties. We are currently experiencing a staggering rate of inflation, well up into the double digits (at this writing, pressing 15 percent a year). At the same time, contrary to all economic theory, we are experiencing a severe recession, as the unemployment rate has risen above 7 percent and the Gross National Product has steadily declined, sure symptoms of a recession that might well mushroom into a full-scale depression. This double bind of rampant inflation and recession has given rise to a new coinage by economists, "stagflation," or even more dramatically, "slump-flation."

Just as the Great Depression was a worldwide phenomenon, so the current rampant inflation is devastating all the major countries of the world. In Britain the rate of inflation has risen beyond 16 percent; in Japan, inflation is beyond 25 percent a year, an inflationary rate comparable to that of Italy; in Brazil, inflation is running better than 15 percent a year and, of all the Western nations, Greece is hardest hit with an inflation rate of 34 percent, although Israel is not far behind. Canada, Sweden, and West Germany have managed to keep their inflation rates well below 15 percent.

Economists have diagnosed the current inflation as both "demand-pull" inflation in which consumer demand far exceeds the supply of goods and services (too much money pursuing too few goods) and as "cost-push" inflation in which rising costs of labor push prices ever higher. The general consensus is that both of these forces are now at work, reinforcing each other in an ever upward spiral of prices. Underlying these inflationary pressures are decidedly new features of the world economy, such as the energy crisis and the general scarcity of essential resources. The consensus of most scholars is that the current inflation, with or without recession, is a long-range phenomenon not likely to recede in the near future. In fact, we may be on the verge of a new society, one in which inflation is endemic to our way of life. In a variety of circles, the alarm has been raised that hyperinflation can lead to the downfall of our democratic society. Thus President Ford has identified inflation as "public enemy number 1" and the conservative Arthus Burns, Chairman of the Federal Reserve, recently observed, "if long continued, inflation at anything like the present rate would threaten the very foundations of our society." The highly prestigious journal *Skeptic*, published by the Forum of Contemporary History, recently devoted a special issue to inflation. The lead editorial of this issue warns that inflation can sap our freedom and bring down our democratic society, in much the way that Uruguay in the past decade has been transformed from a thriving democracy into a bankrupt dictatorship under the pressure of inflation. To quote from this editorial,

> As stiff as inflation's toll has been up to now, it is nothing compared to the cost which confronts us at the end of the road. Unless we check inflation, it will cost us our freedom. And if that sounds too apocalyptic, consider the ways in which inflation already has chipped away at freedoms we have taken for granted. Our

*From *Grants Magazine*, **1**, No. 2 (June 1978). 166–172

options in the marketplace are more limited than they used to be . . . Our freedom of movement is circumscribed by the rising costs of operating a car . . . Our freedom to locate where we choose is limited by soaring rents and real estate prices . . . Our freedom to make plans of every imaginable sort, from having a baby to taking a vacation, has been diminished by inflation . . . Inflation has narrowed our choices and options. In the end it threatens to eliminate them entirely.[1]

Hovering over this period of rampant inflation is the specter of Weimar Germany in which the finances of whole classes of the population were wiped out by hyperinflation and the way was paved for the rise of Naziism.

Whether these apocalyptic events ever come to pass, it is clear that rampant inflation now joined by a dangerous recession has already had a dramatic impact on the way of life of many Americans.

Whether rampant inflation or widespread unemployment is the major problem at the time the proposed study is carried out remains to be seen. In either event, families in all walks of life will have been touched by these economic conditions, and, for some, the pressures will be so great that their very survival will be threatened. A basic thesis of this proposal is that stagflation has caused and will continue to cause considerable hardship for many American families and poses a serious threat to the mental health of a substantial proportion of the population.

OBJECTIVES

The proposed research has two fundamental objectives. First, through a household survey, we plan to identify those segments of the population which have been most hurt by inflation and, conversely, those which have managed to escape the ravages of inflation. A critical concept in the proposed research is what we call "inflation crunch," meaning the degree to which a family has been hurt by inflation. We plan to measure "inflation crunch" in both objective and subjective terms. This distinction is spelled out below in the section dealing with specific aims. As the sampling plan indicates, particular attention will be paid to the two groups widely assumed to suffer most from inflation, the retired who live on fixed incomes and the poor. The sampling plan that has been devised insures that ample numbers of these groups will be included in the household survey for statistical analysis.

The second major objective of this research is to document in a systematic way how families that have experienced varying degrees of "inflation crunch" have adjusted to or tried to adapt to this pressure. We will examine the way in which their lifestyles have changed, the coping strategies they have evolved, and the impact that inflation has had on family structure, marriages, mental health, and basic value orientations.

The ultimate purpose of the proposed research is to provide information that will be useful to policymakers who must weigh the costs and benefits of the current inflationary pressures in contrast to a severe recession. We are convinced that this objective will be realized by research that documents the trends that are developing in the American way of life in response to hyperinflation. These trends are likely to have repercussions for all the major institutions of our society, from the occupational world, to higher education, to leisure time activities, to the functioning of local government, to the

---

[1] *Skeptic* Special Issue Number 3, October, 1974, p. 5.

organization of the family.[2] In short, a careful study of the impact of inflation on American families will provide valuable insights into the future directions of American society which, in turn, will be of value to policymakers.

BACKGROUND

Surprisingly enough, there have been virtually no sociological studies of the impact of inflation on American society or, for that matter, on any society.[3] The mass media have been flooded with anecdotal materials on how one or another typical family has been trying to cope with inflation. For example, last Spring the *Wall Street Journal* had a series of such articles and more recently the major networks have been presenting profiles of families coping with inflation.

A careful search of the sociological literature has uncovered only one study of inflation by a sociologist and that is a doctoral dissertation at Columbia in 1962 by Sam Sieber, entitled *Union Members, the Public and Inflation*. Much of the Sieber analysis is based on a survey of 400 steel union members and 400 members of unions other than steel in Pittsburgh that was carried out in 1959. In addition to this survey, Sieber culls the various public opinion polls conducted since World War II to find out what the public attitude toward inflation and its causes has been over this period. Sieber's analysis of these polls indicates that inflation has been a major worry of the American people through much of the postwar period up through 1960. Sieber notes that most Americans considered inflation a serious problem even though the rate of inflation during these years was quite low (with the exception of the Korean war period) and even though income more than kept pace with inflationary pressures. To account for this public concern over a pseudo-problem, Sieber advances the interesting thesis that people were concerned not so much with making ends meet as they were with the threat of inflation to their realizing the American dream of steadily improving their lifestyles. This idea will be pursued in the proposed research as a possible explanation of why some people feel hurt by inflation (subjective inflation crunch) even though their incomes have kept pace with the rising cost of living (objective inflation crunch).

The Sieber analysis is primarily concerned with the reasons that the public at large and union members, particularly the steelworkers, gave for inflation. There was considerable debate at the time about the causes of inflation and the mass media, mouthing the propaganda of management, tended to place the cause on the unreasonable demands of the unions for salary boosts. The survey analyzed by Sieber took place during the long contract negotiations that eventually broke down and resulted in the longest steel strike in the history of the country in 1959. A major finding of the Sieber study was that many workers, even steelworkers, tended to buy the management line and blamed their union officials for causing inflation. Contrary to the assumptions of many labor economists who take it for granted that workers have an insatiable demand

---

[2]Focusing on the impact of inflation on American families as we propose is only one way of studying the impact of inflation on American society. As is described below, during the Depression, the Social Science Research Council sponsored a series of monographs which examined the impact of the Depression on various phases of American life, e.g., education, the family, recreation, health, the church, etc. A similar series of studies of the impact of inflation on various institutional spheres of society would be highly desirable. We are proposing a study of the impact on a single highly strategic institution, the family, but, of course, inflation's impact on other institutions is deserving of study as well.

[3]To be sure there is a vast literature dealing with inflation in economics but this deals exclusively with the causes of inflation and its impact on the economy rather than its impact on people.

for higher wages. Sieber found that many workers were prepared to forego wage increases if this would check inflation. This question of whom the public blames for inflation will be pursued in the proposed study. It will be interesting to see whether the distribution of blame by the public among business, labor, and government is the same today as it was in 1959 and, if not, the ways in which it has changed.

If inflation has been largely ignored by sociologists, the same is not true for the opposite catastrophic economic event, depression. The Great Depression of the thirties gave rise to an untold number of studies by social scientists dealing with the impact of the Depression on various institutions of society. Although diametrically opposite phenomena, depressions and inflations have a number of similarities with respect to their impacts on individuals and families. Both involve adjusting to lowered standards of living, in the one case because the dollar won't buy as much and in the other because the opportunity to earn dollars has declined. But, of course, of the two, depression, meaning unemployment, is the much more severe problem—at least in the short run. If rampant inflation means, for many people, a reduction in living standards by 10 or 15 percent, unemployment means a reduction on the order of 50 percent or more (assuming that there are relief programs and insurance programs that prevent the reduction from going all the way to zero). In light of these similarities between depression and inflation, the proposed research has much to gain from a review of the vast body of Depression literature, and a more thorough review of that literature than is reported here will be one of the first tasks of the proposed research. Unfortunately, the research technology of the thirties was not nearly as advanced as it is today; hardly any of the Depression studies were on the scale of the proposed study. Whereas we plan to survey some 2500 households, these Depression studies are based largely on case studies of between fifty and one hundred or so families. One of the earliest of these ethnographic accounts of the impact of the Depression was carried out by Lazarsfeld and his colleagues who studied unemployment in a small town in Austria.[4] Other classic studies of the impact of the Depression were carried out by Komarovsky, Bakke, and Angell.[5] These Depression studies document the devastating effects of umemployment on the self-esteem of the breadwinner and the strains that developed within the family. A major theme of this research was the extent to which the unemployed male lost moral authority within his family. The Angell study is particularly interesting in light of the proposed research. Angell was concerned with the strengths and weaknesses of families that allowed some to withstand the pressures of the Depression while others succumbed to these pressures and became disorganized. He attempted to study the impact of two properties of families on their adjustment to the Depression, the degree to which they were integrated, that is, the degree to which the family members assisted and respected each other and helped each other grow, and what he called adaptability or flexibility, that is, the readiness of the family to adjust in good spirits to radically changed circumstances. Angell makes the very telling point that rigid, inflexible families are likely to be the ones deeply committed to material possessions and a lifestyle based on such possessions. Such families are likely to fall apart if they experience only a moderate reduction of income, in contrast with more flexible families that experience

[4]Maria Jahoda, Paul F. Lazarsfeld, and Hans Zeisel, *The Unemployed of Marienthal*, Allensback and Bonn: Verlag für Demoskopie, 1960. Reprinted by Aldine Press, Chicago, 1974.
[5]Mirra Komarovsky, *The Unemployed Man and His Family*, New York: Dryden Press, 1940. W. Wight Bakke, *The Unemployed Worker: A Study of the Task of Making a Living without a Job*, New Haven: Yale University Press, 1940. Robert Cooley Angell, *The Family Encounters the Depression*, New York: Charles Scribner's Sons, 1936.

much larger reductions in income. This idea of Angell's is directly applicable to the proposed research and is at the core of the distinction between objective and subjective inflation crunch.

By far the most ambitious project to assess the impact of the Depression on American society was carried out in 1936 and 1937 by the Social Science Research Council. The SSRC sponsored a series of 13 studies assessing the impact of the Depression on various facets of American society and institutions. This overall project was supervised by Samuel Stouffer and the various volumes were authored by experts in the various fields who culled a vast array of secondary sources for information. The title for the overall series was *Studies in the Social Aspects of the Depression* and each volume was entitled *A Research Memorandum on _____ and the Depression*. The topics that filled the blank included crime, recreation, the family, consumption, minority groups, reading, education, religion, health, rural life, etc.

These volumes are filled with nuggets of information—findings and hypotheses relevant to the proposed research on stagflation/inflation–recession. A cursory sample of the findings and hypotheses include the following:

1. Crimes against property (theft) increased during the Depression.
2. People became more tolerant, less morally indignant, of such crimes.
3. Attendance of high school increased sharply during the Depression even though college attendance declined.
4. "Depression colleges," i.e., junior colleges and adult education programs, came into being to absorb the energies of the unemployed.
5. There was a sharp expansion in leisure time and a sharp growth in recreational facilities. Use of inexpensive recreational facilities, such as parks and beaches, increased greatly. Automobile tours were very popular.
6. There was sharp curtailment of consumption of major durables. Many found relief in escape from conspicuous consumption, especially those who were having difficulty realizing their high consumer aspirations.
7. Marriage rates, birth rates, and divorce rates declined, but illegitimacy rates increased, findings stemming from economic considerations.
8. Youth were particularly hard hit by unemployment with the result that many of the young postponed leaving home and many who left home returned.
9. Reliance of youth on parents was part of a general lengthening of the period of child dependency.
10. The quality of housing decreased sharply as few new homes were built and people moved to cheaper quarters often without electricity and hot water.
11. There was a sharp increase in doubled up families, i.e., two or more families living in the same residence.
12. Mutual aid among relatives, leading to a revival of the extended kinship unit, increased sharply.
13. Mixed marriages and impulsive marriages (e.g., marriages not performed by a minister) increased during the Depression, suggesting breakdown of traditional restraints.
14. There was a sharp increase in symptoms of "war neuroses" as previously stable men "went to pieces," had "nervous breakdowns," and developed neurotic traits.

15. Those in poor health, the handicapped, etc., were most likely to be laid off, in a revival of the survival of the fittest.

16. There was a sharp decline in public expenditures for sanitation and cleanliness, e.g., sewage disposal, street cleaning, etc.

17. There was a sharp decline in occupied hospital beds as people postponed needed operations.

18. Reliance on home entertainment increased sharply, e.g., radio listening, card playing, jigsaw puzzles, board games, like Monopoly.

19. The Depression stimulated the co-op movement.

20. The *Readers Digest* thrived during the Depression as did pulp magazines of the *True Story* variety at the expense of serious magazines and humor magazines.

21. Employed women, because of the industries they were in, were not as likely to lose their jobs as men, with the result that women assumed more of a responsibility relative to men for support of the family.

22. Unemployed men were likely to have their parental authority undermined.

23. Suicide rates increased sharply during the Depression.

24. Racial tensions among workers tended to increase during the Depression, as a result of the competition for scarce jobs.

As these findings indicate, the Depression had a profound impact on the mental health of the unemployed, on family structure, on style of life, on moral attitudes, and on social relations between families. These themes will be studied in the proposed research to see the ways in which the consequences of inflation are similar to and different from those of the Depression. The findings listed above and many more can be found in the following volumes:

Thorstein Sellin, *Crime in the Depression*, SSRC Bulletin 27, 1937.
Educational Policies Commission, *Education and the Depression*, SSRC Bulletin 28.
Samuel A. Stouffer and Paul F. Lazarsfeld, *The Family in the Depression*, SSRC Bulletin 29.
Warren S. Thompson, *Internal Migration in the Depression*, SSRC Bulletin 30.
Donald Young, *Minority Peoples in the Depression*, SSRC Bulletin 31.
Jessie Steiner, *Recreation in the Depression*, SSRC Bulletin 32.
Samuel C. Kineheloe, *Religion in the Depression*, SSRC Bulletin 33.
Dwight Anderson, *Rural Life in the Depression*, SSRC Bulletin 34.
Ronald S. Vaile, *Consumption in the Depression*, SSRC Bulletin 35.
Selwyn D. Collins and Clark Tibbitts, *Health in the Depression*, SSRC Bulletin 36.
Douglas Waples, *Reading in the Depression*, SSRC Bulletin 37.
R. Clyde White and Mary K. White, *Relief Policies in the Depression*, SSRC Bulletin 38.
F. Stuart Chapin and Stuart A. Queen, *Social Work in the Depression*, SSRC Bulletin 39.

Apart from the literature relevant to the proposed study, one facet of the principal investigator's experience should be mentioned as part of the background for this proposal. As is noted below, one theme that will be explored in the household survey is the extent to which families try to cope with inflationary pressures by making use of credit. The principal investigator recently completed a study of people deeply entangled in installment debt.[6] This research disclosed that debt troubles result in a series of debilitating consequences for the debtor and his family. It is widely assumed that rampant inflation is pushing people deeper and deeper into debt and the principal investigator's knowledge of this problem area will strengthen the proposed research in this respect. For example, the problem of measuring debt entanglement has been solved and we will apply it to families under study to test the hypothesis that one result of inflation crunch is debt entanglement.

Earlier in his career, the principal investigator was associated with another study that is quite relevant to the present research, a study of subjective feeling states, known as the happiness study. A major effort in the proposed research will be to measure the impact of inflation on the psychological well-being of the respondents and the principal investigator has considerable experience with questionnaire indicators that measure feeling states.[7]

Specific Aims

The proposed study encompasses three research strategies enumerated in the next section: a household survey of 2500 families, field work involving case studies of 100 families, and an econometric analysis of inflation–unemployment data for the country as a whole and for a sample of large cities. Of these, the household survey is perhaps most critical and almost all the specific aims of the research can be described by identifying the goals of the household survey.

The household survey has four major objectives: (1) identifying the kinds of families that are suffering most from stagflation, i.e., rampant inflation and unemployment; (2) examining the strategies that families have employed in their efforts to cope with inflation–unemployment, strategies that for the most part involve radical changes in lifestyles; (3) identifying the impact of inflation–recession on the well-being of families, on the mental health of family members, and on basic value orientations of family members; and (4) learning how the public interprets the causes of inflation and which critical groups it blames for our economic troubles.

MEASURING THE IMPACT OF HYPERINFLATION AND IDENTIFYING ITS VICTIMS

It is extremely misleading to assume that people in all walks of life are equally affected by the sharp rise in the cost of living over the past several years. Even during the most traumatic economic crisis in our history, the Depression of the thirties, a majority of wage earners were able to escape the ravages of unemployment. The overall unemployment rate during the height of the Depression did not exceed 25 percent. Similarly, not all Americans are currently suffering because of hyperinflation. Partly as a result of cost of living clauses in union contracts and partly because many professional classes are free to raise the cost of their services, large segments of the population have been able to keep abreast of rampant inflation by raising their incomes, and their styles of life have not suffered in any material way. But, by the same token, equally large, if not larger, segments of the population have suffered because of the hyperinflation and stagflation we are now experiencing. For these families, hyperinflation has posed a

---

[6]David Caplovitz, *Consumers in Trouble: A Study of Debtors in Default*, New York: The Free Press, 1974.
[7]See Norman Bradburn and David Caplovitz, *Reports on Happiness*, Chicago: Aldine Press, 1965.

series of difficult choices ranging from finding new sources of income to keep abreast of rising prices to deciding how to lower one's standard of living so as to make ends meet. The notion of the impact of inflation on families gives rise to a concept like inflation crunch. A major task of the proposed research will be to measure inflation crunch and identify the families who are experiencing inflation crunch and the families who are managing to avoid it. The concept of inflation crunch will be measured in two ways: objectively and subjectively. By *objective inflation crunch* we mean the degree to which the family's *normal* sources of income have failed to keep up with the rise in the cost of living. We will know how much the cost of living has risen in each of the sample cities included in the household survey over the two- or three-year period prior to the survey. We will then find out how much the earnings of the chief wage earners have risen during this period. The ratio of these numbers will serve as our measure of objective inflation crunch. In measuring objective inflation crunch we shall be careful to take into account new sources of income stimulated by the inflation, such as the chief wage earner taking on a second job or a secondary wage earner entering the labor force during this period. Expansions in family income due to such measures will be treated as consequences of inflation crunch and will not be included in the measure of objective inflation crunch.[8] In addition to objective inflation crunch the proposed research will measure the degree to which the family feels that it is hurting because of inflation. This will yield a measure of *subjective inflation crunch*. Presumably these two measures will be highly correlated but, as the Angell study of families during the Depression makes clear, a critical intervening variable is the degree of adaptability or flexibility of the family. Families deeply committed to materialism, to "keeping up with the Joneses," will experience more subjective deprivation than families less committed to such values who experience the same degree of objective inflation crunch. These measures of inflation crunch will then be related to the various demographic characteristics of the respondents. In this fashion we shall be able to identify the social groups suffering most from inflation. As noted in the methodological section, the research plan will insure that the poor and the retired, two groups widely assumed to be hurt hardest by inflation, will be included in the study. Thus the first major objective of the study will be to identify the social groups that are being hurt by inflation and the groups that for whatever reasons are not being hurt.

RESPONSES TO THE IMBALANCE BETWEEN INCOME AND STANDARD OF LIVING

Rampant inflation and unemployment represent for many families a sudden imbalance between their income and their standard of living. They find themselves unable to maintain the standard of living that their income previously permitted. Confronted with such a problem, two possible solutions emerge: either income can be raised to keep up with inflation or standard of living can be lowered.

RAISING INCOME.   Should families find that normal increments in the salary of the chief wage earner are insufficient to keep up with inflation, they have several options for increasing family income. The chief wage earner can work harder by doing more overtime work or by taking a second job. Also, a second potential wage earner, typically a spouse but also a teenage child, can enter the labor market. A major objective of the proposed research will be to document the extent to which efforts to raise the family

---

[8]Measuring objective inflation crunch is more complicated than this discussion indicates. Some housewives may have mixed motives for entering the labor force. For example, their children may be grown, they may be bored, and at the same time they may want to help make ends meet. Considerable care will be given to measuring this concept.

income have occurred. It should be noted that pressures that lead additional family members to enter the labor force provide one link between inflation and unemployment. During the period that new entrants to the labor force are looking for work but have not found it, they are counted as unemployed and it may well be that one way that hyperinflation contributes to unemployment is by forcing secondary wage earners into the labor force. To the extent that these adjustments have been made by family members to raise family income, the structure of the family is likely to change and strains may develop within the families. These potential impacts of rampant inflation are discussed below in the section dealing with inflation and family well-being.

REDUCING STANDARD OF LIVING.   The anecdotal materials that has appeared in the mass media has pointed to sharp reductions in standards of living on the part of families who are experiencing inflation crunch. In family menus, steaks have given way to hamburger and casseroles. A shocking discovery has been that many of the poor and the retired have been forced to eat pet food. According to the issue of *Skeptic* cited above, there has been a sharp increase in the sales of pet food even though the number of pets in America has not increased. This can only mean that pet food is being used for human consumption.[9] Families have learned to postpone the purchase of new merchandise, especially major durables, as is now being witnessed by the sharp slump in the automobile industry. Home repairs are either being neglected or are being made by the family members themselves, perhaps with the help of neighbors. Women who never consulted cook books before are now doing so in large numbers as they try to learn to prepare tasty but inexpensive meals. Shopping trips are more and more infused with bargain-hunting and many housewives are shopping around and learning the habits of the "good consumer." Similarly, when it comes to clothing, many housewives are learning to make clothes for themselves and other family members. In these ways, husbands and wives are being forced to develop new competencies which in turn may have implications for mental health (discussed below).

Apart from efforts to scrimp on the necessities of life, families confronted with inflation crunch are no doubt making drastic changes in their ways of life regarding leisure time activities. Rampant inflation has caused a sharp restriction in the geographic scope of vacations. Not only are fewer people vacationing abroad but domestic pleasure spots such as Miami Beach are experiencing hard times because many of their traditional clientele can no longer afford the journey.

Just as the Depression saw a marked increase in home-centered leisure time activities, such as card playing, puzzle solving, and Monopoly games, so the current inflation in conjunction with the energy crunch has led to a sharp rise in home entertainment. Parker Brothers, the manufacturers of the most popular board game, Monopoly, and numerous other board games, has experienced a dramatic increase in sales over the past year.

A major theme of the household survey will be to document in a systematic way the degree to which standards of living have been lowered and the ways in which lifestyles have been altered because of inflation—recession. Most importantly, the research will measure the family's response to such reductions in standard of living, ranging from acceptance with equanimity to severe stress, in much the way that Angell tried to measure the degree of adaptability of families to the deprivations of the Depression.

---

[9]A recent article in the *Wall Street Journal* called attention to a serious health hazard stemming from the consumption of pet food. Apparently fuel pollution has resulted in a sharp increase in the lead content of the grass eaten by cattle. This lead tends to concentrate in the livers of animals and livers constitute the chief meat in pet food. Thus the poor who eat pet food run the risk of lead poisoning.

RELIANCE ON CREDIT AS AN ADAPTIVE MECHANISM

Inflationary pressures are forcing more and more families to rely on credit as a mechanism for bridging the gap between their needs and wants and their ability to pay. Long before rampant inflation struck America, consumer credit grew by leaps and bounds. Between 1966 and 1970, outstanding installment debt increased from $66 billion to $100 billion, a growth of $34 billion in the four-year period. But in the next four-year period, 1970 to 1974, characterized by rampant inflation, outstanding consumer debt climbed from $100 billion to $150 billion, a growth of $50 billion. At first glance, going into debt seems to be a sensible way of coping with inflation because the debtor can pay back his loan with cheaper dollars. But this is true only to a certain point. The debtor heavily in debt has committed a considerable portion of his future income to debt payments and he runs the risk of getting into debt over his head. A recent study by the Morgan Guaranty bank has shown that consumer debt has increased by 42 percent between the end of 1970 and the middle of 1974, but, after taxes, personal income in this period rose by only 37 percent. As a result "a bigger share than in the past of people's incomes is already committed just to make payments on past purchases." The imbalance in family finances caused by inflation is evident in the sharply increasing numbers of people deeply entangled in debt. Lenders and creditors are experiencing record default rates, and personal bankruptcy, one of the few remedies available to overextended debtors, has risen sharply in the past several years. (In fiscal 1974 personal bankruptcies increased by 8.4 percent over fiscal 1973, from 155,643 cases to 168,657. Only a tiny fraction of the families eligible for bankruptcy utilize this drastic remedy.) Debt entanglements induced by rampant inflation may well be wreaking havoc with many families in the patterns identified in *Consumers in Trouble* (see footnote 6).

Changes in the use of credit and the impact of credit use on families will be carefully measured in the household survey.

THE EMERGENCE OF COMMUNAL RESPONSES TO INFLATION

The Depression literature, as noted, documents a sharp rise in mutual aid among members of the extended kinship group and among neighbors, as people joined together to help fight the common enemy, the Depression. Neighboring, i.e., neighborly visits, increased sharply in rural communities and the number of multiple families sharing the same dwelling unit increased sharply during the Depression. Also, the co-op movement flourished. Similarly, communal responses to the current pressures of rampant inflation can be detected. Food-buying clubs, car pools, and babysitting pools have become increasingly popular as neighbors turn to mutual aid to cut down costs. There has even been an increase in doubled up households just as there was in the Depression. Numerous news stories have documented instances of families on Long Island and in other residential areas sharing large houses to cut down costs.

The development of community has been a surprisingly consistent response to adversity. The sharp rise in the crime rate in New York has resulted in the emergence of block associations, organizations whose main task is to raise funds to hire a private guard for the block. These block associations have turned the cold, anonymous big city of New York into a myriad of small neighborhoods in which people on the block have come to know each other. Similarly, the adversity of rampant inflation is having similar effects. These communal responses are quite different from the spirit of communality that thrived among the hippies and flower children of the sixties, who turned their backs on "straight" society. But it is of some interest whether rampant inflation is contributing to a new more communal lifestyle that in some strange way is bringing "straight people" closer to the values of the hippies of yesterday.

IMPACT OF INFLATION – RECESSION ON FAMILY STRUCTURE, MENTAL HEALTH, AND VALUES

In the previous section we reviewed the various strategies that families might employ to maintain the balance between income and standard of living. But these strategies have their consequences for families and family members. Some no doubt exact a heavy psychic toll, ranging from undermining the self-confidence of the chief wage earner to increasing marital strains. But diametrically opposite psychological effects might result. Breadwinners may feel proud that they have been able to keep their heads above water through self-help activities and they may develop new bases for self-esteem. To the extent that wives and teenages are forced to work, major changes are likely to result in the family structure. And finally, just as in the Depression, the drastic changes forced upon families as a result of rampant inflation – recession may lead to major changes in value orientations. Some families may become radicalized by the hard times they are experiencing, others may abandon their blind pursuit of material wealth, and still others may have their faith in major institutions, especially government, seriously undermined. These ramifications of inflation – recession for the well-being of families and individual family members will be carefully studied in the household survey and the case study.

MODIFICATIONS IN FAMILY STRUCTURE

The Depression literature demonstrates that unemployment results in considerable strain in the marital relationship as husbands become less capable of fulfilling their responsibilities. Do comparable strains and changes in marital relationships occur as a result of rampant inflation? To the extent that changes in labor force participation occur on the part of either or both spouses, then changes in the marriage are likely to occur. Wives may learn to be more independent; husbands may feel less in command. A potential for strain exists with respect to expenditures made by one or the other spouse. A husband's drinking habits may be more or less tolerated in times of prosperity, but, in times of rampant inflation, money squandered in this fashion may be a source of considerable strain. Similarly, the housewife who fails to economize on the household budget or who insists on indulging her vanity with expenditures on cosmetics risks the wrath of her husband. In short, rampant inflation reduces sharply the slack in the system for frivolous, irrational expenditures and, in so doing, raises sharply the inflammatory potential of such expenditures.

For some families, the kind that Angell would call well integrated, the pressures of rampant inflation might result not in familial strain but rather in closer cooperation and mutual support as the spouses make extra efforts to "make ends meet." In so doing, the tie between the spouses may grow stronger. It remains for empirical research to document the frequency of these outcomes and the conditions under which marital strains increase or lessen under inflationary pressure.

Apart from the relationship between spouses, rampant inflation is likely to have consequences for the relationship between parents and their children. The Depression studies documented that young adults were unable to find work and thus continued to live with their parents and those who had left home returned home. Rampant inflation may well have the similar effect of prolonging the period of dependency of children on their parents. Inflation is particularly likely to place a strain on the plans for higher education of children. College enrollments appear to be turning downward as many high school graduates find that their families cannot afford to send them to college. Rampant inflation may well be forcing youth who would have gone to college into the labor force and during the period that they are looking for work they contribute to unemployment, yet another way in which inflation is linked to the basic symptom of recession. The failure of grown children to leave home as they would in more normal times might well contribute to further strain in the family, this time between the parents and the children. Parents might well resent the frustrations stemming from the pro- longed dependency of their children.

MODIFICATIONS IN MENTAL HEALTH OF CHIEF WAGE EARNER AND SPOUSE

A major theme of the proposed research will be the impact of inflation on the mental health of the chief wage earner and his spouse. How do people feel when they find they must give up a wide range of aspirations (expensive consumption plans)? To what extent do people worry and suffer from anxiety because of the uncertainty of making ends meet? To what extent do housewives develop feelings of inadequacy because they are unable to cut down significantly on household expenses? To what extent do parents feel guilty because they must deny their children new clothes, summer camps, and expensive recreational activities, to say nothing of a college education?

Apart from the negative impact of rampant inflation on mental health, to what extent does it make a *positive* contribution to mental health? As noted, unemployment tends to undermine mental health by destroying the self-esteem of the breadwinner. But the psychological impact of inflation may be quite different for many people. Inasmuch as most breadwinners are still employed, they are likely to blame the system rather than themselves. In their efforts to make ends meet, both husband and wife may discover inner strengths and resources that they were unaware of, such as being able to make do with less expensive food, making one's own clothes, making household repairs, etc. Whether the negative consequences of rampant inflation for mental health outweigh the positive consequences and vice versa is again a matter for research. To some extent it will be possible to study these subtle psychological issues through standard form questionnaires in the household survey, but in this area, as in others, the proposed field work involving in-depth studies of 100 or so families will make a major contribution.

MODIFICATIONS IN BASIC VALUE ORIENTATIONS

Rampant inflation, for those who are vulnerable to its impact, represents a sudden, drastic reordering of life's priorities. In this process of rapid change it is quite possible that long-held, deep-seated value orientations may well change. The proposed re- search will seek to determine whether value orientations in four basic areas will have been modified by rampant inflation: (a) commitment to materialism, (b) the work ethic, (c) confidence in government, and (d) political orientation on a left–right continuum.

The dominant ethos of American society, one which served quite well until very recently, was a deep commitment to materialism, "getting and spending," acquiring in a never-ending way the symbols of the good life, from color TV sets to new cars and power boats and a home of one's own. Rampant inflation, like a deep recession, makes the pursuit of such consumer goals impossible. Many families not only must go without, but also a number of them may come to question the old values that told them that they should pursue these consumer goals. We may suggest that one consequence of rampant inflation is to seriously undermine the materialistic ethos that has been dominant in our society. In its place new dominant values may be emerging, such as a new sense of communality, kinship with others, or a commitment to simple pleasures, or a commitment to higher values, such as learning and the arts, as dominant goals of life. The impact of rampant inflation on materialistic values will thus be one theme of the research.

Another basic value that may be seriously threatened by rampant inflation is commitment to the work ethic. The sociologist Richard Sennett has suggested that the work ethic may well be undermined as people discover that their hard work not only fails to buy more goods, but also buys even less goods than formerly.[10] Americans are told from the time they are very small that if they work hard they will get the good things in life but rampant inflation tends to make a mockery of this precept. The man who was able to rationalize the aches and pains that he received from work on the grounds that his efforts would allow the family to buy a swimming pool may well wonder why he tolerates such aches and pains when the swimming pool is clearly only a pipe dream. He may decide not to work as hard and in the extreme to give up work altogether for some version of the "drop out" lifestyle. Again, attitudes toward work will be measured in the research to see if there is any merit to Sennett's idea.

Another basic value to be examined in the research will be confidence in government. In order for an administration to govern successfully there must be some minimal level of confidence in it. To what extent do those hurting from inflation turn cynical about government and political leaders because of government's inability to solve the problem that is hurting them? Economic issues have long been recognized as the most salient in the voting booth. To what extent is rampant inflation, coupled with recession, a force capable of making people cynical *about* the voting booth, that is, about their control over their lives and the democratic process itself. These questions border on the fourth basic value orientation to be considered in the light of rampant inflation, political orientation. Has rampant inflation coupled with recession, by pointing up fundamental weaknesses in our capitalistic economy, made people more ready to move to the left and consider socialistic solutions to their problems? Several questions will be asked of the respondents regarding their faith in capitalism and whether it has changed in recent years.

INTERPRETATIONS OF INFLATION

Yet another major goal of the household survey and the field research will be to find out who and what people blame for rampant inflation. This was a major theme of Sieber's research of fifteen years ago and one of his major findings was that at that time even members of a militant union like the steelworkers union were as inclined to blame the excessive wage demands of their leaders as they were to blame corporations for seeking excessive profits by raising prices. At the time of the Sieber study the culprits for inflation were limited to three groups—management, labor, and government. But today a fourth group and a new factor enter the picture, the Arabs and the energy crisis. The research will ask the respondents to rate the role of each of these groups in the current inflation. It will be extremely interesting to see whether there is now consensus within both the blue-collar and white-collar groups and whether these social classes hold similar or different views on the causes of inflation. The analysis of the data collected will deal with the relationships between the locus of blame and certain impacts of inflation crunch.

[10]See *Time Magazine*, November 4, 1974, p. 104.

Methods of Procedure

The proposed research makes use of three well-established research strategies: (1) a large-scale *sample survey*; (2) *case studies* in the form of repeated depth interviews with 100 "representative" families; and (3) *econometric analysis*, primarily of official statistics of cities and the economy as a whole but also of the survey data.

THE HOUSEHOLD SURVEY

At the heart of the proposed research is a large-scale sample survey of households. Instead of a national sample of households, we shall limit the survey to five cities of varying degrees of unemployment. In this way we shall be able to study the impact of inflation in the context of high and low unemployment. Two high unemployment cities will be selected (tentatively Detroit and Seattle) and two low unemployment cities (tentatively Chicago and Atlanta) with one city to represent the middle range of unemployment (tentatively New York). Within each city stratified random samples of 500 families will be selected, for a total of 2500 in all five cities. To insure adequate representation of the groups believed to be hardest hit by inflation, the poor and the retired, within each city, a random sample of 100 poor families and 100 retired persons will be interviewed. The remaining 300 interviews in each city will be split evenly between blue-collar and white-collar workers. Thus the final sample of 2500 households will consist of 500 poor families, defined as families living in the sampled cities who are earning below $8000 or so in the summer of 1976 when the survey will be conducted (by then such an income should be the equivalent of the $4000 poverty level set for urban families during the mid-sixties when war was declared on poverty), 500 retired persons, 750 blue-collar households, and 750 white-collar households. The survey of blue-collar and white-collar families will be limited to complete families, that is, those in which both the husband and wife are residing in the household. The reason for this is to permit examining the inflation strategies of having additional wage earners go to work and the stresses and strains that inflation may be imposing on marriages. The requirement of a complete family will be dropped in the samples of poor and retired persons. In at least half the cases the interview will be conducted with the chief wage earner and in the other cases with his or her spouse.

The research design specified above means that the city unemployment rate will be a key contextual variable in the analysis. We shall be able to assess whether the impact of inflation crunch is the same or different in high and low unemployment cities. It may well be, for example, that the specter of losing a job in a high unemployment community may make those who do have jobs more ready to accept the deprivations of rampant inflation. Given the sampling procedures described above it is quite likely that the final sample will contain several hundred or more households in which the chief wage earner has lost his job and thus we shall be able to compare the deprivations and feeling states of the unemployed with the employed who are experiencing severe inflation crunch.

The household survey will attempt to cover most if not all of the themes described above under "Specific Aims." It is anticipated that this will require about an hour-and-a-half interview employing a standard form questionnaire. This interviewing will be subcontracted to a national interviewing agency. Estimates of costs have been obtained from two such organizations. One gave a figure in the $50 to $60 per case range, the exact figure depending on when the interviewing is done, the length of the interview, and the number of cities in which the survey is done. The other national interviewing agency quoted a lower price, ranging from $42 to $52 per case, depending on similar contingencies. The estimated cost for the 2500 interviews in the budget section of this proposal is based on these estimates.

THE CASE STUDIES

Many of the themes enumerated in the discussion of the specific aims of the research, such as the shifting roles of family members as a result of inflation, the possible decline of authority of the chief wage earner within the family, and tensions between spouses, cannot be fully studied through a static interview employing a standard form questionnaire. Rather, depth interviews at different times with the same family are needed to study these more subtle effects of rampant inflation. For this reason we plan to interview in depth some 100 families at several different times over the course of the research. Approximately 20 of these will be poor families, 20 retired families, 30 blue-collar families, and 30 white-collar families. Each family will be interviewed at least three times at approximately four- or five-month intervals. These case studies will serve a number of functions for the proposed research. First, the information obtained from these depth interviews will be of great help in designing the questionnaire for the household survey. Second, these case studies will greatly enrich our analysis of the impact of inflation on families by providing qualitative information and even crude statistical data on the dynamics of familial responses to rampant inflation—recession.

Seventy of the 100 case studies will be conducted in the New York area, chiefly for reasons of economy. Thus the 20 poor families, the 20 retired families, and the 30 white-collar families will be recruited from the metropolitan area of New York. But the 30 blue-collar families that will participate in the case study will be recruited from among steelworkers in the Chicago, Gary, Joliet area, the district of the steelworkers union that was recently the scene of a triumph of union democracy as an insurgent, Edward Sadlowski, successfully challenged the old guard union leadership by winning an election by a two-to-one margin. It happens that the person who will be in charge of this field work, Professor William Kornblum, has a very close relationship with the new leadership in this district and many members of the union, stemming from his doctoral research.[11] By interviewing steelworkers in depth it will be possible to compare their responses to the current inflation with what Sieber found in his analysis of survey data collected from steelworkers in 1959 regarding their views of inflation. This comparison will be bolstered by the strong likelihood that a number of the 150 blue-collar workers to be interviewed in the Chicago sample of the household survey will also be steelworkers. In short, by taking advantage of Professor Kornblum's close ties with the steelworkers of Union District #31, we will be able to tie our research more closely to the earlier work of Sieber.

The repeated depth interviews with poor families and retired families should be particularly revealing. As our interviewers come to know these families they may well learn about practices that the families would at first want to hide, such as eating pet food or engaging in petty thievery in order to make ends meet.

The case studies are viewed as complementary to the household survey, adding depth to the statistical analysis with qualitative information on subtle processes. At the same time, the household survey can provide some idea of the frequency of certain themes or adaptations uncovered by the case studies.

[11]See William Kornblum, *Blue Collar Community*, Chicago: University of Chicago Press, 1974.

ECONOMETRIC ANALYSES OF INFLATION AND UNEMPLOYMENT

Governmental agencies, particularly the Bureau of Labor Statistics, have kept a running record of inflation and unemployment, the two key economic conditions of concern in this research, over a number of decades. These data exist not only for the economy as a whole but also for most if not all of the large cities of the country. We propose to carry out a series of econometric analyses of these official statistics to learn more about the forces making for inflation and unemployment and the forces that may be establishing a positive, rather than the traditionally negative relationship between the two.

To some extent the econometric analysis will be based on time-series data dealing with the economy as a whole. For example, changes in the composition of the labor force, e.g., percent female, percent youth, etc., will be related to changes in unemployment. Similarly, variables such as productivity and wage settlements will be related to inflation over time for the economy as a whole. But most of the econometric analysis of inflation and unemployment will deal with data on cities in America. Under the direction of Professor Michael Aiken, a large data bank on over 1500 American cities is maintained at the University of Wisconsin. Each city in this collection is characterized by several hundred variables, ranging from demographic characteristics of its population to the kinds of industries it has, to the amount of federal funds it raises for various programs, etc. The Aiken city data bank is a vast resource for analysis of the causes and consequences of inflation and unemployment. By plugging in measurements of the rates of inflation and unemployment into the city data bank, it will be possible through econometric analysis to learn why some cities have high inflation and high unemployment; others, high unemployment and low inflation; others high inflation and low unemployment; and still others, both low inflation and low unemployment. We have been assured by Professor Aiken that the information in his data bank will be available for this analysis. Most likely we shall deal only with the 100 largest cities or so for which time-series data on unemployment and inflation are readily available. The econometric analysis described above, like the case studies, will fill in the background picture of the household survey. The household survey will tell us what kinds of families are hurting from inflation–unemployment and how they are responding, but the analysis of the city data and the data for the economy as a whole will tell us about the forces that are causing the inflation–recession pressures which people are experiencing. A still more direct tie between the econometric analysis and the household survey is envisioned. The critical variables of the household survey, objective and subjective inflation crunch, will be subjected to the refined methods of econometric analysis to learn more about the forces that produce them and their consequences for families. In short, the economists on the research team will have a role to play in the household survey as well as in the analysis of city data.

The Research Team

Each of the three styles of research represented in this proposal—the household survey, the field work or case studies, and the econometric analysis—will be the responsibility of a leading expert in that research tradition. Dr. Caplovitz, the principal investigator, has had considerable experience conducting large-scale social surveys and has demonstrated his ability to translate large-scale research into significant monographs. He will be in charge of the household survey of 2500 families in five cities.

Dr. William Kornblum is a specialist in field work. His recently published book about blue-collar life is based on intensive case studies of the type envisioned in the proposed study.

Dr. Roger Alcaly is one of the better known members of the younger generation of econometricians. For a number of years he was closely associated with some of the leading econometricians at Columbia, Gary Becker and Jacob Mincner among them.

The principal investigator has had the good fortune of persuading Dr. Sam Sieber, the author of the only known investigation of inflation by a sociologist, to serve as a consultant to the proposed study. Dr. Sieber will serve several functions. He will contribute to the development of the questionnaire to be used in the household survey; he will consult with Dr. Kornblum with regard to the depth interviews of the steelworker families, and, on the basis of his extensive review of public opinion polls regarding inflation since World War II, he will prepare an appendix on this subject for the final report of this research. His dissertation summarizes many of these polls up through 1959. For the purpose of the planned appendix, he will update this review of poll data regarding inflation, taking the portrait of public opinion up to the seventies. The preparation of this appendix will be done by Dr. Sieber mainly during the second year of the proposed study.

Time Schedule for the Proposed Study

The first eight months of the proposed study will be spent on a variety of activities. These include analyzing in detail the empirical studies dealing with the effects of the Depression; devising the research instrument to be used in the household survey and pre-testing the various drafts of this questionnaire (experience indicates that the instrument for a study of this scope usually goes through five or six drafts); carrying out the first round of interviews with the 100 families selected for the case study, an activity that will contribute to the development of the household survey questionnaire; and collecting official statistics on inflation, unemployment, and characteristics of the labor force for the economy as a whole and for major cities, data that will be used in the econometric analysis. The last third of the first year will be devoted to the survey data and the official statistics on inflation and unemployment for computer analysis. By the end of the first year or so, the survey data and the data for the econometric analysis will be on computer tapes. During the second year of the study, the 100 families in the case study will be interviewed at least two more times and the various sets of data will be analyzed and research reports will be written. By the end of the project we envision a series of reports, at least one of which will be of book length and suitable for publication.

Significance

On at least two grounds, the proposed research promises to make a significant contribution to knowledge directly relevant to policymakers. First, the research program outlined above is intended to provide insights into changes in family lifestyles as a result of a crescive and chronic condition of modern society: inflation, currently coupled with an even greater economic evil, recession. How American families are adapting to and adjusting to these twin disasters and, equally important, how they are failing to adapt and adjust will be the primary foci of the research. This knowledge should prove of great value to policymakers who must devise programs that will help people cope with these problems. Second, our program of research may provide some answers to the most perplexing problem confronting economists today, namely, how it is possible to have both rampant inflation and a recession at the same time. Finally, apart from its value to policymakers, we envision our research as making an important contribution to knowledge. Just as the Social Science Research Council studies and many other studies documented the impact of the Great Depression on American life, so we believe that our research will achieve the same goal with respect to the rampant inflation of the seventies.

Facilities Available

The proposed research will be carried out at the Graduate School and University Center of the City University of New York. Not only will the Graduate School of CUNY provide space for the project, but also it will provide the graduate students who will serve as research assistants. In addition, the Graduate School of CUNY has at its disposal an advanced computer center. The system is so efficient that within minutes of our request for tables or any other form of computer output the relevant output will be forthcoming.

The undersigned agrees to accept responsibility for the scientific and technical conduct of the research project and for provision of required progress reports if a grant is awarded as a result of this application.

January 20, 1975	*David Caplovitz*
Date	Principal Investigator

THE HISTORY OF THE INFLATION–RECESSION PROPOSAL

David Caplovitz

The idea of studying inflation occurred to me in April of 1974. At that time, the inflation rate was soaring to over 10 percent and unemployment was also climbing sharply, a state of affairs that economists had long insisted could not happen. Conventional economic wisdom held that, when inflation was high, unemployment would be low and vice-versa. The anomaly of high unemployment and high inflation was shaking not only economics but also the political establishment as well.

The idea for doing research came to me from reading an article in the *Wall Street Journal* on unemployment. I had naively assumed that the unemployed were people who had lost their jobs, but from the *Wall Street Journal* article I learned that a significant portion of the unemployed consists of people who are looking for their first job. The unemployed are defined as people who want to work but do not have a job, and of course this group includes new workers who have entered the labor market. I became quite excited for I felt I had an important clue to the enigma of high unemployment and high inflation. Trying to cope with rising prices was forcing new family members into the labor market. Many housewives, I assumed, were looking for work in order to make ends meet and were being counted as unemployed. A few days later, I told an economist friend that I was going to apply for a grant to find out how many of the unemployed were people who had been forced into the labor market because of inflation. My friend promptly discouraged me, explaining that there is an enormous body of economic literature on inflation and unemployment and, unless I was familiar with that literature, no one would take me seriously. This was discouraging because I could not see myself spending months getting familiar with this literature. I asked my friend if she did not think it important to know how many of the unemployed were new workers suffering from inflation. She persisted in her criticism and I tried to develop a new tack. Forget the economics literature, I said. Suppose I do a sociological study of the impact of inflation on families, how they are coping with inflation and who is hurting the most. She had no objection to this approach and so it was through this dialogue that the idea of a study of the impact of inflation on families was born.

A few days later I telephoned Elliot Liebow, the director of the Center for the Study of Metropolitan Problems of the National Institute of Mental Health (NIMH) to find out whether the Center would be interested in funding such a study. He thought it was a pretty good idea and toward the end of April I sent him an eight-page memorandum spelling out the specific themes of the proposed study. In early May he called me and told me that he liked the memo and encouraged me to write a proposal; he reminded me that his was a center for the study of *metropolitan* problems. We agreed that, instead of doing a national survey, the research would focus on five large cities.

By the June 1 deadline, I submitted a proposal entitled "The Impact of Inflation on Families in American Cities," the phrase, "American Cities," being my homage to the Metro Center. This proposal was nineteen pages long, and ten of them consisted of various required forms such as budget pages and biographical sketches of the principal participants. I had decided to ask two colleagues to collaborate on the study, one a fellow sociology professor at CUNY's graduate school and the other an economics professor, with the result that six of the opening pages were biographical sketches. The entire research plan, its objectives and methods, was described in nine single-spaced pages. This description of the research plan followed the outline provided by NIMH: (1) a statement of Objectives; (2) Background, meaning a review of relevant literature; (3) Specific Aims; and (4) Methods of Procedure. The final proposal has been presented, but I would like to provide some idea of the content as it appeared in the first proposal submitted in June 1974.

The original proposal began by identifying the problem of rampant inflation in a time of high unemployment. It argued that the current inflation was a relatively new phenomenon because, unlike past inflationary cycles which were relatively brief, this inflation seemed to be part of a long-term process—that inflation was becoming part of our way of life. It then argued that this long-range inflation should have a profound impact on the American way of life and that dramatic changes in that way of life were beginning to develop. Under "Objectives," I stated that the purpose of the proposed research was to document systematically the various ways in which the current era of inflation has affected the way of life of families in American cities. I added that the "ultimate purpose of the research is to provide information that will be useful to policymakers who must weigh the costs and benefits of the current inflationary pressures."

Under "Background" I pointed out that there was very little sociological literature on inflation and that perhaps the most relevant literature for such a study was the literature on poverty that had emerged in the sixties in connection with the "war on poverty." As I pointed out in the proposal, "the more well-to-do families of the middle class have in the past few years found themselves confronting a problem that the poor have always faced." The poor have long since learned to feed themselves on inexpensive foods, e.g., the various ingredients that constitute "soul food" in the black culture, and the middle class, in this period of hyperinflation, would appear to be following in the footsteps of the perennially poor. The proposed research would examine the ways in which the middle class is learning lifestyles formerly associated with the poor, a process that might be called the "proletarianization" of the middle class. This concept did not appear in the final proposal because in that proposal the recession element was equal in importance to inflation and there was an enormous body of recession literature to be summarized for background. In short, the final proposal made no reference to poverty research for I no longer had to struggle with the "Background" section. Not only was the interesting idea of the proletarianization of the middle class dropped from the final proposal, but it was also omitted in the final report, although the report did document the ways in which middle-class families curtailed consumption. I am currently revising that report for publication and, when I reread the original proposal in order to prepare this paper, I fortunately rediscovered this idea in time to work it into the final manuscript. (I am, of course, taking advantage of this assignment to indulge myself in a tiny piece of intellectual history.)

Under "Specific Aims," I listed six topics that would be examined in the research: (1) changes in labor force participation, e.g., the extent to which housewives were being forced to seek work; (2) changes in providing for necessities, e.g., food, clothing, and household repairs; (3) changes in expenditures for nonessentials, e.g., leisure and recreational activities; (4) changes in family relations; (5) changes in mental health of family members; and (6) changes in social organization—the development of communal responses to inflation. It is perhaps useful to compare these themes with those listed under "Specific Aims" in the final proposal.

Under the heading "Methods of Procedure" I enumerated the three types of study that were planned in much the same way that they are described in the final proposal. These three types of study were closely connected to the research team I had assembled. The basic study was to be a large household survey of which I, an old hand at survey research, was to be in charge.

The second kind of study I built into the proposal was one based on field work, consisting of a series of depth interviews with people in different social strata to find out how they were coping with inflation. Building this kind of field work, which would generate qualitative data into the study, was done for two reasons. These data would undoubtedly enrich the survey, but the main reason was political. I was convinced that this would increase the likelihood that the proposal would be funded. Members of review committees that act on proposals typically come from a wide range of backgrounds. Some are experienced in survey research and feel comfortable with it; others are likely to be qualitative researchers who do field work. It was to appeal to this latter faction that I made certain to include qualitative research in the proposal. This turned out to be the correct decision. The qualitative data enrich the revised report and greatly improve its overall quality. My colleague, William Kornblum, an expert in field work, supervised the depth interviews that were carried out by research assistants during the early months of the study while the questionnaire was being formulated.

The third type of research proposed under "Methods of Procedure" called for econometric studies of inflation and unemployment to be carried out by an economist working with the kinds of data collected by the Bureau of Labor Statistics. An economist at the City University, Roger Alcaly, agreed to fill this role.

The initial proposal submitted to NIMH asked for $258,582 in direct costs for a two-year study. By far the biggest item in this budget was the cost of the envisioned 2500 interviews in five cities, for which $137,000 was requested.

Several months after the proposal was submitted, I was notified by NIMH (the Metro Center) that I was to be site visited in mid-August. The visitors raised a number of questions and suggested that they be answered in an addendum to the proposal.

The first question had to do with the sampling plan for the household survey. The original proposal talked about sampling five cities with populations of 200,000 or more. The five sampled cities were to represent differing degrees of inflation. By late August 1974, when the addendum was prepared, unemployment was vying with inflation as the major problem and in the addendum I said we would sample two high-unemployment cities, probably Detroit and Seattle, two low-unemployment cities, Chicago and Atlanta, and one city representing the middle range of unemployment, New York.

A second question raised by the site visitors dealt with our conceptual orientation and the logic of the analysis. The addendum pointed out that the various topics for investigation listed in the proposal dealt with two themes: strategies for coping with inflation, and the impact of inflation on the well-being of the individual and the family. I then developed a new idea in the addendum. The proposal as written focused on *responses* to inflationary pressures. As such, it made the unwitting and erroneous assumption that all families to be surveyed would experience the same degree of inflationary pressure. But of course some families would be harder hit by rising prices than others. Therefore, I pointed out that a central concept to be measured in the research " is the impact of inflation on the family, a variable that might be called 'inflation crunch.' " This idea would be developed by both objective and subjective measures of the effect of inflation. "Objective crunch" was defined as the extent to which family income fell behind rising prices. "Subjective crunch" referred to the degree to which the family is hurting from inflation. These ideas which were developed in the addendum to the first proposal became central in the final proposal and in the research report.

One site visitor wanted more detail about the methods and functions of the field work. The addendum explained that fifty or so working-class and middle-class families would be periodically interviewed over the life of the project. These depth interviews would serve two functions: they would provide input for the questionnaire by alerting us to lines of inquiry that were not anticipated, and they would greatly increase our understanding of the impact of inflation.

Still another question had to do with the costs of the survey. In the proposal, the estimated cost of each interview was fifty-five dollars. To satisfy this site visitor, I called up several interviewing agencies and got estimates ranging from forty-two dollars to sixty dollars, suggesting that my original estimate was a good one.

One site visitor had suggested that the survey inquire about perceived causes of inflation and in the addendum we agreed to do this.

The review committee met in September of 1974 and I learned from the director of the Metro Center that there was considerable dissension about the merits of our proposal. Some review committee members thought we were asking for too much money for such a short (nineteen pages) proposal. By an extremely narrow vote the reviewers decided to reject the proposal as it was, but recommended that we be encouraged to submit a new proposal for the next round, by February 1, 1975, which I agreed to do.

By October 1974, unemployment had replaced inflation as the number one problem and I took this into account in revising the proposal. The title of the proposal was changed from "The Impact of Inflation on Families in American Cities" to "The Impact of Inflation—Recession on Families in Cities." If there was virtually no sociological literature on inflation, there was an abundance of literature on the Great Depression. I discovered, by chance, that the Social Science Research Council (SSRC) had, in the thirties, sponsored thirteen studies of the impact of the Depression on American institutions, and I spent the next two weeks at the SSRC reading these studies. This background was reflected in the revised proposal which had five single-spaced pages devoted to a review of the literature, mainly these SSRC Depression studies. The revised proposal, unlike the original one, talked about objective and subjective inflation crunch, the impact of inflation on basic values and attitudes, and interpretations of the causes of inflation and recession held by the respondents to be sampled. Once the review of the Depression literature was completed, it took about three days to draft the revised and final proposal. Although it was completed in November, it was not submitted until January of 1975 for the proposal deadline of February 1.

The revised proposal was thirty-one pages long compared with nineteen pages for the original proposal; personnel costs were increased by about $45,000 over the two-year period bringing the total of direct costs to $303,062.

The review committee met in April and approved the proposal in principle. I was told that, although they liked the proposal, they thought it was too expensive and should be cut in half. They also felt that the econometric analysis I had proposed was unnecessary and should be eliminated. I was ready to acquiesce to the decision to eliminate the econometric study, which meant eliminating the economist, and thus reducing the personnel budget by $29,000 over the two-year period. But I was not prepared to settle for only half of the amount of money I asked for. I proposed reducing the sample size, doing the research in four cities instead of five, and reducing the household sample from 2500 cases to 2000. This meant a saving of another $28,000 or so, for a total saving of about $57,000. This brought the budget down to $246,000 in direct costs and I insisted that we needed this much, that a good study could not be done for the $150,000 the review committee had recommended. We finally agreed on $215,000 in direct costs over the two-year period.

So much for the history of the inflation–recession proposal. I have one closing comment. The research began in September of 1975 and was to be terminated in August of 1977. I asked for a three-month extension, without additional funds, to December 1977 which the funding agency readily granted. At the end of the grant period, the funding agency received a 268-page final report. They were extremely happy for it had been their experience to recieve final reports many months, and even years, late and in some instances never to receive a report at all. One sure way to win friends and obtain influence with funding agencies is to deliver final reports on time. Knowing how to write a winning proposal is, of course, extremely important. But it is just as important to deliver the final goods and, unfortunately, many academic researchers fail to do so.

THE UNIQUE OPPORTUNITY

PAUL HENNESSEY

UNIQUE (u-nek), adj. 1. one and only; single; sole. 2. different from all others; having no like or equal. 3. singular; unusual; extraordinary; rare.
Webster's New World Dictionary
of the American Language

At its most basic level, proposal writing is an attempt to convince a funder that your project is more deserving than others sitting on his desk. Perhaps the most powerful argument in favor of your case is that your proposed work is *unique*, as Webster says, "singular; unusual; extraordinary; rare."

Surprisingly, many grant writers do not deal with this important issue. They supply the vita of their principal investigator, but do not say why that person is best suited to lead this particular project. They point out the need, but do not emphasize the particular urgency of the need today. In short, they look on their proposal as a mere explanation of what they hope to do—and not as a description of the unique opportunity it offers the funder.

This important shift in emphasis—from "our project" to "your opportunity"—can make a world of difference to your fundability. The proposal reproduced in this issue, "The Impact of Inflation–Recession on Families in Cities," is a fine example of the right way to present your case. In readable, jargon-free language, David Caplovitz's grant winning application offers the National Institute of Mental Health (NIMH) a unique opportunity to solve a pressing problem.

Caplovitz accomplishes this by pointing out four important facts:

1. The problem he addresses is particularly pressing now.
2. Past attempts to deal with similar problems suggest this study will uncover important new findings.
3. Each staff member of the research team is uniquely qualified to work on his part of the project; in addition, the combination of these people represents a unique opportunity to tackle the task at hand.
4. There will be important, concrete, and practical applications as a result of this study.

By emphasizing these aspects of his project, he makes it appear more than a good investment—it also offers the opportunity to put a unique group of people to work on a problem that will never be more important.

Let's take a closer look at the application and see how this is done.

Throughout "The Impact of Inflation–Recession on Families in Cities," the problem of inflation–recession is described as a two-part issue:

1. As an important social threat.
2. As a particularly difficult fact of life for both individuals and families.

Caplovitz doesn't treat inflation as an abstract academic subject. On the contrary, he describes it as a problem threatening the American way of life. As the quoted editorial from *Skeptic* points out, "Unless we check inflation, it will cost us our freedom." He never loses track of inflation as a problem faced by *people*. The emphasis throughout is on families: "Families in all walks of life will have been touched by these economic conditions, and, for some, the pressures will be so great that their very survival will be threatened." His emphasis on the family, and especially his interest in doing in-depth case studies on selected families, reflects his deep interest in the human side of this economic problem.

Emphasizing both the societal *and* individual dimensions of inflation makes all the difference. Funders are certainly interested in solving large problems, but they are also motivated by the desire to help individual people.

After the problem is outlined, Caplovitz goes on to describe the next unique aspect of his project: its potential to produce important findings. Interestingly, this is done in the "Background" section of the application. Rather than merely cataloging other works in the field, Caplovitz describes key work done in the past. The best example of this is the listing of "nuggets of information" from studies done on the Great Depression of the 1930s. The effect is striking: The reviewer senses the possibility that *this* study may produce similar or better information on important issues of today, such as crime, education, marriage, and mental health.

The effective focus on uniqueness is perhaps most clear in the proposal's description of project staffing and significance.

When the investigators (Caplovitz, Kornblum, and Alcaly) are introduced, they are described as more than competent researchers. Caplovitz's background is outlined as it directly relates to the proposed project: "It is widely assumed that rampant inflation is pushing people deeper and deeper into debt and the principal investigator's knowledge of this problem area will strengthen the proposed research in this respect."

Professor Kornblum's participation in the project is described as a unique opportunity to tie past research findings (of Dr. Sam Sieber, who we find is the only sociologist to have done a study of inflation) to the proposed project. "In short, by taking advantage of Professor Kornblum's close ties with the steelworkers of Union District #31, we will be able to tie our research more closely to the earlier work of Sieber." To make this opportunity seem even more attractive, we later find that Dr. Sieber himself will be part of the project, thus lending the credibility of an important earlier study to the proposed project.

The overall sense of the proposal is thus that an unusually qualified group is coming together to work as a team on an important contemporary problem.

The fourth unique aspect of the project that is emphasized is its potential for practical application. This becomes evident in both the "Objectives" and the "Significance" sections of the application.

Like many scholars, Caplovitz and his researchers are interested in "making a contribution to knowledge" (their own words). But the main thrust of their project is on two important practical applications of that knowledge: an improved understanding of the perplexing relationship between inflation and recession; and an improved ability of policymakers to act to help those most affected by that inflation–recession.

APPLICATIONS

What can we learn from "The Impact of Inflation–Recession on Families in Cities"? Simply this: Each time you write a grant proposal, ask yourself "What makes this project a unique opportunity for the funder?"

Do you have particularly good facilities? A unique team of investigators? The potential to produce practically applicable results? A problem that is particularly important right now? The answers to these questions should become the key foci of your application.

One advantage of having my proposal appear in *Grants Magazine* is that it provided me with the opportunity to write the history of the proposal. Paul Lazarsfeld was a great believer in preparing histories of all phases of the research process and Chapter 6 presents histories of questionnaires that he encouraged his students to prepare. Perhaps this sample of a history of a proposal will encourage other researchers to prepare histories of their proposals, documents that might well facilitate the process of proposal writing.

The next chapter presents a losing proposal that I wrote. The reader would do well to compare closely the winning proposal of this chapter with the losing proposal of the next. The writing style is the same, the format is the same, and, in my opinion, the quality of the two documents is quite similar. And yet one succeeded and the other failed. The discerning reader might well figure out why.

4

A Losing Proposal

Examples of winning proposals are easy to come by, but researchers are reluctant to parade their failures. To avoid embarrassing the author of a losing proposal, I again turn to my own work. In 1980 I was turned down twice, by two different funding sources, for the same proposal, a study of divorce. I initially submitted this proposal to NIMH as part of my application for a research scientist award. The terms of such awards require applicants to submit research proposals indicating the research interests they will pursue during the five-year period that the government will support them. The research scientist award covers only a major portion of the researcher's salary over a five-year period but does not cover the costs of proposed research. I then submitted the proposal to another branch of NIMH for actual funding.

Under the freedom of information act, the government is required to supply the applicant for a grant with the comments of the review committee when a proposal is rejected. The color of rejection in American society is pink. The worker who is being discharged is given a pink slip. The review committee's comments on losing proposals appear on pink paper and the term for this document is "the pink sheets." I requested and was duly sent the pink sheets on this proposal from each of the funding sources. I therefore have two pink sheets for this proposal. The comments on these pink sheets appear after the proposal in this chapter. In short, this chapter presents a losing proposal and the reviewers' criticisms of it. As the author of the chapter, I reserve the last word for myself. I end the chapter with my comments on the criticisms and some observations on the differences between my winning proposal in Chapter 3 and my losing proposal in this chapter.

The Causes and Consequences of Divorce

RESEARCH PLANS AND SUPPORTING DATA—THE CAUSES AND CONSEQUENCES OF INFLATION

A. Research Plan

1. SPECIFIC AIMS

The divorce rate in the United States has grown at an astronomical rate over the past several decades. Today, almost fifty percent of all marriages will end in divorce. Millions of children are now being reared in broken homes and the instability of the American family is a cause of great concern to social scientists and policy makers alike.

In the past twenty years a great deal has been written in popular journals about divorce and many books of advice have appeared addressed to the victims of divorce. These books range from how to find and evaluate divorce lawyers to how to rear children in the absence of a father. And divorce has been a popular theme in fiction. But oddly enough, social scientists have ignored divorce until the past fifteen years or so. In 1948, a sociologist, William J. Goode, did a pioneering survey of 425 divorced women and his book on this research appeared in 1956 (*After Divorce*, Glencoe, Ill.: The Free Press, 1956). More than a decade passed before any other social scientists did research on divorce. The last twelve years or so have seen a rather large number of studies of the causes and consequences of divorce, but these studies have serious shortcomings that the proposed research that I will carry out will remedy.

First, apart from the pioneering study by Goode, almost all the divorce studies have been based on qualitative rather than quantitative data. The researchers have interviewed small numbers of divorced people and on the basis of these depth interviews have explored various themes such as causes, problems of adjustment and the impact of divorce on the children. Second, except for one study now in progress (Sussman and Kitson), none of these divorce studies have been longitudinal in nature, studying the same people over time. Only through such longitudinal studies is it possible to do definitive studies of social processes and causes and effects. Third, none of the divorce studies published to date are based on interviews with both spouses to the marriage. Invariably the researchers have interviewed only one partner and they point out that the reasons for the divorce given by the one partner must be discounted somewhat because the other partner's interpretation is not known. The divorce researchers have found that each partner tends to develop an explanation of the divorce that places the blame on the other partner and without the views of both partners the explanations offered are likely to be distorted. Fourth, with one major exception, all the divorce studies in the literature are based only on divorced people. They make no effort to compare divorced people with people in intact marriages. The exception is a major study recently published in England in which a sample of divorced people is compared with a sample of married people (Barbara Thornes and Jean Collard, *Who Divorces?*, London: Routledge and Kegan Paul, 1979). As is explained below, under Methods of

Procedure, the study that I will carry out will correct for these deficiencies in that it will be a quantitative (as well as qualitative) study, it will be longitudinal, it will involve interviews with both partners, and it will have a control group of married people.

The proposed study will deal with the causes and consequences of separation and divorce, more specifically, the reasons for the marital breakup as offered by the two partners and the mechanisms that allow the parties to the divorce to cope with their situation, that is, their patterns of adjustment. The focus will be on the divorced partners rather than on the children of divorce although the role of children in facilitating or hindering processes of adjustment will be examined. Among the myriad of questions to be answered by the proposed study are the following:

REASONS FOR DISSOLVING THE MARRIAGE.   In many instances, marriages break up because of major flaws in the personality of one of the partners, for example, alcoholism, gambling, violence, occupational instability and infidelity. In other instances, marriages break up because of incompatibility between the partners. The incompatibilities may be quite specific, such as sexual incompatibility, or sharp differences in values, or they may be quite diffuse, with the partners having difficulty articulating them. The research will disclose the frequency of these broad categories of reasons.

Informal interviews with a number of divorced people show that communication problems are quite prevalent in marriages that go sour. The spouses lose the capacity to talk to each other and make their views known to the other partner. A major theme of the research will be to document the frequency of these communication problems and examine the obstacles to communication between the spouses.

What was the sex life of the separated and divorced couple like? A prevalent view is that marriages that end in divorce were characterized by sexual problems and a low level of sexual gratification. How correct is this view? And to what extent do marriages break up even though the sexual relationship was a good one that gave the partners considerable satisfaction?

Another view of divorce is that it is caused by the partners changing over the course of the marriage and growing apart. What one spouse needed from the other during the early years of the marriage no longer holds in the later years. Will accounts of such growth and change be common among separated and divorced couples?

Still another view of divorce is that it is the by-product of neurotic problems that the partners have been unable to resolve. The common symptoms of neuroses, such as guilt feelings and self-loathing, may well lead one spouse to want to dissolve the marriage as a way of punishing oneself. As we shall see in the review of the literature, at least one leading psychiatrist holds to this view. The proposed research will make use of instruments which will allow us to measure the mental health of the partners and conversely the degree to which their mental health is impaired by neuroses.

ADJUSTMENTS TO SEPARATION AND DIVORCE.   Separation and divorce represent failure on the part of the marital partners, perhaps an even more serious form of failure than losing one's job. Failure in turn is extremely damaging to the egos and self-images of those who experience it. This proposed study of divorce will thus be concerned with the processes through which damaged egos are somehow repaired and restored. Of course, not all separated and divorced people do recover their self-esteem. For some unknown number the damage is more or less permanent. One of the objectives of the research is to find out the frequency of recovery and permanent damage. Special attention will be paid to the various mechanisms through which self-esteem is restored.

In perhaps a minority of divorces the decision to end the marriage is a mutual one with both spouses agreeing that the marriage should be dissolved. But in a substantial majority of cases, the decision to end the marriage is made by one spouse, whom we might call the rejector, with the other spouse being the rejected person. The proposed research will be sensitive to this distinction and the patterns of adjustment of both the rejector and the rejected will be studied. The person who breaks up the marriage, the rejector, is presumably someone who feels that he or she will be better off not married to his or her spouse. But, in fact, is the rejector better off? Does he or she feel happier? Has his or her life improved? Or does even the rejector experience considerable stress and strain following the dissolution of the marriage? More precisely, under what conditions does the rejector feel relieved and happier and under what conditions does the rejector experience stress and strain? The rejected party is someone whose ego has been shattered by the rejection and he or she is presumably in a state of despair. But how long does this despair last and how does the rejected party regain his or her self-esteem, and after a period of time, say two or three years after the separation, which party has made the better adjustment, the rejector or the rejectee?

Which party is more likely to remarry, the rejector or the rejectee? What are the differences in adjustment between men and women? Are men or women more likely to recover from the divorce irrespective of which party broke up the marriage? Census data show that divorced men are more likely to remarry than divorced women. What are the obstacles to remarriage for the women and what are the inducements to remarriage for the men?

A major theme of the research will be the economics of divorce. The dissolution of a marriage places enormous economic strains on both spouses. The husband frequently finds that he must pay alimony and child support in addition to the expenses of setting up another household. The wife, in turn, frequently experiences downward social mobility following separation and divorce. Unless she has a substantial income of her own, she finds that her standard of living declines without the full benefits of her husband's income. How do both spouses adjust to these economic pressures and to what extent do economic problems continue to be sources of friction between the spouses after the marriage is dissolved. Do some wives develop new patterns of living to make ends meet such as sharing households with other divorced women?

What role do children play in facilitating or impeding the adjustments of the spouses? Is there a trend toward joint custody of children and, if so, does joint custody contribute to the adjustment of the parents, especially the father?

What roles do friends play in the adjustment process? Is the spouse with a number of friends better off than the spouse with few or no friends? How does the divorce affect friendships? Are many friendships severed because of the divorce?

To what extent do the separated and divorced spouses try to make major changes in their lives, such as taking up new interests, activities, and hobbies? To what extent do they undergo major changes in their personalities, such as becoming socially active when previously they were socially passive? To what extent do they become casual about sexual encounters and develop themselves sexually?

What kinds of relationships evolve between the divorced partners? Is the anger, characteristic of the time of the breakup, replaced by more benign feelings? How often do the divorced remain emotionally involved with their former partners and to what extent do one or both partners want to resume the relationship and, in fact, how often do such reconciliations occur?

This is a mere sampling of the types of questions dealing with the causes and consequences of divorce to be explored in the proposed research.

2. METHODS OF PROCEDURE

The proposed study of separated and divorced couples will be based on a large sample of broken marriages and intact marriages and because of the large sample, quantitative analysis of the data will be possible. The study will not only be quantitative; it will be qualitative as well in that in depth interviews will be conducted with approximately 70 couples (40 divorced couples and 30 currently married couples). A survey will be conducted of 400 separated and divorced couples and 300 currently married couples. Since both spouses will be interviewed, we will have a sample of 800 separated and divorced people and 600 married people for a total sample of 1400.

The study will be longitudinal in that the respondents will be reinterviewed a year and a half later. The longitudinal or panel design will permit us to study the dynamics of the adjustments of the separated and divorced partners. For example, the research will develop measures of adjustment and a number of stress measures currently used in the psychological literature will be included. The panel design will allow us to study four types of persons: (a) those who are in relatively good shape at both time periods, (b) those who are in relatively poor shape at both times, (c) those who have moved from bad to good shape, and (d) those whose adjustments would seem to deteriorate over time, moving from good to bad shape.

As already noted, the study will be based on interviews with both spouses. The versions of the breakup given by one spouse can be checked against the versions given by the other. A major phenomenon to be studied in this research is the consensus–dissensus between the spouses as to why the marriage broke up.

In addition to the 400 separated and divorced couples the sample will include a random sample of 300 currently married couples. The purpose of studying married couples is to permit comparisons with the divorced couples. One major way in which "causes" of divorce can be uncovered is to carry out comparisons of divorced couples with intact couples. Such an analysis should reveal the strengths of the couples that remain married and the weaknesses of the couples that divorce. Another benefit of including married couples in this longitudinal study is that we will be able to identify marriages that end in separation or divorce over the course of the research, for of the 300 married couples initially sampled, some will probably be separated in the year and a half period of research. By the same token, some of the 400 initially separated and divorced couples may well become reconciled over the course of the research. In short, our research design permits us to study transitions from marriage to divorce and from divorce to marriage, that is, the reunion of the spouses. No divorce study carried out to date has allowed this transition process to be studied.

The sample of 400 divorced and separated couples will be drawn from court records in New York City. The sample will be stratified along two dimensions: the length of time since the breakup of the marriage and the age of the male partner. On the length of time dimension, two groups will be distinguished: those who have been separated for under two years and those who have been separated for more than two years. On the age dimension, two groups will also be distinguished, those under 40 and those over 40. This sampling frame generates four cells of various combinations of age and time of separation and in each cell one hundred couples will be sampled. The sample of currently married couples will be drawn on a probability basis from the New York City area. This sample will be stratified by age of male head into two groups: those under 40 and those over 40. The sampling of married couples will be done in two stages. Initially a brief telephone interview will be conducted to establish marital status and age. Then appointments will be made for face-to-face interviews.

A central task of the research will be to develop appropriate measures of the critical concepts, notably stress and divorce adjustment. A number of such measures have already been developed by divorce researchers and one scholar, Philip D. Holley, has written an article analyzing the various divorce adjustment measures that have been developed.* In this article, he reviews adjustment measures developed by a host of researchers including Goode (1956), Blair (1969), Heritage (1971), Fisher (1976), Dixon (1976), Raschke (1974, 1977, 1978), Spanier and associates (1978), and Granvold (1979). Goode developed a trauma scale as well as an adjustment scale, his trauma scale measuring how much the person is suffering because of the divorce. Included in his adjustment scale are economic activities (Is the person functioning well?), social adjustment, friendship and opportunities to meet people, and dating and remarriage. Blair developed a Divorce Adjustment Instrument consisting of 80 items that deal with life satisfaction, feelings about the divorce and dating behavior. Fisher developed a 54 item adjustment scale that dealt with four dimensions: feelings of anger, symptoms of grief, disentanglement from the love relationship and rebuilding social relationships. Of all the scholars, Raschke has expended perhaps the greatest effort on developing a divorce adjustment scale. In a series of publications, she has built a 56 item adjustment scale that is based on three dimensions of the concept of divorce adjustment: perceived unpleasant and unfavorable emotional states, perceived satisfaction with new roles and perceived ability to fulfil or deal with new roles. As Holley notes in his article, the various divorce adjustment scales tend to tap one or more of six dimensions: life satisfaction and happiness, self concept or esteem, stress or trauma, current behavior, items relating to the former marriage and divorce process, and dating, going steady and remarrying. In addition to scales specifically designed to measure divorce adjustment, the researchers frequently use scales developed in other contexts, such as anxiety scales, Rosenberg's measure of self-esteem and Bradburn's measure of happiness based on the balance of positive and negative feelings. This literature will guide our own efforts to develop appropriate measures of stresses and adjustments that follow upon divorce.

The proposed research will shed considerable light on the causes of divorce and the processes of adjustment through which the partners go after the marital separation. In addition to tabular analysis, the methods of regression analysis will be used to examine the causes of key dependent variables. The research design presented in this proposal, a longitudinal quantitative and qualitative study, based on interviews with both spouses and with a control group of married couples, insures that the field of divorce research will be advanced considerably. And by uncovering the reasons for marital breakdowns, the proposed research should be of great value to the development of social policy.

In sum, the proposed research will consider a number of themes relating to divorce and separation, such as:

1. The reasons for the breakup of the marriage.
2. The stresses and strains experienced by both partners as a result of separation and divorce.
3. The involvement of the spouses in new social relationships and the role of new relationships in the adjustment process.

*Philip D. Holley, "An Analysis of Divorce Adjustment Measures," paper presented at the Southwestern Sociological Association Meetings, April 1980.

4. The different forms of custody arrangements and their consequences.

5. The role of various forms of counseling in the adjustment process.

6. The economics of divorce.

The longitudinal research design will permit a dynamic study of these themes and will greatly enhance the possibilities of establishing causal connections among the various variables under study.

TIME FRAME.   The first year of the study will be spent on the 140 depth interviews, the development of the samples for the survey and the construction of the questionnaire to be used in the interviews with divorced and married people. The second wave of interviews will take place a year and a half after the first wave, with the first wave taking place toward the end of the first year. The data will be analyzed throughout the project but the bulk of the data analysis will occur in the third year when a report, suitable for publication as a book, will be prepared.

3. SIGNIFICANCE OF THIS RESEARCH

Divorce is increasing in America at an alarming rate and is considered by social scientists and policy makers alike to be a major social problem. In spite of the considerable attention that has been given to this problem and the growing amount of research that has been done on it, relatively little is known about the causes and consequences of divorce, consequences for the partners and their children. The proposed research, by virtue of its superior design, should contribute greatly to our knowledge of the causes and consequences of divorce. Precisely because the problem it is studying is so important, the proposed research is highly significant. It will not only increase greatly our knowledge of this major crisis in peoples' lives but it may even make a contribution toward lessening the stresses and strains of divorce. It might do so by making people more aware of the pitfalls of marriage, by documenting the kinds of actions that facilitate adjustment and by showing the consequences of various types of custody arrangements.

4. FACILITIES AVAILABLE

The research will be carried out at the Graduate School and University Center of the City University of New York. Not only will the Graduate School of CUNY provide space for the project, but it will provide the graduate students who will serve as research assistants. In addition, the Graduate School has at its disposal an advanced computer center. The System is so efficient that within minutes of our request for tables or other forms of computer output, the relevant data are forthcoming.

B. Supporting Data

1. PREVIOUS WORK DONE ON PROPOSED RESEARCH

After many decades of neglect, separation and divorce have been the subjects of a good deal of research in the past fifteen years. At least three bibliographies of books and articles dealing with separation and divorce have appeared (Israel, 1974; McKenney, 1975; Sell, 1976, 1977, 1978, 1979), and a recent collection of essays on this topic (Levinger & Moles, 1979) lists more than 500 books and journal articles in its bibliography. But in spite of this enormous literature, relatively few studies in this field have been based on large-scale surveys that permit sophisticated quantitative analysis. The pattern has been to interview relatively small numbers of divorced persons in depth. One of the early studies in this field was based on the survey method (Goode, 1956). Goode interviewed 425 divorced women in Detroit in 1948 and, based on these interviews, he generated statistical data dealing with the causes and consequences of their divorces. Almost thirty years passed before another extensive survey of divorced people was attempted. Hunt and Hunt collected questionnaires from 984 separated and divorced people, but their book is based largely on some 200 depth interviews they conducted and their review of the divorce literature. They use their survey material sparingly to provide figures on the characteristics of divorced and separated people with virtually no analysis of their quantitative data (Hunt & Hunt, 1977). By far the most sophisticated quantitative study on divorce based on a large-scale survey has just been published in England (Thornes & Collard, 1979). So recently has this book been published that it has yet to appear in major libraries in New York and knowledge of it is based on the publisher's advertisement. According to the publisher, the book, entitled *Who Divorces?*, presents findings of a large-scale study into the characteristics of those who divorce. The book looks at the childhood, adolescence and premarital and marital characteristics and experiences of a random sample of men and women who divorced and compares them with those of a random sample of men and women whose marriages are still intact. The research findings relate to the causes and consequences of divorce for both the individual and society.

Similar to the Hunt and Hunt book in that it is based largely on qualitative data from depth interviews is another recent book entitled *Marital Separation* (Weiss, 1975). The books by Goode, Hunt and Hunt, Levinger and Moles, Thornes and Collard, and Weiss represent the major works in this field. Their organizations are similar. They first take up the topic of the causes of marital separation and divorce. They then consider the stresses and strains that the marital partners experience after the marriage breaks up. They take up the impact of the marital breakup on the social networks of the spouses, typically relatives and friends. They then consider patterns of adjustment including involvement in new social relationships and eventual remarriage. And all the studies of divorce and separation deal with the impact of the crisis on the children of broken marriages.

For some years now, a study has been in progress in Cleveland that is not only quantitative in nature, being based on a sample of four hundred divorces, but also is a longitudinal study, the first longitudinal study of divorce ever attempted in the United States (Kitson & Sussman). This research has generated several articles, but the main findings have still to be written up.

2. RESULTS OBTAINED BY OTHERS

The findings in the literature on divorce will be organized in terms of the major themes covered in the studies reviewed above, more specifically under the broad headings of Causes and Consequences.

CAUSES OF DIVORCE.   The causes of divorce discussed in the literature fall into four general categories: historical, cultural, sociological and psychological.

Historical Causes.   All the studies of divorce place major blame for the rising divorce rate on macroscopic changes that have taken place in society over the past several hundred years, notably the industrial revolution. As a result of the industrial revolution, the traditional family lost many of its functions; the extended family was replaced by the more fragile nuclear family. This view of the rising divorce rate is to be found in Weiss (1975), Goode (1956), Hunt and Hunt (1977), and Levinger and Moles (1979). The trend toward urbanization has also been associated with divorce. As society has become more urbanized, the divorce rate has increased and at any given moment in time urban areas have a much higher divorce rate than small towns and rural areas (Carter & Glick, 1976).

In a book dealing with the historical change in marital roles, Scanzoni has argued that divorce has increased as the role of wife has shifted from being submissive and passive to one of more equality with the husband (Scanzoni, 1968). According to Scanzoni there has been a historical trend toward increased power of the wife in the family setting.

Cultural Causes.   A number of scholars have pointed to sharp changes in values in American culture as causes of the rise in divorce rates. In particular, the emphasis on individualism and self-realization that became paramount in the sixties has been linked to divorce (Goode, 1956; Pang, 1968; Weiss, 1975; Hunt & Hunt, 1977; Lasch, 1978). The rising divorce rate has also been linked to a dramatic cultural change toward divorce itself. Whereas fifty years ago, divorce was strongly disapproved of and the divorced person was treated as a second class citizen, today divorce is accepted as a rather normal process and no stigma is attached to the divorced person. This change in values has presumably made it easier for people to end unhappy marriages through separation and divorce (Carter & Glick,1976). One manifestation of this change in the cultural definition of divorce has been the rapid growth of no-fault divorce laws in many states. Presumably no-fault laws, by making divorce easier, have contributed to the sharp rise in the divorce rate. But one recent study failed to show a correlation between divorce rate and no-fault divorce laws (Wright & Stetson, 1978).

Sociological Causes.   Divorce rates have been found to be linked to a wide range of social statuses and characteristics. Numerous studies have shown that divorce is inversely related to socio-economic status. The higher the income, the higher the occupational status, the lower the divorce rate (Goode, 1956; Carter & Glick, 1976; Norton & Glick, 1979, Cutright, 1971; Coombs & Zumeta, 1970). But further specification shows that these socio-economic status differences vary with sex. Among men there is a strong negative relationship between income and education and divorce, but among women the opposite tends to be true. Better educated women and women who earn a lot of money tend to have higher divorce rates than more poorly educated women and women who earn less or no money at all (Carter & Glick, 1976).

Although numerous studies have shown that divorce is inversely related to socio-economic status, recent work has shown that the gap is narrowing between social classes because of the rise in the divorce rates of the higher classes (Norton & Glick, 1979). Divorce has been shown to vary not only in terms of broad occupational categories of different prestige, but also within occupational categories of similar prestige. For example, certain professionals, such as social scientists, authors and architects, have much higher divorce rates than other professionals, such as doctors, dentists and accountants (Rosow & Rose,1972). Although income is inversely related to divorce, among the relatively poor income has the opposite effect. Thus recent experiments of income maintenance have shown that low-income families provided with subsidies were more likely to have their marriages break up than low-income families in the control group without subsidies. One interpretation of this finding is that the income subsidy gave the unhappy couple an opportunity to dissolve their marriage (Hannan, Tuma, & Groenweld, 1977).

Race is another important characteristic related to divorce. Blacks have much higher divorce rates and especially much higher separation rates than whites (Bernard 1966; Udry, 1976; Crain & Weissman, 1972; Carter & Glick, 1976; Norton & Glick, 1979). The greater racial gap with respect to separation is explained on the grounds that many blacks lack economic resources to get a divorce.

Age is another social characteristic strongly related to divorce. The younger the spouses at the time of marriage, the higher the divorce rate. For those under twenty the rate in 1970 was 26.6 per thousand married men and 30.7 per thousand married women, a rate that fell to 15.5 among men twenty-five to thirty and 11.1 for women of this age, and to 6.8 among men and women in the thirty-five to forty age group (Carter & Glick, 1976). Nativity has also been found to be related to divorce, with the native-born having higher divorce rates than the foreign-born (Carter & Glick, 1976).

The changing position of women in the occupational structure has also contributed to divorce. Women who are employed have higher divorce rates than women who are not employed, a finding partially explained on the grounds that women who work can afford divorce more readily than women who do not work (Booth & White, 1979; Glick and Norton, 1977).

Several studies have shown that marriages that result from pregnancies are not as stable as marriages that are not forced by such a circumstance (Furstenburg, 1976; Christenson & Rubenstein, 1956). Still another factor that has been found to contribute to marital instability is the instability of the marriages of the parental generation. Pope and Mueller, in reviewing five probability surveys, found that divorce rates were higher among those whose parents were divorced, a finding supported by other research, which suggests that parents serve as role models for their children (Pope & Mueller, 1979; Bumpass & Sweet, 1972).

Psychological Causes. Innumerable studies have shown that divorced people experience more psychological stress than married people, but this finding raises the time order problem. Is psychological stress a consequence of the marital breakup or is psychological stress in the forms of neuroses and even psychoses a cause of separation and divorce? Several studies have shown that separated and divorced people were more likely to have had psychological problems before their marriages broke up, suggesting that these problems contributed to the breakup of the marriage (Briscoe & Smith, 1973; Rushing, 1979). An eminent psychiatrist wrote a book based on this thesis, arguing that divorce is the product of neurotic interaction and is thus symptomatic of psychological problems rather than being a solution to problems (Bergler, 1948). Implicit in this thesis is the notion that divorced people are more neurotic than married people but some studies have shown that unhappily married people have more health problems and experience more psychic stress than divorced people, findings that suggest that divorce can contribute to the solution of problems (Renne, 1971).

A number of studies have asked divorced people to list the reasons for their divorce and these studies show characteristic differences in the reasons offered by men and women. Women complain about physical and verbal abuse, drinking, financial problems and neglect, whereas men tend to complain about in-laws and sexual incompatibility (Levinger, 1965). A very recent study casts strong doubts on the reasons spouses give for the breakup of their marriage. Based on 36 depth interviews with divorced persons, Rasmussen and Ferraro found that, in almost every case, the divorce was blamed on such fundamental problems as alcoholism, economic instability and infidelity. But the depth interviews revealed that these problems were frequently present prior to the marriage and during the years when the marriage was viable and yet these so-called problems did not prevent the marriage from taking place nor did they break up the marriage when they became evident during the "good" years of the marriage, but rather are used by the spouse who wants to break up the marriage as tools for creating a crisis that will end the marriage (Rasmussen & Ferraro, 1979). What the actual causes are, according to these authors, remain murky and difficult to pinpoint. Since uncovering the reasons for the dissolution of marriage is one of the major goals of the proposed research, care will be taken to locate the reasons offered in the time sequence of the marriage. Was the behavior complained about present prior to the marriage; was it present during the early years of the marriage? How does the complainer explain his or her growing intolerance of the behavior complained about?

The historical, cultural, sociological and psychological reasons for divorce discussed above are by no means exhaustive, but they do provide some idea of what divorce researchers have been learning about the divorce process.

CONSEQUENCES OF DIVORCE

Emotional Impact of Divorce and Separation.   Numerous studies have found that separated and divorced people experience more mental stress than married people (Raschke, 1974; Rose, 1973; Spanier & Casto, 1979; Spanier & Hanson, 1979; Weiss, 1976; Dixon, 1976; Holley, 1980). One study found that divorced or separated white women had significantly higher depression scores than married, single or widowed white women (Radloff,1975). Men in particular tend to suffer acute mental stress when their marriages break up. Such indicators of stress as psychiatric hospital admissions, disease morbidity and mortality, suicide and motor vehicle accidents have been found to be much more prevalent among divorced men than married men, the gap between divorced and married men on these indicators being much greater than the gap between divorced and married women (Bloom, White, & Asher, 1979; Chiraboga & Cutler, 1977; Gove, 1972). These findings confirm what Durkheim found long ago in his study of suicide. Durkheim found that married men were much less likely to commit suicide than single men, a difference far greater than the comparable one for women. Durkheim concluded that men benefit from and need marriage more than women do (Durkheim, 1951). One study found that lingering attachment to the former spouse contributed to the stress experienced (Marroni, 1977). Age has been found to influence the emotional stress produced by separation and divorce. Older people, less likely to divorce in the first place, suffer more than younger people when they do divorce, especially older women (Blair, 1970).

Some researchers have found pronounced alterations in the moods of separated and divorced people, from extreme depression to elation and euphoria (Weiss, 1975; Hunt & Hunt, 1977). Somewhat surprisingly, studies have shown that the person who initiates the divorce, the rejector, undergoes almost as severe stress and depression as the partner who is rejected (Weiss, 1975; Hunt & Hunt, 1977; Goode, 1956). But the types of negative feelings that the rejector and the rejectee experience tend to differ. The rejector's depression is laced with guilt feelings, whereas the rejectee feels hurt and abandoned (Weiss, 1975). It has been estimated that it takes from two to four years for the stress produced by divorce to completely disappear (Weiss, 1975). Although age affects the level of stress experienced, education does not. The well educated are just as vulnerable to stress induced by separation and divorce as the poorly educated (Barringer, 1973; Blair, 1970; Goode, 1956).

Impact of Divorce on the Social Networks of the Spouses.   Weiss found that kin react in various ways to the news of separation and divorce. In many instances they are supportive and sympathetic to the person whose marriage has broken up. In other instances they are disapproving and condemning and, as Weiss notes, separation can diminish the person's standing in the family (Weiss, 1975). Goode found that the wife's family is more inclined to approve of the separation and divorce, whereas the husband's family tends to disapprove (Goode, 1956). This difference in the response of the spouses' families is in keeping with the findings that suggest that men get more social-psychological comfort from marriage than do women. Relations with friends tend to undergo drastic changes as a result of separation or divorce. At first friends are very supportive, but inasmuch as the friends tend to be married, over time the separated or divorced person, by changing into a single person, tends to drift away from his or her married friends (Weiss, 1975; Hunt & Hunt, 1977).

Adjustment to New Social Relationships.   Several studies have shown that adjustment and regaining mental health are strongly influenced by social participation. The more active the divorced person is socially the lower the level of stress (Edward & Klemmack, 1973; Brown & Manela, 1976; Hynes, 1979; Raschke, 1977). In time the separated and divorced person becomes socialized into a new world made up of the formerly married. A variety of institutions exist whereby the newly separated person is able to meet others in the same boat as himself (from singles bars, to personal ads, to clubs and other organizations). In time the separated person tends to have a variety of sexual relationships with new partners that he meets in the world of the formerly married. This process of immersion in a new culture of the formerly married is well documented in Hunt and Hunt (1977). Eventually, the divorced develop new emotional relationships and most of them remarry. A quarter of the divorced remarry in one year and half remarry within three years of the divorce. Eventually four out of five of the men and three out of four of the divorced women remarry (Glick & Norton, 1971; Carter & Glick, 1976). Studies have shown that these remarriages are not as stable as first marriages, having a somewhat higher divorce rate, but most remarried compare their new marriages highly favorable with their first marriages, which ended in failure. In short, most divorced people get remarried and are happy with their new marriages, even though somewhat more than average get divorced a second time (Hunt & Hunt, 1977; Weiss, 1975; Goode, 1956). The fact that the remarried are somewhat more likely to divorce again may well be the result of their having learned a solution to an unhappy marriage.

The Role of Professional Help.   A number of works have appeared about the role of professionals in the divorce process. Many of these focus on divorce lawyers and offer advice on how to choose and deal with divorce lawyers. Of more relevance are studies that have tried to evaluate the role of marriage counselors in restoring marriages that were headed toward divorce or assisting in the adjustment of divorces. Several studies have shown that marriage counseling has resulted in improved relations between the spouses (Beck, 1975; Brown & Manela, 1976).

Consequences for Children.   Considerable research has been done on the effects of divorce on the children. The results of this research present a somewhat mixed picture. On many indicators, the children of the divorced tend to have more social and psychological problems; for example, delinquency rates are higher, there tend to be more school and learning problems and signs of emotional disturbance (Weiss, 1975; Goode, 1956; Ryker, 1971). A major review article of some sixty rigorous studies documents a state of confusion regarding the harm to children stemming from divorce. Twenty-four of these studies concluded that father-absence was linked to undesirable traits of behavior in the child; twenty concluded that it was not; and sixteen were unable to arrive at any firm conclusion at all (Herzog & Sudia, 1971). Several researchers have argued that unhappy intact families in which the parents are frequently fighting are more psychologically damaging to children than broken families (Longfellow, 1979).

In sum, the literature on divorce and separation provides a good deal of information on the causes of marital dissolution and the psychic stress to the spouses following the breakup of the marriage and the impact of divorce on the children. But, as noted, there are notable gaps in the literature. Few of the studies are based on quantitative data; with one exception of a study now in progress, none of them are longitudinal in nature in which the same people are followed over time; none of the studies are based on data collected from both spouses; and none of the studies compare divorced people with those whose marriages have survived. The proposed research will correct for these glaring defects and should greatly advance our knowledge of marital dissolution.

PERTINENT LITERATURE REFERENCES

Bane, M.J., "Marital Disruption and the Lives of Children," in G. Levinger and O. Moles, eds., *Divorce and Separation*, New York: Basic Books, 1979

Barringer, K.D., "Self-Perception of the Quality of Adjustment of Single Parents in Divorce Participating in Parents Without Partners," Ph.D. Dissertation, College of Education, University of Iowa, 1973

Beck, D.F. "Research Findings on the Outcomes of Marital Counseling," *Social Casework*, 1975, 56, 153–181

Bergler, E. *Divorce Won't Help*, New York: Harper and Brothers, 1948

Bernard, J. "Marital Stability and Patterns of Status Variables," *Journal of Marriage and the Family*, 1966, 18, 421–429

Blair, M. "Divorce Adjustment and Attitudinal Changes about Life," *Dissertation Abstracts*, 1970, 30, 5541–42, University Microfilms No. 70-11099

Bloom, B.L., Whilte, S.W. and Asher, S., "Marital Disruption as a Stressful Life Event," in Levinger and Moles, eds., *Divorce and Separation*, New York: Basic Books, 1979

Booth, A. and White, L., "Thinking about Divorce," paper presented at the meetings of the Midwest Sociological Society, Minneapolis, Minnesota, 1979

Briscoe, C.W. and Smith, J.B., "Depression and Marital Turmoil," *Archives of General Psychiatry*, 1973, 29, 811–817

Brown, P. and Manela, R., "Client Satisfaction with Divorce Counseling," *The Family Coordinator*, 1976,.26, 294–303

Brown, P., Perry, L. and Harburg, E. "Sex Role Attitudes and Psychological Outcomes for Black and White Women Experiencing Marital Dissolution," *Journal of Marriage and the Family*, 1977, 39, 549–561

Chiraboga, D.A. and Cutler, L., "Stress Responses Among Divorcing Men and Women," *Journal of Divorce*, 1977, 1, 95–105

Christenson, H.G., and Rubinstein, B.B. "Premarital Pregnancy and Divorce," *Marriage and Family Living*, 1956, 18, 114–123

Coombs, L.C. and Zumeta, Z. "Correlates of Marital Dissolution in a Prospective Fertility Study," *Social Problems*, 1970, 92–102

Crain, R.L. and Weissman, C.S. *Discrimination, Personality and Achievement: A Survey of Northern Blacks*, New York: Seminar Press, 1972

Cull, J.C. and Hardy, R.E., *Deciding on Divorce*, Springfield, Illinois: Charles C. Thomas, 1974

Cutright, P. "Income and Family Events: Marital Instability," *Journal of Marriage and the Family*, 1971, 33, 291–306

Dixon, B. "Adjustment to Divorce," *Free Inquiry*, 1976, 4, 26–39

Durkheim, E. *Suicide*, Glencoe, Illinois: The Free Press, 1951

Edwards, J.N. and Klemmack, D.L., "Correlates of Life Satisfaction: A Reexamination," *Journal of Gerontology*, 1973, 28, 497–502

Furstenberg, F.F., "Premarital Pregnancy and Divorce," *Journal of Social Issues*, 1976, 22, 67–86

Glick, P.C. and Norton, A.J. "Frequency, Duration, and Probability of Marriage and Divorce," *Journal of Marriage and the Family*, 1971, 33, 307–317

Goode, W.J., *After Divorce*, Glencoe, Illinois: The Free Press, 1956

Gove, W. R., "Sex, Marital Status and Suicide," *Journal of Health and Social Behavior*, 1972, 13, 204–213

Hannan, M.T., Tuma, N.B. and Groenweld, L.P., "Income and Marital Events: Evidence from an Income Maintenance Experiment," *American Journal of Sociology*, 1977, 82, 1186–1211

Holley, P.D. "An Analysis of Divorce Adjustment Measures," paper presented at Southwestern Sociological Association Meetings, Houston, Texas, 1980

Hunt, M. *The World of the Formerly Married*, New York: McGraw-Hill, 1966

Hunt, M. and Hunt, B. *The Divorce Experience*, New York: McGraw-Hill, 1977

Hynes, W.J., "Single Parent Mothers and Distress: Relationships Between Selected Social and Psychological Factors and Distress in Low-Income Single Parents," Unpublished Ph.D. Dissertation, Catholic University of America, 1979

Israel, S. *A Bibliography of Divorce*, New York: Bloch, 1974

Kitson, G.C. and Sussman, M.B. A Study of Divorce, Western Reserve University, Cleveland, Ohio, now in progress

Kitson, G.C., Lopata, H.Z., Holmes, W.M. and Meyerling, S.M. "Divorcees and Widows: Similarities and Differences," *Journal of Orthopsychiatry*, 1980, 50

Lasch, C., *The Culture of Narcissism: American Life in the Age of Diminishing Expectations*, New York: Norton, 1978

Levinger, G. "Marital Cohesiveness and Dissolution: An Integrative Review," *Journal of Marriage and the Family*, 1965, 27, 19–28

Levinger, G., and Moles, O.C. eds., *Divorce and Separation: Context, Causes and Consequences*, New York: Basic Books, 1979

Locke, H.J., *Predicting Adjustment in Marriage: A Comparison of a Divorced and Happily Married Group*. New York: Holt, 1951

Longfellow, C., "Divorce in Context: Its Impact on Children," in Levinger and Moles, eds., *Divorce and Separation*, New York: Basic Books, 1979

Marroni, E.L., "Fathers Influencing the Adjustment of Separated or Divorced Catholics, Unpublished M.S.W. thesis, the Graduate School of Social Work, Norfolk State College, Norfolk, Virginia, 1977

McKenny, M., *Divorce: A Selected Annotated Bibliography*, Metuchen, New Jersey: Scarecrow Press, 1975

Norton, A.J., and Glick, P.C., "Marital Instability in America: Past, Present and Future," in Levinger and Moles, eds., *Divorce and Separation*, New York: Basic Books, 1979

O'Neill, W.L., *Divorce in the Progressive Era*, New Haven: Yale University Press, 1973

Pang, H. and Hanson, S.M., "Highest Divorce Rates in Western United States," *Sociology and Social Research*, 1968, 52, 228–236

Pope, H., and Mueller, C.W., "The Intergenerational Transmission of Marital Instability: Comparisons by Race and Sex," in Levinger and Moles, eds., *Divorce and Separation*, New York: Basic Books, 1979

Radloff, L., "Sex Differences in Depression: The Effects of Occupation and Marital Status," *Sex Roles: A Journal of Research*, 1975, 1, 249–265

Raschke, H. "Social and Psychological Factors in Voluntary Postmarital Dissolution Adjustment," Ph.D. dissertation, University of Minnesota, 1976

Raschke, H., "The Role of Social Participation in Postseparation and Postdivorce Adjustment," *Journal of Divorce*, 1977, 1, 129–140

Rasmussen, P.K. and Ferraro, K.J., "The Divorce Process," *Alternative Life Styles*, 1979, 2, 443–460

Renne, K. "Health and Marital Experience in an Urban Population," *Journal of Marriage and the Family*, 1971, 33, 338–350

Rosow, I. and Rose, K.D., "Divorce among Doctors," *Journal of Marriage and the Family*, 1972, 34, 587–598

Ross, H.L. and Sawhill, I.V. "Time of Transition: The Growth of Families Headed by Women," Washington, D.C.: The Urban Institute, 1975

Rushing, W.A., "Marital Status and Mental Disorder: Evidence in Favor of a Behavioral Model," *Social Forces*, 1979, 58, 540–556

Ryker, M.J., "Sex Selected Factors Influencing Educational Achievement of Children from Broken Homes," *Education*, 91, 1971

Scanzoni, J., "A Historical Perspective on Husband–Wife Bargaining Power and Marital Dissolution," in Levinger and Moles, eds., *Divorce and Separation*. New York: Basic Books, 1979

Scanzoni, J., *Sexual Bargaining: Power Politics in American Marriage*. Englewood Cliffs, New Jersey: Prentice-Hall, 1972

Sell, K.D., *Divorce in the 1970's: A Subject Guide to Books, Articles, Dissertations, Government Documents, and Film on Divorce in the United States*, 1970–79

Spanier, G. and Anderson, E., "The Impact of the Legal System on Adjustment to Marital Separation," *Journal of Marriage and the Family*, 1979, 41, 605–613

Spanier, G. and Hanson, S. "The Role of Extended Kin in the Adjustment of Marital Separation," paper presented at the Southern Sociological Society meetings, New Orleans, Louisiana, 1978

Thornes, T. and Collard, J., *Who Divorces?*, London: Routledge and Kegan Paul, 1979

Udry, J.R. "Marital Instability by Race, Sex, Education and Occupation Using 1960 Census Data," *American Journal of Sociology*, 1966, 72, 203–209

Weiss, R.S., *Marital Separation*, New York: Basic Books, 1975

Weiss, R.S. *Going It Alone: The Family Life and Social Situation of the Single Parent*, New York: Basic Books, 1979

Wright, G.C., and Stetson, D.M., "The Impact of No-Fault Divorce Law Reform on Divorce in American States," *Journal of Marriage and the Family*, 1978, 40, 575–580

THE PINK SHEETS

As noted, I received two pink sheets for this proposal, one from the NIMH Research Scientist Development Review Committee and the other from the NIMH Life Course Review Committee, Child and Family Subcommittee. The Life Course Review Committee's document is identified as Pink Sheet I (PS I) and the Research Scientist Development Committee's document is identifed as Pink Sheet II (PS II).

PS I—Résumé

Disapproval was recommended unanimously for this three-year proposal to explore the causes and consequences of marital dissolution. Reviewers thought that the application was far too undeveloped and flawed to merit a recommendation of approval. The sampling procedures and lack of fully developed analysis plans were seen as particularly troublesome. The budget was seen as excessive and poorly justified. Relatively little is known about the impact of divorce on the mental health of divorcing couples; consequently, a study delineating some causes and consequences of marital dissolution is timely and relevant.

PS II—Summary

This is a new application for a Research Scientist Award to study the "Causes and Consequences of Marital Dissolution." Reviewers were impressed by the applicant's intelligence and dedication; they believed that his publications would be helpful to decision makers concerned with specific social issues. However, they considered the proposal to be seriously flawed in both theory and methodology. The Committee unanimously recommends disapproval of the application.

PS I—Human Subjects

Subjects will be divorced or separated couples and married couples. They will be interviewed about their marriages. The purpose of the study will be explained, and written consent will be obtained. Numbers will be substituted for the names of respondents. Reviewers thought the consent and confidentiality procedures were adequate and that subjects were not likely to be at risk. No further action is necessary.

PS II—Human Subjects

Further action required. Evidence is not presented with the proposal that the privacy of subjects would be protected, nor does the investigator discuss how subjects would be protected from damage that might result from intensive questioning in sensitive areas related to divorce and/or serious indebtedness. The required Human Subjects Statement (HEW 596) is not submitted.

PS I—Critique

Reviewers thought that the proposed research addressed an important topic. However, they also agreed that this proposal was undeveloped, ambiguous, and inaccurate in its claim to advance considerably the field of divorce research. It was noted in the application that there has been almost no good longitudinal research on the causes and consequences of divorce and that qualitative as well as quantitative data are necessary if the phenomenon is to be understood. The importance of a longitudinal approach and of an approach that compares married with divorced and separated couples was also noted in the application. The advantage of talking to both the husband and wife, rather than only to one spouse, was also noted. Reviewers agreed that a proposal which adequately addressed all of the above issues would, indeed, make a major contribution to the area. However, this application had failed to do so, and the sampling approach and analysis plans were seen as particularly troublesome.

Reviewers thought it extremely unlikely that the proposed number of couples could be obtained in the amount of time that would likely be devoted to that task. Previous research in this area has demonstrated that it is extremely difficult to elicit the cooperation of both spouses of a divorced couple. It was noted that response rates in the six most comprehensive studies of divorce average around 30 percent, and these studies have included only one spouse. It was thought likely that an initial sampling in the thousands would be required if both spouses of a divorced couple were to be obtained. Reviewers were concerned that there seemed to be no awareness of the difficulties of interviewing both members of a divorced couple. Furthermore, it was not clear what kind of probability sample procedure would be used to select the currently married couples. There was no justification for using the age of the male partner as a variable for stratification nor for choosing 40 as the age for dividing the sample. It was unclear if the two samples were to be equated along any dimensions relevant to the quality of their marriage, psychological factors, or other variables. Apparently, the married sample was to be seen as some type of comparison group. However, if they were to be a comparison group, reviewers thought that some criteria or basis for comparison would need to be described, justified, and reflected in the sampling and design procedures. A final sampling problem was thought to be the difficulty of locating respondents who had been separated for more than two years. Reviewers noted that there is 20 percent mobility in the general population each year, approximately, and this mobility may be higher in New York City. It is much higher among divorced individuals. Those who have done research in this area report the difficulty of locating respondents; however, this application did not indicate awareness of some of the specific issues and problems of obtaining the type of sample proposed. It was thought that addendum materials on attrition did not adequately address the unique problems of sampling divorced couples.

The analysis plans were seen as vague and undeveloped. Neither the proposal nor the addendum presented a plan that would insure that the data would be managed and analyzed appropriately. It was noted that "regression analysis will be used in the analysis of the critical concepts." Apparently this was the only multivariate procedure planned, even though the design of the study seemed to suggest the need for a number of sophisticated multivariate techniques typically used in longitudinal survey designs.

Other major problems included the lack of clear definitions of critical concepts and the lack of a conceptual framework for tying these concepts together. The literature review was seen as incomplete, poorly organized, and incorrect. For example, it seemed to be suggested that a substantial proportion of divorce studies have been based on qualitative rather than quantitative data and that there is only one longitudinal study in progress. Reviewers disagreed with both these assertions. Other claims were also challenged by review committee members. For example, it appeared to be suggested that in many instances marriages break up because of major flaws in the personalities of the partners. Review committee members suggested that many researchers would dispute that this explanation accounted for a substantial proportion of divorces. Rather, current work in the area suggests that marriage and divorce are extremely complex and characterized by subtle patterns of interaction. It was thought that this proposal presented a far too simple and static model of marriage and divorce.

It was thought unrealistic to propose that measures could be developed in the time that would likely be devoted to this task. Furthermore, the discussion of possible measures was seen as inadequate. Since a conceptual framework had not been developed, reviewers were not clear why particular concepts had been chosen, and even less clear about how they might be measured. Procedures to assure that measures would be reliable and valid were not developed. Although the problem of attrition was mentioned in the addendum, that discussion did not provide any information about how the problem would be handled in the data analysis. Reviewers doubted that the technique of obtaining the names of people who might know where the respondent is at a later point in time would be particularly effective, but the complexities of the problem were not adequately addressed. Finally, although the economic consequences of divorce and the consequences for children would be studied, neither of these topics was adequately reviewed, and it appeared that major studies in each of these areas had not been evaluated (e.g., Hetherington's work on the effects of divorce on children).

Finally, reviewers had no clear idea of what the instrument might look like. Although topic areas were mentioned, there were no examples of sample questions or detailed discussions of criteria that would be used in developing or selecting questions. Since many studies have been done in this area, there are a number of instruments and measures that could be used, and reviewers were concerned that the proposal indicated no awareness of items and indices that could be adapted or adopted. Since many of these questions would be on topics apt to elicit defensiveness, anxiety, or other strong reactions, it would be essential to devise questions and interviewing strategies that would take these factors into account. However, these factors were not addressed in the proposal, and examples of specific questions were not presented.

In sum, reviewers thought that there were far too many problems with this too brief and undeveloped application to permit a recommendation of approval. Every major aspect of the application, including the conceptual framework, literature review, procedures, instruments, and analysis plans were seen as inadequately developed. Overall, it was thought that a far too simple picture of a most complex process had been presented, and disapproval was recommended unanimously.

PS II—Evaluation

Without doubt Dr. Caplovitz has been a productive worker: He obtains grants, conducts extensive studies, and publishes the results. The topics covered by his research are undoubtedly of importance for public policy; and some of his books have been helpful to, and influential among, policy makers. What is missing is any theoretical statement of what his findings mean as contributions to his discipline as a science. The consequence is that his publications seem to read more like specialized almanacs than like scientific monographs. The reviewers did not find in all his books a single test of significance or a single measure of association. This strategy is perhaps not unjustified, since the applicant typically employs large samples and his presentation is primarily descriptive. However, as a consequence of the strategy Dr. Caplovitz occasionally discusses non-significant differences and also capitalizes substantially on chance since analyses are not shaped by theory. His publications proceed by a series of 2- or 3-way tables of percentages followed by illustrative quotes, a style which typified much good work in the 1950s. In the current proposal more analytic strategies are alluded to; however, there is no evidence that the applicant is likely to change his approach at this point in his career, nor that he has the training and background to do so.

Similarly, Dr. Caplovitz's research does not demonstrate appreciation of scaling or reliability methods. Plans discussed indicate he will combine two or three dichotomous items to create three or four response category groups for ad hoc examination in tables. All treatments, even of what appear to be ordered responses to items, are categorical rather than ordinal. No reliabilities of any kind are ever mentioned, nor apparently to be computed.

His most recent book, *Making Ends Meet*, has major problems in measurement and analysis. For example, the applicant is concerned with the effects of inflation/recession on mental health. Despite the considerable progress in psychiatric epidemiology, progress that has yielded a number of usuable instruments for surveys of this type, the applicant chooses to measure mental health by a very small number of rather simple questions on subjective distress. Further, all data are analyzed only by cross-tabulations without even simple tests of significance being applied. This seems particularly pertinent in view of the fact that the current proposal plans to collect panel data which requires some of the most sophisticated statistical models now available.

The proposal itself is inadequate in many respects. Most generally, it is simply too brief, too undefended, and too poorly conceptualized. More specifically the applicant's review of existing literature on divorce and separation is superficial. Although he has touched on most of the studies (he has left out some quite significant work, such as the recent studies of Wallestein, who interviewed both parents over a two-year period), he sorts the literature into poorly defined conceptual bins. For example, in reviewing the literature on causes of divorce, he reviews work under four headings: historical causes, cultural causes, sociological causes, and psychological causes. There is clearly overlap among these four domains, and any new, extensive study must take responsibility for extracting and synthesizing the existing literature beyond this form of simple categorization. Indeed, we don't have a sense of what issues in separation and divorce the applicant will focus on and explore in this current study; rather, he seems to be trying to touch all bases without adequate attention to any.

From a methodological perspective, the proposal itself falls short. The sampling strategy is barely described. In particular, it does not describe how the control group— the married couples—will be selected or matched with the divorced and separated couples. More than that, there is no clear statement of how data from the married sample will be used. The applicant argues that such data will help illumine the causes of divorce, but inferences of that kind are exceedingly complex and intricate, and none of the strategies to be employed are even mentioned. The nature of the questions to be asked of the respondents is also not clarified. There is not a single example of a question to be posed to the sample. Clearly, inquiries of respondents about the causes and consequences of their divorce—including inquiries about the adequacy of their sexual experience with their partners—are among the most sensitive survey researchers can pose to a random sample. It behooves the applicant to clarify just what his approach here will be and to present some preliminary data supporting that approach. For example, in a recent survey study, Straus and his colleagues have been able to elicit information on the sensitive issue of family violence but have done so by a very carefully conceptualized and field-tested approach. Finally, the applicant says nothing of how his data will be analyzed. He is collecting his data in two waves, and he hopes to make longitudinal, if not causal, inferences from his panel design. Recent developments in measurement theory and the analysis of longitudinal data have been very rapid. For example, the reliability of a measure at any single time influences how it can enter into the analysis of the relationship between the underlying variable from the first to the second time of measurement. This is only one of the many analytical problems faced by panel designs, and nothing about the author's previous work or current proposal is reassuring that he can handle these.

Therefore, because of serious theoretical and methodological weaknesses in the proposal, the Committee unanimously recommends disapproval.

PS I—Resources and Facilities

The resources and facilities of the Graduate School of the City University of New York are excellent for the proposed research. Reviewers doubted, however, that the proposed number of subjects could be obtained, given the unwillingness of many divorced couples to participate in research that involves the other partner and focuses on the reasons for the failure of their marriage.

PS II—Environment

The environment is highly supportive in terms of administrative backing, colleagues, graduate students, and facilities.

MY COMMENTARY ON THE PINK SHEETS

The first thing to be noted about these pink sheets is that the review committees were unanimous in rejecting my divorce proposal. A review committee typically has about nine members; thus 18 social scientists acting as reviewers voted against my proposal. In research on review committees Cole and Cole found that there is considerable disagreement among reviewers about the merits of proposals.* Presumably good proposals are severely criticized and presumably bad ones have their supporters among reviewers. I was shocked that my proposal had no advocates among the reviewers. I happened to think it was a good proposal, probably as good as my inflation proposal. I was proud of having identified four major weaknesses in the divorce literature: almost all the studies were qualitative rather than quantitative, they were all static rather than longitudinal, only one spouse was interviewed, and there was never a control group of married couples. My study was designed to plug these loopholes, but this did not impress the reviewers.

In asking myself why the inflation proposal was funded and the divorce proposal was not, I have come up with two theories. First, the inflation proposal was submitted in 1974 and the divorce proposal in 1980. Over that six-year period, reviewers became much more sophisticated about methodology. Advanced statistical procedures such as regression analysis and path analysis have become standard. My application for a research scientist award required my submitting all my publications as well as proposals indicating the type of research I wanted to do. The members of that review committee, who were in a position to assess my style of research, were

*Steven Cole, Jonathon R. Cole, and Gary Simon, "Chance and Consensus in Peer Review," *Science,* **214,** 881–886 (November 20, 1981).

critical of my adherence to the Columbia tradition, pointing out that it was 25 years out of date. Nowhere in my published work are there tests of significance or measures of correlation, to say nothing about regression analysis, all marks of the Columbia tradition. At least one of the reviewers was ready to admit that given my large samples, I did not need tests of significance. This lack of methodological sophistication was particularly damaging in the eyes of the reviewers because in my proposal I planned to do a panel study, and panel techniques have become rather complicated in the past several decades. Since I was a product of the institution that invented panel studies, The Bureau of Applied Social Research, I thought that I was qualified to do such a study, but I now realize that in my proposal I should have indicated my awareness of the problems of panel studies and my knowledge of the advances that have been made in that field.

My second theory as to the difference between the inflation proposal and the divorce proposal is based on the amount of work that has been done in these areas. As I note in my inflation proposal, there had been no sociological research on inflation and my proposal was staking out new ground. But divorce is an area in which there has been considerable research and in writing such a proposal I was vulnerable to the criticism that I had not covered the literature adequately or conceptualized divorce properly.

As for the specific criticisms of the reviewers, some of them strike me as well taken, but others border on nitpicking. Both review committees came down hard on my sampling plans. They point out that although I planned to compare divorced and married people, I say nothing about how I will ensure that the groups would be comparable in relevant respects. I do not specify the dimensions along which I will sample married couples to make them comparable to the divorced couples. This criticism is on target. Members of both review committees saw considerable difficulty in my finding both spouses, and they were convinced that my response rates would be low. The methodological criticism relating to panel studies was also mentioned by both review committees.

Both review committees were critical of my review of the literature, considering it superficial, incomplete, and poorly organized. This criticism strikes me as unfair. I made a considerable effort to review the vast divorce literature and my bibliography on divorce is much longer than the bibliography I came up with for inflation and recession. The research scientist review committee faulted me on my organization of the literature on the causes of divorce, considering my categories overlapping and simple. I see nothing wrong with my organization of the literature on causes but I leave it to the readers of this chapter to judge.

Another surprising criticism that both review committees made was my failure to present the kinds of questions that I would be asking of my respondents. In all the proposals I have written, I have never presented sample questions. Precise questions emerge only as a result of a lengthy process of drafting, pretesting, and rewriting. Moreover, in this particular proposal, I identify a number of scales that have been developed by other researchers to measure the critical concept of divorce adjustment. Perhaps I should have given examples of the items in these scales, but I at least established that I was aware of the existence of scales that I could use to measure my key concepts of adjustment and stress.

The Life Course Review Committee also criticized my proposal for its theoretical shortcomings, its failure to define the critical concepts and provide a conceptual framework for tying these concepts together. This criticism, too, surprises me. I view the divorce proposal as problem oriented rather than theory oriented. I saw myself collecting data that might provide the basis for a theory of divorce, but I did not plan to test some theory that I already had. In the proposal I identified various factors that might contribute to divorce and said that the research would find out how frequent each type of factor is. This is a descriptive function essential for subsequent theory building.

As for the lessons that might be learned from the pink sheets, an important one is that proposals submitted in the eighties must be methodologically sophisticated. The era of simple cross-tabulations may well be over. Second, when one is proposing to do research in a highly sensitive, emotional, stressful area such as divorce, one must specify in the proposal the types of questions that will be asked and how the respondents' anxieties will be faced. Perhaps a special section on the research instruments is needed in the methodology section. Third, a section on methods of data analysis should be included, perhaps with a flow chart showing the critical variables and the arrows of causation linking them. Fourth, care should be taken to explain the nature of the samples to be studied and how the samples are to be drawn. But given the Coles' findings on review committees, there is no guarantee that proposals that pay attention to all these points will be funded.

PART TWO

Data Collection

Every textbook on research methods has chapters on data collection dealing with observation and field methods, questionnaires, and survey research as a method of data collection. This text considers related topics in an original form. Chapter 5 is based on a historical survey of questionnaires from 1940 to 1980. It describes how questionnaires have evolved and changed over this 40-year period. Next, Chapter 6 is a tribute to Paul Lazarsfeld's insistence that we write histories of our questionnaires. It presents three of the six histories that Lazarsfeld's students developed in the late 1950s and 1960s. Chapter 7 celebrates qualitative data and the role they can play in quantitative research. The moral of this chapter is that quantitative researchers should make room for qualitative data in their research instruments. Drawing upon material from a particular study (Lazarsfeld's *Academic Mind*), this chapter shows how qualitative data can perform the important function of interpreting quantitative data.

5

The Nature of Questionnaires

Once the researcher has written a proposal and raised the money for research, the data on which the research is based must be collected. Researchers have used a number of methods for collecting data, the most common being observation through field work and asking questions of respondents, the subjects of the research. Survey research, which is probably the most frequently used method for collecting data in the social sciences, is based on asking questions of people, and in this chapter we are concerned with this method of collecting data.

The survey method involves a number of techniques or tasks. First, the researcher must draw a *sample* of respondents from the population under study. Sampling is a complex topic in its own right and a number of theories and methods of sampling have been developed. The essence of sampling is to ensure that the sample of respondents is representative of the population to which it belongs. Cases must be selected according to the laws of probability, so that each case in the population has the same chance of falling into the sample. Numerous books have been written about sampling, and the reader who wants to know more about sampling should consult one of these books.

The major task in the survey method of collecting data is the development of the basic research instrument, the questionnaire. Once the data are collected, they must be processed and the processing of survey data involves additional tasks, which are only mentioned here. An important task in processing the data is *coding*, that is, classifying the respondent's answers to the questions into a set of categories. These categories, which presumably exhaust all possible answers to the question, are assigned numbers to represent names for the categories. Just as military messages are sent in code to maintain their secrecy, so the answers of respondents in surveys are assigned numbers which serve as the code names for the response categories. Developing the categories of answers is known in the trade as "building the codes."

Once the questionnaires are coded, the information is transferred to IBM punchcards as an essential preliminary step toward the eventual use of the computer in the analysis of the data. This task is known as *keypunching*,* that is, punching into an IBM card the code numbers for the responses to the various questions. An IBM card has 80 columns and 12 possible punches in each column. Generally, each question is assigned a column, and the number punched in that column stands for the response category to that question. For example, if the respondent's sex is recorded in column 10, then punch 1 might stand for male and punch 2 for female.

Once the questionnaire data have been transferred to IBM punch cards, the researcher must engage in an operation known as *card cleaning*, to get rid of the possible errors and mistakes that might have been made in the interviewing, the coding, or the keypunching. Card cleaning involves a number of internal checks, such as making sure that the number of punches in a column equals the number of cases in the sample and that the number of people who answered a contingency question equals the number of people who gave the response on which the contingency question is asked. (For example, the people who said yes to a question might be asked a follow-up question to explain their answer. The number of people who gave these explanations must equal the number who said yes.) Through checking out the number of punches in each column and the contingency questions, the researcher eliminates most of the errors that might have crept into the data processing. Only when the researcher is satisfied that he has a clean deck of cards is he ready to begin the analysis of the data. Coding, keypunching, and card cleaning are relatively simple tasks that do not concern us in this chapter. Rather, we concentrate on the intellectually challenging and difficult task of developing the questionnaire that generates the data the researcher needs to study her problem or test her theories.

QUESTIONNAIRE CONSTRUCTION

Opening Comments

The word "questionnaire" has been used in two different ways in social research. In the early days of survey research, from the 1930s through the 1950s, a "questionnaire" was a method of data collection in which respondents themselves wrote down the answers to the questions on the research instrument. This was also referred to as the "self-administered question-

---

*With advanced technology, the keypunching step can be omitted. Questionnaire data now can be entered directly into the computer.

naire." The questionnaire in this sense was contrasted with the *interview schedule,* a method of data collection in which the interviewer asks the questions and then records the answers on the schedule. A number of the early research methods textbooks used these definitions. The second meaning of the word "questionnaire" in social research refers to the research instrument itself, whether the data are collected by an interviewer or are recorded by the respondent. In this chapter we use the word questionnaire in this second sense, to refer to the research instrument. In recent decades this use has become very common.

The Content of Questionnaires

Whether the research is being done to test a theory or to study a problem, the researcher must collect data that will allow analysis of key concepts. In surveys this means inventing questions that will provide the information needed to classify respondents in terms of the concepts. For example, if the research deals with politics and the researcher wants to study conservative and liberal political orientations, he or she must invent questions that will allow classification of the respondents according to how liberal or conservative they are. Questionnaires are suitable for obtaining a wide range of information about individuals—factual information, information about beliefs, attitudes, values, expectations, reasons, or explanations, and even information about social relations. Factual information includes data about the individual—such as age, religion, occupation, income—or data about occupation (Do you work with your hands? Does your job involve physically hard labor?), or place of employment (How many people work where you work?), or community (How large is the town/city in which you live?). People can be asked about their beliefs or what they think will happen (Is this a safe neighborhood? Do you think there will be a major war in the next 10 years?), about their attitudes, whether they like or dislike things or people (Do you like the president? Do you like football?), about their values (Which is more important to you, your job or your family life?), about their expectations (Do you expect to get a raise this year? Do you have any plans to get married?), and people can even be asked about specific social relations (Name your three best friends. Who is your boss?). The survey method has been used to study an extremely wide range of topics, from voting behavior to prejudice to neurosis to juvenile delinquency, divorce, union democracy, intelligence, social mobility, social class, religion, drug addiction, consumer credit, medical education, to occupational choice.

A question frequently put to the survey researcher concerns the honesty of the respondent: How can the researcher be sure that the respondent is answering the questions truthfully? This concern was greater during the early days of survey research than it is today. Survey research is so common now, so many millions of people have participated in surveys, that the public is accustomed to surveys and considerable confidence has developed about the accuracy of survey results. In many instances, surveys have been proven accurate by the facts. For example, election polling has become highly respectable and everyone concerned, especially the politicians, believes in the validity of election polls. The reason for this confidence is that the polls very accurately predict the outcomes of elections. Surveys of consumer behavior, in which representative samples are asked about their buying intentions, have been shown to be very good predictors of the state of the economy. The assumption of survey researchers is that the great majority of respondents will tell the truth on almost all issues and that if a question is considered too personal, rather than lie, the respondent is likely to refuse to answer or to say "don't know." The frequency of abstentions and "don't knows" is an important clue to the researcher of the adequacy of the questions. Questions that generate large numbers of abstentions or "don't knows" are generally flawed questions that should be dropped from the survey.

Several devices have been employed to test the honesty of respondents. A common procedure is the use of several questions dealing with the same topic. If the response to one of these questions agrees with those to the others, the assumption is made that the respondents are telling the truth. Another way of checking for accuracy is to test common sense expectations about the relationships among variables. For example, in a study of the impact of inflation, families were classified according to how much they were hurting from inflation. The general consensus in society is that low-income families are much harder hit by inflation than well-off families. The measure of inflation impact was related to family income, and, as expected, it was found that income was negatively related to inflation crunch. The lower-income families were suffering much more than the higher-income families. In another study, dealing with socially disapproved behavior, cheating, an index of cheating was constructed and this index was verified by relating it to grades. The assumption was that students who received relatively poor grades would be under more pressure to cheat and the data confirmed this expectation. These confirmations of expectations give us confidence in the validity of the data collected in surveys.

The Format of Questions: Open- Versus Close-Ended Questions

Questions that appear on questionnaires fall into two basic types, open-ended and close-ended, or checklist, questions. In the open-ended question, the respondent is allowed to respond in any way. The interviewer tries to record the verbatim response. In the close-ended question, a set of response categories is provided with the question and the respondent is asked to choose the response that comes closest to his or her position. An open-ended question is: What do you think about the present state of the economy. A close-ended question is: Do you think in the current state of the economy that (a) wages are too high, (b) wages are too low, or (c) wages are about right? Another close-ended question is: What do you think about gun controls, are you strongly in favor of gun controls, somewhat in favor, somewhat opposed to gun controls, or strongly opposed to gun controls?

There are pros and cons about each of these types of question. The open-ended question is especially suitable when researchers are not sure of the range of responses to the question. For example, the dimensions of public opinion on such issues as the Soviet invasion of Afghanistan and the war between Iran and Iraq are not at all clear. A simple question—like What do you think about the Soviet invasion of Afghanistan—might reveal (a) the strength of disapproval, (b) the degree that it is perceived as a threat to world peace, (c) the degree to which it is viewed as damaging to detente, and (d) the degree to which the public is concerned at all about the issue. A major problem of the open-ended question is that the respondents might address different dimensions of the question, so that their answers would not be comparable. For example, when asked why they bought a book, some respondents might say because they like to read, others might say because the book was not in their local library, still others might say because a friend told them about it, and still others might say because it was cheap. These answers are not really comparable because they refer to different dimensions of the issue. The person who likes to read would rather buy books than, say, records, because reading is more important than listening to music. The person who referred to the book's being missing from the local library is explaining why he bought the book rather than borrowing it, the person who mentions a friend's recommendation is explaining how he heard of the book, and finally the person who mentions the price is referring to yet another dimension.

The drawback of checklist questions is that the responses offered may not capture the nuances of the respondent's sentiments and feelings; there is also the risk of "putting words in the respondent's mouth," distorting his views. But there are many virtues to close-ended questions. They tend to clarify the meaning of the question, specifying the dimensions of the question that are important to the researcher. Instead of an open-ended question—How do you feel about your marriage?—a close-ended question— How happy are you with your marriage: very happy, pretty happy, or not too happy?—specifies the type of evaluation of marriage the researcher wants the respondent to make.

Checklist questions are much easier to process than open-ended questions. Each open-ended question requires the researcher to build a code for classifying the answers and a rather lengthy operation of data processing, known as coding, must take place. In short, open-ended questions add considerable time and cost to the data processing phase of the research. On balance, checklist questions seem to be superior to open-ended questions and the history of survey research shows, as we shall see, a steady trend from open-ended to close-ended questions. Even so, open-ended questions perform valuable functions for the researcher and they are seldom excluded entirely from surveys. Open-ended questions are particularly valuable during the early phases of the research, when the researcher is developing the questionnaire. Generally, the first draft of a questionnaire will have a number of open-ended questions that will generate the range of responses to the question. After pretests involving open-ended questions, the researcher usually has learned enough about the questions to convert them to checklists. But even in the final version, some open-ended questions are likely to be retained (their role is discussed in Chapter 7).

Types of Question

The questions that appear in questionnaires are one of three types: main questions, contingency questions, and batteries of questions. The main questions are numbered. Contingency questions are questions that are asked if the main questions are answered in a certain way. A contingency question is contingent on a particular answer to the main question. An example of a series of contingency questions is provided by *The Poor Pay More.**

Q.43.   Do you always pay cash at food stores or
        do you sometimes buy on credit?   Always cash _____
                                                Sometimes credit _____

   If Credit:
   A. How high do you let your food bill go? $ _____
   B. Do you owe any money *now* to a food store?   Yes _____
                                                         No _____

       If Yes
       How much? $ _____
   C. What's your main reason for buying food on credit?
   D. Would you buy at that store if you didn't need the
       credit?   Yes _____
                                                         No _____

The main question, number 43, is asked of all respondents. The five contingency questions are asked only of those respondents who said that they sometimes buy food on credit. The contingency questions are identified by letters, a standard practice in questionnaire construction. Contingency question B is followed by another contingency question dependent on the yes answer to B. Secondary contingency questions are also common on questionnaires.

Batteries of questions consist of a series of questions that have the same response categories. For example, scales named after the psychologist

*David Caplovitz, *The Poor Pay More*, New York: Free Press, 1963.

Rensis Likert, which permit opinions to be expressed on a five-point continuum from strong agreement to strong disagreement, are used frequently in social research. The response categories are set out along the top of the page as follows:

Agree Strongly	Agree Somewhat	No Opinion	Disagree Somewhat	Disagree Strongly

The specific questions are then listed down the left side. The battery represents a very convenient format for asking a series of questions that can be answered in the same way. Since batteries are readily understood, their use is much more common in self-administered questionnaires than in questionnaires involving interviews. In the face-to-face interview, interviewers explain that they are about to ask the respondent a series of questions that can be answered in a consistent way and then read off the response categories. One tactic frequently employed in interview surveys is to hand the respondent a card on which the response categories appear so that the respondent may read off the response category that best expresses his or her opinion on each question.

Batteries are frequently used when the researcher has developed a series of indicators to measure the concept. For example, in the happiness research done by Norman Bradburn at the National Opinion Research Center during the 1960s, a balance of feelings battery was developed to measure the critical concept of happiness.* This battery contained five positive feelings and five negative feelings; since the number of positive feelings was strongly correlated with the simple question "How happy are you?" and the number of negative feelings was negatively related to the happiness question, Bradburn developed as his index of happiness the respondent's positive feeling score minus his or her negative feeling score. The following battery of items went into this index:

H.6 Now let's talk about something else. We are interested in the way people are feeling these days. During the past few weeks, did you ever feel—

		Yes	/	No
A.	Particularly excited or interested in something?	38	1	2
B.	Did you ever feel so restless that you couldn't sit long in a chair?	39	1	2
C.	Proud because someone complimented you on something you had done?	40	1	2
D.	Very lonely and remote from other people?	41	1	2
E.	Pleased about having accomplished something?	42	1	2

*Norman Bradburn and David Caplovitz, *Reports on Happiness*, Chicago: Aldine Press, 1965. Norman Bradburn, *The Structure of Psychological Well-Being*, Chicago: Aldine Press, 1969.

F.	Bored?	43	1	2
G.	On top of the world?	44	1	2
H.	Depressed or very unhappy?	45	1	2
I.	That things were going your way?	46	1	2
J.	Upset because someone had criticized you?	47	1	2

All of these questions could be answered either yes or no, lending them to the battery format. This battery illustrates another principle of questionnaire construction, the *precoding* of the response categories. In the early days of survey research, responses to questions had to be coded, meaning that column numbers and punch numbers had to be assigned to each response by coders who would write these numbers on to the questionnaires. Coding frequently took several weeks of labor on the part of a team of coders. Precoding means assigning column and punch numbers to the response categories on the questionnaire. Thus by circling the numbers under the Yes and No headings the interviewer is simultaneously recording and coding the answer. The numbers 38 to 47 to the left of the response categories stand for column numbers and numbers under Yes and No stand for punch numbers within the columns. Precoding was a major invention that greatly facilitated the data processing.

Types of Response Category

The response categories for the questions asked in surveys are of various types and complexity. Over time, response categories have become ever more sophisticated, permitting more and more powerful measurements. In the early days of survey research, the response categories were simple, generally dichotomies like Yes or No and Agree or Disagree. At the most, the respondent would be presented with three categories. For example, in a 1944 survey for the War Department, NORC had questions that could be answered Too Many, About Right, Not Enough; Up, Down, Some Up, Some Down; and Higher, About the Same, Lower. These response categories providing three positions are primitive ordinal scales, that is, the type of scale that ranks respondents in terms of more and less of some attribute. In subsequent years response categories became more refined, eventually becoming true ordinal scales. Many opinions and attitudes in surveys were measured by five-point scales like the Likert scale:

Strongly agree	_____
Agree	_____
Neutral	_____
Disagree	_____
Strongly disagree	_____

Survey researchers have even invented seven-point scales made up of qualitative labels such as the following, which appeared on an NORC questionnaire:

Extremely liberal	_____
Liberal	_____
Slightly liberal	_____
Moderate or middle of the road	_____
Slightly conservative	_____
Conservative	_____
Extremely conservative	_____

Another seven-point scale used by NORC was for a question concerning the frequency of various social activities. The categories were:

Almost Every Day	Once or Twice a Week	Several Times a Month	About Once a Month	Several Times a Year	Once a Year	Never

   As questionnaires continued to evolve, researchers discovered ways of designing the response categories so that they approximated interval scales, which permitted using much more powerful statistics in the data analysis. In a national survey of public opinion in 1974, NORC asked the respondents to evaluate various countries. The question read:

> The boxes on this card go from the highest position of "plus 5" for a country that you *like* very much to the lowest position of "minus 5" for the country that you *dislike* very much. How far up or down the scale would you rate the following countries?

$$+5 \quad +4 \quad +3 \quad +2 \quad +1 \quad -1 \quad -2 \quad -3 \quad -4 \quad -5$$

In place of qualitative labels, NORC used numbers that are located on the page equally distant from each other, the mark of the interval scale.* And the number of categories has been increased to 10.

   In another survey NORC invented a way of getting interval readings of a complex concept such as feelings of closeness to people, institutions, and things. In a survey of basic beliefs conducted in 1972, NORC presented the respondents with a series of concentric rings (see Figure 5.1) signifying degrees of closeness. The question read:

> Please look at the circle on this card. The rings are meant to represent how close or how far you may feel in certain kinds of relationships. The inside ring, 1,

*Ordinal and interval scales will be discussed in more detail in Chapter 8.

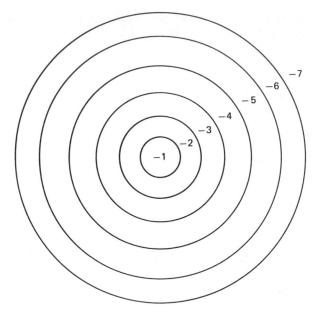

Figure 5.1. Response card for closeness.

stands for "very close." Outside the circle, −6 stands for "not at all close." The other rings stand for different degrees of closeness in between. For each relationship that I'm going to ask you about, please tell me which numbered ring best represents how close you feel.

A. How close do you feel to God most of the time?
B. How close do you feel to your church most of the time?
C. How close do you feel to your husband/wife most of the time?

The concept of closeness is a spatial concept and NORC's concentric circles evoke the concept very well.

In the 1950s the psychologist Charles Osgood invented the semantic differential scale, a device for measuring personality traits and attitudes toward things. The semantic differential scale has frequently been used by survey researchers. The scale consists of polar opposite adjectives separated by seven or eight numbers, which the respondent is asked to use to locate his opinion or attitude about the object under study. For example, the following question appeared on an NORC questionnaire in 1978:

> This list has pairs of adjectives on it which can be used to describe the groups listed above. Taking them one at a time, please tell me which of the two adjectives best describes (the group named) in your personal view. [The groups provided were Socialists, Communists, Ku Klux Klan, John Birch Society, Atheists, Pro-Abortionists and Anti-Abortionists.] For example, the first pair of adjectives is strong−weak. If you think the (group named) are

very strong give me the number 1. If you think they are very weak, give me
the number 7. Let the numbers 2 to 6 represent various degrees of strength
with 4 in the middle (neither strong nor weak). So you are to give me a number
between 1 and 7. Do you understand the instructions? OK, let's begin. What
about _____ ?

		1	2	3	4	5	6		7		8
A.	Strong							Weak		Don't know	
		1	2	3	4	5	6		7		8
B.	Dishonest							Honest		Don't know	
		1	2	3	4	5	6		7		8
C.	Trustworthy							Untrustworthy		Don't know	
		1	2	3	4	5	6		7		8
D.	Predictable							Unpredictable		Don't know	
		1	2	3	4	5	6		7		8
E.	Dangerous							Safe		Don't know	
		1	2	3	4	5	6		7		8
F.	Important							Unimportant		Don't know	
		1	2	3	4	5	6		7		8
G.	Violent							Nonviolent		Don't know	
		1	2	3	4	5	6		7		8
H.	Good							Bad		Don't know	
		1	2	3	4	5	6		7		8

If an interview is supposed to approximate a conversation, this question
developed by NORC would appear to violate the rules of good questionnaire design for the simple reason that the interviewer has to read a rather
lengthy speech in introducing the question. By and large, the shorter the
question and the less talking done by the interviewer, the better.

In another NORC survey a clever device was invented for measuring the
importance that people attached to various areas of their lives. They were
presented with a large circle broken up into equal-sized sectors representing
different areas of their lives, such as family, work, leisure activities, and
voluntary associations. They were then given a number of cardboard tokens
and told to allocate the tokens to the various sectors of the circle according to
how important that sector was to them. The more important the sector, the
more tokens they would place in it.

In a study of leisure time activities carried out in the mid-sixties, NORC
evolved an even more complex way of measuring the importance of various
activities. The respondents were presented with a seven-page booklet based
on the trading stamp idea. The booklet listed a large number of leisure time
activities on the left side of the page corresponding to stamp-size squares on
the right which represented hours of time. The respondents were given
stamps and told to paste in stamps representing the number of hours per

day or week they would want to devote to the activity—the more hours, the more stamps they would paste in.

Still another example of response categories in the form of an interval scale appeared on another NORC questionnaire. The respondents were presented with a card with a ladder drawn on it with 10 rungs that looked like Figure 5.2. The question read:

> All of us want certain things out of life. Think about what really matters in your own life. What your hopes and wishes are for the future; what your life has been like in the past. The figure on this card represents the "ladder of life." The top rung represents the best that your life could be. The bottom rung represents the worst that it could be. Please tell me the number of the rung that represents. . . .
>
> A. Where you were as a child?
> B. Where you were as an adolescent?
> C. Where you are right now?
> D. Where you think you will be in five years?

This question too suffers from being rather wordy. This scale, like some of the others presented earlier, contains at least 10 scores. A final example of response categories that are interval scales covers a much larger range, fully 100 different scores. During the 1970s it became fashionable for survey researchers to make use of a "feelings thermometer." The Survey Research

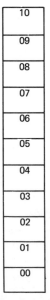

Figure 5.2.   Interval scale in the form of a ladder.

Center at the University of Michigan did a survey in 1974 dealing with political attitudes. The questionnaire had the following question:

This next card is called a "feeling thermometer," and we would like to use it to measure your feelings toward various groups. If you don't feel particularly warm or cold toward a group, then you should place it at the 50° mark. If you have a warm feeling toward a group, you would give it a score somewhere between 50° and 100°. On the other hand, if you don't feel very favorably toward a group, then you would place it somewhere between 0° and 50°.

The first group is small businessmen. Where would you put them on the thermometer?

Group	Feelings Thermometer	
Small businessmen	100°	Warm
The Democratic Party	−95°	
The Women's Liberation Movement	−90°	
Revolutionary groups	−85°	
The Military	−80°	
Blacks	−75°	
The Republican Party	−70°	
Student protesters	−65°	
Civil Service employees	−60°	
The Police	−55°	
Big business	−50°	
Clergymen	−45°	
Whites	−40°	
Labor unions	−35°	
Migrant workers	−30°	
	−25°	
	−20°	
	−15°	
	−10°	
	−05°	
	−00°	Cold

With feelings thermometers survey research has truly come of age, pushing measurement in the social sciences to a level of refinement approximating that of the physical sciences.

THE EVOLUTION OF QUESTIONNAIRES

Survey research began to flourish in the 1930s and 1940s, when the major institutions that carried out survey research were founded. Lazarsfeld had founded the Office of Radio Research in the 1930s, moving it to Columbia University in 1940 when its name was changed to The Bureau of Applied Social Research. The National Opinion Research Center (NORC) was founded in 1941, and the Survey Research Center at the University of Michigan came into existence in 1946. The major national polling organizations, those of Gallup, Roper, and Harris, were founded in 1935, 1936, and 1955, respectively.

To show the evolution of questionnaires, I conducted a survey of questionnaires over a 40-year period from the forties through the seventies. This survey was made possible by the good offices of the National Opinion Research Center, which allowed me to go through its library of questionnaires. In addition, I have access to a number of surveys conducted by the Bureau of Applied Social Research and some surveys that I recently carried out at the Graduate School of the City University of New York.

In all I have sampled more than 40 questionnaires used in face-to-face interviews over a period of 37 years. I paid particular attention to four features of these research instruments: their length in pages, their length in number of questions of various types, the number of batteries of questions they contain, and the number of open-ended questions they have. This research has uncovered a number of trends in questionnaires. First, they have grown enormously in size through the years, both in number of pages and number of questions. Second, the number of batteries has increased substantially, and third, the number of open-ended questions has declined markedly through the years. This can be shown by presenting the statistics on the questionnaires sampled in tabular form by decade. Table 5.1 presents the results for seven questionnaires that were administered during the 1940s. As can be seen, the questionnaires of the 1940s were extremely short, ranging from three to nine pages carrying from 31 to 84 questions. Only one of these early questionnaires, the 1948 survey, used a battery of questions, and the number of open-ended questions ranged from 10 to 27 percent.

The fact that the early questionnaires were short is related to both the norms of the profession at the time and the state of the technology. The early survey researchers were convinced that respondents were unwilling to give more than 15 minutes or so of their time to an interviewer, and the technology for processing data was so primitive that the researcher had no way of handling a large amount of data. In the very early days of survey research the answers obtained on questionnaires were transferred to McBee cards for processing. A McBee card was about 5 by 8 inches marked off in columns or sections representing questions. A hole puncher was used to punch holes on the card representing answers to the questions. The counting of answers would involve sorting the cards with the aid of a needle. The needle would be inserted in the holes and the cards that did not have a punch in that location would drop out. The cards thus would be sorted into different piles representing different answers. The researcher would then count the cards in each pile to find out how many respondents gave the various answers.

Table 5.1. Characteristics of Questionnaires from the Forties[a]

Organization	Year	Pages	Questions		Battery Items	Total Questions	Number of Batteries	Open-Ended Questions	
			Main	Contingency				N	%
1. NORC	1944	4	40	21	0	61	0	9	15
2. NORC	1945	4	20	11	0	31	0	3	10
3. NORC	1945	5	34	11	0	45	0	6	13
4. NORC	1947	4	21	14	0	35	0	7	19
5. NORC	1947	6	42	15	0	57	0	6	11
6. NORC	1948	9	41	31	12	84	1	23	27
7. NORC	1949	3	21	10	0	31	0	5	16

[a]These questionnaires were for the following studies: 1 = study of opinions for the U.S. Office of War Information; 2 = a survey of physicians; 3 = a study of foreign affairs for the State Department; 4 = a survey of opinions about T.B. for the National Tuberculosis Society; 5 = a survey of hospital interns relating to army service; 6 = a survey of medical students, interns, and physicians regarding army service; 7 = a survey for the Denver Tuberculosis Society.

The McBee card was replaced in the mid-forties by the counter sorter, a machine developed by IBM for counting IBM cards. The counter sorter represented an enormous advance in data processing. The answers to questions were now punched on IBM cards and the counter sorter allowed the researcher to sort cards according to the categories on one variable and then count the various punches in another column. In this way the researcher was able to construct a table. Since each pile of cards had to be inserted by hand into the counter sorter, it could easily take 5 or 10 minutes to generate a single table, so that researchers spent many long hours over the counter sorter analyzing data. It was not until the early 1960s that the counter sorter was replaced by the computer—capable of generating hundreds of tables in minutes.

The relatively large number of open-ended questions in the early surveys also reflects the state of art at that time. There was considerable controversy in the early days about the relative merits of open-ended and close-ended questions. Many people thought that checklist questions failed to do justice to the richness and complexity of opinions and attitudes, a criticism that intimidated early survey researchers. To protect themselves, they made sure that surveys contained a number of open-ended as well as checklist questions.

By the 1950s, when survey researchers were still dependent on the counter sorter for processing their data, questionnaires grew substantially in size, as can be seen from Table 5.2. The last questionnaire in Table 5.2, from the end of the decade, is a deviant case, more characteristic of the questionnaires of the 1970s. It is extremely long, 71 pages, and contains 408 questions. The other questionnaires sampled from the 1950s range from 13 to 32 pages containing 99 to 247 questions. Open-ended questions were still prevalent in the 1950s, ranging from 9 to 40 percent of the questions. These questionnaires all contain batteries of questions, but the number of batteries is relatively small. The very long 1959 questionnaire had eight batteries, but most of the 1950s questionnaires had only one or two.

In the 1960s the number of batteries increased sharply and the number of open-ended questions declined substantially (see Table 5.3). The questionnaires are much longer than the questionnaires of the 1950s, ranging from 21 to 60 pages containing 141 to 442 questions. The number of batteries increases over the 1950s. Perhaps the most startling characteristic of these questionnaires is the sharp decline in open-ended questions. Of the 11 questionnaires only two have more than 10 percent open-ended questions. As we shall see, this trend continues into the 1970s. Just as one of the questionnaires sampled in the 1950s was unusually long, so one in the 1960s sample is unusually long, the fifth item in the table, the 1964 questionnaire of 57 pages and 442 questions. The other questionnaires of the 1950s sample ranged from 133 to 391 questions.

Table 5.2. *Characteristics of Questionnaires from the Fifties*[a]

Organization	Year	Pages	Questions Main	Questions Contingency	Battery Items	Total Questions	Number of Batteries	Open-Ended Questions N	Open-Ended Questions %
1. NORC	1950	29	39	69	20	124	2	50	40
2. BASR	1951	32	93	141	13	247	3	37	15
3. NORC	1952	13	59	35	15	99	1	27	26
4. BASR	1953	25	72	85	26	183	2	24	13
5. NORC	1953	16	53	112	22	187	2	17	9
6. NORC	1953	15	40	99	15	154	1	17	11
7. NORC	1953	14	39	123	5	167	1	23	17
8. NORC	1955	32	95	91	50	236	4	50	21
9. NORC	1957	24	50	74	37	161	6	18	11
10. NORC	1957	28	72	69	11	152	2	18	12
11. NORC	1959	71	127	235	46	408	8	62	15

[a]The studies are: 1 = Survey of attitudes toward mental illness; 2 = Lipset's study on union democracy; 3 = survey of reactions to aircraft noise; 4 = Lazarsfeld's study of McCarthyism on campus published as *The Academic Mind*; 5 = a survey of health and medical care in the United States; 6 = survey of health and medical care in the United States; 7 = survey of health and medical care in Boston; 8 = survey of doctors; 9 = survey of family health in New York; 10 = survey of physicians' knowledge and values; 11 = survey of dental attitudes and practices.

Table 5.3. *Characteristics of Questionnaires from the Sixties*[a]

Organization	Year	Pages	Questions Main	Questions Contingency	Battery Items	Total Questions	Number of Batteries	Open-Ended Questions N	Open-Ended Questions %
1. BASR	1960	25	159	175	57	391	4	30	8
2. NORC	1960	24	67	69	5	141	1	43	30
3. NORC	1963	42	141	105	44	290	5	23	8
4. NORC	1963	22	45	44	88	177	8	10	6
5. NORC	1964	34	67	102	55	224	8	28	13
6. NORC	1964	57	167	157	118	442	9	34	8
7. NORC	1964	29	77	44	115	236	11	12	5
8. NORC	1966	60	176	101	102	379	13	16	4
9. NORC	1968	21	76	38	19	133	4	3	2
10. NORC	1968	52	77	212	69	359	11	14	4
11. BASR	1968	27	143	89	7	239	1	25	10

[a]The studies are: 1 = Caplovitz-Consumer Practices of Poor: *The Poor Pay More*; 2 = Massachusetts hospital study; 3 = Bradburn-Caplovitz happiness study; 4 = first amalgam survey (multitude of clients); 5 = central Harlem community survey; 6 = occupation study; 7 = survey of interviewers; 8 = utilization of health-related services; 9 = amalgam survey; 10 = survey for Bar Association of Problem Solving by the Poor; 11 = Caplovitz study of small businessmen in Harlem (*The Merchants of Harlem*).

The trends shown by the 1960s questionnaires continue into the 1970s, as can he seen from Table 5.4. The three trends noted in the 1960s continued: the questionnaires got much longer, the number of batteries increased sharply, and the number of open-ended questions declined precipitously. In the 1970s sample there are two unusually long questionnaires, the one from 1974 and the one from 1979. Each more than 90 pages, one has 541 questions and the other the incredible number of 809. The other questionnaires average about 300 questions and close to 40 pages in length. The figures for the open-ended questions are startling. Not a single questionnaire had at least 10 percent open-ended questions. In fact, the largest number is a mere 6 percent and almost all the questionnaires had well below 5 percent open-ended questions. The battle between the proponents of open-ended questions and the proponents of close-ended questions, fought so vigorously in the forties and fifties, had clearly been won by the close-ended advocates by the 1970s.

The trends in questionnaires can most easily be seen from the averages for samples of questionnaires for each decade, seen in Table 5.5. We computed the averages in two ways, first with all the questionnaires and second with the longest questionnaire of the 1950s to 1970s eliminated. Whether one looks at the top half of the table, which refers to all the questionnaires, or the bottom half, which eliminates the longest questionnaire, the trends are clear: the numbers of pages and questions steadily increase, the number of batteries increases sharply, and the number of open-ended questions drops sharply between the fifties and the sixties. In the forties and fifties 16 and 17 percent of the questions were open-ended; in the sixties the open-ended rate dropped to 9 percent, and the decline continued into the seventies, when the rate fell to 3 percent.

We already noted that a major factor contributing to the growth of questionnaires was the technological revolution brought about by the computer. The computer makes it possible to process large amounts of data in a simple fashion. But another factor contributed to the growth of questionnaires: the institutionalization of survey research. As noted, in the early days of survey research, the researcher was worried about imposing upon the respondent and felt that 15 minutes or so was the maximum time for an interview. But through the years, many thousands of surveys have been conducted and millions of Americans have been interviewed. The public is now very familiar with survey research, and as survey research became more and more institutionalized the researchers felt that they could get away with longer and longer interviews. Today an interview frequently takes 1½ to 2 hours.

Self-Administered Questionnaires

The interview has been central to survey research since its earliest days, but, survey researchers are relying increasingly on the self-administered ques-

Table 5.1. Characteristics of Questionnaires from the Seventies[a]

Organization	Year	Pages	Questions		Battery Items	Total Questions	Number of Batteries	Open-Ended Questions	
			Main	Contingency				N	%
1. BASR	1972	57	165	78	86	329	15	16	5
2. NORC	1972	24	52	41	102	195	13	2	1
3. NORC	1973	65	128	104	124	356	26	0	
4. NORC	1974	90	218	164	159	541	16	28	5
5. NORC	1975	49	118	106	63	287	7	4	1
6. NORC	1975	30	60	51	67	178	7	2	1
7. CUNY	1976	33	134	60	52	246	5	14	6
8. NORC	1976	55	178	113	91	382	8	19	5
9. CUNY	1977	21	66	35	78	179	7	7	4
10. NORC	1978	40	111	40	60	211	8	4	2
11. NORC	1979	94	350	371	88	809	4	19	2

[a]The studies are: 1 = study of New York City neighborhoods; 2 = survey of basic beliefs; 3 = amalgam survey (multitude of clients); 4 = survey of life events and various aspects of health; 5 = amalgam survey (multitude of clients); 6 = leisure activity survey; 7 = Caplovitz–impact of inflation (Making Ends Meet); 8 = adolescent and young adult health project; 9 = Caplovitz: Youngsters experimenting with drugs; 10 = amalgam survey (multitude of clients); 11 = national medical care utilization and expenditure survey.

Table 5.5. Average Characteristics of Questionnaires by Decade

Decade	Pages	Questions		Battery Items	Total Questions	Number of Batteries	Open-Ended Questions	
		Main	Contingency				N	%
A. All Questionnaires								
Forties	5	31	16	—	49	—	8	16
Fifties	27	67	103	24	193	3	31	17
Sixties	36	109	103	62	274	7	22	9
Seventies	51	144	106	88	338	11	10	3
B. Minus Longest								
Forties	5	31	16	—	49	—	8	16
Fifties	23	61	90	22	171	3	28	17
Sixties	34	103	98	56	257	7	21	9
Seventies	47	123	80	88	291	12	9	3

tionnaire. The respondent reads the questions and answers them by writing on the questionnaire, thus alleviating the expense of interviews. The interviewing is almost always the most expensive item in a project's budget. During the 1960s interviews cost about $50 each; by the 1970s the cost had climbed to $60 to $100 a case. Given the expense of interviews, surveys never exceeded several thousand respondents and most surveys worked with considerably smaller samples. The self-administered questionnaire, in contrast to the interview, is very inexpensive. The biggest expense is the mailing to and from the respondent. Self-administered questionnaires cost anywhere from a few dollars to 10 dollars each. Since they are relatively cheap, self-administered questionnaires make it possible to develop very large samples. For example, back in the sixties, NORC launched a massive panel study of college graduates in the class of 1961. They sampled 40,000 graduates and followed them over a three-year period. Each year the graduates were sent a self-administered questionnaire, which they filled out and mailed back. (To ensure a high response rate NORC asked the students for the name and address of someone who would know where they were a year later.) About that time in a Columbia study of cheating on campus mail questionnaires were collected from about 20,000 college students.

The samples in the two studies cited above were college students. Self-administered questionnaires are most appropriate for studies of special populations of reasonably high education such as lawyers, doctors, teachers, students. In surveys based on random samples of the entire adult population, as in the Gallup and Harris polls, self-administered questionnaires are never used, the researcher relying on the interview instead. Not only did self-administered questionnaires make it possible to study very large samples, but they made it possible to ask more questions through the economy of the battery of questions. The respondent staring at the battery does not need complicated instructions on how to answer batteries of questions, and the researcher can therefore rely more heavily on the battery format. The battery makes it possible to ask a large number of questions in a short space, a page or half a page of a questionnaire. Thus self-administered questionnaires tend to contain more questions than the research instrument in an interview study. These characteristics of self-administered questionnaires can be seen from Table 5.6, which shows the results for a sample of open-ended questionnaires.

The self-administered questionnaires varied considerably in length. Three had fewer than 20 pages and three had under 200 questions. At the other extreme were four questionnaires over 40 pages long and four with over 400 questions. The economy of self-administered questionnaires is shown by the fact that the average number of pages is 33, which is smaller than the average number of pages in the questionnaires used in interview surveys during the sixties and seventies, yet the average number of questions on the self-administered questionnaires is substantially larger. Indeed,

Table 5.6. Characteristics of Self-Administered Questionnaires[a]

| Organization | Year | Pages | Questions | | Battery Items | Total Questions | Number of Batteries | Open-Ended Questions | |
			Main	Contingency				N	%
1. NORC	1961	19	62	28	37	127	5	0	—
2. BASR	1962	14	61	14	183	253	28	2	0.5
3. NORC	1964	43	184	130	448	762	82	3	0.4
4. NORC	1964	24	85	29	72	186	9	0	—
5. NORC	1969	30	156	38	351	545	32	1	0.2
6. NORC	1969	46	112	41	409	562	35	3	0.5
7. NORC	1970	34	68	57	253	378	25	6	1.6
8. NORC	1973	17	96	42	66	204	7	0	—
9. NORC[b]	1977	46	111	16	92	229	12	0	—
10. NORC	1978	29	58	26	29	113	3	3	3.0
11. NORC	1979	63	147	59	257	463	33	5	1
Average		33	104	44	200	347	25	2	0.65%

[a]The studies are: 1 = the first wave of the three year panel study of the College Class of 1961; 2 = a study of cheating in college; 3 = the fourth wave of the panel study of the Class of 1961; 4 = a survey of the college class of 1964; 5 = study of Franciscan order of priests; 6 = study of Catholic priests; 7 = study of resigned priests; 8 = national study of physicians; 9 = study of family life and achievement; 10 = evaluation of National Science Foundation Regional Program; 11 = study of religious values in Montreal.
[b]Although this questionnaire has the second most pages, it is in the bottom third in terms of number of questions. The reason for this is that it is the only questionnaire set in pica type. All the others are set in elite type, which is considerably smaller.

the average number of questions for the self-administered questionnaires is 347 compared with 257 for the questionnaires of the sixties and 291 for the questionnaires of the seventies. The reason for this economy is the battery format, which permits asking a large number of questions in a relatively small space. And it is the battery format that accounts for most of the questions in the self-administered questionnaires. The average number of main questions is comparable to the questionnaires of the sixties and seventies, but the average number of contingency questions is substantially lower (44 compared with 98 and 80). The self-administered questionnaires have an average of 200 battery items (compared to 56 and 88 in the sixties and seventies) and 25 batteries. As noted, the battery is highly compatible with the self-administered questionnaire format.

What is especially striking is that open-ended questions virtually disappear on self-administered questionnaires. Only one questionnaire studied had more than 1 percent open-ended questions. Four of them had no open-ended questions at all, and the remainder had less than 1 percent. It should also be noted that this sample of self-administered questionnaires is limited to the sixties and the seventies. Prior to the sixties, self-administered questionnaires were rarely used. And from the description of the studies in the footnote below the table, it is clear that these self-administered questionnaires were used in studies of highly literate populations, college students, physicians, and priests. Only two of them, a study of family life and of religious values, had more general populations.

DELICATE QUESTIONS

For many years debates raged over the types of questions that survey researchers could ask. It was believed in the early days of survey research that a wide range of personal questions must be avoided if rapport with respondents was to be maintained. In many instances government watchdog agencies, like the Office of Management and Budget, which evaluates questionnaires developed for research under government contracts, discouraged survey researchers from asking personal questions relating to religion and income and even more personal questions dealing with such private matters as sex and crime. But through the years, survey researchers became more daring and did ask about a range of personal and private matters; to their pleasant surprise, they found that the public was prepared to answer personal questions. Thus over time there has been a steady decline in questions that are taboo. Some questions dealing with deviant behavior and questions dealing with highly personal matters such as sex illustrate the types of delicate questions that have been successfully asked in surveys.

Questions about Deviant Behavior

In my study of youngsters experimenting with drugs, boys aged 10 to 14 were asked about their use of various drugs. To find out about marijuana use, the youngsters were asked a deliberately loaded question, one that assumed they had used marijuana, to wit:

40. How old were you when you first smoked marijuana.

In spite of the question being loaded, the great majority denied that they had used marijuana, but 25 percent responded affirmatively. They were then asked whether any of their friends smoked "Angel Dust" and if they themselves had smoked it. They were then asked comparable questions about cocaine and heroin.

In the same study the youngsters were asked a battery of questions about the activities they engaged in with their friends that included the following items:

		True	False
1.	Sometimes we steal things from stores.	6%	94%
2.	My friends and I carry weapons to protect ourselves.	7%	93%
3.	My friends have gotten into trouble with the police.	17%	83%
32.	Have you ever had trouble with the police?	Yes 9%	No 91%

A number of surveys have been done on juvenile delinquency and questions that deal with crimes such as stealing are fairly common.

In an unpublished study of cheating in college, William Bowers, then with the Bureau of Applied Social Research at Columbia, asked a large sample of college students a series of questions about cheating that included the following:

How often since you have been in college have you:

Copied from another student during an exam?

Plagiarized from published materials on papers?

Turned in papers done entirely or in part by other students?

Used crib notes during an exam?

Fully 50 percent of the sample of college students admitted to at least one of these four forms of cheating.

In a study of adolescent health based on a sample of black youth in a low-income community, Dr. Ann Brunswick asked a series of questions about drug use and pregnancy.* The girls were asked:

28. Have you ever been pregnant? If yes: Are you pregnant now?
29. What about miscarriages or abortions—have you ever had a miscarriage or abortion?

The sample was also asked about their use of a series of drugs, including marijuana, LSD, cocaine, heroin, Methadone, uppers, and downers.

Not only have questions about drugs been asked in surveys of special populations such as preteens from a low-income community or black youth, but such questions have been asked in national surveys of the general population. In a study of leisure activities carried out in 1975, NORC asked the following questions about marijuana:

28. Marijuana is commonly used. Have you yourself, at any time in your life, smoked marijuana?

Yes _____
No _____

If No:
A. Not at all, not even once?

Yes _____
No _____

If Yes:
B. Have you smoked marijuana during the past year?

Yes _____
No _____

If yes to B: Have you smoked marijuana in the past month?

Yes _____
No _____

C. Has there ever been a time when you were smoking marijuana at least three times a week?

Yes _____
No _____

D. When you smoked marijuana, how many cigarettes or pipes did you usually smoke on an average day?

2 or less _____
3–4 _____
5–6 _____
7–8 _____
More than 8 _____

*Ann Brunswick, "Black Youths and Drug Use Behavior," in George M. Beschner and Alfred S. Friedman (Eds.), *Youth Drug Abuse*, Lexington, Massachusetts: Lexington Books, 1979, Chapter 18.

As these examples make clear, questions about a wide range of deviant activities have been asked in surveys.

Questions about Very Personal Matters: Sex

The same NORC survey of leisure activities also included a number of questions about sex. Thus at one point the national sample was asked:

33. In the past month, have you engaged in sexual intercourse?

                                         Yes _____
                                          No _____
                      Prefers not to answer _____

    If Yes:

  A. On the average, how often did you engage in intercourse during the month?

                                        Daily _____
                            4–6 times a week _____
                            2–3 times a week _____
                                 Once a week _____
                          2–3 times a month _____
                        Once a month or less _____

  B. Have you engaged in intercourse during the past 24 hours?

                                         Yes _____
                                          No _____

Nor did the NORC researchers stop there. Their next question asked:

34. In the past month, have you masturbated?

                                         Yes _____
                                          No _____
                      Prefers not to answer _____

    If Yes:

  A. On the average, how often did you masturbate in the past month?

                                        Daily _____
                            4–6 times a week _____
                            2–3 times a week _____
                                 Once a week _____
                          2–3 times a month _____
                        Once a month or less _____

  B. Did you masturbate during the past 24 hours?

                                         Yes _____
                                          No _____

Not only is sexual intercourse fair game for the survey researcher, but even such extremely private behavior as masturbation does not escape the spotlight of survey research.

Whereas the leisure activity survey dealt with many topics besides sex, in 1970 NORC did a survey for the Institute of Sex Research (The Kinsey Institute) at Indiana University which dealt exclusively with sex. This survey used a combination of an interview schedule and self-administered questionnaire. In the interview the respondents were asked whether they approved or disapproved of premarital sex, extramarital sex, and masturbation. They were asked whether they knew any homosexuals and lesbians and they were asked whether they felt there should be laws banning various sexual practices. They were even asked whether they had any desires to be of the opposite sex in the following question:

34. How often have you . . .

	Often	Sometimes	Rarely	Never
A. felt you would have been happier as a (OPPOSITE SEX)?	_____	_____	_____	_____
B. felt more like a (OPPOSITE SEX)?	_____	_____	_____	_____
C. felt you would prefer to wear (OPPOSITE SEX)'s clothes?	_____	_____	_____	_____

Whereas the interview schedule was used to elicit attitudes and feelings, the self-administered questionnaire handed to the respondents was designed to reveal their sexual experiences. In this questionnaire, the respondents were asked how old they were when they first masturbated, when they first had sexual intercourse, and the age of their partner. They were asked a number of questions about childhood sex play such as the following:

1. When you were a child, before your body was developed sexually, did you ever have playmates, brothers or sisters, or anyone else, who had any kind of sex play or sex games with you?

Yes _____
No _____

If Yes:

A. Was the sex play with children of your own sex, of the opposite sex or of both sexes?

Only of my sex _____
Only of opposite sex _____
Of both sexes _____

They were then asked how their parents responded when they found out about this sex play. This survey even inquired about homosexual experience. In a deliberately loaded question, the respondents were asked:

9.   What was your age the first time you had sexual
     experience with someone of the *same sex*, when
     either you or your partner came to a sexual climax?

                                             Age _____ # years.

     IF YOU HAVE *NEVER* HAD THIS EXPERIENCE
     WRITE NEVER AND SKIP TO Q.12 ON PAGE 11.

Those who said they had had this experience were than asked a series of questions about it, such as the frequency of their homosexual experiences, the number of different people they had these experiences with, their age, and the age of their partners. They were asked a series of questions about their feelings about homosexual experiences and if anyone they knew had found out about their homosexual activity.

Income

Although it is possible to ask about a wide range of deviant behavior and about such highly personal matters as sexual behavior, one question many respondents are reluctant to answer is the question of their income. In survey after survey the income question generates the largest number of "no answers." To minimize the no answers to the income question, survey researchers have tried to devise methods that would be less painful to respondents. A very common technique is to hand the respondent a card with anywhere from seven to 10 income categories identified by letters. The interviewer then asks the respondent to read off the letter of the category that represents his income. Rather than ask about the respondent's income, many surveys inquire about total family income, as in the following sample question:

Which of the following categories best describes your *total* family income from *all* sources—before taxes—for the year 1976?

This question appeared on a self-administered questionnaire that was sent out in February 1977.

In a number of surveys researchers inquire about monthly or weekly income on the assumption that this may provoke less resistance than yearly income. In a fifth wave administered to the graduates of the class of 1961 in 1968, when they were seven years out of college, NORC asked a rather complicated income question as follows:

42.   How much money do you earn and do you expect to earn per year from

your own employment and from *all* sources for your entire family?

	My Own Employment	Total Family Income
Now	$ _____,000	$ _____,000
Six years from now	$ _____,000	$ _____,000
When you are 45 years old	$ _____,000	$ _____,000

An innovation in asking the income question occurred in the survey of youngsters experimenting with drugs. In that study the mothers of the boys were also interviewed, and they were asked about family income. These were all relatively poor families and the mothers were asked whether their family income was above or below $10,000 a year. If they said above, they were asked a follow-up question, whether their income was above or below $15,000. If they said their income was below $10,000, the follow-up question asked whether it was above or below $5,000. In this way four income categories were generated. In a study of the general population, the same technique could be used, increasing the cutoff point in the first question to $25,000 a year. Questions about income generally generate "no answer" rates of 10 percent or more. The efficacy of the two-part question described above is shown by the fact that the "no answer" rate for income in that study was only 6 percent.

The problem of asking about income brings to a close our examination of the development of questionnaires. As we have seen, questionnaires have become more complex over time, interviews have become much longer, the measurements made in surveys have become more refined, and the battery format has made it possible to ask a large number of questions in limited space. Behind these innovations and developments in questionnaires has been the changing technology of data processing from McBee cards to counter sorters to the 101 statistical sorter to computers. Cultural changes have also contributed to the development of questionnaires. The "sexual revolution" is reflected in the intimate questions that can now be asked in surveys. Moreover, survey research itself has become institutionalized in our society, with most people aware of surveys and many millions of people participating in surveys as respondents.

6

The History of Questionnaires

Having seen how questionnaires have developed over time, we turn in this chapter to the rather complicated task of constructing a questionnaire. The topics to be covered in a questionnaire are indicated by the research problem, and the task of questionnaire construction involves developing suitable questions that bear on these topics. This process goes through a series of stages which represent successive approximations of the final product. Questionnaires evolve through a sequence of drafts. The typical questionnaire may have four, five, six, or more, drafts. Each draft generally is pretested on a small sample of people who represent the population to be studied. Through the pretests researchers learn about the flaws of the questions and may get ideas for new questions. After each pretest the questionnaire is revised and then tested again. Eventually the point of diminishing returns is reached and the researcher is satisfied that the questionnaire will accomplish its objectives.

The best way to learn about questionnaire construction, according to Paul F. Lazarsfeld, is the case method, that is, systematic accounts of how particular questionnaires were developed, what changes were made from draft to draft, and the reasons for changes. He encouraged his students to write histories of the questionnaires they were developing to document the changes that took place from draft to draft and the results of the pretests. About a half dozen of these histories were written during the fifties and sixties at the Bureau of Applied Social Research at Columbia, and this chapter draws on these histories to elucidate some principles of questionnaire construction and the cross-pressures, dilemmas, and conflicts that frequently influence the writing of questionnaires.

CASE STUDY I

In the late 1950s I worked with a graduate student named Rapael Gill on the history of one section of the questionnaire developed by Lazarsfeld in his study of the impact of McCarthyism on college professors.* A critical variable in this study was "apprehension," the degree to which college professors were intimidated or afraid of McCarthyism. A number of questions were developed as indicators of apprehension, and this variable was finally measured by a subset of these questions. An extract of the paper that was developed on these questions follows.

=====

History of the Apprehension Battery in the Academic Mind Questionnaire by Paul F. Lazarsfeld and Wagner Thielens, Jr.

RAPHAEL GILL AND DAVID CAPLOVITZ

In contrast with some studies where the problem under investigation only becomes gradually defined during the exploratory stage, the problem in this study was defined at the outset by the client—the Fund for the Republic—to what extent had college teachers become frightened or apprehensive because of the attacks leveled against them during the McCarthy era? When we say that the problem was fairly clear from the beginning we do not mean to imply that the meaning of apprehension was clear or even how to measure it. On the contrary, the researchers started out with only a vague image of apprehension and the problem of how to measure it was by no means clear.

At one time or another during the questionnaire construction phase, some 30 questions were drafted to serve as indicators of apprehension. Of these, 21 survived and appeared in the final version of the schedule. And once the data were collected, it was found that only six of the items met all the tests of suitable indicators and were used in an index of apprehension. Each of these items inquired about some particular attitude or behavior on the part of the respondents which on common sense grounds seemed to be related to the phenomenon of apprehension. These questions could all be answered either "yes" or "no." Examples of items that appeared in the final battery are the following:

1. Have you worried about the possibility that some student might inadvertently pass on a warped version of what you said and lead to a false impression of your political views?

Yes _____
No _____

*Paul F. Lazarsfeld and Wagner Thielens, Jr., *The Academic Mind: Social Scientists in a Time of Crisis*, New York: Free Press, 1958.

2. Have you ever wondered that some political opinion you have expressed might affect your job security or promotion at this college?

Yes _____

No _____

3. Have you toned down anything you have written lately because you were worried that it might cause too much controversy?

Yes _____

No _____

4. Do you find in your conversations with your fellow faculty members that there's a lot more talk these days about teacher firings and other political security problems?

Yes _____

No _____

Some idea of the kinds and amount of change that took place in the formulation of the apprehension questions is provided by the following statistics. First, the number of items fluctuated a great deal. In the very first draft, when the method of measuring apprehension was not clear, only 11 of the 30 items which were eventually drafted appeared. Moreover, they were scattered throughout the questionnaire and their form was not consistent. Between the first and second drafts, the researchers decided to have a battery of apprehension questions and in the second draft, there were 28 items grouped together. The list was cut to 16 items in the third version. In the fourth draft, four questions were resurrected and one was discarded so that the list now numbered 19. In the seventh draft, two new questions were added and the list was brought to the final total of 21. As for changes in wording through the various drafts, only seven of the 21 items finally used did *not* undergo any changes; six were changed once and eight underwent at least two modifications in wording; one particularly troublesome item was worded somewhat differently in six of the eight drafts. However, the location of the battery within the questionnaire shifted throughout the various versions. Because of these many changes, this battery provides good material for examining the processes involved in questionnaire construction.

Of the various types of changes, three will be discussed and illustrated: (a) changes in the techniques of inquiring about apprehension; (b) changes in the content of the battery and (c) changes in the wording of questions.

I. CHANGES IN THE TECHNIQUES OF INQUIRING ABOUT APPREHENSION

The method of studying apprehension was still very unsettled when the first version of the questionnaire was being drafted. In part, the changes that subsequently took place in the approach to the problem stemmed from further reflection on the kind of measure that was needed and in part the changes grew out of the pre-tests which led to the revision of certain preconceptions held by the researchers about college teachers and how they would react.

One of the initial assumptions of the researchers was that the topic of apprehension was an extremely delicate one and therefore had best be approached in a cautious and indirect manner. The very first version of the questionnaire, in comparison with subsequent ones, reflects this more cautious approach in several ways. First, the relatively few questions dealing directly with apprehension were scattered throughout the questionnaire and they were always preceded by queries about the fears of either colleagues or students on the theory that the respondents would find it easier to talk about others than about themselves. For example, one series of questions began with the query whether students were less inclined to express unpopular views in the classroom. The next question asked whether the respondent himself had any fears about expressing his own views in the classroom and if so to explain in detail. Actually, questions about the respondent's *perceptions* of colleagues and students were intended to serve several functions. They were viewed as a way of leading into questions about the respondent's own fears; secondly, they were seen as providing information about the climate or atmosphere at the respondent's college; and third, it was felt that such questions might be projective, that is, they might be treated as indicators of the respondent's own state of apprehension. Although the trend from the first draft to subsequent ones was toward inquiring more directly about the respondent's own fears, some questions about the fears of colleagues survived into the final version. [Chapter 14 shows how these questions were used in contextual analysis.] One such example is question 4 cited above.

A second indicator of the more cautious approach to apprehension was that the first draft gave more emphasis to open-ended questions than did the subsequent versions. Not only were there a few unstructured questions about the kinds of things the respondent worries about, but the check list apprehension questions were followed by probing questions asking for detailed explanations. The purpose of these probes was not only to gather qualitative data but also to give the respondent the opportunity to qualify his answer on the theory that he would be more cooperative this way than if restricted to a "yes" or "no" answer.

Between the first and second draft of the questionnaire, the decision was made to pull the various apprehension indicators together into a single battery, to expand greatly the list of items and to standardize the response categories so that each item could be answered either "yes" or "no." One reason for this change in approach was the growing realization that in the analysis it would be necessary to construct a quantifiable index of apprehension. A second reason behind this more direct approach was that the pre-test of the first draft indicated that teachers were not as reluctant to comment on their attitudes and fears as had been assumed. This is perhaps a frequent discovery of pre-tests. Researchers generally tend to underestimate the respondents' willingness to talk about the issues in question.

Another set of assumptions made by the study directors which affected their initial formulation of questions concerned their images of American colleges. They began the study with the rather naive notion that American colleges were similar to the ones that they personally were familiar with. As a consequence they formulated questions which seemed to make sense at the large, high prestige universities they knew about but which did *not* make sense at many of the teachers colleges and small denominational schools that make up such a large proportion of the colleges in the United States. For example, respondents were asked whether they had toned down their recent writings (see question 3 above) the assumption being that all teachers write; another question asked whether teachers were less willing to act as advisors to student political groups, again the existence of such groups being taken for granted. The pre-tests quickly revealed that these assumptions were incorrect. The discovery of the extreme diversity of American colleges led to two kinds of modifications. First, in some questions the response category "never encountered" or "does not apply" was added. Second, some questions which took a particular situation as given were changed to hypothetical questions. The two versions of question 5 below illustrate such a change.

> **5.** *First version: When* you have hired a teaching assistant, *have you ever wondered* if his political background might possibly be embarrassing to you?
>
> *Final version: If you were to hire* a teaching assistant, *would you wonder* if his political background might possibly be embarrassing to you?

Instead of asking what happens when an assistant is hired, the language was changed to make the hiring of an assistant hypothetical. Such a change introduces its own difficulties. While the question can now be answered by all the respondents, it is no longer possible to distinguish those teachers for whom the question is a reality, that is, teachers who do have teaching assistants and presumably are reporting on their behavior, and teachers for whom the question is only hypothetical. The diversity of American colleges and trying to come to terms with it is another major factor which influenced the development of the questionnaire.

Certain preconceptions of the researchers led them to omit entirely some lines of inquiry that they would have liked to have included. *The Academic Mind* was a rather unusual study in that it is one of the few in which the respondents were much more sophisticated than the interviewers. One suggestion that was made by a consultant to the study was that it would be important to distinguish between the apprehension created by the McCarthy era and the general level of anxiety of the respondents characteristic of their personalities. Although considered desirable, it was decided not to act on this suggestion on the grounds that the college teachers would see through and resent any attempt to administer a psychological test measuring anxiety.

Changes in the Content of the Battery

The second class of changes deals with the content of the apprehension battery, the deletions and additions of items.

Omissions

Items 6 through 8 are examples of questions that were dropped before the final draft.

> **6.** If you were teaching economics, would you hesitate to criticize the system of private property for fear that your remarks might be misunderstood?
>
> **7.** Have you ever refused any speaking engagements or turned down attending any meetings because of the possible political repercussions?
>
> **8.** Have you ever refrained from writing for a particular publication because of possible political repercussions?

A general problem of questionnaire construction is that of length. Budgets as well as interviewer and respondent fatigue make long questionnaires impractical. A rather typical outcome of pre-tests is the discovery that the schedule is too long. This was true in the *Academic Mind* study. The interviewers all felt that the 28 item apprehension battery was too long and should be cut. Were the researcher to have the benefit of the analysis at this stage, he would be able to make sound decisions about what to omit, but, of course, this is not the case. As a result, an element of arbitrariness enters into the decision process. At this point the researcher is at the mercy of the interviewers who did the pre-testing. Items which posed some difficulty for the interviewers tend to head the list of candidates for omission. This was true, for example, of question 6. Several pre-test interviewers reported that respondents had difficulty understanding the meaning of "system of private property." The specific reasons for dropping the other two questions are not now known; to some extent they are similar to other items, such as the question on toning down writings and may have been considered repetitious. But they may have been dropped because they assume experiences that many professors probably never have. For example, many professors may never have speaking engagements and may not be inclined to write journal articles. And the decision to drop them may well have been arbitrary; some questions had to be omitted. These two items (7 and 8) call attention to a major dilemma in the research process. Precisely because the researcher knows more about what he is studying after he has studied it, he must inevitably make decisions in the early phases which in retrospect are regrettable. Proof that the study directors had only a vague image of apprehension at the start of the study is provided by the omission of these items. The subsequent analysis showed that apprehension has several dimensions, one a component of "worry," a mental state, and another, a component of "caution"—a reference to behavior. A person might be frightened or worried and yet not change his way of behaving. Since the distinction between worry and caution was not formulated at the outset, the final apprehension battery had more indicators of "worry" than of "caution." It was not until work began on the history of the questionnaire that it was discovered that indicators of caution, such as questions 7 and 8, had been discarded.

The Addition of Items

Once the apprehension battery had been drafted for the second version of the questionnaire, no new items were added until the seventh draft when the following items were formulated.

9. Have you ever wanted to join an organization and despite the possibility of personal criticism for joining it, you went ahead and became a member anyway?

10. Have you recently wanted to express publicly a political point of view on something and despite your worry that you might be criticized for saying what you did, you said it just the same?

The reason for adding these was that a consultant to the project warned the study directors to be aware of response set. The apprehension indicators were to be answered "yes" or "no" and the "yes" answer was always the apprehensive response. To guard against response set, items 9 and 10 were drafted. A "yes" answer to these questions would indicate that the respondent was not intimidated and presumably not apprehensive. The seventh draft was produced only a short time before the field work began; in fact, this draft was not pre-tested. As a consequence, the good intention of these questions was spoiled by a flaw which went undetected; the meaning of the negative answer is unclear. If a person says "no" to question 9 we do not know whether he would have joined an organization if he weren't worried about criticism, or whether he had no intention of joining, worry or no worry. In this instance, the effort to correct one problem led to the unwitting creation of another. It should be pointed out that these items were not without value. The meaning of the yes answer is still clear. In some instances, the researcher may only be interested in one response category and treat all others as residual. Lazarsfeld was able to use these items to gauge the activism or courage of teachers. Nonetheless, if the questions had been formulated earlier in the process, the error would probably have been corrected. At this point we might formalize a concept which should be taken seriously by those who study the development of questionnaires, the concept of "questionnaire construction fatigue." As the questionnaire goes through numerous revisions and the deadline for the field work approaches, writers of questionnaires are apt to become fatigued and anxious to start the next phase of the research. Questions drafted in the terminal stages of this fatigue may well be the ones that violate the rules of writing questions.

Changes in Wording

The third major category of changes in the development of the apprehension battery consists of changes in wording. The numerous wording changes in these items can for the most part be classified under three headings. The first of these is "sharpening the focus," that is, getting the question to focus on the subject matter of the study. In the following three examples, the word "political" was inserted in order to link the source of worry to the subject matter of the research.

11. *First version:* Have some colleagues ever given you advice on how to avoid getting into trouble on campus?
     Final version: Have some colleagues *here on campus* ever given you advice on how to avoid getting into *political* trouble at *this college*?

12. *First version:* Do you find yourself worrying sometimes that you might be the subject of gossip in the community?
     Final version: Do you *ever* find yourself *wondering if because of your politics or something political* you said or did that you might be subject to gossip in the community?

13. *First version:* Have *you ever considered* the possibility that some student might inadvertently pass on a warped version of what you have said and lead to false ideas about you?
     Final version: Have you worried about the possibility . . . false ideas about *your political views*?

A second focusing problem had to do with the time period under investigation. The point of the study was to examine the impact of recent political events on college teachers. Initially, the researchers concentrated on the theme of a question and it was not until several pre-tests had taken place that they were reminded of the time focusing problem. As a consequence, in later versions of the questionnaire, such words as "lately," "recently," "these days," and "more of a tendency," were inserted in the questions. Questions 14 and 15 are examples of such changes.

14. *First version:* Have you *ever* toned down anything you have written because you were worried that it would cause too much controversy?
     Final version: Have you toned down anything you have written *lately* because you were worried . . .?

15. *First version:* Have you ever wanted to express a point of view on something and despite your worry that you might be criticized for saying what you did, you said it just the same?
Final version: Have you *recently* wanted to express *publicly* a *political* point of view . . .?

Item 15 is actually item 10 presented above as an addition to the battery, only here we see it in its two different versions. Not only was *ever* changed to *recently*, but the words *publicly* and *political* were added to improve the focus of the question.

A troublesome word in the time focusing of questions was "ever." Ever was used in the first version of many questions to capture incidents or thoughts that had occurred at least once. But, of course, in addition to the frequency meaning of once, the word "ever" refers to the indefinite past, especially when used with the past tense or with the present or past perfect verb form. In most questions where "ever" was first used it was changed to focus the question on the recent past. But there were a few where the word survived into the final version. For example, the value of question 9 concerning joining organizations in spite of criticism was further reduced by the word "ever." And again, the word "ever" appears in the final version of question 11 above and 17 below.

Still a third way in which the focus of some questions was sharpened was in the matter of place. For example, in item 11, the words "here" and "at this college" were added to clarify the intent of the question.

Apart from wording changes intended to sharpen the focus of the questionnaire, a number of changes can be classified as finding synonyms to avoid monotonous repetition. The word "worry" used in some of the early versions was subsequently changed to "wonder" or "thought about" and conversely, in some instances, the word "wonder" was changed in later versions to "worry." Items 12 and 13 contain examples of such changes. The direction of the change was in part dictated by where the item happened to be located in the battery. If there were several successive questions which used the word "worry" in the early drafts, efforts were made to find synonyms for the word in subsequent drafts. The problem of whether to use synonyms for "worry" posed an interesting dilemma. On the one hand the researchers did not want the questionnaire to sound monotonous nor did they want to drive home the point that they were focusing on worries. On the other hand, by using synonyms they ran the risk of making the questions non-comparable. Wisely or not, they decided to make the questionnaire less monotonous by using synonyms rather than repeating the word "worry" over and over again. There has since been some criticism of *The Academic Mind* on precisely these grounds—that is, whether such words as "wonder" are the equivalent of "worry." Of course, this depends on the context. If the question refers to a very serious matter then even such a mild word as "wonder" might be indicative of apprehension. Elmo Roper pointed this out rather dramatically to one critic who felt that "wonder" did not imply "worry" by formulating the following question: "Have you ever wondered whether your wife was sleeping with another man?"

A third category of wording changes consists of words or phrases that the pre-tests showed were either ambiguous or too affect-laden. For example, item 16, which inquires about worries over job security due to politics, used the word "tenure" in the first version. Somewhat surprisingly, there were some pre-test respondents who either were not sure of the meaning of the word or were at schools without a tenure system.

16. *First version:* Have you ever wondered that some political opinion you've expressed might affect your tenure or promotion at this college?

Final version: Have you ever wondered . . . might affect your *job security* or promotion at this college?

As can be seen, the word tenure was changed to job security. Question 17 originally contained the colloquial phrase "against the tide" in order to lend an informal and more conventional tone to the question. However, the pre-test uncovered some respondents who were troubled by the vagueness of the phrase and so the word "unpopular" was used in later versions.

17. *First version:* When you have private talks outside the classroom with a student whose views are *against the tide* do you try to help him conform to the prevailing views on campus?

    Final version: When you have private talks outside the classroom with a student whose views are *unpopular . . .*?

This example touches perhaps on a general problem of question writing, the use of informal conversational terms in order to make the interview more natural versus the danger of introducing ambiguities of meaning.

The last example, item 18, is a question that was particularly difficult to word. This question actually underwent six wording changes although only four are shown here. Pre-tests indicated that the word "unpleasant" was too loaded; who would deliberately want to discuss unpleasant and presumably offensive topics? The word "argument" was tried but interviewers reported that respondents were bothered by this word, too. Finally, the word "controversial" was decided on and then other revisions were necessary to sharpen the focus of the question.

18. *First version:* Have you noticed a tendency in social gatherings on the campus to avoid *unpleasant* political topics?

    Second version: . . . on the campus to avoid political topics that might *start an argument*?

    Third version: . . . on the campus to avoid political topics that might be *controversial*?

    Final version: Have you noticed *more* of a tendency *lately* in social gatherings on campus to avoid controversial political topics?

To summarize, this paper has reported on some of the experiences in formulating questions for a particular study. The attempt was made to identify some of the cross-pressures and considerations that affect the final outcome of a questionnaire and that occasionally may lead to violations of what are listed in textbooks as basic rules of question design. We have tried to show how pre-tests can serve the function not only of pointing up ambiguities or gaps in questions but also the function of correcting various preconceptions held by the researchers about what can and cannot be asked.

———————————

Before moving on to other histories of questionnaires, some comments are in order on the history just presented. The Gill–Caplovitz history of the questions in the apprehension battery of the *Academic Mind* study was written in 1959; 24 years later, some of its concerns and conclusions seem naive. For example, the paper points out that a general problem of questionnaire construction is length and that study directors are under pressure to keep their questionnaires relatively short. In the last chapter, we saw that through the decades questionnaires got longer and longer and study directors were much less concerned about length. The *Academic Mind* questionnaire was listed as item 4 in Table 5.2 as an example of a questionnaire from the fifties. It was 25 pages long and contained 183 questions, far fewer than the average of 47 pages and 291 questions of the questionnaires of the seventies. A second concern of the drafters of the *Academic Mind* questionnaire that seems naive today is their concern with repetitious wording. A number of questions changed to avoid repeating the word "worry" were cited. As the battery has become a major device for formulating questions, words like "worry" appear in the main part of the question followed by a series of items that complete the question, each item being a separate question. For example, the sample of a battery question presented in Chapter 5 was Bradburn's battery of positive and negative feelings. The core question read as follows:

During the past few weeks, did you ever feel . . .?

This was followed by a list of eight feelings. Lazarsfeld could have developed his apprehension battery in the same way. His core question could have read like this: "Recently, have you ever worried that . . .?" This could have been followed with 10, 15, or 21 worries. Note that the core question just made up contains the word "recently" to focus the time span as well as the word "ever" to capture events that happened only once. In short, just as Bradburn's battery contains the word "feel" in every item in the battery, so Lazarsfeld could have used the word "worry" in every item in his battery.

The Gill–Caplovitz paper pointed up a third concern of the researchers, which, although probably misplaced, still concerns researchers today, and that is the issue of response set. It was noted that a consultant to the project warned Lazarsfeld that his apprehension items might be vulnerable to response set since the yes answer always meant apprehension. If there were some people inclined to answer affirmatively to any question, these people would be scored as highly apprehensive when in reality they were only being agreeable, saying yes to everything. Because of this criticism, Lazarsfeld added items 9 and 10, which referred to courageous acts in the face of possible political criticism. Presumably professors who would take such actions were not apprehensive and intimidated. According to the theory of response set, the people who said yes to these acts of courage would say no to the other questions that asked about apprehension. In fact, Lazarsfeld found that the same people who said yes to these acts of courage were also more likely to say yes to the questions about worry. Such findings pointed to the likelihood of response set, but Lazarsfeld refused to believe that he had uncovered response set. Rather the pattern suggested to him a new concept, the "cautious or worried activists," people who behaved bravely in spite of their worries.

A similar concern with response set led to an even more profound theoretical breakthrough in Bradburn's happiness research. Bradburn, just like Lazarsfeld, was warned by a consultant to be careful of response set. In the original draft of his questionnaire, Bradburn made up five questions measuring negative feelings, a sign of unhappiness. But his consultant told him that people prone to response set might answer all these questions positively, giving the false impression that they were unhappy. To guard against this, Bradburn made up five items measuring positive feelings. The assumption was that respondents who scored high on negative feelings would score low on positive feelings, and that the converse would be true. But when the data were analyzed, it was found that there was no relationship between positive and negative feelings. People could have lots or little of both. Rather than suspect response set, Bradburn discovered that happiness was made up of two independent dimensions, positive feelings and negative feelings, with one's happiness score being the net of positive and negative feelings, that is, the number of positive feelings minus the number of negative feelings. Psychologists place much store in response set and are constantly guarding against it. But from these examples, it would seem that sociologists are more likely to develop new concepts rather than accept response set. Bradburn was perhaps more justified in doing so than Lazarsfeld, for instead of finding a positive relationship, he found no relationship (although he expected a negative one).

CASE STUDY II

During the early sixties, Lazarsfeld and Sieber did a study of the quality of educational research on behalf of the College Entrance Examination Board, which was worried about the generally low quality of educational research. Lazarsfeld and Thielens designed a study of the organizational aspects of educational research on the theory that the organizational context was a major factor influencing quality of research. They developed a questionnaire for the deans of graduate schools of education and the chairmen of departments of education. Some four years after this questionnaire was developed, Sam Sieber and his student Walter Schenkel wrote a lengthy history of this questionnaire. What follows are excerpts from their paper.

History of the Questionnaire for Administrators of Graduate Schools or Departments of Education for a Study of the Organizational Aspects of Education Research by Paul F. Lazarsfeld and Sam Sieber

WALTER SCHENKEL AND SAM SIEBER

Each phase in the process of questionnaire construction will, for the purpose of this paper, deal with the construction of a single draft. Phase 1 will range from a discussion of the initial steps to a description of the instrument's first draft; Phase 2 will deal with the development from the first to the second draft; Phase 3 with the development from the second to the third draft, etc. Since there were five drafts and a final questionnaire, the process of developing the instrument will be discussed in terms of six phases.

Although the investigators had clarified the major concepts in which they were interested in the monograph *Organizing Educational Research*,* they did not preclude the inclusion of concepts that might emerge during the data-gathering stage or during the analysis. In short, they were alert to the possibilities of measuring "unanticipated concepts." This is exemplified in the notion of *research climate*, which was presented in the final report as an index of the number of status groups in the school (dean, faculty, etc.) that ranked research above teaching and service as responsibilities of the faculty. Similarly, such important concepts as "styles of research leadership," "innovativeness of the director," and "production of researchers" were not contemplated when the questionnaire was constructed, but were nonetheless measurable later on and figured prominently in the final report. In short, by drawing upon *domains* of variables concerned with the social organization of research, such as "interest in research," "activities of directors," "occupations of graduates," it was possible to delineate more powerful concepts later on and to find appropriate measures for them in the questionnaire.

Of the questionnaire's many drafts, only one was submitted to a proper pre-test that involved a sample very similar to the ultimate sample of respondents. The instrument was constructed for self-administration by the respondents, but with the help of field representatives to deliver and retrieve the questionnaire. The field representatives were chosen from among the junior faculty and advanced graduate students at the institutions in which the dean or head of department was located. (For a detailed description of the use of field representatives, see Appendix E of the final report.)

Lazarsfeld and Sieber were assisted by two types of advisors. One was a formally established *advisory committee* composed of six persons who were very knowledgeable about educational research and its organizational context. This advisory committee performed a function that could be termed "strategic" inasmuch as its major task was to guarantee that the investigators would pursue the most relevant questions. The second, more informal group was composed of *local colleagues* of the investigators whose task was chiefly "tactical"—that is, to advise the investigators on how to improve the wording of questions and organize the instrument. (Local colleagues were convened formally on two occasions.)

Although it took the investigators *six months* to arrive at the final version of the instrument for deans, not all of their time was spent on the project. Both investigators

---

*Paul F. Lazarsfeld and Sam D. Sieber, *Organizing Educational Research*, Englewood Cliffs, New Jersey: Prentice-Hall, 1964.

had other university tasks; also, a certain lapse of time occurred after each draft had been subjected to either a pre-test or a "simulated pre-test."

THE SIX PHASES OF THE QUESTIONNAIRE

Phase 1: From the Initial Steps to the First Draft

Preparatory work for the first draft of the instrument was started in early July 1963. The exploratory research for *Organizing Educational Research* had provided the investigators with three types of conceptual guidelines:

(a)   A general *problem* to be investigated: what were the effects of organizational arrangements on educational research activities?

(b)   A number of *hypotheses*, or propositional corollaries, of the problem. For example: educational research that is carried out in research "bureaus" within graduate departments of education is of higher quality and of broader significance than research done in an uncoordinated way by individual scholars.

(c)   Several *domains of variables*, such as the following: history of the organization, its internal structure, its external relationships, and the leadership styles of research coordinators and bureau directors. It was this third type of conceptual guideline that turned out to be especially important later on.

When an investigator starts to work on the first draft of his instrument he sometimes looks for other questionnaires which have successfully elicited information about the variables he intends to study. Thus, Sieber borrowed questions from instruments used by Berelson (a study of graduate school deans), Milavsky (a study of graduate business school deans), and Wilder (a study of reading researchers and experts). The instruments from which the investigators borrowed had one feature in common: they contained questions that sought to gather data about the organization of university research and research training. One of the questions borrowed from Berelson, for example, dealt with the attitudes of deans toward certain criticisms directed at the structure of graduate schools (Question 1 on the first draft):

> The following specific points have been made in the criticisms directed at the graduate schools over the past few years. On the whole, how do you feel about each of them? ("agree strongly," "agree," "can't say," "disagree," "disagree strongly")
>
> > With the numbers of students now involved in doctoral study, it has become almost impossible to provide the basic necessity of research training, namely, proper apprenticeship relations.
> >
> > The quality of doctoral work is limited these days by the fact that most students are motivated by the practical objective of getting a job rather than the objective of becoming a research scholar.
> >
> > Doctoral candidates are too often allowed or encouraged to attempt a major contribution as their dissertation rather than to take on a manageable topic that can be finished in a reasonable time.
> >
> > Doctoral work is conceived too much as professional training, oriented to practice, rather than as academic learning, oriented to scholarship.
> >
> > The graduate schools unduly stress research and research training at the cost of properly preparing college teachers.

> Two degree programs should be set up at the doctoral level—one for re-
> searchers, one for college teachers.

Another battery of questions was borrowed from Wilder's questionnaire developed for
reading researchers:

> . . . The following is a list of factors that some people claim have hindered the
> advancement of educational research. If you think any of these has hindered
> educational research, place a check in the appropriate box (leave blank if you
> think it has not hindered research). [The two response categories were "major
> hindrance" and "minor hindrance."]

Fifteen statements followed, and a sixteenth statement was added because of its
special relevance to schools of education:

> Isolation of schools of education from the liberal arts division.

While about half a dozen batteries were borrowed from the three questionnaires
mentioned, most of the material in the first draft of the instrument was newly formulated.

The major *domains* of variables assembled for the first draft of the dean's instrument
were:

- *(a)* Problems of educational research
- *(b)* Problems of graduate schools
- *(c)* Arrangements for educational research
- *(d)* Purposes of the school's graduate program
- *(e)* Financing of research
- *(f)* General educational opinions of deans
- *(g)* Institutional data
- *(h)* Personal information about the dean

As mentioned before, our attention will be mainly devoted to revisions in the section
on "Institutional Data" because this is the section which is best documented.

The questions borrowed from the Berelson and Milavsky instruments were included
in the first draft not only because they had already been addressed to deans, but also in
order to permit *comparisons* between the Berelson and Milavsky data and those of the
present study. The necessity of adding questions that were of immediate relevance to
education, however, caused the gradual *deletion* of these borrowed items from later
versions of the questionnaire.

It is noteworthy that the section on "Institutional Data" was very brief in the first draft,
consisting of three questions only (the first of which was borrowed from Berelson, the
second and third from Milavsky):

1. Please provide the following figures for new graduate students
   for the academic year 1963–64.
   Applied for admission to graduate school   _____
   Accepted for admission   _____
   Actually registered   _____
2. As of September, 1963, what is the total number of students
   working for the *doctorate* in the School or Department of Education?   _____

3.   What is the salary level for each of the following faculty positions
     in your school?
     [The faculty categories were: Instructor, Asst. Professor, Assoc.
     Professor, and Full Professor. Salary ranges were provided in
     the question.]

Later on, as a refinement in the first draft, the following question was inserted between
Questions 2 and 3 in order to disclose the *relative* importance of the school or
graduate department of education within the particular university:

Of the total number of doctoral degrees awarded by the university last year,
approximately what percentage were awarded by the school or graduate department of education?

Despite this additional question, the domain of variables dealing with "Institutional
Data" in the first draft was still only slightly covered. This first version of the questionnaire was not presented for discussion to the advisory committee; instead, the investigators discussed it with a few of their colleagues.

Phase 2: From the First Draft to the Second Draft

The section on "Institutional Data" remained the same in the second draft; however,
changes were made in other sections. Thus, in the section dealing with "Arrangements
for Research" in the first draft, Question 5 had been as follows:

5.   How satisfied are you at present with the administrative provisions for
     research in the School or Department of Education?
     Very satisfied
     Satisfied
     Dissatisfied
     Very dissatisfied

The investigators decided *(a)* to reduce the number of answer categories from four to
three, and *(b)* to follow up on the dissatisfied responses with an open-end probe. Thus,
Question 5 looked as follows in the second draft:

5.   How satisfied are you at present with the administrative provisions for
     research in the school or department of education?
     Extremely satisfied
     Moderately satisfied
     Not satisfied

If you are not Satisfied:
What improvements would you like to see?

The open-end question about possible improvements was intended to allow the
investigator to delve directly into problems of research organization.
    A second major change in the second draft dealt with another question under the
heading of "Arrangements for Research." The second draft contained two completely

new questions on this topic. The first concerned the position of *graduate students* within the institution's research program:

> In an average school year (excluding the summer), approximately what percentage of the doctoral students are research assistants for faculty members who are doing research *outside of any research organization that may exist*? ____ %
>
> Do graduate students provide teaching or supervisory assistance in order to relieve faculty members for research?   ____ Yes   ____ No
>
> *If they do*, about what percentage of the entire faculty is relieved in this way to do research?   ____ %

The second addition concerned the relationship between faculties on education and liberal arts:

> Which of the following arrangements with liberal arts faculties exist? (Please check as many as apply.)
>
> ____ Students are sent from the liberal arts departments into the school or department of education for courses
>
> ____ Students are sent from the school or department of education into liberal arts departments for courses
>
> ____ Joint appointments with liberal arts departments for *teaching*
>
> ____ Joint appointments with liberal arts departments for *research*
>
> ____ Visiting professorships for *teaching*
>
> ____ Visiting professorships for *research*
>
> ____ Full-time appointment of professors entirely trained in the liberal arts division of a university
>
> ____ Distinct departments within the school of education which are staffed mostly by professors trained entirely in the liberal arts division of a university
>
> ____ Interdisciplinary committees or similar groups which include profesors appointed to a liberal arts department
>
> ____ Other (please specify) _____

These two additions reflected a growing concern on the part of the questionnaire designers with *research training* and *interdisciplinary relations*. The final report devoted a good deal of attention to these aspects of research organization, drawing upon the data in a way not anticipated when developing the instrument. For example, the list of interdisciplinary relations was used to construct an index of *formal* ties with other departments.

Phase 3: From the Second Draft to the Third Draft

A discussion of the second draft by the advisors, and a "simulated pre-test" with the same advisors, produced a number of suggestions for revision. Thus, the third draft differed from the second in the following respects:

(a) The draft submitted for discussion to the committee was preceded by an introductory letter addressed to the deans explaining the purpose of the project. A suggestion was then made—stemming from fear that the instrument might become too long—that the questions should be divided into two major groups, "Institutional Data" and "Opinions and Experiences of Deans and Chairmen." This division was made so that the respondents could have the section on "Institutional Data" filled in by their assistants. As a result of this suggestion, the introductory letter in the third draft was changed to clarify this procedure. All the sections of the instrument not relating to "Institutional Data" were rearranged under the general heading "Opinions and Experiences of Deans or Chairmen."

(b) With respect to the section on "Institutional Data," a new question was introduced:

Is either a teaching certificate or professional experience in the schools a formal requirement for admission to the graduate program?

	Yes	No
Teaching Certificate	————	————
Professional Experience	————	————

This question was aimed at discovering whether the schools or graduate departments of education were narrowly occupational in their selection procedure.

(c) With regard to changes in other parts of the questionnaire, there were very few deletions but a good number of additions, and in all cases the new additions were questions that originated with the investigators. Thus, as already mentioned, the third draft contained a higher proportion of questions drawn up by the investigators than did either the first or the second draft. Also, the borrowed questions now began to disappear.

Many of these new questions stemmed from the meeting with the advisors. For example, in an effort to take into account the varied meanings of certain major terms used in the questionnaire, the following question was introduced:

Since the term "educational research" is used in a variety of ways, it is often difficult to know what a person means by it. To which of the following kinds of activity do you ordinarily apply the term "educational research"? (Check as many as you wish)

——— Collecting statistics on school practices and educational outcomes, sometimes called "school status studies"

——— Designing new curricula and methods of instruction

_____ Evaluating the effectiveness of new curricula and methods

_____ Local school surveys (curriculum, financial, plant, etc.)

_____ Investigating factors which affect the teaching–learning process in the classroom

_____ Disseminating new curricula, methods of instruction, or other school practices

_____ Investigating factors which affect school administration

_____ General psychological studies of human learning or development

_____ Presenting evidence to legislators of the need for greater support for the schools

_____ Developing new tests and measurements

_____ Analyzing the key concepts or philosophical assumptions underlying current educational issues

_____ Studying the educational research journals for lecture materials

Phase 4: From the Third Draft to the Fourth Draft

The third draft was revised and resubmitted to the committee as draft number four. The section on "Institutional Data" was considerably expanded; instead of the *five* questions that made up the section in the earlier draft, the new section now contained *fourteen* questions. Some of the additions follow:

Approximately what percentage of the graduate faculty of education was trained *entirely* in the liberal arts and sciences outside of any college, school, or department of education?
_____ None
_____ 1–5%
_____ 6–10%
_____ 11–25%
_____ 26–50%
_____ More than 50%

Are there any distinct departments within the graduate program of education which are staffed *mostly* with professors trained *entirely* in the liberal arts and sciences? _____ Yes _____ No

If yes: Which department(s)? _____

Are professors who apply for sabbatical leaves required to state the purpose of the leave? _____ No _____ Yes

If yes: Is research an acceptable justification? _____ Yes _____ No

To the best of your knowledge, about what percentage of professors who have taken sabbaticals in the past five years have conducted research while on leave?
_____ %

At the end of the sabbatical, are professors who have done research required to report their work to the administration?   ＿＿ No ＿＿ Yes

If yes: What form does this report usually take? ＿＿＿＿＿＿＿＿＿＿＿＿＿＿＿＿＿

＿＿

Are leaves of absence without pay given to faculty members who wish to do research?   ＿＿ No ＿＿ Yes

If yes: About what percentage of the faculty has taken such leaves in the past five years?   ＿＿ %

And at the end of the questionnaire:

Would you please send us any materials which describe the faculty research program, for example, a list of faculty publications, or a history of research in your institution.

If you have reports which indicate the types of positions which doctorate recipients hold, we would appreciate receiving a copy.

Phase 5: From the Fourth to the Fifth Draft

The fifth draft was to be the crucial one because it was to be pre-tested systematically with a group of retired deans, a solution that was adopted because the ultimate sample was too small to "use up" respondents in pre-tests. Since the fifth draft took over the questions of institutional data from the fourth draft exactly as they were, we shall not dwell on this version.

Phase 6: From the Fifth to the Sixth Draft

The pre-tests introduced greater realism into the questionnaire. For example, here are two versions of a question, one before and one following the pre-tests:

BEFORE PRE-TEST:

Approximately what percentage of the graduate faculty of education was trained *entirely* in the liberal arts and sciences outside of any college, school, or department of education?

Are there any distinct departments within the graduate program of education which are staffed *mostly* with professors trained *entirely* in the liberal arts and sciences?

FOLLOWING PRE-TEST:

Approximately what percentage of the graduate faculty of education received their highest degrees from a liberal arts and science department rather than from a school or department of education?

Are there any distinct departments within the graduate program of education which are staffed *mostly* with professors who received their highest degree from liberal arts and science departments?

The responses in the pre-test indicated that the request to enumerate faculty who were "trained entirely in the liberal arts and sciences" was unrealistic. First, deans were not in a position to know this datum; and second, virtually *no* faculty members in education were trained *entirely* outside education. By replacing the inadequate phrase "trained entirely in . . ." with "recieved their highest degree from . . ." the respondents' knowledge was not overtaxed, since it can be assumed that a dean knows roughly how many teachers on his staff have doctorates or master's degrees in education, and how many have degrees in academic disciplines.

When the fifth draft was sent out for pre-testing, the investigators sent the committee a *new* memorandum, the purpose of which was to justify the inclusion of new questions. Here is an illustrative excerpt:

DEANS' EXPERIENCES WITH EDUCATIONAL RESEARCH

As in the case of bureau directors, in order to fully understand the deans' policies and opinions, we need to know something about their past experiences with research. First, we want to measure their personal involvement in teaching and conducting research . . . . Also, we asked several questions about personal background which might have a bearing on professional careers.

Second, we are interested in their observations about research, especially in their own school. Here we shall get into the problems that arise from allowing time off from teaching, from accepting funds from outside the university, and from other administrative responsibilities associated with the faculty's research. Their opinions about what constitutes educational research, the hindrances to the advancement of educational research, and the utility of research to practitioners also fall under this heading.

With regard to the section "Institutional Data," the major change entailed moving the section from the end of the questionnaire to the beginning. The rationale behind this change was that deans should be able to hand the instrument to their assistants for completion of the section before supplying us with information that they might regard as confidential. Also, it was decided *not* to make the institutional section detachable because of the danger of its being mislaid.

In the section "Institutional Data," the *order* of the questions was modified, and the two following questions were dropped altogether:

Is there a residency requirement for the doctorate in education?
_____ Yes _____ No

If there is: Which of the following residence requirements apply to the Ed.D. and which to the Ph.D. program? [5 categories]

An open-end question regarding interchange between academic department and the school of education was extended somewhat:

Former version: In general, how fruitful have interchanges been with the *academic* departments in the university; and what *problems* have been encountered, if any?

Revised version: In general, how *fruitful* have interchanges been with the academic departments in the university; what *problems* have been encountered, if any; and what *directions* would you like future interchange to take?

With hindsight, it is surprising that the *size* of the education faculty had not been asked in any previous versions. Hence, a question was added:

How many instructors are teaching courses to graduate students in the school or department of education?

━━━━━━━━━━

As Schenkel and Sieber explain, their history deals with only one section of the questionnaire. Of the many valuable cues to questionnaire construction that their account provides, notice should be given to the various sources of input into questionnaire construction. Lazarsfeld and Sieber set up an advisory committee of experts for their study. This is a fairly common procedure for large-scale studies. An earlier study that Lazarsfeld did on the impact of McCarthyism on academia also had an advisory committee. The advisory committee performs several functions. First, its members verify the importance of the themes and ideas that study directors are building into their research. Second, they often suggest new ideas and themes. Third, they serve as first-rate critics of the various drafts of the questionnaire, suggesting wording changes and new questions. And fourth, the advisory committee is the first audience of the final report. Their comments on the draft of the final report frequently contribute to improvements in the report. In addition to the advisory committee, Lazarsfeld and Sieber got valuable help on the questionnaire from their colleagues' reactions to various drafts. They even called two formal meetings of their colleagues to discuss the questionnaire. Finally, valuable input into questionnaires comes from the pretests with respondents similar to those to be surveyed. Through pretests, researchers learn which questions work and which are troublesome and confusing.

CASE HISTORY III

Developing histories of questionnaires was Paul Lazarsfeld's idea; studies that he was connected with at the Bureau of Applied Social Research in the fifties and sixties had histories of their questionnaires prepared as a matter of course. Our last example is from a study of financial aid officers that was also done on behalf of the College Entrance Examination Board.

History of the Questionnaire Used in a Study of College Financial Aid Officers Directed by Paul F. Lazarsfeld and Patricia Nash

PATRICIA NASH

BACKGROUND OF THE STUDY

The Sponsor

In the Spring of 1965, the College Entrance Examination Board (CEEB) asked the Bureau of Applied Social Research to undertake a study of financial aid directors. Their interest in such a study stemmed from the fact that one of the main services provided by the CEEB is the College Scholarship Service. The College Board supplies colleges with forms on which parents of applicants for financial aid describe their financial situation. The College Scholarship Service processes and evaluates these forms in order to determine the applicants' eligibility. This service has increased 40% in the last three years. The Annual Report of the CEEB indicated some disagreement about where the function should be placed in the organization:

> The committee was unable to resolve fully the organizational questions pertaining to the College Scholarship Service and its relationship to other elements of the Board's structure. On the one hand, it recognized that important distinctions existed between financial aid and admissions activities on the college and university campuses. These distinctions, considered alone, argue for a CSS which is independent of the Board. On the other hand, the committee recognized that in many other ways financial aid and admissions activities are closely interrelated and require close coordination. This circumstance argues against any separation of the CSS from the Board.*

Further study of this problem was recommended. The CEEB wanted to know more about the financial aid director; his background, needs and satisfactions as well as the organizational structure in which he worked. The focus of the study was, therefore, primarily determined by the sponsor. It was to be a descriptive study of financial aid directors. In many ways it was considered to be a companion to the study recently completed by the Bureau on admissions officers.

Our early field work pointed to the fact that the financial aid function was administered by a variety of individuals differentially located in the academic hierarchy . . . from president down to clerk. This brought the subject for study into focus. When a function is performed by individuals differentially located in the social structure, what are the implications for the organization in relation to the effectiveness of the program and the satisfaction of the administrator?

---

*Report of the President, *Annual Report of the College Board*: College Entrance Examination Board, Princeton, New Jersey, page 19.

The Proposal

The original proposal outlined a two phase mailing to financial aid directors. One Spring mailing of a short questionnaire was to determine who the financial aid director was and in what kind of organizational structure he worked. This was to be followed by a mailing in the Fall of a long questionnaire asking the financial aid director how the job was done, inquiring about his background and future plans, studying the relationship of the financial aid director with admissions and asking for an evaluation of the effectiveness of the aid program at his college.

We subsequently decided that only one mailing should be made. In addition to the costs involved in a two phase mailing, we anticipated a problem in lack of comparability among respondents. That is, not all respondents to the first mailing would answer the second mailing. Further, two mailings would have required duplication of a number of questions. For example, if in the first questionnaire we asked the financial aid director to whom did he report and in the second we wanted to know about relations with his superior, we would have had to repeat the question, "To whom do you report?" in order to focus the attention of the respondent on a specific referent. Finally, the anticipated problem of locating the financial aid director at the college was unfounded. Each college provides routing services both for mail and telephone calls. A telephone canvas of financial aid officers at 18 colleges in the East showed that the proper person was easily reached when a phone call or letter was addressed to the Director of Financial Aid. For these reasons one, rather than two questionnaires was sent to financial aid directors.

Pre-Test of a Questionnaire

We proceeded to draw up the first draft of the questionnaire. Pre-tests of this questionnaire were made by personal visits to financial aid directors. We asked them to fill it out as if they had just received it in the mail. Although we were present, technically, we did not administer the questionnaire. We noted the time it took to fill in the questionnaire. This was approximately 30 minutes. When they were finished, we asked if we had excluded any area they felt to be important, which questions were difficult to understand, if they objected to any questions and if so, which. We asked if they thought any questions could be excluded. This information was taken into consideration when preparing subsequent drafts. We wanted to maintain rapport since we would have to be calling on these people again in the near future with the final questionnaire. No less than 65 preliminary interviews and pre-tests of the questionnaire were conducted.

GENERAL OVERVIEW OF THE QUESTIONNAIRE

In addition to two preliminary drafts prepared over the summer, there were seven actual drafts drawn up between September and November of 1965. Major revisions occurred on three of these drafts.

1. A major change was made between the preliminary drafts and the actual first draft. This was as a result of the depth interviews which were conducted at the workshops.

2. A major change was made between Draft 1 and Draft 2. This was primarily the result of the pre-test given to the Board of Advisors.

3. A major change was made between Draft 5 and 6 . . . most likely because we were getting close to the deadline for mailing. (As a result of talking with members of the advisory board, we had decided to mail the questionnaires late in the fall . . . sometime around the end of November. They felt that this would be a time when work at the college would be more evenly paced and we would be able to secure their cooperation.)

Preliminary Draft A

Preliminary Draft A, which was drawn up in June of 1965, consisted of a series of questions which we felt to be most relevant in understanding the job of the financial aid director and the organizational structure of financial aid. The major concentration of this draft was on the organization and administration of financial aid.

There were, however, some questions incorporated in this draft which were not, even at the time of incorporation, considered to be questions for the final schedule. The following are some examples:

1. *Deciding on a definition of financial aid.* We needed to know, "Are jobs considered financial aid?" in order to construct questions on the administration of financial aid. The researchers had to determine whether jobs were considered a type of financial aid to be included in the definition of financial aid along with scholarships and loans.

2. *Obtaining additional information on financial aid practices.* The question, "Is aid packaged?" was included. We knew that some colleges had a practice of packaging aid. That is, a student received financial aid in the form of a combination of scholarship, loan and job. We needed to know how extensive was the practice of packaging aid in order to construct questions on financial aid policies and practices which would be meaningful to most of the respondents to the mailed questionnaire.

3. *Logical extensions of other questions.* Some questions give rise to further inquiry. The subject matter is not necessarily relevant to the immediate focus of the questionnaire. For example, "Are you aware of any changes in the college's planning and administration of financial aid?" (Logical extension: "Would they result in more deprived students being brought to the campus?") Many such questions were subsequently dropped due to the limitations of time and space in the questionnaire.

4. *Questions pertaining to the total data collected.* Some questions which were included required data collected on all colleges and not just from one respondent. For example, "What per cent of colleges have each type of aid program?"

These questions were not intended for the final questionnaire. Our intent was to get these questions down on paper in order to give us something to work from or refer to at a future time. Question areas in Preliminary Draft A were very general. For example: "Who are the sources of support?" and, "Are there problems in the administration of financial aid at your college? What sort?" These questions were to be made more specific.

Preliminary Draft B

The second preliminary draft was drawn up during the month of July. This was the questionnaire administered to the two regional financial aid workshops of the College Entrance Examination Board. It was from this draft that the 18 depth interviews were obtained. Questions which were included in Preliminary Draft A, such as definitional questions, background, logical extensions and questions for the analysis were excluded. Only questions on substantive areas were drafted. The question, "Who are the sources of support?" was also excluded; although questions seeking to uncover the sources of problems were included. In addition to asking for information on the organization and administration of financial aid, a substantial number of questions were included on the financial aid director as a person: his background, frustrations, opportunities, etc.

The difference between Preliminary Drafts A and B is that the latter attempted to focus on the attitudes of the financial aid director as well as the more objective problems in the administration of financial aid.

Draft 1

As we mentioned, in the two months between Preliminary Draft B of July 1965 and the actual first draft of September 1965, major changes were made. These resulted from the analysis of the 18 depth interviews, discussions with financial aid directors at their colleges and meetings with the sponsor and fellow researchers. The general questions pertaining to the problems in the administration of financial aid had been rewritten for the first draft and were now much more explicit. Very few of the questions which appeared in Draft 1 were open-ended, whereas, the preliminary drafts were composed wholly of unstructured questions.

One of the major aims of the questionnaire was to nail down the structure of aid administration. In the depth interviews we did not have much difficulty since the interviewer had the opportunity to probe. From the responses to the depth interviews and discussions with a number of financial aid directors we were able to locate three components of the aid structure: type of aid, type of recipient, and office administering the aid.

In Draft 1, the first battery of questions on the organization of financial aid administration was drawn up. Seven questions were needed. The questions were designed to obtain information on which offices were involved in financial aid, the type of aid and the type of recipient serviced by each office, the title and initials of the administrator of each office and the persons to whom each administrator reported. We also wanted to relate aid to other functions at the college. What was the relationship with the office that admitted students and with the office that collected loans? Was aid to graduates and undergraduate students administered separately?

Although we were able to include questions on all the information we wanted, our colleagues at the Bureau felt that the format was too complex for a respondent to follow. At their prodding, we simplified the section without sacrificing any question we considered necessary. However, in simplifying the question, we made coding the response more complex.

By applying what we learned from our preparatory work, we were able to:

1. *Eliminate an area*. From our content analysis of catalogs, we had come to feel that religion was a major factor in the awarding of aid. Further discus-

sions with the advisory board and with a group of administrators at a conference convinced us that this was not the case. We dropped this section from the questionnaire.

2. *Make an inquiry more subtle.* Conversations with administrators at some colleges led us to the realization that grants to athletes were a problem. We originally intended to ask questions about how many athletes received aid, but this proved impractical. Since the subject was controversial, we simply added three statements on athletics to a routine and noncontroversial section on opinions on aid. To answer this section, the respondent merely needed to indicate whether he agreed or disagreed. This worked very well.

3. *Enlarged the focus of an inquiry.* We were interested in the problems of administrators in general and not just those of financial aid directors. To this end, we used the aid director as a reporter on the administration at his college. We asked him what positions existed, to which did he aspire, how each of the administrators ranked in relation to himself, and the degree to which each was involved in the administration of financial aid.

The major change made between the preliminary drafts and the first draft of the questionnaire was in making questions more specific. The 18 depth interviews furnished categories so that each of the answers was made multiple choice rather than open end. Draft 1 included entirely new substantive areas such as the relations of the financial aid directors with others (i.e., relatives, other aid directors and the administration and faculty).

Subsequent Drafts

Table 6.1 shows that once we had completed a working instrument, that is, the first draft, different types of changes were made in subsequent drafts.

The majority of questions were not changed in Drafts 3, 4, and 5. New questions were more likely to be introduced in the 2nd and 6th drafts. Major revisions in existing questions were made in the 2nd, 6th and 7th drafts. We can note also that the actual number of questions asked in each draft fluctuated as a result of the additions, deletions, separations and combinations of various question parts. From this draft to draft comparison we see that changes vary and that drafts differ from one another in different ways.

Table 6.1. Per Cent of Changes Made in the Questionnaire

	Draft					
	2	3	4	5	6	7
Questions not changed	24%	71%	65%	58%	15%	22%
New questions	23	5	5	4	10	6
Questions changed	53	24	30	38	75	72
Total	100%	100%	100%	100%	100%	100%
N	105	136	131	128	119	120

(Reads: Of the 105 questions which appeared in Draft 2, 24% were exactly the same as questions found in Draft 1; 23% were completely new questions; and 53% were questions which appeared in Draft 1 but were changed in some way for Draft 2.)

We focused first on the organization and administration of financial aid and then upon taking a fresh look at the questionnaire, prepared a battery of questions to deal with the aid director, himself. Once these two major areas had been delineated, our responsibility in the remaining drafts was to integrate and blend these questions to sharpen the focus and clarify terminology. Little change occurred in ordering of questions.

DESIGNING QUESTIONS TO MEASURE THE DEPENDENT VARIABLE: SATISFACTION OF THE ADMINISTRATOR

As previously stated, in studying financial aid officers, we were primarily studying a function performed by individuals differentially located in the social structure. We wanted to determine the implications of this for the organization in relation to the effectiveness of the program and the satisfaction of the administrator. While it is impossible to review the entire conceptual process of the questionnaire, it might be well at this point to review the development of a series of questions constructed to measure the dependent variable: satisfaction of the administrator.

Using the standard definition of satisfaction, "the relative quiescent condition resulting from the fulfillment of any need or desire," (Webster) we could identify several dimensions of satisfaction for a financial aid administrator. These included:

1. Satisfaction with existing policies and decisions made which directly or indirectly affect the financial aid director.
2. Satisfaction with the work that the financial aid director must perform.
3. Satisfaction with the working conditions.
4. Satisfaction with the amount of recognition given to the individual performing the job of financial aid director.
5. Satisfaction with the amount of recognition given to the function of financial aid administration by others.
6. Satisfaction with the social relations the financial aid director has with other administrators.
7. Satisfaction with the work performed other than that of financial aid.

While it is not feasible to deal with all aspects of satisfaction in this paper, we can demonstrate one case in point: satisfaction with the amount of recognition given to the individual performing the job of financial aid director.

Our first step was to outline what would be considered indicators of recognition. That is, if we were to consider a financial aid director satisfied with the amount of recognition he received, with what should he be satisfied? We decided to measure his satisfaction on the following items:

1. Salary
2. Authority (decision making)
3. Prestige (rank)
4. Promotion
5. Status (recognition by students and parents)
6. Fringe benefits

During the process of constructing the questionnaire, 35 questions were designed to tap these indicators. Of these 35 questions, only 13 survived and were included in the final questionnaire. We were able to reduce a number of questions by making them much more specific and collapsing them into more comprehensive questions. Some questions were dropped because they duplicated other questions. A few questions, however, were excluded because pre-tests showed that the respondents were unable to answer them. Such was the case with the questions constructed to determine the respondent's satisfaction with promotion possibilities.

We wanted to find out the requisites for promotion, how fair the aid director thought they were and how important promotion was to him as an individual. We included questions in which the respondent was asked to compare what should matter and what does matter for promotion in a battery of 16 items. We also listed 12 academic positions and asked the respondent which position he would like to hold and which position he felt he could be promoted to at his college. These two comparisons would have enabled us to measure the degree of discrepancy in recognition. However, in each case, respondents to the pre-test told us that they could not answer these questions. It might have been possible to ask their superior but the director not doing the promoting would not presume to be an authority on promotion criteria. Although we kept the questions asking respondents to indicate the positions they would like to hold, we dropped the other questions and replaced them with the question, "How well do you feel that you understand the criteria for promotion within the administration at your college?"

Another question dealing with promotion, "What are the chances of your succeeding your present superior eventually?" had to be dropped. This question encountered resistance in that the aid director would be reluctant to show the completed questionnaire to his colleagues.

We were able to construct satisfactory questions for all indicators of recognition with one exception, fringe benefits. Fringe benefits can vary widely. We could not construct a satisfactory question which would be meaningful to all respondents.

CHANGES IN THE ORGANIZATION OF THE QUESTIONNAIRE

Table 6.2 outlines changes made in the organization of the questionnaire. The questions were arranged within substantive sections. Of the eight sections which appeared in Draft 1, five survived to appear in the printed questionnaire. Three of these five were subject to some change. The three sections which did not survive were absorbed into the existing or subsequent categories which were added. Four new sections were added in succeeding drafts of the questionnaire. Most of these changes were made in the 2nd draft. The order of the categories did not change through various drafts. Sections B, C, and D of Draft 1 were merged into Section A.

Of the new sections which were added, only one, "Background and Career Plans," had been planned in the initial stages of the questionnaire design. Two sections, "Your Opinions on Financial Aid Matters Based on Your Own Experience as Financial Aid Administrator" and "Financial Aid Policies and Practices" were added as a result of our attending the financial aid workshops. The section which covered the adequacy of the College Scholarship Service was added because of its special interest to the sponsor. No sections were designed and subsequently dropped. All areas focused upon by the researchers found their way to the final printed questionnaire.

Table 6.2. Organization of Questionnaire

Sections of the Drafts (as originated in Draft 1)	Draft					
	2	3	4	5	6	7
A. Your position and the variety of work you perform	−	−	−	−	/[1]	A
B. The organization of financial aid administration to full time under-graduate students	+	−	−	−	X	
C. The relationship of your office to those other offices listed above (refers to other offices involved in financial aid)	X					
D. Part time jobs as financial aid	X					
E. The financial aid committee	−	−	+[2]	−	−	B
F. (Letter not used)						
G. Financial aid work	−	+[3]	−	−	−	C
H. Relations with others	−	−	−	−	−	D
I. The administration at your college	−	−	−	−	−	E
New areas						
Your Opinions on Financial Aid Matters Based on Your Own Experience as a Financial Aid Administrator	*	−	−	−	−	F
Financial Aid Policies and Practices	*	−	+[4]	−	−	G
Adequacy of College Scholarship Service				*	−	H
Your Background and Career Plans	*	−	−	−	−	J

Explanation of symbols:
− Same as previous questionnaire
/ Major title change (Section A)
+ Minor title change (Sections E, G)
X Absorbed into other categories (Sections B, C, D)
* New areas

[1]The administration of financial aid at your college
[2]The financial aid committee and financial aid policy
[3]Financial aid work at your college
[4]Financial aid policies and practices at your college

SURVIVAL RATE OF QUESTIONS

To measure the survival rate of questions, we charted the flow of questions through the succeeding drafts. This was difficult because the question numbers vary from draft to draft. In addition, although certain whole questions were dropped or added, parts of questions were also dropped or added. To simplify the process, we decided to classify a question as having survived if any part of the question found its way into the printed questionnaire. On the other hand, if a new part was added to a question, this was not considered a new question unless it was sufficiently important to be assigned its own number. If two questions were collapsed into one or one question separated into two questions, we checked to be sure that in substance they either survived or did not survive. The results of checking the flow of questions in order to determine their survival rate are as follows:

1. Of the 92 questions which appeared in Draft 1, 61% survived through all other drafts and appeared in the final questionnaire.

2. All questions which appeared in Draft 1 and survived through the final questionnaire were changed in some way (form, technical, or substantive).

3. Of the 92 questions constructed after the 1st draft of the questionnaire, 70 survived through to the final draft; 22 were dropped. This is a 76% survival rate for subsequent questions.

4. Of the 128 questions* which survived to the final questionnaire, 57 were in the first draft and 71 were subsequently added. This means that 45% of the questions which appeared in the printed draft had survived through all drafts since the 1st draft and 55% of the questions in the printed questionnaire had been subsequently constructed.

5. Only seven new questions were added to the printed questionnaire subsequent to the 6th draft. Of these, however, three had appeared in a previous draft but had been dropped prior to inclusion in the printed version.

6. Only two questions (in addition to the three mentioned above) which had been dropped in a previous draft were reinstated in the printed questionnaire.

Nash's history of a questionnaire shows the wide range of themes that can be covered. She presents tables showing the number and types of changes in each draft, changes in the organization of the various sections of the questionnaire, the number of changes made in specific questions, and how the number of changes made is related to "no answers." Although omitted from this condensation of her paper, she investigates the hypothesis that questions become more refined and better with each change and therefore the greater the number of changes, the higher the response rate should be; she then presents data confirming this hypothesis. And Nash

*Actually, 120 questions appeared on the final draft. This, however, is a condensation of 128 questions which had appeared in previous drafts.

gives a complete accounting of the various groups that have an influence over the questionnaire, from the sponsor to the advisory committee to colleagues to the pretest subjects.

In presenting these histories, I hope to encourage other researchers to record the histories of the questionnaires they have developed. I am convinced that Lazarsfeld was correct in emphasizing the case method as a way of learning about social research. Once a large body of case histories of questionnaires exists it will be possible to write a meaningful textbook on questionnaire construction.

7

The Role of Qualitative Data in Quantitative Research

It is customary in social science to think of qualitative methods as alternatives to quantitative methods. A study is presumably qualitative or quantitative—not both. In fact, however, most quantitative studies make use of qualitative data and incorporate qualitative methods of data collection. During the early stages of a quantitative study that will use a questionnaire to collect data from a large sample of people, depth interviews frequently are carried out with a small number of respondents. These depth interviews provide ideas for questions for the questionnaire. By giving the respondents an opportunity to discuss in detail the topics under study, the researcher may discover new aspects of the problem. For example, in a study I did of the impact of inflation on families, almost 80 people were interviewed in depth while we were making up the questionnaire for the survey. (The grant provided me with five half-time graduate research assistants who I kept busy interviewing people in depth about inflation.) One respondent said that inflation had caused him to lose confidence in the American dream, and this comment led us to make up a question on this very theme for the survey.

Moreover, depth interviews provide rich qualitative data to blend in with the quantitative data in the final report. The report for my inflation study was based primarily on a survey of almost 2000 families. But two chapters in that report* are based on the 80 depth interviews that were completed before

*The report was later published as a book. David Caplovitz, *Making Ends Meet: The Impact of Inflation and Recession on American Families*, Beverly Hills, California: Sage Publications, 1979.

the survey. Two critical variables in this study were the degree to which families found their income falling behind rising prices, which we called *objective inflation crunch,* and the degree to which families were hurting because of inflation, which we called *subjective inflation crunch.* An early chapter identified the types of people whose salaries fell behind and the next chapter described the types of people who were suffering. It was found that the poor were especially likely to be victims of objective and subjective inflation crunch, with the retired and the working class following. These chapters, which consisted of tables, were followed by a chapter entitled "The Voice of the People" with extensive quotes from the poor and working-class people we interviewed in depth. Mothers on welfare described how, because of inflation, they had cut back to one or two meals a day and how they had to face agonizing decisions about which child to buy new clothes for when there was not enough money to buy clothes for more than one child. The qualitative data presented in this chapter made the plight of the poor, and the working class as well, come alive in a way that the tables could not. Not only do the qualitative data enrich the quantitative report, but they make it more readable as well and broaden the audience for the report. And as noted in Chapter 1, the researcher who promises to do qualitative along with quantitative research enhances the chances of having a proposal funded. For all these reasons, quantitative researchers would be well advised to do depth interviews before they develop their questionnaires.

Qualitative analysis has still another role to play in quantitative research: helping the researcher interpret the quantitative findings. Paul F. Lazarsfeld, who pioneered in this use of qualitative analysis, used a skilled qualitative researcher to analyze the questionnaires of deviant or unusual cases in his study *The Academic Mind.* Jeannette Green, who had worked for Lazarsfeld earlier as a depth interviewer, prepared more than a dozen memoranda offering interpretations of deviant and extreme cases based on her reading of the entire questionnaire of the cases under study. Puzzled as to why some people bucked the trend, Lazarsfeld would turn to Green for an answer. For example, Lazarsfeld found that his key dependent variable, apprehension, was strongly correlated with political orientation. The more liberal faculty members were much more likely to be apprehensive during the McCarthy era. But he found some highly conservative people who were apprehensive and some very liberal ones who were not. By studying the entire questionnaire of these deviant cases, Green would frequently find cues to explain their seemingly deviant responses. Studying the entire questionnaire, she would learn what type of person the respondent was from the demographic data, and answers to other questions might provide clues to answers to the questions under study. Comments written in on the questionnaire by the interviewer were also helpful. The various memoranda that Green prepared provided the basis for a paper that I wrote on this role of qualitative analysis in quantitative research which is excerpted below. As for the functions of qualitative data in developing questionnaires and enriching the final report, Sam Sieber has prepared an unpublished paper on this topic which is presented below as well. The Sieber paper is presented first, followed by sections of the Green–Caplovitz paper.

=====

The Integration of Survey Research and Field Work*

SAM D. SIEBER

In a paper written several years ago[†] I noted that the advantages of integrating surveys and qualitative field methods are seldom recognized and rarely exploited. And indeed, it would appear that most social research either utilizes only a single method of investigation or assigns a second to an extremely weak role. To demonstrate the benefits that flow from the integration of these techniques, I gave examples of research wherein one method had contributed to the other in each of three phases: (1) Research design, (2) Data collection, and (3) Analysis. In the present paper I will elaborate on the contributions of qualitative field methods to survey data collection by reference to my own recent research in which efforts were made to exploit the integration of these techniques. But first let me review the history of the separation of field work and surveys.

Prior to World War II, field work (by which I mean participant observation), informant interviewing and use of available records to supplement these techniques predominated in social research. Such classics as the Hawthorne studies, the Middletown volumes, the Yankee City series and the Chicago studies of deviant groups (not to mention the anthropological contributions) attest to the early preeminence of field work. Following the war, the balance of work shifted markedly to surveys. This shift was largely a consequence of the development of public opinion polling in the 'thirties. Mosteller, Cantril, Likert, Stouffer and Lazarsfeld were perhaps the major developers of the newer survey techniques.

With the rapid growth of this vigorous infant, there emerged a polemic between the advocates of the older field methods and the proponents of the newer survey techniques. In fact, two methodological subcultures seemed to be in the making, one professing the superiority of "deep, rich" observational data and the other the virtues of "hard, generalizable" survey data. That the field workers were more vocal about the informational weaknesses of surveys than were survey researchers with respect to field work suggests the felt security of the latter and the defensive stance of the former. An extreme point in the polemic was reached by Becker and Geer's statement that ". . . the most complete form of the sociological datum, after all, is the form in which the participant observer gathers it . . . ." Such a datum gives us more information about the event under study than data gathered by any other sociological method . . . ."

This position was strongly contested in a rebuttal by Trow (1957), who pointed out that no single technique could claim a monopoly on plausibility of inference; and,

*This paper was prepared for presentation at the 1973 meetings of the American Educational Research Association, New Orleans.
[†]Sam D. Sieber, "The Integration of Field Methods and Survey Research," *American Journal of Sociology*, Spring 1973.

indeed, as Trow argued, many sociological observations can be made only on the basis of a large population. In his brief rebuttal, Trow did not seek to propose a scheme for determining the suitability of field work or survey research for the collection of given types of data. This task was undertaken a few years later by Zelditch (1962), who applied the criteria of efficiency and informational adequacy to surveys, participant observation and informant interviewing in gathering three kinds of data: (1) Frequency distributions, (2) Incidents and histories, and (3) Institutionalized norms and statuses. Thus, if the objective is to ascertain a frequency distribution, then the sample survey or census is the "prototypical and best form," but not so with incidents and histories, which render the survey both "inefficient and inadequate," according to Zelditch. This contribution was a long step forward in mediating between the two historically antagonistic styles of research.

But even this formulation showed the traces of an assumption that undergirded the earlier polemic, namely, that one uses either survey or field methods. The fact of the matter is that these techniques are sometimes combined in the same study. If all three types of information noted by Zelditch are sought within the framework of a single investigation, then all three techniques are properly called into play. In such cases, the inefficiency of a survey for studying institutionalized norms and statuses falls by the wayside: if one is conducting a survey anyway, then why not proceed to measure norms and statuses in the questionnaire? Likewise with the investigation of incidents and histories by means of a survey.

It is curious that so little attention has been paid to the intellectual and organizational problems and prospects of integrating different methods. A few methodologists have sought to compare the results of different approaches, but these endeavors were conceived within the traditional framework of mutually exclusive techniques, inasmuch as the problem was to determine the consequences of using *either* one *or* another technique.

The authors of a compendium of "unobtrusive measures" have noted our doggedness in viewing social research as a single-method enterprise and have made a plea for multioperationalism. But they were prompted to raise the issue on the assumption that every technique suffers from inherent weaknesses that can be corrected only by cross-checking with other techniques. To be sure, there are areas of informational overlap between methods, but there are also large areas of information which can be gained only by a particular technique. If each technique has an inherent weakness, it also has an inherent strength unmatched by others. Therefore, by drawing upon its special strengths, one technique can contribute substantially to the utilization of the other. While this principle can be demonstrated for every phase of research, here we confine ourselves to the benefits of field work for survey data collection.

There are four ways in which qualitative field work can contribute to data collection in surveys. First, it can provide legitimation for a survey; second, it can afford a basis for formulating a sampling frame; third, it can contribute fundamentally to the development of the survey instrument; and last, it can be used to increase return rates.

GAINING LEGITIMATION

It is well known that contacts with the leaders of a population will often smooth the way for contacts with followers. This applies to gaining legitimacy for a survey among followers as well as to gaining access for qualitative research purposes. If there are conflicts among leaders, of course, then the endorsement of only a single leader may set a large number of people in opposition to the survey. But information about political in-fighting and other conflicts should come to the attention of a field worker in the normal course of informant interviewing or observation, thereby prompting him to gain endorsements in a way that will appeal to all sectors of the population. In social research on schools, leadership may reside in superintendents, school board members, union officials, heads of parent groups, principals or informal opinion leaders anywhere on the staff.

The importance of identifying and gaining support from the appropriate authority during the exploratory phase preceding a survey, and of grasping the political context in which approval is sought, are perhaps best demonstrated by a negative instance. Voss describes the case of a school survey that was terminated by the superintendent on the grounds that it was "unauthorized by the school." Although in reality the superintendent was responding to pressures from a group of right wing parents, the survey having been duly approved by lower level administrators, he was able to claim that he had not *personally* endorsed the study and could therefore cancel it. Voss concludes from this experience that ". . . lack of familiarity with the structure of the organization may spell disaster . . . . The only means of avoiding such a problem is to obtain unequivocal support from the highest level possible."

My study of two suburban districts affords a case at the opposite end of the spectrum of cooperation. After conducting field work for several months in the schools, there was never really any question of gaining endorsements for the survey. Every administrator in the two districts cooperated fully in urging teachers to respond and in collecting the completed questionnaires in a box in their outer office. And the many helpful, marginal comments of the teachers, some addressing the survey designer by name, suggested that the questionnaire was completed with uncommon seriousness. The return rate was about 90 percent of the entire staff.

The two project histories are not exactly parallel since Voss surveyed students rather than staff members, but the problems encountered by Voss are also faced in gaining access to school staff for survey research. Apparently, the impersonality of a survey can be counteracted by the respondent's personal acquaintance with the investigator and the goals of his study.

In a more recent study in which we employed part-time field observers to help us evaluate an educational extension system in three states, a great deal of qualitative data were gathered over the period of a year preceding our survey of clients of the service. Cassette tape recorders were used to record interactions between extension agents and school personnel, follow-up interviews with clients and the random observations of both agents and our observers. These tapes were then coded in our New York office and the responses placed on 3 × 5 cards for easy reference while preparing the questionnaire or writing reports. And it seems clear that the familiarity of clients with our observers substantially smoothed the way for our survey. Where the observers had established the highest rapport with clients, response to the survey was highest. Two of our observers were local professors of education who had contributed directly to the extension program by organizing workshops or new courses, and these individuals were especially useful in gaining legitimation for our survey. Thus, in many instances the questionnaire was not viewed as a sudden intrusion from some remote university researchers, but as part of an on-going study with which many of the respondents were personally familiar through contact with our observers. And because of the close relations which had developed between observers and agents, the agents themselves vouched for the authenticity and value of the survey. Approximately a third of the clients responded to the first mailing of our eight page questionnaire without a follow-up letter. (Incidentally, one should bear in mind that these clients were mainly *rural* school teachers and administrators.) Further, in only one of the many school districts that received our questionnaire did we fail to gain the support of an administrator, and this occurred in an area where the field observer had had the poorest relationships with school personnel.

FORMULATING THE SAMPLING FRAME

In the course of conducting field work in the study mentioned above it had become clear that certain strategic subpopulations would have to be oversampled in order to treat them separately in our analysis. The importance of differentiating among these sub-populations was impressed upon us by the field work. For example, our field observers had found that experiences with administrators were quite different from those with teachers. Administrators were overwhelmed with reading material and therefore needed to be prodded to give serious attention to the information that was delivered to them by the extension agents. Also, their informational needs were more often for long range planning than for immediate application. Thus, the information they received was of a very special character. Finally, because of the importance of their gatekeeper role, which had emerged quite clearly from field observations, it occurred to us that their satisfaction with the service might be more significant than the satisfaction of their teaching staff, even though the latter might outnumber them by 20 to 1. For these reasons we decided to take a 100 percent sample of administrators in the rural areas of the three states. Similar observations of specialists prompted us to build them into the design as a separate group—which then raised the knotty problem of differentiating between specialists and administrators on the basis of mere formal titles in the state directories. In sum, experiences in the field demonstrated the advisability of adopting a sampling design based on certain status and job differentials.

CONTRIBUTIONS TO THE QUESTIONNAIRE

It is difficult to imagine how we could have formulated our questionnaire in the survey mentioned above without the long period of intensive observation which preceded it. Since the extension program was unique in education, we could not fall back on other studies or experiences. Let me give just one dramatic example of how our field work dictated an item which one would have considered doubtful without the contribution of field observations.

We gave the respondents a checklist of nine different activities or traits of the field agents and invited them to appraise the agent on each of these criteria. A five point scale was used with the option of saying that the activity did not occur at all. One of these critieria was "understanding of his role or job." When we submitted our question-naire for clearance, a USOE official in the forms management office responded that the item was meaningless because respondents could not possibly appraise a field agent's understanding of his role. Now, for a year we had been listening to tape recorded sessions with clients in which the agents had sought to explain their job. Frequently the clients reacted with confusion, and occasionally the agents themselves professed their own uncertainty. And in our interviews with clients, several felt that the agents did not know what their proper duties were. This was indeed the case because the role was entirely new to both client and agent, and it was quite evident that the role could not be performed unless there was consensus between agent and client about its goals and limitations. In short, it did not take much sophistication for a client to realize when an agent was unable to understand or articulate his role.

The item was retained in the final questionnaire, making it possible to measure the extent to which role definitions were still problematic after a year of working in the field. In fact, it was isolated statistically as one of two items concerned with what we later called "presentation of self and program." These two items were not only the most frequently observed, but received the highest marks from clients in their appraisal of the agents. This finding showed that regardless of how ambiguous and troublesome the field agent role was at the outset, a year's experience was sufficient for it to have taken firm shape.

Our field observers were also quite helpful in making suggestions for the questionnaire. In one case an observer sent us a short checklist of different aspects of the program to which clients might have been exposed. The checklist was incorporated into the questionnaire for all clients. Of course, the observers were also available for pretest interviewing, and as a result of this input hardly a single item remained in its original form. In sum, without the assistance and direct input of our field observers who had become experts on all phases of the program the survey instrument would have been seriously defective.

INCREASING THE RETURN RATE

The use of field representatives to increase return rates was clearly demonstrated in our survey of school of education deans in 1965. In most universities we were able to commission junior faculty in sociology departments to deliver the questionnaire, explain its intent, assist in filling it out, retrieve it and review it for complete responses, and then forward it to our office. Since the questionnaire was about 25 pages in length and requested a good deal of statistical data, the use of field representatives appeared to be obligatory. And indeed the difference in return rates between schools with and without field representatives was about 40 percent. Clearly, had we failed to recruit field representatives, our survey response would have been so poor that the data would have been worthless.

In our more recent study of extension agents, the field observers were sent the names of all nonrespondents after two follow-up letters and requested to call them by telephone or speak to them on their visits in the schools. In all areas the response rate increased by approximately 15 percent after the observers had contacted the clients. The final return rates from each of the three states was 61 percent, 77 percent and 85 percent. In order to study response bias, a one page questionnaire was mailed to collect background information and inquire about satisfaction with the service. Including responses to this one page instrument, the overall response rates were 72 percent, 86 percent and 93 percent respectively in the three states. Without the legitimizing and follow-up roles of our field observers, it is highly doubtful that we could have succeeded in reaching this largely rural population with our survey.

CONCLUDING REMARKS

The neglect of field work by survey researchers is most unfortunate, not only because certain data are missed, but also because the survey itself will suffer. The necessity of overcoming cynicism toward survey research, of identifying subpopulations for sampling purposes, of fitting the questionnaire to the respondents' frame of reference and of inducing reluctant or busy respondents to return questionnaires dictate the use of qualitative field work for data collection purposes. At the very least, field representatives are often methodologically obligatory. Until such time as multiple techniques are applied, the results of most of our survey research will remain plausible rather than conclusive.

═══════════════

Sam Sieber, the author of this paper, is a product of Columbia University's Bureau of Applied Social Research, the organization created by Paul F. Lazarsfeld. As one of the leading practitioners of survey research and the author of a number of quantitative methodologies, Lazarsfeld was nonetheless a firm believer in qualitative research and wrote several theoretical articles on the subject. He strongly believed that qualitative research was important to quantitative studies, and he passed this belief on to his students, including Sam Sieber and me. The following paper is based on his study of the impact of McCarthyism on academia, published as *The Academic Mind*.

═══════════════

Qualitative Analysis in the Context of Quantitative Research

JEANNETTE GREEN AND DAVID CAPLOVITZ

INTRODUCTION

Although *The Academic Mind* was based mainly on statistical data, it made extensive use of qualitative material, primarily in the form of verbatim quotations from the respondents. In this respect *The Academic Mind* is similar to many other studies which have managed to blend qualitative and quantitative data. In most statistical studies, however, qualitative data, when used, are assigned a *descriptive* function of illustrating and enriching concepts and quantitative findings bearing on them. Less frequently do we find qualitative material used to interpret statistical results, or put more generally, to resolve problems arising from statistical analysis.

In *The Academic Mind* qualitative data were used for both of these purposes. Since the more traditional descriptive function of qualitative analysis is familiar to the readers of social research literature, the present paper will concentrate on the interpretive role that qualitative analysis played in *The Academic Mind*.

An examination of what was done in the research process indicates at least four types of reasons for turning to qualitative analysis for interpretive purposes: *(a)* assessing the validity of check list responses which were to be treated statistically; *(b)*. accounting for unexpected statistical results; *(c)* shedding light on the deviant cases in a cross tabulation between two variables; and *(d)* examining extreme and unusual cases too few in number to be studied statistically. Each of these occasions for turning to qualitative analysis will be described and illustrated with data from the study of college teachers.

QUALITATIVE ANALYSIS TO ASSESS THE VALIDITY OF RESPONSE CATEGORIES

Qualitative analyses were carried out on several occasions to clarify the meaning of check list responses and in particular to check on the possibility that respondents were misclassified. In spite of all the precautions of pre-tests, some questions invariably appear in the final version which contain an ambiguous term or else have response categories which do not fully cover the subtleties of reactions. The analyst is alerted to the possibility of a faulty question by the qualifying comments spontaneously offered by respondents and recorded by the interviewers next to the check marks. Such a problem presented itself when the analysts noticed a large number of qualifications accompanying the "yes" and "no" answers to the six items that were to be used to measure the basic dependent variable of apprehension. The sheer volume of these comments put the analysts on guard and raised questions about the validity of an index based on them.

A group of 400 questionnaires were selected at random and all qualifying comments to the six questions were examined to see whether they negated the checklist response. The results of this analysis are reported on pp. 86–88 of *The Academic Mind*. As the authors note, the analysis showed that the great majority of the spontaneous comments reinforced the meaning of the check list response. For example, one professor who was worried that students would pass on a warped version of his comments, which would create a false impression of his political views, added:

> I don't ever like to be misquoted by students particularly at a time when we are most hysterical about things.

Another respondent who answered "yes" to this question pointed out that he was particularly conscious of the problem at his present college.

> I feel much more hesitant here at _____ to make references to Marxism than at the U. of _____ where I taught before.

A respondent who was worried that his political opinions might affect his job security specified the area of his concern:

> You have to be careful in domestic and state politics. I avoid them.

Conversely, a number of non-apprehensive teachers often explained their "no" answers. Some stated after their negative checkmarks that they either did not have controversial opinions or did not deal with controversial subject matter and so had nothing to fear.

> It happens that my political opinions are not such as affect my job and promotions adversely.

Most of the stuff I assign is not too controversial anyway.

Others were not afraid to express themselves even though their opinions might be considered controversial because of the favorable climate of opinion at their colleges.

It is clearly and emphatically "no." I am not aware of any pressure from the administration.

In contrast with the majority of the comments, which reinforced the checkmarks, about one in every ten appeared to contradict the checkmark answer. In qualifying "yes" answers, some respondents went on to say that although the thought had crossed their minds they were not really worried. The following are typical:

It has been just an incidental thought on my part as to what effect my words might have—but has *not* been in any sense a fear.

I've thought about it (political opinions affecting job) but I don't worry about it.

Similarly, the qualifications to some "no" responses indicated that the respondents in fact manifested the kind of apprehension that the index was measuring. For example, when asked whether he had toned down his recent writings in order to make them less controversial one respondent replied "no" and went on to say:

Although I have toned material because the public attitude has changed and one must take account of that.

In answer to the question, "Do you find in your recommendations of reference material to students that you are more careful today not to recommend something that might be later criticized for being too controversial?," some respondents answered "no" and then proceeded to show how careful they were not to be placed in a controversial position:

I would be more careful to recommend both sides so as not to be criticized for giving only one side. But I would point out which side was Communist.

But I might point out to students that what they are going to read might be criticized by some people.

The crucial question posed by the qualifications which seemed to contradict the meaning of the checkmarks was whether an index based on the uncorrect responses would lead to biased results. The outcome of the qualitative analysis was to show that reclassification was not necessary for, in the aggregate, the qualifications tended to cancel out. As the authors point out, "an affirmative answer qualified to a 'no' occurred as often as a qualification in the other direction." Consequently, the proportion of teachers who were apprehensive would be about the same, and the relationship between apprehension and other variables would not change, except possibly they would be greater in strength if all the errors were removed. In this instance, a combination of qualitative and quantitative analysis (counting the number of qualifications in each direction) served to lend validity to the measurement of a basic variable of the study.

In the preceding account, it was the large number of qualifications which directed the analysts' attention to the adequacy of the check list alternatives. In another instance, it was the accidental discovery of a qualifying comment pointing up an ambiguous word in the body of a question which stimulated a systematic assessment of the check list responses. At one point in the interview, respondents were asked a series of check list and free answer questions dealing with the issue of loyalty oaths, whether they had signed oaths, whether they would if asked, and their reasons for signing or not signing. In the course of a qualitative analysis of the free answer material (concerning reasons for signing or not signing), it was discovered that some respondents who said they had signed an oath were referring to oaths to uphold the state constitution rather than to the special loyalty oaths instituted at certain colleges during the height of the McCarthy era. For example, one respondent explained:

Yes, I signed the Massachusetts state oath in 1938 when I came here.

The discovery of this comment led to a systematic check of the responses of the 500 teachers in the sample who said they had signed a loyalty oath. Although the great majority in this group did not bother to qualify their affirmative answer, the few qualifications which did appear suggested that a number were referring to state oaths. The extent of the inflation of the "yes" answers could not be accurately determined but the limitations of the statistical result were pointed up by the qualitative analysis.

QUALITATIVE ANALYSIS IN THE EXPLICATION OF UNEXPECTED OR SURPRISING STATISTICAL RESULTS

A fairly common experience in the analysis of quantitative data is the "surprising" statistical result. The study director may have included a response category to a question for purposes of logical completeness with no expectation that respondents do in fact have the attitude, only to discover that there are indeed such cases. An even greater source of surprise is the discovery that two variables are related to each other in an opposite way from what common sense or theoretically derived hypotheses would lead one to expect. Such findings are, of course, a stimulus to new ideas, but, in large part, because they *are* unexpected, the analyst frequently finds that he lacks the necessary statistical information to test his new interpretations. It is in such situations that the analyst is apt to turn to less systematic, qualitative data which might either support the new ideas or uncover other reasons for the surprising result.* In the course of the analysis of *The Academic Mind* data, unexpected results both in response to single questions and in the cross-tabulation of two variables occurred and gave rise to qualitative analysis. We shall first consider the "unexpected response" and then deal with an instance where qualitative data shed light on an unexpected correlation.

The "Optimistic" Professors

A number of questions required the respondents to compare the current academic climate at their colleges with the situation six or seven years earlier prior to the

*See Patricia Kendall and Paul F. Lazarsfeld, "Problems in Survey Analysis," in Robert K. Merton and Paul F. Lazarsfeld (Eds.), *Continuities in the American Soldier*, Glencoe, Illinois: Free Press, 1950, pp. 165–168, for a discussion of the use of qualitative data in the elaboration of a statistical relationship.

McCarthy era. In one series of questions professors were asked whether they had noticed any change in the behavior of their colleagues regarding controversial political issues. These questions read as follows:

Q.24.   Is it your impression that members of the social science faculty are less willing to express unpopular views, than they were six or seven years ago, more willing or hasn't there been much change? [Each part answered separately]

A.   To express unpopular political views in the classroom.
B.   To express unpopular political views publicly in the community.
C.   To serve as faculty advisors to student political groups that might advocate unpopular causes.

Another question asked about whether some of their colleagues in their writings and speeches were more likely now to avoid controversial political subjects than they were six or seven years earlier, less likely to, or whether there had been no change. And another question, with the same response categories, referred to the avoidance of controversial material on reading lists. For the sake of logical completeness, all of these questions provided the alternative that colleagues were more ready to assume risk today than formerly, but given the climate of McCarthyism, the researchers assumed that no one would choose this alternative. In short, it was not expected that any respondents would report that matters had improved. Of course, the overall distribution of responses did bear out this assumption. On each of these questions, the majority felt that their colleagues had not changed much. Of those who did report changes, most said that their colleagues were less willing to engage in controversy than they had been prior to the McCarthy period. But the important point is that each of these questions turned up some respondents who felt that their colleagues were more willing to take a controversial stand than they had been previously. In all, there were 268 teachers (out of the sample of 2451) who indicated by their checkmarks a greater willingness on the part of their colleagues to take a controversial position on at least one of these questions.

An indicator of the surprise element in these responses is that no provision was made for respondents to give reasons for their opinions. These "optimistic" responses suggested the new idea that on some campuses the faculty may have been mobilized to fight back against encroachments on academic freedom and was more motivated than ever to tackle controversial issues. To test this hypothesis a sample of 100 questionnaires was taken from the group of 268 and carefully examined for possible explanations. Only about one in five contained spontaneous comments to these questions which gave some reason for the response. It was necessary, therefore, to look elsewhere in the questionnaire for clues to the optimism of this minority.

While the analysis did indicate some support for the "reaction to threat" hypothesis, it uncovered other explanations as well. A major theme in these interviews was that favorable changes had occurred in the external conditions which made consideration of controversial matters more possible. Yet another kind of explanation offered was that during the intervening period there had been an increase in the amount of controversial subject matter that had to be dealt with in courses.

The awakening of the faculty by the threats to their freedom was mentioned by a professor at a major West Coast university who felt that his colleagues were less inclined to avoid controversial issues in their writings:

> In the history department I think a lot of people have done civil liberties writings that they wouldn't have done otherwise. I think they have gone out to fight the evil—I've done it and others have too. (Mentions name of book on civil liberties written recently by a colleague.)

Under this general heading might be placed several explanations offered by teachers concerning the greater need to make students aware of controversial matters. A professor at an Eastern university felt that his colleagues were more willing to take up controversial matters in the classroom and implied that this was necessary to combat the lethargy of the students:

> I feel that students need to be blasted more than before.

And in similar vein an instructor at a Southern university said:

> Because it is necessary to expose students to ideas now more than it was six or seven years ago.

In some interviews comments were found in other parts of the questionnaire which implied that the greater willingness of the faculty to deal with controversial matters had been stimulated by the threats to academic freedom. Thus, one respondent who felt that his colleagues were more oriented toward controversy explained the effect of an academic freedom incident that had occurred:

> It brought the faculty together and made them reach a conscious policy on it—facing the issue and agreeing it solidified opinion.

The spontaneous comments to these questions indicated that a more prevalent explanation was that changes in the external situation, either in the nation at-large or within the school, had contributed to a freer atmosphere. Significantly enough, those who felt that the greater interest in controversy stemmed from a lessening of tension in the community were people who misinterpreted the time period specified by the questions. Rather than comparing the present with six or seven years ago, these people were comparing the present with the situation that prevailed at the height of the McCarthy era, a year or so prior to the study. These comments are typical:

> I think people are relatively freer now than they were a few months or a couple of years ago, since the McCarthy peak dropped.

> As soon as we got rid of McCarthy. Now we can speak up far better than we could *two years ago*. Now we are swinging back to normal.

Some of the "optimists" attributed the more conducive atmosphere to changes in the personnel of the faculty. A professor at an Eastern university explained:

> If anything, the department has become more liberal because of change of personnel in the last few years. Many older men have retired. They are bolder

today only because different people are here compared with six or seven years ago.

A professor at a teachers college gave a similar explanation for his belief that his colleagues are more willing to express unpopular political views:

We have a new man in charge here and on that basis I'd say they are more willing to express themselves on politics.

Still another kind of change within the college was mentioned by a teacher at a Catholic college. He attributed the greater willingness to assign controversial reading material to a change in the student body:

We used to have only nuns and now we have lay students and can use more of two sides to issues.

A third kind of explanation for the greater willingness to deal with controversial matters was that there had been an increase in the amount of controversial matters that required attention and a greater interest in such topics on the part of students. This viewpoint is expressed in the following comments:

Nowadays there is more talk on controversial subjects because there are more controversial things to talk about.

There is more frequent reference to controversial subjects because of the interest of the students. My impression is that there are more courses now in which students read about Communism.

To summarize, this qualitative analysis was stimulated by the unexpected finding that some respondents felt that their colleagues were more willing to take stands on controversial issues than they had been before the onset of the "difficult years."

The Cautious Activists: An Unexpected Correlation

A paradoxical finding emerging from the statistical analysis was that apprehensive professors were more willing than nonapprehensive ones to engage in activities which were likely to subject them to criticism. It was found that apprehensive professors were more likely to belong to controversial organizations and in response to two hypothetical questions they were more likely to protest strongly any administration effort to ban a controversial speaker or a student debate on a controversial topic and when asked whether they had recently expressed in public a political opinion in spite of possible repercussions, they were more likely to say they had done so than the nonapprehensive teachers. Each of these behaviors indicates a greater willingness to take action in face of criticism on the part of the apprehensive teachers. The puzzlement arises from the fact that the statistical analysis showed one of the dimensions of apprehension to be cautious behavior. In the words of the authors, "How can we explain the fact that many professors who refrain from discussing politics, express fewer controversial opinions in public and are more circumspect in their writings, at the same time read magazines and belong to organizations which are known to be controversial and are confident that they would vigorously oppose a president who interfered with campus intellectual activities?"

Qualitative analysis entered into the explanation of this seemingly anomalous finding in two quite different ways: a study of the cautious activists and a study of the content of the relevant questions. The first procedure was to go through the questionnaires of the highly "activistic" apprehensive respondents to see what explanations they themselves offered for their cautious behavior in response to the apprehensive items. The questionnaires of the teachers who manifested activism on all the indicators described above—46 cases in all—were scrutinized for comments which might explain their tendency toward caution. That these people were inclined to be cautious is evidenced by 25 of them admitting that they "go out of their way to make statements or tell anecdotes in order to bring home the point that [they] have no extreme leftist or rightist leanings." Only 28 per cent of the entire sample answered this question in the affirmative.

The analysis of spontaneous comments uncovered several reasons for the apparent contradiction. For a number of respondents the simultaneous expression of both caution and activism seemed to be due to a distinction they made between "off-campus" and "on-campus" behavior. These respondents were willing to be active within the confines of the college or their homes, but were prone to be cautious when dealing with the outside community. A professor of government at a state university explained why he was worried that something political he had said might cause him to be unpopular with the alumni:

> I have an obligation not to hurt the university as I speak throughout the state all the time. The institutions are under such pressure, I don't want to say the wrong thing.

A West Coast professor of political science also called attention to the distinction between "on campus" and "off campus" when he said:

> There is no pressure put on me within the university about what I do in the classroom. There has been pressure outside the university on the administration by groups to get me fired because of public statements I have made. These activities and statements are off campus.

A second theme in the spontaneous comments of some "cautious activists" is that of strategy. Some of these men admit that they occasionally make concessions in order to achieve more important goals. Presumably, these men will become more cautious in some circumstances in order to increase their effectiveness in others. A professor of history, when asked whether he had toned down his writings, answered:

> Sometimes I have toned down when writing to Congressmen when I felt it would harm what I was saying.

A professor of government who said he would protest vigorously if the president of the college banned Owen Lattimore, a Johns Hopkins professor accused by McCarthy of being a Russian agent, from speaking on campus qualified his answer:

> But it is a hypothetical question. There may be circumstances under which the President might feel this action a better way to protect academic interests in freedom. There are times when we do need to make concessions on some more important matter; other times we cannot make them without compromising principle.

Perhaps the most prevalent explanation offered by these respondents for their cautious behavior in some circumstances in spite of their activism in others was the need to disassociate themselves from Communism. A professor of political science at a New England college explained why he occasionally went out of his way to show that he had no extreme leanings:

When I was a member of the Progressive Party, many critics equated support for the Progressive Party with sympathy toward Communism. It therefore became necessary for me and other academicians supporting the Progressive Party to explain repeatedly that our support had nothing to do with sympathy toward Communism.

A West Coast professor of economics explained how this need to protect himself from being mistaken for a Communist led him to sign a loyalty oath:

I nearly got fired because of the loyalty oath. I resented very deeply the fact that it had to be signed and before the Korean War I refused to sign and helped lead the opposition. Then South Korea was invaded and I was afraid the issues would get mixed up with patriotism and Communism and so I signed.

The need to avoid being misinterpreted as a Communist or Communist sympathizer affected the style of teaching of a number of these teachers. A history professor at a small Eastern liberal arts college said:

When I lecture on Marxism, I probably am led to spend greater time giving my disagreements with it than previously.

And a similar comment was made by an anthropologist at a New England college:

If you say something critical of the American government, you feel obligated to say something equally critical of Russia. You go out of your way in this respect to make your position clear. That's one of the bad effects of the whole current climate.

The analysis of the spontaneous comments of the "cautious activists" indicated that their position could be explained in terms of such factors as the distinction between on-campus and off-campus behavior, the need to make concessions in order to achieve other goals and the need to dispel the stigma of Communism.

The second way in which qualitative analysis was done to explain the cautious activists was to analyze the questions themselves in more detail. Further scrutiny of the questions used to measure "caution" and "activism" showed that the items tapping "activism" tended to refer to visible and public behavior while the items dealing with "caution" were more private and not as likely to be noticed by one's colleagues. As the authors note, whether one does or does not protest against the president's interference with the academic freedom of students is apt to be known by one's colleagues. The same might be said of the kinds of organizations to which one belongs and the kinds of magazines one reads. "Friends would notice if one were not to sign a protest, or if one were suddenly to drop one's membership or to a lesser degree, cancel a subscription. In addition, these are reactions requiring a decision one way or another."

In contrast, the items measuring "caution" involve the notion of refraining from doing something when there is no specific reason for doing it. Not bringing up certain political topics with one's colleagues is not apt to be noticed. Similarly, "toning down one's writings" or being more circumspect with one's reading lists can easily go unnoticed by colleagues. Further specification of the caution and activism indicators thus led to a distinction between "public" and "private" courage. This in turn gave rise to speculations about the role of the "collegial" group in reinforcing the norms of academic freedom. Where deviations from these norms were apt to be visible to colleagues, the professors were less inclined to be "cautious" than in those areas where the behavior was not likely to be observed by the peer group. In a way, it might be said that professors were likely to act courageously when they could count on the support of their colleagues, or at least when their lack of courage would be noticed by them.

QUALITATIVE ANALYSIS OF DEVIANT CASES

There were frequent occasions in the course of the statistical analysis when qualitative data were analyzed in order to shed light on the deviant cases in the cross-tabulation of two variables. As Kendall and Wolff have pointed out, the analysis of deviant cases can serve two functions.* First, it can lead to a refinement of the indicators of the concepts under study by uncovering misclassifications. Second, deviant case analysis can result in the discovery of new conditions under which a relationship holds and thus lead to an improvement in the interpretive scheme. As will be illustrated, the analysis of deviant cases in *The Academic Mind* served both of these purposes.

Several of the deviant case analyses dealt with the items which were to be used in an index of a permissive orientation toward political unorthodoxy. In these instances, the deviant cases were especially puzzling since the items being related were so similar in content. The analysts went about measuring this value-orientation by first constructing separate indices of permissiveness and conservatism which they then later combined into a single index. As a measure of permissiveness they selected two items dealing with the issue of Communists on campus. One asked whether an admitted Communist should be allowed to teach in a college and the other whether students who wanted to should be allowed to form a Communist student organization. When these seemingly similar items are cross-tabulated, a substantial number of deviant cases are found. This cross tabulation is shown in Table 7.1. Most professors are either permissive on both counts or are not permissive on either. However, there are 343 professors who give

Table 7.1. The Relationship between Two Permissive Responses

Young Communist League	Communist Professors	
	Should Be Fired	Should Not Be Fired
Should not be allowed	888	198
Should be allowed	145	596

*Patricia Kendall and Katherine M. Wolff, "Two Functions of Deviant Case Analysis," in Paul F. Lazarsfeld and Morris Rosenberg (Eds.), *The Language of Social Research*, New York: Free Press, 1955.

inconsistent responses. The problem posed by the deviant cases was how to explain the fact that a number of respondents were willing to accept unorthodox ideas in one sector of the college but not in another.

The questionnaires of about half the cases in each of the deviant cells were examined. The qualifying comments to these questions pointed up a basic distinction in the minds of the respondents between Communism as an international conspiracy which presented a physical danger to American security and communism as an intellectual position, a distinction which some respondents phrased as the difference between "Big C" and "little c" communism. Both of the deviant groups in the table were opposed to conspiratorial Communism. Where they differed was in their assessment of which group—Communist teachers or Communist students—was likely to represent the conspiratorial aspects of communism as opposed to the expression of heretic opinions. By and large, those who would fire the Communist teacher but would allow the Young Communist League saw the teacher as an agent of conspiratorial Communism under orders to indoctrinate and convert unsuspecting students to Communism, while the Young Communist League was viewed more as a study group concerned with the intellectual aspects of communism.

A professor of economics in a Midwestern university who perceived the two questions in these different terms made the following comments:

> (After checking "yes" to firing a Communist teacher:) If a party member, he should be dropped. There should be a big distinction made between a man who is a true Communist party member and one who advocates communist philosophy.

> (After checking that the Young Communist League should be allowed:) I'm in favor of all groups having the right to talk. If merely advocating communism as a subject of study, the Young Communist League should be allowed.

A sociology professor at a Western university made no comment when he checked "yes" to the question on firing the admitted Communist teacher, but in explaining his answer to a similar question about whether a social science professor who is an admitted Communist can be a fit teacher, he implied that a Communist teacher is part of a conspiracy:

> Such a person is a member of a military organization in a sense.

Yet this same man would allow a Communist student organization because he sees such a group as just another student club:

> They would be subject to the rules of all student clubs.

Closely related to the theme that the Communist teacher is an active agent in a conspiracy is the idea that a member of the Communist Party is no longer a free agent and therefore incapable of manifesting the characteristics of a good teacher. These respondents feel that the Communist teacher should be fired on the grounds of incompetence. This position is suggested by such comments as these:

> My objection to a Communist teacher is that he has already committed himself to rigid ideas and he is not a free intellectual agent.

If they were not under orders from the Communist Party they could teach, but they are under discipline and therefore unfit to teach.

In contrast, those who would prohibit a Young Communist League but would not fire a Communist tended to perceive the student organization as representative of "big C" Communism capable of doing harm to society and to the students themselves, while the teacher was seen as the advocate of an intellectual position. In explaining why they would not allow the Communist student organization, these people offered such comments as these:

By definition a Young Communist League wouldn't be a political party in the usual sense, but would be dedicated to the overthrow of the existing government.

My negative answer is dictated largely by the fact that the party itself has been made extralegal.

A few respondents were concerned about the negative consequences belonging to such an organization would have for the students. In explaining why he would prohibit a Communist student organization, a professor said:

We should protect students from the harm it will do them in the future if they have joined a Communist League.

In justifying their opinion on not firing the Communist teacher these same respondents suggested that teachers are abstract thinkers who are relatively harmless. One in this group qualifies his refusal to fire the Communist teacher by saying:

There could be a communist who subscribes to the economic system and not the political; a person who subscribes to the overthrow of government shouldn't be left in a position to cause danger, but profession of social and economic beliefs should not be grounds for dismissal.

Another professor in this group said in answer to the question about the teacher:

It depends on whether he used the classroom as a rostrum for indoctrination.

And one respondent saw the Communist teacher serving an educational function:

As a matter of policy, every college ought to have a resident Communist. More people would know what they are against. But I don't mean an underground one, or all the benefits would be lost.

For the most part, the inconsistencies between the responses to the questions on the Communist teacher and the Communist student organization can be interpreted by the different frames of reference in which the word "Communist" was perceived. In a few instances, the seemingly inconsistent response pattern was more the result of an error in classification. For example, one respondent who believed that the Communist teacher should be fired said that the student organization should be allowed so that it would be easier "to watch them" and make it possible to "ferret out the undesirables."

For this respondent a Communist organization should exist not because students have a right to unorthodox opinions, but rather because it makes it easier to combat Communism on campus.

[Green and Caplovitz provide a second example of the qualitative analysis of deviant cases, those that emerge in the cross-tabulation of the permissive and conservative indices, but this example will be omitted for the sake of brevity.]

QUALITATIVE ANALYSIS OF EXTREME CASES

A fourth reason for turning to qualitative data was to analyze unusual or extreme cases which, almost by definition, are too few in number to be analyzed statistically. Precisely because these cases manifest some characteristic in the extreme, they are a potentially rich source of information on the determinants and correlates of the characteristic in question. Several of the qualitative analyses undertaken in the course of the study fell into this category.

The Highly Apprehensive Teachers at the Nonapprehensive Schools

This example of the study of extreme cases has some of the properties of a deviant case analysis since the cases were generated by a cross-tabulation of two variables, the school rate of apprehension (a group property) and the teacher's own score on the apprehension index (an individual property). However, this example differs from what we ordinarily consider deviant case analysis in an important respect. Typically, when an analyst examines deviant cases, he is primarily interested in the degree of association between two variables. He will study the deviant cases if, for some reason, they weaken his argument, or if he has a hunch about what accounts for them, or if he is confronted with the problem of how to score them when constructing an index. But his interest in the deviants is secondary to his interest in the correlation between the two variables.

In contrast, the *only* reason for relating the school rate of apprehension to the apprehension of teachers was to locate the "deviant" cases. The relationship is obviously tautological for by definition the school rate is related to the existence of apprehensive teachers. The technique used to locate these cases is a further indication of the difference. To insure a representative sample of cases, all the colleges were classified simultaneously according to type of control, size and quality. Within each of the resulting cells, the school with the lowest rate of apprehension was selected and from that school, the professor with the highest apprehension score was singled out for study. In this way, 22 cases of apprehensive teachers at nonapprehensive schools were selected.*

The reason for singling out these extreme cases was to find out why people could be apprehensive in an environment which did not generate apprehension. Were these teachers who were by nature prone to apprehension or were there special circumstances which made them apprehensive during the difficult years? The analysis proceeded by examining the entire questionnaire of these respondents and comparing their characteristics with those of their less apprehensive colleagues. These cases documented many of the factors that the statistical analysis showed to be related to apprehension. Among them were many who had once belonged to a controversial organization; as a group, they tended to be more permissive and "activistic" than their

---

*The schools were actually classified in 26 groups. But in four of the cells, the school with the lowest apprehension rate failed to have a single apprehensive respondent.

colleagues; perhaps their most distinguishing characteristic was that they were much more likely than their colleagues to have personally experienced pressures or to have been the victim of a clear attack during the McCarthy period. Of the 22 teachers in this group, 16 reported some pressure on them. In contrast, only two of these teachers were located at schools where at least half of their colleagues also reported being under pressure.

A variety of special factors conducive to apprehension seemed to differentiate these people from their colleagues. The apprehension of one seemed to stem from his teaching a course on Russia at a comparatively conservative school. Others in the group are clearly deviant from their colleagues in the area of politics. Among these cases are a former "Wallaceite" at a conservative school and a "McCarthyite" at a liberal school. Several of these highly apprehensive teachers voted contrary to the majority of their colleagues in the 1952 election. Included in the group is a Negro who had considerable difficulty finding a home in the community in which he teaches, and a women teacher at a Southern school who had been criticized for being outspoken on the subject of Negro rights. One person in the group was foreign born and reported having difficulty getting citizenship papers. In a few instances there did not seem to be any external stimulus for the unusual amount of apprehension and perhaps in these cases apprehension stemmed from a general tendency toward anxiety.

Excerpts from these "case histories" point out the varied characteristics of the highly apprehensive at the nonapprehensive schools. A young instructor at a West Coast state university, who was very permissive as well as apprehensive, revealed attitudes of suspicion, intimidation, insecurity and bitterness both toward his school and the political climate of the day as the following quotes illustrate:

I've frequently worried about the possibility of students passing on a warped version of what I say. I habitually keep all my classes as confused as possible about my own views.

(Have you wondered that a political opinion might affect your job security?) Emphatically yes. As a matter of fact, I'm extremely careful to make a reconnaissance of a person's potential effect on my security position.

(Have you thought about the possibility that the administration keeps a dossier on every faculty member?) Yes and I have further taken action to find out whether they have such a dossier.

(In explanation of his refusal to answer a question about political periodicals he reads:) I prefer not to tell anybody that and I prefer not to begin here. I have been asked that question by most of the representatives of the security agencies who have interviewed me and I consider it a trespass of the fundamental political rights of the individual.

Another teacher in this group is a professor of sociology at a Northeastern private university who had been subjected to pressures for being highly active in liberal politics in his traditionally conservative state. Perhaps because he has tenure he seems to be undaunted by the pressures and continued to be active in the political life of his community for at the time of the interview he was chairman of the local chapter of

Americans for Democratic Action. The following comments convey the nature of the pressures on him:

> I'm chairman of Americans for Democratic Action and every ten days somebody tells me that it is not good for me.

> I've been subject to gossip about how liberal or "pink" I am. I used to be a popular lecturer. Today I get almost no paid lectures, no radio sponsorship. My income has suffered considerably by lack of lectures. I have had editorials in papers against me, lying editorials.

> Occasionally, I used to hear that word got back to the administration that I was a radical.

The women teacher at a small Southern college who was deeply concerned about the problem of Negro rights revealed her difficulties in the following comments:

> I was warned by the President of the college that I should not have attended a meeting at a Negro school. My honest opinion has kept me back professionally. Stool pigeons are watching me constantly and reporting on me. I would probably be dismissed but I have lots of relatives who graduated from here and I am well known in the community.

> A new teacher told me that the President of the college told him to stay away from me because of the stand I have taken for Negroes.

> I feel that it takes courage and shows strong character to come out in the open with your opinions on all matters helping to improve America. I know that I could be a full professor now with my qualifications if I went along with the President's ideas but I am courageous enough to state how I feel and I am in hot water all the time.

As the last example from the "case histories" of the highly apprehensive at nonapprehensive schools, the voice of the only clearly conservative professor in the group may be heard (this man teaches at a Northeastern public school):

> People have told me I'd get ahead if I agreed with the department head. There have been very intense social pressures. It's hard to associate with fellows when they disagree with McCarthy and you happen to believe in him. You have to be a frontiersman and live by yourself. At social gatherings people can make pretty insulting statements to you.

And his economic philosophy is revealed by this comment:

> I've always been an individualist, a capitalist. So I've subscribed to capitalistic publications and given money to the NAM. People on this faculty have warned me about salary raises and that I'll lose friends. But I haven't any friends here and so how can I lose them?

What is so striking about these excerpts from the interview with the "McCarthyite" is the similarity between the pressures he experienced and those reported by the extremely liberal apprehensive professors. Like the professor of sociology who is chairman of ADA and the women spokesman for Negro rights, this respondent reports pressures toward conformity from both administrators and colleagues. Like them, he recounts attempts at social ostracism. His case differs from those of his liberal counterparts in one important respect: unlike them, he does not experience any pressures from the outside community for the mood of the country was much like his own.

Extreme Case II: Teachers Turned Down for Government Jobs or Projects

A second example of the use of qualitative data to shed light on unusual cases deals with the affirmative responses to the following question:

> Have you ever been turned down for a government job or for work on a government project for what you suspect have been political reasons?

Out of the 2451 teachers interviewed, 35 answered this question in the affirmative. These cases were singled out for special analysis to find out whether they were extreme radicals and potential "subversives."

A few preliminary statistical comparisons cast doubt on the assumption that these professors were uniformly radicals and potential security risks. For example, a somewhat greater proportion of them voted Republican in 1952 than was true for the entire sample and they were no more likely to say they were more liberal than their colleagues than were respondents in the entire sample.

With these somewhat puzzling statistical facts as background, the interviews of the 35 teachers were studied for comments which might explain why they had been turned down for government jobs. In only seven of the 35 cases were explicit explanations of the affirmative answer offered. In about a dozen other cases answers to such questions as membership in a controversial organization could be used to infer reasons for being turned down by the government while in almost half the cases no explanation at all could be garnered from the questionnaire. Nonetheless, the qualitative data that were available in these interviews were sufficient to indicate that political radicalism and suspected subversion were not the only reasons for having been turned down by the government.

Among those who gave explicit explanations for their being refused government positions for political reasons were two Republicans who had been rejected for patronage positions under a Democratic administration. This interpretation was not at all anticipated by the writers of the question. Thus, one of these professors explained:

> I was turned down for a job in Washington 20 years ago. I believe the grounds were political. They did not see how I could work on a job I had in Pennsylvania for so long without being a Republican and they did not want a Republican.

And another teacher among the minority who offered an explanation said:

> Yes, I was turned down for a job because I voted in the wrong primary.

Included among the thirty-five cases were some teachers who had belonged to radical organizations a number of years ago and had since developed a more conservative ideology. A few of these men explicitly cited their past association as the reason for their being refused a government job. An independent who had voted for Eisenhower and had been promised a government post which did not materialize explained:

> Thirty years ago I belonged to the Socialist Party that broke over Lenin's 21 points and became the Communist Labor Party. I couldn't get a job in government today for an indiscretion committed over thirty years ago.

The theme of "guilt by association" which was so highly publicized in many security hearings appears in the explanation of another teacher who answered "yes" to this question:

> Yes, I've been turned down. I always thought it was because my mother had been a member of the IWW in Massachusetts.

One respondent gave as the reason for his being turned down his current membership in a liberal organization:

> I have been denied in the past year provisional security clearance for the National War College because of my acknowledged membership in ADA and the American Civil Liberties Union.

Membership in pacifist organizations seems to be the reason for being turned down in some of these cases. One professor at an Eastern university cites his strong pacifist views along with his belief in socialism as the reason for his being refused clearance:

> I am a pacifist. The French government, Mexican government and others have begged me to work on research. I turned them down. The U.S. government with its present security checks wouldn't even consider me. I've always been a controversial figure—a pacifist and a socialist.

Some others who did not give explicit explanations for their affirmative answer mentioned elsewhere in their interviews membership in pacifist groups. A young historian at a Middle Atlantic college answered a question on whether he had ever been criticized for belonging to an organization by saying:

> I'd been a member of a pacifist group, the Fellowship of Reconciliation, during World War II and was criticized for it. I haven't been interested in pacifism since 1945, but it still affects my future.

Far from flushing out suspected Communists, the qualitative analysis of the 35 cases turned down for government posts uncovered Republicans who had patronage difficulties, ex-radicals whose youthful indiscretions were still being held against them, activists in liberal organizations and former and present pacifists.

SOME TECHNIQUES OF QUALITATIVE ANALYSIS

Selecting Cases for Analysis

As the preceding analysis makes clear, qualitative analysis carried out for interpretive purposes is almost always concerned with cases that are determined statistically. The cases to be analyzed are those which exhibit a response pattern of interest to the analyst. They may be located by a single variable or by a cross-tabulation of two or more variables. When qualitative analysis is carried out for *descriptive* purposes, the cases under examination are not determined beforehand. The analyst starts out with some theme in mind and searches the questionnaires for data which illustrate the theme. He may use check list responses as guides for locating potentially rich qualitative data but he is not limited to a particular set of questionnaires. For example, in order to find qualitative data illustrating the various ways in which professors became cautious, the analyst might start his search with those cases that scored very high on the apprehension index. But he is not committed to studying only these cases nor does he attempt to explain why these teachers are so apprehensive.

In some of the analyses described above, the number of cases exhibiting the response pattern of interest was so large that it was necessary to draw a sample for detailed analysis. This was true in the analysis of the deviant cases in the cross-tabulation of the two permissiveness indicators. In this instance, the cases that were examined were selected at random. A somewhat different approach seemed advisable when the analysis was undertaken to explain an unexpected correlation, such as the positive relationship between caution and activism. Here the response pattern of interest was exhibited by a majority of cases and consequently some sampling procedure was necessary. In order to minimize the likelihood of selecting cases which might be the result of coding errors, the analysis concentrated on "pure" cases—those teachers who were highly active and yet were also cautious.

Utilization of the Entire Questionnaire

The search for explanatory data was not limited to the spontaneous comments offered by the respondents to explain their checkmarks. In addition, the entire questionnaire was examined for data which might shed light on the problem. Frequently check list responses to other questions were used to provide a portrait of the teachers whose attitudes were under analysis. For example, it was often helpful to know whether the respondent was a Republican or a Democrat, apprehensive or nonapprehensive, young or old, a professor or an instructor, a newcomer or an oldtimer at his school, with or without tenure. By studying the entire questionnaire as a unit, it was frequently possible to form an image of the respondent and the forces impinging on him which would help explain the particular response pattern under analysis. While quantitative analysis consists of the simultaneous study of a few variables on a large number of cases, qualitative analysis of the kind we have been describing focuses upon a small number of cases and a large number of variables, approximating the "case history" technique.

The Subdivision of Cases into More Homogeneous Sub-Groups

A fairly common technique in these analyses was to use data not involved in the response pattern under study to sub-divide the cases into more homogeneous sub-groups. This procedure is the microscopic equivalent of introducing additional variables in traditional statistical analysis. Its purpose is to separate respondents who are likely to have different explanations for their response patterns.

One occasion on which this was done was in the analysis of the apprehensive teachers at nonapprehensive colleges. Preliminary analysis of these cases showed that a large number had been subjected to pressures. The question then arose as to whether they were different from their colleagues in this respect. While most were located at schools where hardly any teachers had been under attack, there were some who were at schools where at least a third of the teachers also reported pressures on them. The group was thus sub-divided according to whether they had colleagues who also had been attacked. For those who were virtually alone in being subjected to pressures, this fact alone would go a long way toward explaining their unusual apprehension. But additional factors would seem necessary to explain the high apprehension of those who had a number of colleagues who also experienced pressures and yet were not apprehensive. At this point the analysis was expanded to include the questionnaires of these colleagues. One impression gained from this analysis was that the pressures the colleagues had experienced were more vague and trivial than those exerted upon the highly apprehensive. The analysis was not extended beyond this point but further work might have uncovered differences in security and protection between the two groups. Tenure and length of stay at the college might have explained why some teachers under attack at these schools became very apprehensive while others did not.

Other Uses of Qualitative Analysis

The four reasons for turning to qualitative data in the course of a quantitative study which we have illustrated are not intended to be exhaustive. Other possibilities for qualitative analysis were suggested by the data of this study even though they were not carried out. For example, one intriguing problem which seems particularly suited to qualitative analysis would be the study of variations in accounts of the same incident by respondents at the same school. As is reported in *The Academic Mind*, an incident count for each school was obtained by pooling the observations of all the respondents at the school. In the course of this work it was noted that respondents varied considerably in how fully they reported the incident, what features of it they reported, their evaluation of it and, of course, whether they even recalled the incident. It was noticed, for example, that at schools where widely publicized incidents occurred, some teachers did not even mention the case. Qualitative analysis might well suggest explanations for the processes of selective perception at work in these accounts.

Qualitative Analysis Where the Units are Groups Rather Than Individuals

In all the examples of qualitative analysis that have been given, the units of analysis were individuals. But many of the same reasons for turning to qualitative data apply equally well where the units are groups. *The Academic Mind*, after all, is a study of colleges as well as teachers, and in a number of places tables are presented in which the units are schools. Just as individuals who are extreme or deviant can be studied qualitatively, so qualitative data can shed light on extreme or deviant schools. One important difference is that when the units of analysis are groups the level of explanation shifts from individual or psychological factors to social or structural ones. For example, suppose school rates of permissiveness and conservatism had been related in an ecological table.* Had we then found that there were some deviant schools that were high on both permissiveness and conservatism we could no longer be satisfied with an explanation that individuals happened to give special interpretations to the questions for these special interpretations would now be socially patterned. We would want to look for some structural characteristic of the school which would explain why the

*See Chapter 14 of this book for a discussion of ecological tables.

permissive faculty felt, for example, that a nonconformist teacher was a luxury that their school could not afford.

Qualitative data were, in fact, used on several occasions to analyze extreme and deviant schools. On page 165 in *The Academic Mind*, for example, a table is presented showing that the proportion of teachers who report pressure on the administration increases with the quality of the school. There is a slight reversal in this table, however. Teachers in the lowest quality schools report more pressure on their administration than teachers at the medium low quality schools. The schools in the lowest quality group with high rates of pressure on the administration were identified and it was found that they tended to be either Negro colleges in the South or large but comparatively poor private universities located in big cities, the commuter colleges. It was conjectured that the integration issue in the South and the dependency of the "streetcar" colleges on local money accounted for the reports of pressure on the administrations of these schools.

═══════════════

The Academic Mind study was done in the mid-fifties and the Green–Caplovitz paper was written in 1959. Like many other papers produced at Columbia by graduate students at that time, it was never published. The pattern was to produce papers for internal consumption only. Lazarsfeld's work on qualitative analysis in quantitative studies did not spread to other institutions and since the world did not know about the Green–Caplovitz paper, hardly any quantitative researchers have followed in Lazarsfeld's footsteps in doing qualitative analysis to help interpret quantitative findings. Perhaps the situation will now change.

PART THREE

Data Analysis

Data analysis is a topic covered in all research methods texts, yet even this part of the book has unique features. Chapter 8 deals with an important topic that is not dealt with in other texts: the presentation of tables. The novice does not know how to convert data into tables and this chapter is designed to teach him how. This is, of course, extremely elementary and yet my students over the years have appreciated its themes very much, as well may the readers of this text.

Chapter 9 deals with the Columbia tradition of index construction. It reviews the principles of index construction and introduces Lazarsfeld's idea of the interchangeability of indices. It then contrasts indices with typologies. It presents some new ideas on the origins of typologies and their functions in social research. Chapter 10 is on bivariate analysis and deals with the common themes of statistical significance and correlation. It also takes up a seldom discussed topic, the time order of the two variables under analysis.

Chapter 11 is about multivariate analysis—the effects of introducing a third variable into the analysis. This chapter presents an improvement on Lazarsfeld's elaboration scheme by identifying a third outcome apart from interpretation and specification, what Rosenberg labels "distortion or suppression."* It presents a way of showing the outcomes of elaboration that is an alternative to Lazarsfeld's famous fourfold table.

Chapter 12 pays homage to the modern technique of regression analysis, which was ignored in the Columbia tradition. Since I am a product of that

*Morris Rosenberg, *The Logic of Survey Analysis*, New York: Basic Books, 1968.

tradition, I did not feel comfortable enough to write this chapter myself and I commissioned a colleague, Mark Gallops, to write it. I am extremely grateful to him for carrying out this task so well. This chapter is intended to provide some balance to the discussion of tabular analysis in the preceding chapters.

Chapter 13 treats longitudinal research design by examining three longitudinal studies, the trend study, the cohort study, and the panel study. The complexities of panel analysis are reviewed.

Finally Chapter 14 deals with the analysis of group properties, notably, contextual analysis. It is based largely on a paper I wrote in 1956. It, too, is innovative in that it identifies a heretofore unanalyzed fallacy—the opposite of Robinson's ecological fallacy—what might be called the contextual fallacy.

8

The Presentation of Tables

Tables are devices for organizing research findings and communicating them to readers. They tell us about the distribution of the cases under study in terms of one or more dimensions, called *variables*. The concept of a variable is perhaps the most basic of all research concepts. It is used continuously by all researchers. With this in mind, it is perhaps a good idea to make this concept clear at the outset before we consider the transformation of variables into tables.

The term variable refers to a property of the units under study. The property is one that varies from one unit to another in that one unit may have more or less of the property than another unit. A *variable* is contrasted with a *constant*. A constant is a property shared by all the units under study. For example, all the people in a survey share the properties of being human beings, alive, breathing air, eating food. Such properties are constants rather than variables. Scientists have little interest in studying constants.*
Rather they want to study properties that vary from one unit to another and show the relationships that exist among such varying properties. If property X increases, will property Y increase? This is the basic concern of the researcher.

TYPES OF VARIABLES AND SCALES

Variables can be thought of as *classificatory schemes*, schemes for classifying the units under study in terms of a given property. These classificatory

*Some constants, however, such as the family and the the incest taboo, have attracted considerable attention in social science.

schemes consist of a set of categories into which the units are classified. Suppose, for example, one were interested in classifying a national sample of people according to the state in which they live. Such a classificatory scheme would consist of 50 categories, each category representing one of the 50 states. Or suppose the classificatory scheme refers to the variable of sex. Such a scheme would have two categories, male and female, and individuals would be classified into one or the other of these categories depending on their sex.

A classificatory scheme sometimes is called a *scale*, which for most purposes can be treated as a synonym for variable. The variables or scales that social researchers work with are of different types. In a classic article, psychologist S. S. Stevens developed a theory of scales in which he delineates four basic types.* According to Stevens, a scale is a series of numbers assigned to objects according to a rule. The most simple type of scale is the *nominal* scale, a scale in which names are assigned to different objects. The rule in a nominal scale is to assign the same name to objects that are alike and different names to objects that are different. In the nominal scale, the numbers stand for names and have no other meaning. For example, if the problem is to classify people according to the state in which they live, then the first state alphabetically, Alabama, would be assigned the number 1 and the last state, Wyoming, would be assigned the number 50.

A second type of scale, more powerful than the nominal scale, is the *ordinal* scale. The rule for classifying objects in terms of an ordinal scale is to assign a higher number to objects that have more of the property and a lower number to objects that have less of the property. An example of an ordinal scale is the system used for measuring the hardness of minerals. When two minerals are rubbed together, the one that scratches the other is harder and is assigned the higher number, signifying greater hardness. Ordinal scales are used frequently in social science to measure such traits as liberal–conservatism, anxiety, alienation, democracy–authoritarianism, cohesion, and most other social and psychological concepts. On ordinal scales, objects are ordered in terms of more or less, but we do not know how much more or how much less because we do not know the distance between the various scale scores, only that one represents more or less than the other. For example, the true distances between the scale scores might look like this: 1 2   3   4   5 6 or like this: 1   2 3   45   6. With ordinal scales we cannot say that one object has twice as much of the property as another object or three units more of the property than another object.

The next higher order of scale, one in which the distances between the scale scores is known, is the *interval* scale. The problem in creating an interval scale is determining the equality of intervals or differences. The

---

*S. S. Stevens, "On the Theory of Scales of Measurement," *Science* **103**, No. 2684, 677–680, (June 7, 1946).

numbers of an interval scale represent quantities of the property being measured. For example, an object that scores 3 on an interval scale has one more unit of the property than an object that scores 2 and two fewer than an object that scores 5, and so forth, and the units are equivalent. With interval scales it becomes possible for the first time to compute averages. With nominal scales, the only appropriate measure of central tendency is the *mode*, the category with the largest number of cases. With ordinal scales it is possible to compute *medians*, that is, locate the case separating the upper 50 percent from the lower 50 percent. But only with interval scales is it possible to add the scale scores of the various objects and then divide by the number of objects to compute the *mean*, or *average*.

The fourth type of scale is the *ratio* scale, the most powerful of all scales. In addition to having all the properties of an interval scale, the ratio scale has an absolute zero point. Temperature, whether Centigrade or Fahrenheit, is measured by an interval scale because the zero points in these scales are arbitrary. They do not signify no heat at all. But ratio scales have true zero points as in measures of time, weight, distance, and size. With ratio scales it becomes possible for the first time to make ratio statements. For example, a group with 50 people is twice as large as a group with 25 people. A movie that lasts one hour is only one third as long as a movie that lasts three hours. The numbers of a ratio scale take on new meaning. They now stand for given quantities of the property being measured. An object that scores 2 on a ratio scale has two units of the property and an object that scores 4 has four units, or twice as many, as an object that scores 2. Ratio scales in social research include income, years of schooling, and group size.

When doing research, it is always important to know what kind of scale each variable represents, for the kinds of statistical manipulation that can be done depend on the scale.

TABLES

The simplest table reports the distribution of cases on only a single dimension or variable. For example, the responses to any question asked in a survey might be conveyed in a table which shows the number or percentage of respondents who gave each possible answer to the question. Suppose the question asked the respondents to report their religion and the responses were classified into five categories: Protestant, Catholic, Jewish, Other, and None. The responses could then be shown in a one-dimensional table as in Table 8.1. This one-dimensional or single-variable table conveys concisely and clearly the religious composition of the sample. We learn at a glance that Protestants comprise the majority, that Catholics are the next largest religious group, that only 3 percent of the sample belongs to some other religion, and that atheism is limited to a mere 4 percent of the total group. This one-dimensional or single-variable table also has two essential ingre-

Table 8.1. The
Distribution of
Respondents on Religion

Protestant	59%
Catholic	27
Jewish	7
Other	3
None	4
$N = 1000$	100%

dients of all tables—a total percentage and the base figure on which the percentages were calculated. We learn that the response categories are exhaustive, totaling 100 percent, and that the entire sample consisted of 1000 people, a number more than large enough to yield stable percentages.

The one-dimensional table is a rarity in social research. The results of a single distribution are so easy to communicate to the reader that the device of a table is in most instances not necessary. Instead of using a table, the researcher can report the religious distribution of the sample in a simple sentence: "On religion, we find that 58 percent of the sample is Protestant, 27 percent Catholic, 7 percent Jewish, 3 percent belong to some other religion, and 4 percent have no religious affiliation at all."

Whereas the distribution of cases on a single variable can easily be reported in the text, this is not true of distributions in terms of two or more variables. To show how the sample is distributed on two or more variables, it is almost always necessary to resort to the table format. Examining the distribution of cases on two variables, in what is known as a cross-tabulation, is the heart of the basic task of the researcher: establishing causal connections among variables. Most research is carried out to shed light on the causes of some phenomenon or the consequences of some phenomenon, and to study causes and consequences it is essential to relate one variable to another. The table is an ideal format for communicating the extent to which two or more variables are related.

An example of the distribution of cases on two variables is seen in Table 8.2. In this hypothetical example, each of the two variables is an ordinal scale consisting of three categories. The totals appearing on the right and at the bottom tell us how many cases were classified as low, medium, and high on each variable. These distributions on each variable appear in the *margins* of the table and, for this reason, the convention has developed to refer to the distribution of cases on single variables as *the marginals*. Before a researcher starts to analyze data by relating variables to each other, he or she spends some time becoming oriented to the data by studying the marginals. The marginals in a survey are typically reported in a code book. The code book reports the location of the data in columns and punches of IBM cards and the distribution of the cases in the various categories on each item or question.

Table 8.2 reports the number of cases in each cell of the table, the cells representing particular combinations of variable X and variable Y. For example, we see that 60 of the 300 cases are low on both variable X and variable Y and 20 are low on X and high on Y. At the other extreme, 30 cases are low on Y and high on X and 45 cases are high on both X and Y. Since the number of cases in each category on each variable varies, it is extremely difficult to study relationships from the number of cases alone. For example, is 60 out of 110 much greater or only slightly greater than 40 out of 95 cases? To study relationships from tables, it is necessary for the researcher to compare the distribution of cases in the various categories of the independent variable. In Table 8.2 we want to know whether Y increases as X increases, that is, does the frequency of cases in the high category on Y increase as we move from the low to the high category on X? In this example, the answer is obviously yes, since the number of cases high on Y increases from 20 to 45 as we move from low to high on X. But how much of an increase has occurred? Given the different number of cases in the X categories, it is extremely difficult to tell from the raw numbers alone. To make the comparisons easier, it is necessary to standardize the raw numbers and make them comparable. This is done by converting them to percentages based on the number of cases in each category. Percentages tell us the rates per 100 for each category of the independent variable (in this example, variable X). Table 8.3 presents the data of Table 8.2 in percentage form.

Table 8.2. **Variable Y by Variable X**

		X		
Y	Low	Medium	High	Total
Low	60	40	30	130
Medium	30	20	20	70
High	20	35	45	100
Total N	110	95	95	300

Table 8.3. **Variable Y by Variable X**

		X	
Y	Low	Medium	High
Low	54%	45%	32%
Medium	27	22	21
High	19	37	47
	100%	100%	100%
N	(110)	(95)	(95)

By converting the raw numbers to percentages, we have standardized the data and have made it possible to compare the columns. As we read across the third row we see that the percentage of those high on variable Y steadily increases as the value of variable X increases. This indicates a positive relationship between variable X and variable Y, and the overall percentage difference of 28 points (47 minus 19) suggests that this is a fairly strong relationship. (In many surveys, a percentage difference of lesser magnitude is common.) Comparing Tables 8.2 and 8.3, we find that in Table 8.3 the row totals are omitted. Omitting these totals is pretty much the norm when presenting tables designed to show relationships between variables. The critical numbers are the percentages showing the relationship and the base figures on which these percentages are computed. Since in Table 8.3 the percentages were computed in the columns rather than the rows, the column Ns appear rather than the row Ns. When percentages are computed on the column Ns, the findings of the table emerge by reading across the rows. The reverse is true when the percentages are computed on the row Ns. In that case the findings emerge by reading down the columns. When the percentages total to 100 for each column, the findings appear when comparing the different categories on the independent variable, that is, by comparing the columns by reading across the rows of percentages.

A common mistake of novices is to read down the columns of percentages and to compare percentages within the same column. For example, the novice might note that almost three times as many of the low cases of variable X are low on variable Y as are high on variable Y (comparing 54 percent and 19 percent in the first column). Although true, this observation has nothing to do with the relationship between variable X and variable Y, the presentation of which is the purpose of the table. That relationship emerges only by comparing the different values on variable X, that is, comparing the different columns with regard to a given value of variable Y. In discussing the finding of Table 8.3,we focused on the percentage high on variable Y and how this varied with the value of variable X. We could have presented pretty much the same finding by focusing on the percentage low on variable Y. In most instances, the pattern at one extreme (e.g., high on variable Y) will be the reverse of the pattern at the other extreme (e.g., low on variable Y). Just as the percentage who are high on variable Y increases as X increases, so the percentage who are low on Y decreases as X increases.

Although in most instances the patterns for the two extreme categories will be the reverse of each other, in a few instances the researcher will find that the pattern signifying a relationship is much more pronounced at one extreme than at the other. In such an event the researcher must consider how best to report the finding. Findings emerge from the patterns shown at the extremes. The middle categories, which vary little, do not show the finding and in most instances can be safely ignored. A common error of novices is to talk about the differences that emerge not only at each extreme of the dependent variable, but in the middle categories as well. Typically, they will observe that major percentage differences emerge in the low and high categories of the dependent variable but not in the middle category. The rare instance in which the relationship between X and Y is curvilinear rather than linear must be considered, however. In a curvilinear relationship the middle categories are either larger or smaller than the extreme categories. Curvilinear relationships do exist in reality and frequently are important. For example, the notion that too much or too little of something is harmful implies a curvilinear relationship.

Before leaving Table 8.3, it should be noted that the variables are clearly labeled and that the table has a title. Table 8.3 was set up so that variable X is the independent variable on which the percentages were computed and variable Y is the dependent variable. The independent variable is the presumed causal variable and the dependent variable the presumed effect. Tables are always percentaged on the independent variable. Some researchers prefer to percentage their tables on the rows and hence will have the independent variable go to the left side of the table and the dependent variable across the top. But most researchers adhere to the convention adopted here of having the independent variable across the top and the dependent variable down the side, with the finding emerging by comparing the columns. In the title of Table 8.3, the dependent variable appears first and is linked to the independent variable by the word "by" or some other connective phrase such as "according to." This is a very common format for the table title, that is, simply identifying in the title the variables presented in the table. But some researchers prefer jazzier titles and will make the key finding of the table the basis of the table title. For example, the table might show that better educated people earn more money than poorly educated people, and the researcher would use this statement for the table title: "Better Educated People Earn More than Poorly Educated People." Not all tables report relationships, however, and the novice is advised to use the more neutral format of identifying the variables in the table title.

In addition to naming the variables in the title of the table, it is important to identify the categories of the variables (low, medium, and high in Table 8.3) and to have the name of the variable appear above the names of the categories. For example, the X that appears above the column labels in Table 8.3 might be Education, and the Y that appears above the row labels might be Income. In this instance, the table title would be Income by Education, and the column categories would be headed by Education and the row categories by Income. Properly labeling the variables in a table and identifying the variables in the table title are very important to the communication process, and judging from students I have had through the years many novices err in failing to label their variables properly.

THE PROBLEM OF SMALL *N*s (CASE BASES)

Tabular analysis requires large samples of cases. Most sophisticated analyses require at least 500 cases, although many studies using tables are based on samples of 200 or 300 cases. Below 200 cases, the researcher runs into the problem of small base figures, which make the percentages unreliable. For example, a three-variable table in which the two independent variables are trichotomies would result in breaking up the sample into nine subclasses. If these subclasses were of equal size, which rarely is the case, then a sample of 200 cases would be divided into nine subgroups of 22 cases each. An *N* of 22 may be too small to yield stable percentages. Each case in such a sample would represent almost 5 percentage points, and if a few cases were misclassified, this would result in an error of 10 to 15 percentage points, an error sufficiently large to create the erroneous impression of a significant finding or vitiate a finding that would actually be significant if the errors were removed.

The question then arises as to how large the *N* should be to justify percentaging. There is no clear answer to this question. Virtually all researchers agree that it is foolish to percentage on an *N* of less than 10 since each case would represent more than 10 percentage points. Many researchers will percentage on *N*s of 10 or more, and many have more stringent rules, not percentaging unless they have 15 or 20 or 30 cases.

What should the researcher do if the base figure in one table is too small to yield stable percentages, say fewer than 10 or 15 cases? Several conventions have developed for handling this problem. One is to present an asterisk instead of a percentage next to the base figure. Another is to present the percentage in parentheses, which indicate that the percentage is not stable. Still a third convention employed by many researchers is to present the raw number in brackets instead of the percentage. For example, suppose the base figure is 9 and 5 of these 9 cases manifested the property in question. The results might be presented as follows:

$$
\begin{array}{cc}
* & (9) \\
(56\%) & (9) \\
[5] & (9)
\end{array}
$$

Whichever convention is employed, the base figure is always shown in parentheses. The asterisk signifies a base figure too small for percentaging; the parentheses, a percentage that is unstable; and the brackets, the number of cases that manifest the trait.

We may now summarize the foregoing principles of table presentation:

1. Convert raw numbers to percentages and present percentages in your table. Never present the raw numbers.
2. Always present the totals for the percentages, usually 100 percent, but sometimes 99 or 101 percent due to rounding.

3. Always show the number of cases on which the percentages are computed.

4. Every table must have a title, usually composed of the names of the variables presented in the table.

5. Identify the dependent variable first in the table title, followed by the names of the independent variable or variables; for example, Income by Education and Occupation (a three-variable table).

6. Present the independent variable in the columns of the table (across the top) and the dependent variable in the rows (down the side).

7. Read the table by comparing columns, that is, by reading across the rows.

8. If the dependent variable has more than two categories, as in Table 8.3, focus on the patterns at the extremes, either the percentage low on the dependent variable or the percentage high on the dependent variable.

9. Never percentage on an *N* less than 10. When *N*s are under 15 use an asterisk rather than percentage, or put percentage in parentheses or put raw number in brackets followed by base figure in parentheses.

FROM COMPUTER OUTPUT TO TABLE

A table like Table 8.3 is specially prepared by the researcher to maximize the process of communication with the reader. Like all communications, tables are effective only if they clearly state their message with a minimum of extraneous data (noise). Just as effective prose must avoid unnecessary words, so tables, which rely on numbers to communicate messages, must avoid all unnecessary numbers. And just as words must be arranged in a logical fashion to communicate messages, so the numbers of a table must be arranged in a logical fashion. The tables that researchers present in their reports are generated in the modern world by computers. Researchers instruct the computer to print out the tables that they want. The computers have been programmed to generate the maximum possible information for the researcher and the tables that are printed out by the computer contain much more information than the researcher wants to communicate to readers. The good researcher knows how to study the computer's output and extract from it the appropriate information for a table. In short, a computer's table is cluttered with all kinds of information that is not germane to the researcher.

Table 8.4 is an example of a raw table generated by a computer. This table is based on the annual NORC survey and shows the relationship between education and attitude toward abortion (this attitude being measured by an index explained in the next chapter). Each of the two variables, education and abortion attitude, is trichotomized, yielding a ninefold table. As can be seen from Table 8.4, this ninefold table as developed by the computer has 50

Table 8.4.   Attitude Toward Abortion by Education (As Produced by the Computer)[a]

ABORTATT FREQUENCY PERCENT ROW PCT COL PCT	EDUC < H.S.	HIGHEST H.S.	SCHOOL SOME COL LEGE	YEAR COMPLETED TOTAL
ANTI	151 9.90 39.95 31.13	128 8.39 33.86 23.66	99 6.49 26.19 19.80	378 24.77
MIXED	197 12.91 36.08 40.62	208 13.63 38.10 38.45	141 9.24 25.82 28.20	546 35.78
PRO	137 8.98 22.76 28.25	205 13.43 34.05 37.89	260 17.04 43.19 52.00	602 39.45
TOTAL	485 31.78	541 35.45	500 32.77	1526 100.00

[a]Notice how the computer identifies in the upper-left-hand corner the numbers that appear in the cells of the table. The first number is the count; the second, the total percentage; the third, the row percentage; and the fourth, the column percentage.

numbers. In the lower right hand corner is the number standing for the number of cases in the study, in this instance 1526, and below it is the number 100 percent. At the bottom of the table are the column totals and the percentage of the total number of cases each column total represents. For example, the table shows that 485 of the total sample of 1526 had low education and that this group represents 31.8 percent of the total sample. On the far right are the row totals, that is, the number of cases in each category of the dependent variable, and below these totals are the numbers that tell us what percentage of the total these row totals represent. Each cell of the table contains four numbers. The first of these is the number of cases that fall into that cell. The next three numbers in the cells are percentages. The second number represents the row percentage, that is, it tells us the percentage that the number of cases in that cell represent, based on the N for that row. The third number in the cell represents the column percentage. Just as the row percentages add to 100 across each row, so the column percentages add to 100 down each column. The fourth number in each cell represents the percentage of the total number of cases in the table that appear in that cell. These total percentages are calculated on the total N that appears in the lower right of the table. Researchers are seldom interested in these total percentages, and they may even instruct the computer not to bother to print them out. Of the four numbers that appear in each cell, only one of them is important to the researcher who wants to show the relationship between variables. If, as is the convention, the table is set up so that the independent variable is across the top, with each column representing a value of the independent variable, then the researcher is concerned only with the column percentages, the third number that appears in the table cells. The row percentage, like the total percentage, is of no value. Furthermore, the researcher is not interested in the raw number of cases that appears in each cell. A common error made by novices is to report these raw Ns alongside the percentages in their tables. This is a most serious error that should be avoided at all costs. Never show the raw N corresponding to the percentage. Given the base figures and the percentages, the curious can always calculate these raw Ns, but to present them in the table is to clutter up the table with noise.

Of the 50 numbers generated by the computer, the researcher is interested in only 12—the nine column percentages and the three column Ns. Table 8.5 shows how these numbers are used in the table that is prepared for the research report. Compare Table 8.5 with the computer output in Table 8.4. The computer felt free to abbreviate the variable labels, but abbreviations should not be used when presenting tables to readers of research reports. Second, percent signs appear in the top row of Table 8.5 to alert the reader to the fact that these numbers are percentages. It is not necessary to present the percent sign next to all the other numbers in the table. The major difference between Table 8.5 and Table 8.4 is that the computer presents percentages in one decimal point, whereas the researcher ignores this spurious refinement and, to facilitate communication, rounds off the percentages to the nearest whole number.

As for the finding in Table 8.5, by reading across the rows of the table (comparing the columns) we find that attitude toward abortion is very much related to education. As education increases, so does a favorable attitude toward legal abortion. As the comparison of Tables 8.4 and 8.5 shows, there is a world of difference between the computer's table and the researcher's table. The researcher, to maximize communication, extracts the relevant numbers from the vast array for presentation to the reader.

Table 8.5. Attitude toward Abortion by Education

Attitude toward Abortion	Education		
	Less than High School	High School	Some College
Anti-abortion	31%	24%	20%
Mixed	41	38	28
Pro-abortion	28	38	52
	100%	100%	100%
N	(485)	(541)	(500)

PRESENTATION OF THREE-VARIABLE TABLES

Thus far we have dealt with the presentation of two-variable tables. To understand the dynamics of the relationships uncovered, researchers frequently find it necessary to introduce third variables into their analysis. For example, the researcher might want to know how the relationship between education and abortion attitude is affected by the respondent's religion. Will education make as much difference for Catholics as for Protestants and Jews? To answer this question the researcher must elaborate the two-variable relationship by introducing religion as a third variable, as is done in Table 8.6.

In Table 8.6, the relationship between education and attitude toward abortion is shown separately for each religious group. Whereas it takes only a single page of computer output for a computer to print out the results of a two-variable table, a three-variable table usually takes as many pages of computer output as there are categories on the third variable—in this instance three, one page for each religion. There are very few Jews in the NORC survey and almost all of them strongly support abortion, especially those who have had a college education. Studying the rows of Table 8.6 shows that education has a very different impact on attitude toward abortion for Protestants and Catholics. As education increases among Protestants, favorable attitudes toward abortion increase. But among Catholics the well educated are more opposed to abortion than the poorly educated. At the other extreme, the pro-legal abortion attitude among Catholics is unaffected by education.

Table 8.6 is a complex table to read. As it is set up, it is fairly easy to see the impact of education on attitude toward abortion, but it is difficult to compare the religious groups. Do Protestants or Catholics have more favorable attitudes toward legal abortion? To answer this question it is necessary to compare comparable columns in the different parts of the table. To facilitate

Table 8.6. *Attitude toward Abortion by Education and Religion*

	Religion								
	Protestant			Catholic			Jewish		
Education:	Low	Medium	High	Low	Medium	High	Low	Medium	High
Abortion attitude									
Anti	33%	23%	17%	28%	31%	38%	—	—	—
Mixed	42	39	33	39	40	30	(1)	50%	—
Pro	25	38	50	33	29	32	(3)	50	100%
	100%	100%	100%	100%	100%	100%		100%	100%
N	(352)	(336)	(289)	(103)	(154)	(126)	(4)	(8)	(16)

the reading of such a complicated table, the convention has developed to present the results in an abbreviated fashion. Where the dependent variable is an ordinal scale, as in this instance, it is always possible to collapse the distribution into two groups, for example, those who are pro-legal abortion versus all the others (grouping the anti- and mixed groups). When this is done, a table can be set up showing only the percentage in one of the dichotomous categories, say, the percentage pro-legal abortion. By dichotomizing the dependent variable and showing the percentage in one category, the data in Table 8.6 can be greatly simplifed, as shown in Table 8.7.

The meaning of the percentages is provided in the title of the table which has the phrase "percentage pro." The base figures that appeared at the bottom of the columns in Table 8.6 now appear in parentheses next to the percentages signifying pro-legal abortion attitude. The findings of Table 8.6 are now easily read by reading across the rows and down the columns of Table 8.7. The columns show the impact of education on abortion attitude when religion is held constant. The rows permit us to compare the religions when education is held constant. From the first column we see that pro-legal abortion attitudes increase among Protestants with education. But the second column shows that education is not related to pro-legal abortion attitude among Catholics. The rows of Table 8.7 tell an interesting story. Among the poorly educated, Catholics turn out to be more pro-abortion than Protestants. But among those of moderate education and the well educated, Protestants are more pro abortion than Catholics. In fact, as education increases, the dominance of Protestants over the Catholics in the pro-legal abortion camp increases, as the gap between Protestants and Catholics is wider among the well educated than the moderately educated.

An abbreviated table such as Table 8.7 sacrifices information in order to increase communication. In this instance we do not know about the people who are anti-abortion or have a mixed view of abortion. In most instances, little information is lost in the abbreviated table, as the pattern at one extreme (e.g., pro-legal abortion) is almost always the reverse of the pattern at the other extreme. In this table, this is true for the Protestants, in that the pro-legal abortion attitude increases with education and the anti-attitude declines with education. But this is not true for the Catholics. Whereas the

Table 8.7.   Percentage Pro-Abortion by Education and Religion

Education	Religion		
	Protestant	Catholic	Jewish
Low	25% (352)	33% (103)	3% (4)
Medium	38% (336)	29% (154)	50% (8)
High	50% (289)	32% (126)	100% (16)

pro-legal abortion percentages show no relationship between education and attitude, the anti- figures increase with education. The abbreviated three-variable table is so easy to read that most researchers prefer it to the more cumbersome complete table like Table 8.6, even though some information is lost.

A TYPOLOGY OF TABLES

The reader of research reports will frequently come across tables very different from Tables 8.5, 8.6 and 8.7. All the tables presented thus far in this chapter show the relationship between two or more properties of the cases in the sample. The Ns in these tables add up to the total sample size minus the no-answers. These tables are examples of unit tables, or what might be called "table-tables." But sometimes the researcher will combine a set of discrete tables into a single table. This can reduce the number of tables in a report, making the document more readable to the lay public and more appealing to publishers, who frown on tables because they increase costs. This can also call attention to the patterns shown by the discrete tables bearing on the same topic. Further, a single table contrasts the discrete tables, highlighting the differences between them. Such tables, which consist of several unit tables, might be called multi-tables, or "multi-table-tables." Table 8.8 is an example of such a multi-table.

Table 8.8 presents four unit tables in a single-table format. To facilitate the presentation, it was necessary to reverse the common order of the independent and dependent variables. The dependent variable is listed across the top and the independent variables down the side. In these four unit tables, the dependent variable is the same, a measure of inflation crunch, and the independent variables represent different social characteristics. The tables are linked in that they bear on the same theme: the more underprivileged groups were hardest hit by inflation.

Table 8.8 presents a cluster of two-variable tables. Even more complicated tables can be presented in a multi-table format. Table 8.9 on page 206, is an example of a cluster of three-variable tables presented under a single table heading.

These tables consist of three variables each—a coping strategy, inflation crunch dichotomized into low and high, and race-ethnicity. The three-variable tables are presented in the abbreviated form, showing only the percentage high on the strategy, and the base figures are presented below.

Multi-tables such as Tables 8.8 and 8.9 are great conservors of space and thus highly functional to an author who wants to avoid burdening a report with excessive tables. Were each of the unit tables in Tables 8.8 and 8.9 presented separately, they would amount to nine tables.

A third type of table sometimes encountered in research reports involves less than the full sample, what might be called a partial table. Whereas a unit table is based on 100 percent of the cases and a multi-table is comprised of

Table 8.8. **Subjective Inflation Crunch by (A) Subsample, (B) Income, (C) Occupation, and (D) Race-Ethnicity**[a]

	Subjective Inflation Crunch					
	Low	Medium Low	Medium High	High		N
A. Subsample						
Poor	6%	11	26	58	100%	(323)
Blue collar	14%	26	23	37	100%	(581)
White collar	34%	29	19	18	100%	(769)
Retired	31%	24	24	21	100%	(309)
B. Income						
Under $7,000	9%	14	26	51	100%	(395)
$7,000–12,999	14%	21	24	41	100%	(390)
$13,000–19,999	20%	27	24	29	100%	(435)
$20,000 and over	38%	33	18	11	100%	(462)
C. Occupation						
Higher white collar	33%	30	18	18	99%	(680)
Lower white collar	34%	23	22	21	100%	(296)
Higher blue collar	14%	26	24	36	100%	(344)
Lower blue collar	12%	18	25	45	100%	(662)
D. Race-Ethnicity						
White	28%	27	21	24	100%	(1,464)
Black	10%	15	26	49	100%	(407)
Spanish-speaking	3%	17	18	61	99%	(88)

[a]From David Caplovitz, *Making Ends Meet: The Impact of Inflation and Recession on Families,* Beverly Hills, California: Sage Publications, 1979, p. 47.

subtables, each of which accounts for 100 percent of the cases, a partial table adds to less than 100 percent. Partial tables are employed when either the independent or dependent variable is made up of many subdivisions or categories. Rather than take on such a complex table that might spread over more than one page, the researcher breaks up the table and shows each of its component parts as a separate table. In a study of apostasy among college graduates, I wanted to show apostasy rates for different types of school. Schools were subdivided into 13 types and rather than present all 13 in a single table, I divided them into three groups, those representing low apostasy rates, those with average apostasy rates, and those with above-average apostasy rates. Each of these subtypes became a separate table (see Tables 8.10, 8.11, and 8.12 on the following pages).

Table 8.10 was discussed and then Table 8.11, representing college types with medium apostasy rates, was presented. Finally, the high-apostasy schools were shown in Table 8.12. It is important to keep in mind that Tables 8.10, 8.11, and 8.12 are really parts of a single-unit table, with each of these

Table 8.9. Strategies for Coping with Inflation by Race/Ethnicity and Subjective Crunch (Percentage High on Strategy)[a]

	Race-Ethnicity		
Coping Strategy	White	Black	Spanish-Speaking
1. Income raising			
Low crunch	25%	21%	39%
High crunch	51	51	44
2. Curtailed expenditures			
Low crunch	30	28	39
High crunch	78	72	68
3. Self-reliance			
Low crunch	25	39	33
High crunch	55	67	77
4. Bargain hunting			
Low crunch	11	18	17
High crunch	55	78	71
5. Sharing			
Low crunch	35	30	61
High crunch	54	52	60
N Low crunch	(812)	(102)	(18)
High crunch	(652)	(305)	(70)

[a]From David Caplovitz, *Making Ends Meet: The Impact of Inflation and Recession on Families*, Beverly Hills, California: Sage Publications, 1979, p. 113.

partial tables representing about a third of the total sample. By breaking up such a complex table into three partial tables, the researcher maintains greater control of the data. Low-apostasy schools can be discussed without the distraction of the medium- and high-apostasy schools. And the reader can be led gradually to the most critical part of the larger table, the subtypes with very high apostasy rates.

Partial tables were also employed in a study that I carried out of consumers who were sued for not maintaining payments on their installment purchases. A major concern of the study was the reasons why consumers

Table 8.10. Apostasy by Religion at Types of Schools with Low Apostasy Rates[a]

School Type	Jewish Rate	Protestant Rate	Catholic Rate	Total School Rate
Catholic colleges	2% (43)	8% (72)	1% (3,630)	1% (3,567)
Teachers colleges	2% (43)	7% (477)	7% (712)	7% (712)
Southern colleges	10% (259)	6% (4,439)	8% (474)	6% (5,172)
Protestant colleges	17% (29)	6% (1,562)	8% (161)	6% (1,752)

[a]From David Caplovitz, *The Religious Dropouts: Apostasy among College Graduates*. Beverly Hills, California: Sage Publications, 1977, p. 113.

Table 8.11. Apostasy by Religion at Types of Schools with Medium Apostasy Rates[a]

School Type	Jewish Rate		Protestant Rate		Catholic Rate		Total School Rate	
Big-city commuter colleges	12%	(1,540)	12%	(1,823)	10%	(1,248)	11%	(4,611)
Midwest/West public	14%	(319)	13%	(5,611)	10%	(1,101)	12%	(7,031)
Middle Atlantic	10%	(113)	10%	(547)	11%	(239)	11%	(899)
Midwest private	13%	(77)	17%	(415)	10%	(80)	15%	(572)
Engineering	13%	(251)	20%	(673)	13%	(433)	16%	(1,357)

[a]From David Caplovitz, *The Religious Dropout: Apostasy among College Graduates*, Beverly Hills, California: Sage Publications, 1977, p. 114.

had stopped paying. The reasons were obtained from several open-ended questions that appeared in the interview schedule. Reasons were initially divided into two very broad categories, those relating to the debtor's mishaps and shortcomings and those which related to the creditor/seller. Within these broad categories, further categories of reasons were delineated. For example, reasons where the debtor was at fault included such categories as loss of income, voluntary overextension, involuntary overextension, marital instability, debtor's third parties, and debtor irresponsibility. Within these categories still more specific reasons were classified. Some five chapters of the book were devoted to describing these reasons for the default. Each of these chapters began with partial tables, showing the distributions of reasons under the more general headings. For example, reasons for default relating to loss of income, one of 13 general categories of reasons, generated Table 8.13. These percentages total to 51 percent, rather than 100 percent, because there are 12 other major categories of reasons apart from loss of income. These percentages were calculated on the N for the total sample, 1326, and the 51 percent represented 665 of the total cases. The reasons for the presentation of partial tables are even more compelling here than in the apostasy study. Whereas in the apostasy study colleges

Table 8.12. Apostasy by Religion at Types of Schools with High Apostasy Rates[a]

School Type	Jewish Rate		Protestant Rate		Catholic Rate		Total School Rate	
Ivy league colleges	15%	(562)	23%	(1,056)	23%	(299)	20%	(1,917)
Small high quality colleges	28%	(101)	22%	(696)	26%	(77)	23%	(874)
Major California universities	23%	(190)	28%	(805)	25%	(197)	27%	(1,192)

[a]From David Caplovitz, *The Religious Dropouts: Apostasy among College Graduates*, Beverly Hills, California: Sage Publications, 1977, p. 114.

Table 8.13. **Types of Income Loss as Reason for Default**[a]

Reason	Percentage
Loss of job	26%
Illness to chief wage earner	16%
Loss of secondary wage earner's income	5%
Debtor goes on welfare	1%
Business failure	2%
Debtor goes to jail	—
Loss of supplementary income	—
All other reasons for loss of income	—
	51%
Subtotal of cases	(665)
Total cases	(1,326)

[a]Reprinted with permission of Macmillan Publishing Co., Inc. from *Consumers in Trouble* by David Caplovitz. Copyright © 1974 by The Free Press, a Division of Macmillan Publishing Co., Inc.

were divided into 13 types, in the debtor study 13 major categories of reasons were further subdivided into a total of 53 specific categories of reasons. Clearly, it would have been extremely difficult to present a variable with 53 categories in a single table. Moreover, since each of the various reasons chapters in the report dealt with one of the major categories of reasons, it was relevant to show in tabular form the more specific reasons within each particular general category.

TWO TWO-VARIABLE TABLES: A SPECIAL TYPE OF MULTI-TABLE

Multi-tables are presented to save space and to show how a set of variables that are conceptually related is linked to a dependent variable. But sometimes researchers are interested in the contrasting patterns of a set of two-variable tables and will present two unit tables in a single table to highlight the contrast. The key finding of such a table is the difference between the two unit tables rather than the pattern within each unit table. Such tables are used frequently in the study by Lipset, Trow, and Coleman on union democracy.* At one point they want to show that involvement in the printer's occupational community ultimately leads to involvement in the politics of the union. To demonstrate this process, they relate both activity in politics and participation in social relations with other printers (the measure of involvement in the occupational community) to age and present the results in graphic form as in Figure 8.1. As the graph shows, activity in politics

*Seymour Martin Lipset, Martin A. Trow, and James S. Coleman, *Union Democracy*, New York: Free Press, 1956.

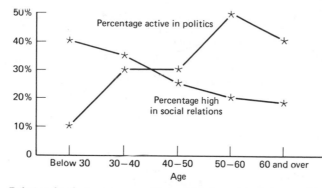

Figure 8.1. Relationship between age and being high in social relations and between age and being active in politics.

	Below 30		30–40		40–50		50–60		60 and over	
Active	11%	(19)	31%	(93)	31%	(141)	47%	(116)	39%	(61)
High soc.	39%	(18)	36%	(90)	28%	(134)	20%	(111)	16%	(55)

Reprinted with permission of Macmillan Publishing Co., Inc. from *Union Democracy* by Seymour M. Lipset, Martin A. Trow, and James S. Coleman. Copyright 1956 by The Free Press, a Corporation.

increases with age, whereas being highly involved socially with other printers declines with age. Lipset et al. infer from these patterns that young printers first get involved socially with other printers and as they get older get drawn into union politics through their social relations with other printers. The graphic form makes these contrasting patterns vivid.

At another point Lipset et al. want to show that printers who are sensitive to ideological issues are likely to be interested in both union politics and national politics (what they call U.S. civil politics), and they plot on a graph the percentage who are interested in these kinds of politics according to ideological sensitivity, as in Figure 8.2. The point of this graph is to show the similarity of the sloping lines, one referring to union politics and the other to national politics.

Later on, Lipset et al. present two two-variable tables in a multi-table like those presented earlier. They want to show that night workers, who are more cut off from normal social relations, are more deeply involved in the printers' occupational community than day workers. They relate type of work shift to three measures of involvement in the occupational community (Table 8.14). On each measure of involvement in the occupational community, night workers score higher than day workers.

Two two-variable tables are common in another famous study carried out at Columbia University's Bureau of Applied Social Research, *The Academic Mind.** At one point Lazarsfeld and Thielens want to show that higher

---

*Paul F. Lazarsfeld and Wagner Thielens, Jr., *The Academic Mind: Social Scientists in a Time of Crisis*, New York: Free Press, 1958.

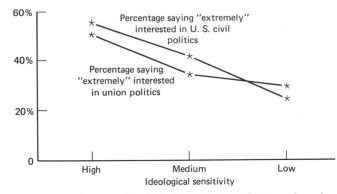

Figure 8.2.   Relationship between ideological sensitivity and interest in union and civil politics.

Percentages	52%	36%	23%
	50%	30%	26%
Total cases	(96)	(220)	(117)

Reprinted with permission of Macmillan Publishing Co., Inc. from *Union Democracy* by Seymour M. Lipset, Martin A. Trow, and James S. Coleman. Copyright 1956 by The Free Press, a Corporation.

quality colleges did a better job of protecting faculty members from McCarthyite attacks than did lower quality colleges. They present two measures, one reporting accusations made against faculty members, the other threats to the academic freedom of faculty members. Their measure of the protectiveness of the college is the discrepancy between accusations and threats. If many faculty are accused but few are actually threatened, then the college administration is doing a good job of protecting its faculty members. Conversely, if as many faculty feel threatened as are accused, then the college is not providing a buffer for its faculty, as accusations are immediately translated into threats. To show the greater efficacy of the higher quality college in protecting faculty members, Lazarsfeld and Thielens present the data in graph form (Figure 8.3).

Table 8.14.   Relationship between Work Shift and Involvement in the Occupational Community[a]

Involvement	Night Workers	Day Workers
High in Social Relations	30%	23%
Two or more printer friends	38%	27%
Member of printers' clubs	36%	26%
N	(200)	(234)

[a]Reprinted with permission of Macmillan Publishing Co., Inc. from *Union Democracy* by Seymour Martin Lipset, Martin A. Trow, and James S. Coleman. Copyright 1956 by The Free Press, a Corporation.

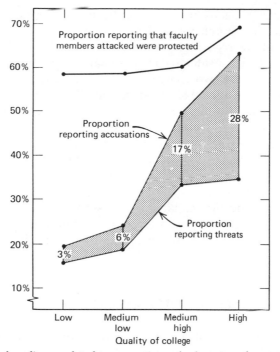

Figure 8.3. School quality as related to accusations of subversion, threats to academic freedom, and the administration's treatment of accused professors.

Reporting faculty members were protected when attacked	58%	(43)	58%	(143)	60%	(379)	69%	(555)
Reporting accusations	19%	(230)	24%	(589)	50%	(752)	63%	(880)
Reporting threats	16%	(230)	18%	(589)	33%	(752)	35%	(880)

Reprinted with permission of Macmillan Publishing Co., Inc. from *The Academic Mind* by Paul F. Lazarsfeld and Wagner Thielens, Jr. Copyright © 1958 by The Free Press, a Corporation.

The key finding in the Lazarsfeld–Thielens graph is the discrepancy between the percentage reporting accusations and the percentage reporting threats, shown by the shaded area in the graph. As the quality of school increases, the discrepancy increases, from a low of 3 percentage points in the low-quality schools to a high of 28 percentage points in the high-quality schools. As in all the multi-tables shown in this chapter, the two unit tables have one variable in common, in this case the quality of colleges, a contextual property of the individual faculty members. In one of the two-variable tables, quality is related to reported accusations and in the other, to reported threats.

Lazarsfeld and Thielens also analyze the two components of their key dependent variable, apprehension. They construct this index by combining items that indicate worry with items that indicate caution, that is, avoiding actions that would be considered controversial. They examine the impact of school quality on these two components of apprehension, showing how worry and caution are related to school quality. The results are presented in a graph where, again, the key point is the discrepancy between the patterns for the two unit tables (Figure 8.4). As the figure shows, as school quality increases the gap between worry and caution increases. Faculty at high-quality schools are worried by McCarthyism, but they are less ready to translate their worry into caution, presumably because they feel protected by their institutions.

As these tables and figures illustrate, researchers will construct multi-tables not only to save space or condense the discussion, but also to present critical findings that depend on the contrast between the patterns of the unit tables.

ON TABLES, GRAPHS, AND BAR CHARTS

As can be seen from the data presented from the Lipset and Lazarsfeld studies, the results of tabular analysis are not always presented in tabular form. Many researchers prefer to convert the tabular results into graphs or bar charts. They make this decision solely on the basis of improving communication with the readers of their reports. It will be noted that both Lipset and Lazarsfeld present the tabular results in percentage form along with the base figures beneath their graphs. Their graphs thus are redundant, but they are presented because the researchers believe that they do a better job of communicating the finding to the reader.

Even more popular than the graph is the bar chart, in which percentages are converted into bars that presumably communicate the finding through their relative height. Table 8.5, which showed the relationship between the attitude toward abortion and education, can be presented as a bar chart, as in Figure 8.5. This bar chart presents all three categories on the dependent variable, utilizing a different shading for each category. Many times researchers will simplify their bar charts by presenting only one category on the dependent variable, as in Figure 8.6.

Bar charts are rather attractive, which is perhaps one reason why some researchers prefer them, and they can communicate with people who are frightened of numbers. Lazarsfeld was so convinced that laymen could not read tables of numbers that he almost always used bar charts. But bar charts have their drawbacks. For one thing, the researcher can easily manipulate the presentation by using either very large gaps or very small gaps between the percentage numbers. By using very large gaps, small differences—for example, the difference between 43 and 49 percent—can be made to look

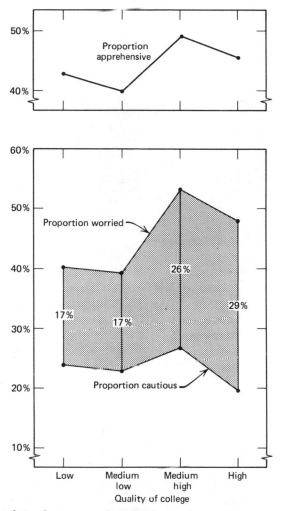

Figure 8.4. The relation between quality of college and apprehension.

Apprehensive	43%	40%	49%	46%
Worried	40%	39%	53%	48%
Cautious	23%	22%	27%	19%
Total cases	(230)	(589)	(752)	(880)

Reprinted with permission of Macmillan Publishing Co., Inc. from *The Academic Mind* by Paul F. Lazarsfeld and Wagner Thielens, Jr. Copyright © 1958 by The Free Press, a Corporation.

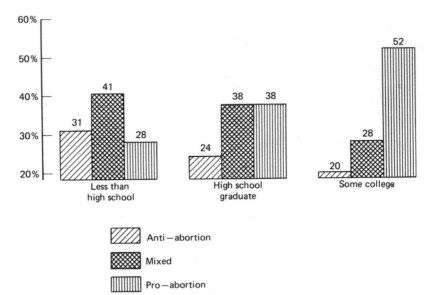

Figure 8.5.   Attitude toward abortion by education.

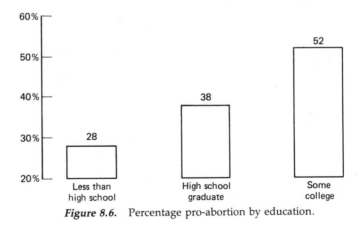

Figure 8.6.   Percentage pro-abortion by education.

substantial; small gaps would make relatively large differences—say 21 percent as compared with 42 percent—look small. This can be seen from the scales below:

A. Exaggerating Small Differences	B. Minimizing Large Differences
60% X	60% X
	50%
55%	40%
X	30% X
50%	20%

The difference between the Xs on the left amounts to 6 percentage points, whereas the same gap between the Xs on the right amounts to 28 percentage points.

Another drawback of bar charts is that they become cumbersome for presenting three-variable or four-variable tables.

The researcher is of course free to use tables, graphs, or charts, but my guess is that the lay audience is not as naive as Lazarsfeld believed and that tables properly presented can communicate research findings clearly.

We may conclude this chapter on the presentation of tables with a few tips about the presentation of tables in the context of a research report. First, it is critical to introduce a table with a sentence explaining why the table is being presented, formulating the question that the table will answer. All too many novices present tables without any introductions, and some novices even begin their research reports with a table. The critical point to bear in mind is that the data never speak for themselves. The researcher must take the reader in hand, explaining why the table is being presented. After such an introduction, the table is presented, then a paragraph or two discuss the findings shown in the table. The introduction might pose a question, for example: Will men or women be more likely to endorse X? The table then is presented, and it will show whether men or women are more likely to support X. But the researcher, proceeding on the assumption that many readers will not understand the table, will then compose sentences after the table which state what the findings of the table are. "As can be seen from Table 1, men are more likely than women to support X" is a typical example. In sum, every table should be introduced by a sentence or two, and after the table is presented the researcher should state clearly what the findings in the table are.

This chapter is intended as a guide to the presentation of tables. All too many students and laymen are frightened of tables, and the good researcher will take them by the hand and lead them through tables in such a way as to remove the element of fear. Essential to this process is the presentation of tables in a clear and concise way so as to maximize communication and minimize noise and static. The researcher who follows the principles laid out in this chapter should succeed in this task.

9

Concepts and Indices: The Process of Measurement

One of the most important and difficult tasks confronting the researcher is classifying the objects under study in terms of the concepts central to the research. The purpose of the research might be to study political liberalism, happiness, anxiety, alienation, authoritarianism, group cohesion, bureaucratization, efficiency, or any of a myriad of individual and group characteristics. Whatever the critical concepts of the research, the researcher must figure out some way of classifying the objects according to how much or how little of these concepts they possess. Not until he or she has developed some scheme for classifying the objects in terms of these concepts will the researcher be able to analyze the data and study the causes and consequences of the key concepts. This process of classifying objects in terms of concepts is a process of measurement, and the task confronting us in this chapter is to determine how the researcher goes about measuring the properties of the objects of the research.*

ON THE NATURE OF SOCIOLOGICAL CONCEPTS

The tasks involved in the classification or measurement process will become clearer when we consider the nature of sociological concepts. We might begin by asking just what are sociological concepts and where do they come

*For more than 30 years Paul F. Lazarsfeld gave a course at Columbia entitled "Concepts and Indices." Much of the material in this chapter is based on the thinking of Lazarsfeld.

from? Students in introductory courses are urged to pay attention to the central concepts of the discipline and are required to learn their definitions, but all too often the students just don't know what a *concept* is. Should they have the temerity to ask their instructor, they might well find the instructor's answer surprising for its uncertainty, for example, "They are abstractions from reality" or "They are the names we give to the things we see." Such answers are not really off the mark, for concepts are abstractions and they do refer to phenomena we observe. Concepts are the products of thought, for they are ideas—ideas that we formulate to describe things out there in the world.

Where do the ideas that we call concepts come from? What do we observe out there that leads us to form ideas? This may well be a large philosophical question that would take much time and effort to answer, but a preliminary answer might go something like this. We notice consistency in a background of change or conversely we notice change in a framework of consistency. For example, we may notice that some people always wait for the traffic light to turn green before they cross the street regardless of the traffic on the road, whereas other people in the same situation will cross the street if no cars are nearby regardless of the traffic light. If we further observe these people, we may notice that the former behave cautiously in a variety of situations, whereas the latter often take risks. To capture this difference in behavior in similar situations we might develop the idea of prudence or its opposite, recklessness; in short, we develop a concept to capture our observation of differences in behavior in similar situations. Or we might be in a position where we can observe army units under battlefield conditions. If we observe a fairly large number of such units, we might notice that when the battle becomes intense, some of these units split apart with the soldiers running off in all directions, whereas other units stand fast and continue fighting. This striking difference between groups under the same conditions might lead us to formulate a concept such as group cohesion. If we are in a position to observe the same people in a variety of situations, we may notice certain consistencies in their behavior that transcend the particular situation they are in. For example, we may notice some people seem afraid to speak in public, they seem nervous when talking to someone of the opposite sex, they are reluctant to ride in elevators, have difficulty sleeping at night, and seem unable to sit still. This array of observations might lead us to an idea; we might formulate the concept of anxiety and say that people who behave in these ways are anxious people.

The concepts of prudence, cohesion, anxiety, and almost an infinite number of others all belong to a particular class of concepts to be distinguished from another class. Samples of this second class would be such concepts as society, person, status, role, organization, group, community, attitude, city. This second class of concepts refers to the units of social science, the units under observation. The first class of concepts, in contrast, refers to properties of these units and might be thought of as classificatory concepts for they are the concepts in terms of which the units under observation are being classified for purposes of scientific study. In this chapter we are concerned not with unit concepts but with classificatory concepts and how they are measured.

Sociological concepts have two properties that are directly relevant to the measurement process: they are not directly observable and they are complex, consisting of a bundle of dimensions. It is important to bear in mind that we never see group cohesion, bureaucracy, democracy, prudence, anxiety, or alienation. For all intents and purposes the concepts of sociology are invisible. We know of them only because of their manifestations, the things they cause that are observable to us. These observables, from which we infer the presence of the concept, are called *indicators*. The process of measuring concepts involves working with the indicators of the concept. For example, we do not see anxiety, but we do see people biting their nails, tapping their feet, blinking their eyes, and wringing their hands; from such observations we infer the presence of anxiety.

SPECIFYING THE DIMENSIONS OF CONCEPTS

The second salient property of sociological concepts is their complexity. They tend to comprise a bundle of separate components or dimensions, and much theoretical development in sociology consists of analyzing concepts and uncovering their various dimensions. For example, in his essay on bureaucracy, Max Weber lists six characteristics of organizations that comprise the bureaucratic syndrome. According to Weber, a bureaucracy has these elements, such as fixed and official jurisdictional areas that are ordered by rules, levels of graded authority organized into a system of superordination and subordination in which there is supervision of the lower offices by the higher ones, and written documents on which the management of the modern office is based, to name only three of the six dimensions that Weber identifies.* In another classic paper, Melvin Seeman analyzes the concept alienation and uncovers five dimensions of alienation: powerlessness, meaninglessness, normlessness, isolation, and self-estrangement.† Still another theorist specifying the dimensions of a concept is John C. Leggett, who analyzed the concept of working-class consciousness. According to Leggett, this concept has four dimensions: class verbalization, skepticism, militance, and equalitarianism.‡ "Class verbalization" refers to the tendency of working-class people to discuss things in class terms; "skepticism" occurs when people believe wealth is allocated to benefit the middle class

*H. S. Gerth and C. Wright Mills, *From Max Weber. Essays in Sociology*, New York: Oxford University Press, 1946.
†Melvin Seeman, "On the Meaning of Alienation," *American Sociological Review* **24** No. 6, 783–791 (December 1959).
‡John C. Leggett, "Uprootedness and Working Class Consciousness," *American Journal of Sociology* **68** No. 6, 682–692 (May 1963).

rather than the working class; "militance" refers to acting to advance the interests of one's class; and "equalitarianism" means favoring a redistribution of wealth to ensure the same amount for everyone.

If the first stage of movement from concepts to measuring devices called indices is the vague formation of an idea, then the second stage consists of specifying the dimensions of the new concept. This process of specifying dimensions is much like working out the definition of the concept. Presumably, the concept is present when all of its dimensions are present. But what about those instances in which only some of the dimensions are present? If a person is powerless, experiences meaninglessness and normlessness, but is neither isolated nor self-estranged, is he still alienated, or partly alienated, or not alienated at all? The possibility that some dimensions of a concept are absent opens the door to the development of typologies of concepts or subconcepts, each type representing a different combination of the basic dimensions. In explicating the process of translating concepts into indices, Lazarsfeld developed the notion of a property space. The various dimensions of a concept can be thought of as dimensions of a space in which the concept and its related concepts are located. Seeman's five dimensions of alienation can be thought of as comprising a five-dimensional property space in which each dimension is dichotomized into present or absent. Such a five-dimensional space consists of 32 sectors, each sector representing a type of alienation or nonalienation. At one extreme are the people who manifest all five dimensions of alienation, the completely alienated; at the other extreme are people who have none of these dimensions, the completely nonalienated. Between are 30 additional types representing various combinations of the presence and absence of these five dimensions. By similarly cross-tabulating his four dimensions of working-class consciousness, Leggett could have developed a typology of 16 types of class-consciousness. This process of constructing a property space by cross-classifying the dimensions of a concept was called by Lazarsfeld the process of *substruction* of a property space. Substruction not only leads to the clarification of a concept, but it frequently leads to the discovery of new concepts or new subconcepts. An example is provided by Merton's essay on prejudice.* The concept Merton had in mind was antagonism toward the out group. He specified two dimensions of the concept, one attitudinal and the other behavioral. The attitudinal dimension refers to feelings of liking or disliking the group, the behavioral dimension, to discriminating or nondiscriminating actions. By cross-tabulating these dimensions, he derived the typology as shown on the following page. By constructing a property space from these dimensions, Merton discovered two new concepts, the fair-weather liberals and the fair-weather illiberals.

*Robert K. Merton, "Discrimination and the American Creed," in Robert M. MacIver (Ed.), *Discrimination and the National Welfare*, Institute for Religious and Social Studies.

| Behavioral | Attitudinal Dimension | |
Dimension	Pro	Anti
Pro	All-weather liberal (unprejudiced nondiscriminator)	Fair-weather illiberal (prejudiced nondiscriminator)
Anti	Fair-weather liberal (unprejudiced discriminator)	All-weather illiberal (prejudiced discriminator)

Constructing a property space from the dimensions of a concept through the process of specification is only one type of substruction. Another type is to develop a property space for typological concepts that already exist. Through such an exercise, one frequently discovers new concepts and types. Durkheim's types of suicide, Riesman's types of character structure, and Linz's types of regime all lend themselves to substruction.[†] In the case of Durkheim the critical dimensions seem to be the presence and absence of norms and whether the norms emphasize the individual or the group. Cross-tabulating these dimensions yields the following property space:

| | Presence of Norms | |
Emphasis of Norms	Yes	No
Individual	Egoistic	A_n
Group	Altruistic	$_o{}_{mic}$

The distinction between individual and group becomes irrelevant in the case of no norms and so substructing the property space for Durkheim's concepts fails to yield a new type. For Riesman's typology the critical dimensions seem to be self versus other and unchanging stable norms (tradition) versus changing norms. The property space for these dimensions follows:

| | Focus of Norms | |
Stability of Norms	Self	Other
Changing	Inner directed	Other directed
Unchanging	?	Tradition directed

[†] Emile Durkheim, *Suicide*, Glencoe, Illinois: Free Press, 1951. David Riesman, Reuel Denney, and Nathan Glazer, *The Lonely Crowd*, New Haven: Yale University Press, 1950. Juan Linz, "Totalitarian and Authoritarian Regimes," in Fred I. Greenstein and Nelson W. Polsby (Eds.), *The Handbook of Political Science*, Vol. III, Reading, Massachusetts: Addison-Wesley, 1975, pp. 175–411.

The question mark in this property space raises the question of whether there might not be a fourth type of character structure. Inasmuch as Riesman's image of the tradition-directed society is the primitive society of anthropology, individualization is extremely low in such societies and the tradition-directed type thus belongs in the fourth cell. But have there been stable, unchanging societies in which the individual or self is emphasized? Linz's typology of regimes consists of three types: democracy, totalitarianism, and authoritarianism. If the United States symbolizes the democratic regime and Nazi Germany and the Soviet Union the totalitarian regime, then Franco's Spain symbolized the authoritarian regime. One dimension of Linz's typology is whether the leaders are elected by the populace or are imposed from above. The other dimension is the number of areas of life controlled by the state, a few or many. Substructing these types yields the following property space:

	Selection of Leaders	
Areas of Life Controlled by State	Elected	Imposed
Few	Laissez faire democracy	Authoritarianism
Many	Social democracy? Welfare state?	Totalitarianism

The new type suggested by this substructing of Linz's typology is the democratic state in which the state attempts to regulate a fairly large number of areas of life, which might be called the welfare state.

SEARCHING FOR INDICATORS OF THE CONCEPT

Once the researcher has specified the dimensions of a concept, the next task is to find indicators of the various dimensions. The indicators are the observable items that stand for the concept. As Lazarsfeld stressed in his lectures, indicators do not have a one to one relationship to the concepts for which they stand, but rather a probabilistic relationship. If an indicator is present, then the chances are that the concept is present; if the indicator is absent, then the chances are that the concept is absent. But this probabilistic relationship between concepts and indicators opens the door to errors in the measurement process. Two types of error can occur: the concept may be present but the indicator absent and, conversely, the indicator may be present but the concept absent. Consider, for example, the previous list of indicators of anxiety. A person might bite his nails not because he is anxious but because he has a hangnail. And a person may not sleep at night because he is experiencing physical pain. And it is possible that such indicators are absent and the person is still anxious, resorting to unusual or less visible indicators of anxiety such as having repeated nightmares.

The probabilistic relationship between concepts and indicators, which opens the door to errors, requires the researcher to rely on more than one indicator when measuring a concept. Using multiple indicators to measure a concept has a number of advantages. First, it reduces the likelihood of error; second, it permits greater refinement in the measurement process. Instead of a dichotomous classificatory scheme in which cases are classified as having the concept or not having the concept, multiple indicators allow a classificatory scheme depicting the degree of having the concept. In short, the classificatory scheme can be an ordinal rather than a nominal scale.

The search for indicators of a concept is usually not a difficult process, for the indicators of any concept tend to be unlimited in number. Consider the concept of intelligence. A number of intelligence tests have been developed, each consisting of dozens and even hundreds of indicators. The Scholastic Aptitude Tests, the Graduate Record Examinations, and the Law School Aptitude Tests are further examples of the vast number of indicators of concepts. Every year the content of these examinations changes as new indicators are devised to replace the old ones, yet the tests are considered comparable from one year to the next. The SAT scores have been declining for years, causing considerable concern in educational circles and yet the items (indicators) used to measure SAT change every year. (As of 1982, the trend seems to have reversed.)

Lazarsfeld saw the development of indices of concepts as a process of selecting a small sample of indicators from a large universe of indicators and combining the sample into an index, the word *index* referring to a set of indicators.

When deciding which indicators to select to measure a concept, the researcher is confronted with the problem of assessing the adequacy of the indicator: How good a job does it do in measuring the concept? Elaborate statistical procedures have evolved for deciding which cluster of indicators hang together to measure a concept, but the amateur and even the more advanced researcher are well advised to avoid factor analysis and rely instead on simpler procedures for constructing indices. Instead of starting out with a concept to be studied, the factor analyst frequently begins with a large bundle of indicators, determines through the statistical procedure which indicators cluster together to form a factor or a concept, then struggles to find a name for this factor or concept. In short, factor analysis results in the discovery of concepts, rather than translating a known concept into a measuring rod, an index.

A researcher who starts with a concept and searches for appropriate indicators to measure it tends to rely on two criteria for assessing the adequacy of the indicators. The first is known as face validity: On the face of it, does the indicator seem to bear on the concept? For example, if the research task is to classify the countries of the world according to how democratic they are, then the institutionalization of elections to choose leaders is an obvious indicator of democracy. On the other hand, freedom of religion is a less obvious indicator. It is conceivable that authoritarian and even totalitarian regimes would tolerate freedom of religion. The second criterion for assessing the adequacy of an indicator is an empirical test: How well correlated is it with the other potential indicators? If one or more of the sample of indicators turn out to be unrelated to the other indicators, it is best to eliminate them from the sample, for the chances are that unrelated indicators are not measuring the same concept as the other indicators. If the items in the sample of indicators are related to each other, this would be evidence that the indicators are measuring the same concept. Although we would expect that indicators of the same concept are empirically related, we would not want to find too strong a correlation between the indicators. If the correlation between two indicators is very strong, then we gain little by using both in the same index. Including them both would be tautological.

In short, we expect indicators of the same concept to be empirically related, but we do not want such strong relationships that the items appear to be identical. Our goal is to have each indicator tap a somewhat different aspect or dimension of the concept so that the set of indicators that we use in the index does a good job of measuring the concept in all its complexity.

COMBINING INDICATORS INTO AN INDEX: REDUCTION OF A PROPERTY SPACE

Just as the dimensions of a concept can be viewed as a property space, so the indicators that are to be used to measure a concept can also be conceived as a property space, each indicator representing one dimension of the space. Inasmuch as the dimensions of a concept are as invisible as the concept, we might think of the property space composed of the dimensions as a *latent* property space, and since the indicators are visible and observable, we might think of the property space made up of the indicators as a *manifest* property space. Index construction is thus a process of reducing a multidimensional manifest property space to a single dimension.

The manifest property space that is to be reduced is made up of the indicators that have been sampled to measure the concept. These indicators have already met the tests of face validity and relatedness to each other. If the indicators are dichotomized, then the sectors of the property space they comprise number 2 to the nth power, n equaling the number of indicators. For example, an index based on three dichotomous indicators comprises a property space of eight (2^3) sectors; one that has four dichotomous indicators consists of 16 (2^4) sectors and one that has five dichotomous indicators makes up a property space of 32 (2^5) sectors. Inasmuch as index construction consists of reducing a multidimensional property space to a single dimension, an index can be thought of as a formula that tells you which sectors of the property space to treat as equivalent. In a classic article about property space, Alan Barton identifies three ways of reducing a property space to form an index, arbitrary numerical reduction, functional reduction, and pragmatic reduction.[*]

[*]Alan Barton, "The Concept of Property Space in Social Research," in Paul F. Lazarsfeld and Morris Rosenberg (Eds.), *The Language of Social Research*, New York: Free Press, 1955.

Arbitrary Numerical Reduction

One way of reducing a multidimensional property space to a single dimension is to assign numerical scores to each value on each dimension and then simply add the scores, called arbitrary numerical reduction. This method of reducing a multidimensional property space to a single dimension can be illustrated by a conventional index of socioeconomic status, comprised of the three indicators of income, education, and occupational prestige. Table 9.1 provides the relevant information for such an index.

In Table 9.1 the three indicators of socioeconomic status are trichotomized into low, medium, and high. The numbers entered into the cells of this three-variable table are fictitious. An inspection of the numbers will show that the three variables are related, indicating that they are suitable measures of the abstract concept of socioeconomic status. The various categories on each variable have been assigned numbers ranging from 0 to 2. This three-dimensional property space can be reduced to a single dimension simply by adding the scores that define each cell of the table. When this is done it will be seen that different cells are treated as equivalent in that they are assigned the same score. The cells of the table have been identified by letters, and since there are 27 cells and only 26 letters in the alphabet, we have identified the last cell as z'. As noted, an index is a formula that tells us which sectors of a property space to treat as equivalent. By applying the principle of arbitrary numerical reduction, that is, simply adding the scores that define each cell, we quickly discover which cells are treated as equivalent. Cell a is unique in that it receives a score of 0. Cell b receives a score of 1 as do cell d and cell j. Thus cell b with 100 cases and cell d with 80 cases and cell j with 60 cases all receive the same index score of 1, a score that accounts for 240 cases. A score of 2 applies to cell e, cell c, cell g, cell m, cell k, and cell s, or a total of 400 cases. The largest number of cells contributes to a score of 3, totaling 510 cases. The complete distribution of cases on this index of socioeconomic status constructed through the method of arbitrary numerical reduction is as follows:

Index Score	N	%
0	150	7
1	240	11
2	400	18
3	510	23
4	480	21
5	290	13
6	170	7
	2240	100%

Table 9.1. Income by Education by Occupational Prestige

	Income								
	Low (0)			Medium (1)			High (1)		
Education:	Low (0)	Medium (1)	High (2)	Low (0)	Medium (1)	High (2)	Low (0)	Medium (1)	High (2)
Occupation									
Low (0)	(a) 150	(b) 100	(c) 40	(j) 60	(k) 55	(l) 40	(s) 50	(t) 40	(u) 40
Index score	0	1	2	1	2	3	2	3	4
Medium (1)	(d) 80	(e) 150	(f) 100	(m) 80	(n) 120	(o) 90	(v) 80	(w) 90	(x) 100
Index score	1	2	3	2	3	4	3	4	5
High (2)	(g) 25	(h) 80	(i) 80	(p) 50	(q) 80	(r) 80	(y) 100	(z) 110	(z') 170
Index score	2	3	4	3	4	5	4	5	6
	255	330	220	190	255	210	230	240	310

Researchers seldom work with so many categories on their critical variables and typically they collapse the distribution into a smaller number of categories. For example, the decision might be made to group the first three categories—scores 0, 1, and 2—into a low-SES group consisting of 36 percent of the cases. Scores 3 and 4 might be combined to provide a middle-SES group with 44 percent of the cases, and scores 5 and 6 could be grouped into a high-SES group with 20 percent of the cases. How such collapsing is done is fairly arbitrary, although the analyst ordinarily tries to achieve subgroups of roughly equal size.

Functional Reduction

Another way of reducing a multidimensional property space to a single dimension rests on the selection of indicators representing differing degrees of the underlying concept or differing degrees of difficulty. When this is done many of the sectors of the property space are empirically empty and the cases tend to fall into a natural order along a single dimension. Barton calls this functional reduction, and it is equivalent to Guttman scaling.[*] Some years ago, Louis Guttman developed a theory of measurement based on a series of indicators of differing degrees of difficulty or acceptability. According to the logic of this theory, those who accept the more difficult indicator naturally accept the less difficult indicators.

A classic example of such Guttman scaling or functional reduction is provided by the Bogardus social distance scale.[†] Bogardus designed a series of indicators for measuring the degree of acceptability or rejection of an out group. Typical of the Bogardus scale were items such as the following:

1. Would you have any objection if a person from group X lived in your neighborhood?
2. Would you have any objection if a person from group X worked at the same place where you work?
3. Would you have any objection if a person from group X came to your house for dinner?
4. Would you have any objection if a person from group X married your daughter?

These questions represent differing degrees of acceptability of a person from group X. The person who would not object to having someone from group X

[*]Louis Guttman, "The Bases for Scalogram Analysis," in Samuel Stouffer, Louis Guttman, Paul F. Lazarsfeld, and Edward Suchman (Eds.), *The American Soldier*, Vol. 4, Princeton, New Jersey: Princeton University Press, 1950, pp. 60–90.
[†]E. S. Bogardus, "Measuring Social Distances," *Journal of Applied Sociology* **9**, 299–308 (1925), and "A Social Distance Scale," *Sociology and Social Research* **17**, 265–271 (1933).

come to dinner presumably would have no objection to the two less intimate degrees of contact, having the member of group *X* live in the neighborhood and work in the same establishment. A scaling error would occur when a person accepts a more intimate contact but rejects a less intimate one. In order for a series of items to meet the test of Guttman scaling, the number of errors must be kept to a minimum. The response patterns one would expect to a set of items such as those that comprise the Bogardus social distance scale would be as follows:

	Item			
1	2	3	4	Scale Score
−	−	−	−	0
+	−	−	−	1
+	+	−	−	2
+	+	+	−	3
+	+	+	+	4

Of the 16 sectors of a property space comprised of these four dichotomous indicators, only five, the response patterns shown above, have any cases in them, and these five response categories are ordered into a single dimension. In short, the property space is reduced to a single dimension automatically as a result of the types of indicators that were selected. It should be noted that those who score 0 are so hostile to the outgroup that they reject even the easiest item, having someone from that group in the same neighborhood. The score of 1 is assigned to those who accept this easiest item but reject the three more difficult ones, and so forth, until those who are totally free of prejudice accept all four items and earn a score of 4.

The scale scores in functional reduction or Guttman scaling have a property that is very different from the scale scores in arbitrary numerical reduction. As we saw above, in arbitrary numerical reduction the same score is assigned to different response patterns. For example, we saw that in the index of SES, six different response patterns were assigned the same score of 2. But in Guttman scaling, the scale score refers to a unique response pattern. It becomes possible to reconstruct the response pattern once the scale score is known. For example, a score of two means that the respondent has accepted the two easier items and rejected the two harder ones and a score of 3 means that he objects only to his daughter marrying someone from the out group, but he will accept this person as a dinner companion, co-worker and neighbor.

Pragmatic Reduction

Sometimes the method of arbitrary numerical reduction works too rigidly and groups categories together too arbitrarily. As Barton notes, "There may be interactions among the different properties such that each combination must be considered in its own right before it can be properly classified."* In such instances, the researcher uses his knowledge of various combinations of the indicators to classify the combination as low, medium, or high on the underlying concept. For example, suppose one wanted to classify people according to their acceptability to the ruling elite of a community in American society, and that all we knew about the people was their education (whether they had gone to college or not), their place of birth (whether they are native Americans or were born abroad), and their race (whether they are white or black). Table 9.2 shows the categories that emerge from a cross-tabulation of these three dimensions. If one were to use a system of arbitrary numerical reduction, assigning the number 1 to the desired trait and 0 to the undesired trait, the cells of the table would be grouped accordingly:

Scale Score	Cells
0	*h*
1	*d, g, f*
2	*b, c, e*
3	*a*

According to this arbitrary numerical reduction, the college educated foreign-born black (cell *f*) is equivalent to the noncollege educated foreign-born white (cell *g*) and the native-born white without college (cell *c*) is equivalent to the native-born black who has been to college (cell *b*). But this arbitrary numerical reduction ignores the fact that race is a bigger deterrent to acceptance by the white elite than either nativity or education. A more pragmatic reduction of the property space would take this into account. At the top of social acceptance to the white elite would be the people in cell *a*, the

Table 9.2. Indicators of Social Acceptability

	Education			
	College (1)		Noncollege (0)	
Race:	White (1)	Black (0)	White (1)	Black (0)
Nativity				
Native born (1)	*a*	*b*	*c*	*d*
Foreign born (0)	*e*	*f*	*g*	*h*

*Allen Barton, "The Concept of Property Space in Social Research," in Paul F. Lazarsfeld and Morris Rosenberg (Eds.), *The Language of Social Research*, New York: Free Press, 1955, pp. 40–53.

native-born whites of high education. But the second category of acceptability might well be native-born whites of lower education. A third category might be the foreign-born whites regardless of education, followed by well-educated blacks irrespective of nativity and finally the poorly educated blacks regardless of nativity. In short, a more pragmatic reduction of the space, one that would reflect greater accuracy, might look like this:

Scale Score	Cells
0	*d, h*
1	*b, f*
2	*c*
3	*e, g*
4	*a*

This pragmatic reduction not only groups the cells differently but generates an additional scale score, five categories instead of four.

THE DOCTRINE OF THE INTERCHANGEABILITY OF INDICES

Given the universe of indicators of any given concept, which subsample should the researcher select to measure the concept? If the indicators have face validity and are empirically related to each other, then according to Lazarsfeld it does not make much difference which set of indicators is selected, for different sets will yield roughly similar results. Lazarsfeld presented this idea by elaborating a theory of the interchangeability of indices. What he meant by interchangeability is that two indices of the same concept, each composed of different indicators, would yield similar results when related to outside criteria, that is, other variables. The theory of interchangeability of indices rests on two properties. First, when two indices of the same concept are related to each other, it will be found that they are strongly correlated but nonetheless there will be a substantial number of errors. Cases classified as high on one index may appear as medium on the other, and some cases classified as high on one index will appear as low on the other. These errors, which stem from the probabilistic relationship between concepts and their indicators, are disturbing to the researcher until he or she discovers the second property, that both indices yield roughly similar correlations when related to other variables.

The errors that creep into the measurement process can be either random or systematic. If systematic, meaning that the errors show up in certain types of case but not other types, then bias is introduced into the measurement process, bias which results in either spurious correlations or spurious noncorrelations. Bias is a serious problem confronting the researcher trying to measure concepts. But random error is much more common than biased error, and it is random error that stems from the probabilistic relationship between concepts and indices. By chance alone, the indicator may be present and the concept absent or the concept present and the indicator absent. Random errors serve only to reduce the correlation between the concept and some outside variable. The errors that show up when two indices of the same concept are related to each other are likely to be random, for when the indices are related to outside criteria they yield similar results.

To illustrate the notion of the interchangeability of indices we shall draw on the six questions that have been used for a number of years in the NORC annual social surveys to measure attitudes toward abortion. The basic question read as follows:

Please tell me whether or not you think it should be possible for a pregnant woman to obtain a *legal* abortion . . .

		Yes	No
147A.	If there is a strong chance of a serious defect in the baby?	84%	16%
147B.	If she is married and does not want any more children?	46%	54%
147C.	If the woman's own health is seriously endangered by the pregnancy?	91%	9%
147D.	If the family has a very low income and cannot afford any more children?	53%	47%
147E.	If she became pregnant as a result of rape?	84%	16%
147F.	If she is not married and does not want to marry the man?	50%	50%

The yes answers to these six questions range from a high of 91 percent to a low of 46 percent. Three of the questions get an overwhelming favorable response, those about a defective baby, the health of the mother, and rape. On the other hand, public opinion on the other three questions is sharply split, close to 50–50. These questions deal with social issues rather than the catastrophes of life or death, rape, and deformity. It would seem that each set of three questions measures a different dimension of attitude toward abortion, a medical dimension and a social dimension.

Inasmuch as the responses to these two sets of questions clearly differ, indices made from them should also be different. Comparing the medical abortion index with the social abortion index should thus provide an extreme test of the doctrine of the interchangeability of indices. Table 9.3 shows the distribution of cases on these two abortion indices. As these distributions show, there is consensus on the medical abortion index and dissensus on the social abortion index. The overwhelming majority turn out to be unqualifiedly for legal abortion on the medical index, whereas the

Table 9.3. The Distribution of Cases on the Medical and Social Abortion Indices

Index Score	Social Abortion Index (Q. 147B, D, F)	Medical Abortion Index (Q. 147A, C, E)
3 Pro-abortion	33%	77%
2	9	10
1	12	6
0 Anti-abortion	46	7
	100%	100%
	(1,412)	(1,443)

tendency is to be against legal abortion on the social index, as almost half are opposed and a third in favor with relatively few in the middle on this index.

The first test of the interchangeability of indices is to see whether the two indices of the same concept are empirically related. It would seem obvious that those who are for legal abortion on the social index would certainly be for it on the medical index, indicating that the indices are indeed related, but the sharp differences in the distribution of cases also indicates that there will be many errors when the indices are related. Table 9.4 shows this relationship. Examination of the numbers in the table shows that the two indices are very strongly related. When the table is percentaged, the percentage difference across the top row is 45 percentage points. But it is equally obvious that a majority of the cases are classified differently on the two indices. Only 579 people, 42 percent of the sample, are classified the same way on the two indices (the cases on the main diagonal). Another 206 people, or 15 percent of the sample, represent a one-step discrepancy in that their scores on the two indices are off by one point. Some 262 people, 19 percent of the sample, represent a two-step discrepancy, and fully 313 people, 23 percent, are completely turned around, scoring in the highest category on the medical index and the lowest category on the social index. This large number of

Table 9.4. Medical Abortion Index by Social Abortion Index

Social Abortion Index	Medical Abortion Index			
	3 (pro)	2	1	0 (anti)
3 (pro)	465	5	2	0
2	116	6	1	0
1	143	16	8	1
0 (anti)	313	117	67	100
	1,037	144	78	101

errors indicates that the two indices are obviously measuring very different dimensions of opinion about abortion. But will these seemingly different indices yield similar correlations when related to outside criteria? The answer is to be found in Tables 9.5 and 9.6, which show how these indices relate to family income and to the respondent's level of education.

Although the percentage who favor legalized abortion differs sharply on the two indices, as we already know from Table 9.3, the correlation of abortion attitude with income is remarkably similar for the two indices, as the percentage difference on the social index is 18 points and on the medical index, 15 points.

Table 9.6 shows the results when these indices are related to education. On this issue, the indices are less interchangeable. Although they both show a positive relationship to education, the difference on the social index is 26 percentage points, whereas on the medical index it is only 13 percentage points. One reason for the absence of greater comparability is that so many people are pro-abortion on the medical index that there is little room for variation on that index. In short, the medical abortion index is close to being a constant rather than a variable.

A second test of the interchangeability of indices is based on a somewhat different mixture of the attitude toward abortion indicators. In this test two of the social items are combined with one of the medical items and two of the medical items are combined with one of the social items. We have grouped arbitrarily two of the social items, 147D, a low-income family unable to afford more children, and 147F, the unmarried pregnant woman who does not want to marry the man, with 147A, the question about a defective baby, to make one arbitrary abortion index. The second arbitrary abortion index

Table 9.5.   Percentage High on Medical and Social Abortion Indices by Income (Score 3—Pro-Abortion)

Income	Social Abortion	Medical Abortion	
Under $7,000	30%	70%	(330)
$7,000–14,999	32	78	(408)
$15,000–19,999	32	80	(389)
$20,000 and over	48	85	(207)

Table 9.6.   Percentage High on Medical and Social Abortion Indices by Education (Score 3—Pro-Abortion)

Education	Social Abortion	Medical Abortion
Less than high school	21%	70%
High school graduate	31	78
Some college	47	83

links two of the medical items, 147C, the mother's health being endangered, and 147E, the pregnancy resulting from rape, with 147B, the social item that asks about abortion for a married woman who does not want any more children. As can be seen from Table 9.7, by mixing social and medical items in a two and one manner, the distribution of cases becomes more similar than was the case in Table 9.3 when the social items were compared with the medical items.

Arbitrary index II, which is based on two of the three medical items, shows more support for the right to legal abortion than arbitrary index I, which is based on two of the social items. But the gap between the distributions on these two indices is much narrower than on the pure medical and social indices seen in Table 9.3. At the extremes, scores of 3 and 0, these two indices are rather similar and only in the two middle categories do the indices diverge. Given the greater similarity in the distributions on the two indices, we can expect fewer errors than was the case with the pure medical and social indices when these two arbitrary indices are related to each other, as is done in Table 9.8.

By comparing Table 9.8 with Table 9.4, we see that interchanging one social item for one medical item has sharply reduced the errors. Table 9.8 shows that 56 percent of the cases (755 cases) are classified the same way on the indices compared with only 42 percent on the pure medical and pure social indices. One-step discrepancies, which represent relatively slight error, are much more common in Table 9.8 than in Table 9.4, 38 compared with 15 percent. But the more serious errors, two-step and three-step discrepancies, are much less common in Table 9.8 than in Table 9.4. In Table 9.8 the two-step errors account for only 6 percent of the cases compared with 19 percent of the cases in Table 9.4, and three-step errors are totally absent in Table 9.8 compared with 23 percent of the sample showing three-step errors in Table 9.4. Thus the shifting of one item from one index to the other greatly reduces the amount of error and increases the chances that the indices are interchangeable. Whether they are in fact interchangeable can be seen from Table 9.9 which tests their interchangeability when related to income.

The overall percentage differences in Table 9.9 are quite similar on the two indices, but index I shows a steady progression whereas index II shows only that the very wealthy are different from all the others. The results for the second test, education, are more supportive of the notion of interchangeability, as can be seen in Table 9.10. In both cases we find a percentage difference of 25 points, with the better educated being more pro-legalized abortion than the poorer educated.

The final test of interchangeability of indices based on the abortion items strives for still more comparability between the indices. Instead of dealing with three-item indices, the third test is based on two-item indices, each composed of one social and one medical indicator, yielding three index scores rather than four. One of the two-item indices is made from item 147B, a married woman who does not want any more children, and 147E, a

Table 9.7. *The Distribution of Cases on Arbitrary Abortion Index I and Arbitrary Abortion Index II*

Index Score	Arbitrary Abortion Index I	Arbitrary Abortion Index II
3 (pro-abortion)	37%	41%
2	15	41
1	31	10
0 (anti-abortion)	17	7
	100%	100%
	(1,420)	(1,424)

Table 9.8. *Arbitrary Abortion Index I by Arbitrary Abortion Index II*

Arbitrary Abortion Index I	Arbitrary Abortion Index II			
	3 (pro)	2	1	0 (anti)
3 (pro)	465	46	2	0
2	75	123	8	1
1	26	322	67	4
0 (anti)	0	57	64	100
	566	548	141	105

Table 9.9. *Percentage Pro-Abortion (Score 3) on Arbitrary Index I and Arbitrary Index II by Income*

Income	Arbitrary Index I	Arbitrary Index II	
Under $7,000	33%	40%	(329)
$7,000–14,999	36	39	(415)
$15,000–19,999	36	39	(392)
$20,000 and over	50	57	(208)

Table 9.10. *Percentage Pro-Abortion (Score 3) on Arbitrary Index I and Arbitrary Index II by Education*

Education	Arbitrary Index I	Arbitrary Index II	
Less than high school	25%	29%	(436)
High school graduate	34	39	(509)
Some college	50	54	(474)

pregnancy resulting from rape; the other index consists of 147D, the family with low income that cannot afford more children, and 147C, where the mother's health is endangered. The distribution of cases on these two indices is much more similar than on the two previous sets of indices, as can be seen from Table 9.11. Somewhat more respondents are pro-right to abortion on index II, based on the health of the mother and a poor family unable to afford more children, than index I, based on rape and the married woman who does not want more children. Conversely, somewhat more are opposed to abortion on the first index, but on balance, the distributions are fairly similar. As a result we should expect fewer errors when these indices are related to each other, as is done in Table 9.12. Fully 1060 cases, or 77 percent, are classified the same way on the two indices, 319 cases represent a one-step discrepancy, amounting to 23 percent of the sample, and only 11 cases, less than 1 percent, represent two-step discrepancies. Clearly the correlation between these two item indices is much stronger than the correlation between the two indices in the previous tests.

Table 9.13 shows how the two indices are related to income. On both indices attitude toward abortion remains pretty much the same through the first three income levels and only rises sharply in the highest income group, those earning over $20,000 a year.

The relationship of these indices to education can be seen from Table 9.14. The first two-item index yields a percentage difference of 23 points and the second, a difference of 20 points, indicating that both indices are strongly related to education.

Lazarsfeld's doctrine of the interchangeability of indices has been supported by the data presented here. We have seen in three separate instances that indices bearing on the same concept made up of different indicators prove to be empirically related to each other although many of the cases turn out to be classified in different ways on the two indices, indictating errors in the measurement process. But when the two indices are related to outside variables they tend to show similar relationships, suggesting that one index is as good as the other for purposes of research.

A CASE OF NONINTERCHANGEABILITY

I have never come across two indices of the same concept that failed to yield similar correlations with outside variables, but I have come across a case of individual indicators of the same concept failing the test of interchangeability. In the mid-sixties I worked with Bradburn on the famous happiness study.* The basic dependent variable was a simple question: How happy

---

*Norman Bradburn and David Caplovitz, *Reports on Happiness*, Chicago: Aldine Press, 1965. Also see Norman Bradburn, *The Structure of Psychological Well Being*, Chicago: Aldine Press, 1969.

Table 9.11. Distribution of Cases on the Two-Item Abortion Indices

Index Score	Two-Item Index I	Two-Item Index II
2 (pro)	41%	48%
1	42	43
0 (anti)	17	9
	100%	100%
	(1,444)	(1,439)

Table 9.12. Two-Item Index I by Two-Item Index II

	Index II		
Index I	2	1	0
2	528	53	2
1	134	429	19
0	9	113	103
	671	595	124

Table 9.13. Percentage High on Two-Item Abortion Indices by Income (Score 2)

Income	Two-Item Index I	Two-Item Index II
Under $7,000	40%	44%
$7,000–14,999	38	47
$15,000–19,999	39	46
$20,000 and over	56	61

Table 9.14. Percentage High on the Two-Item Abortion Indices by Education (Score 2)

Education	Two-Item Index I	Two-Item Index II
Less than high school	30%	39%
High school graduate	39	45
Some college	53	59

would you say you are, very happy, pretty happy or not too happy? In addition, we made up another happiness question that was suggested to us by Hornell Hart in his book *Chart for Happiness.*[†] Hart stressed the notion that the happy man is someone who likes his life as it is and does not desire to change it. The more dissatisfied a person is with his present life, presumably the more unhappy he is and the more he wants to change his life. With this in mind, we constructed the following question:

> Think of how your life is now. Do you want it to continue in much the same way as it's going now, do you wish you could change some parts of it, or do you wish you could change many parts of it?

The marginals (distributions) to these questions are strikingly similar:

Indicator I: How Happy		Indicator 2: Want to Change Life	
Very happy	32%	Same	31%
Pretty happy	56	Some change	56
Not too happy	12	Much change	13
	100%		100%
	(2,789)		(2,789)

The marginals deviate by only a single percentage point. And when the two indicators are related to each other, they show a very strong relationship (Table 9.15). Given the similarity of the marginals, one might have expected all the cases to fall on the main diagonal, that is, to be classified the same way on the two indicators. But as Table 9.15 shows, this is by no means the case. Only 60 percent of the cases are classified the same way on the two indices, 38 percent represent a one-step discrepancy, and 2 percent a complete reversal, a two-step discrepancy.

In spite of the errors, the two indicators behave in much the same way when related to a number of outside criteria. For example, another happiness indicator asked how well the respondent was doing in getting the things he or she wanted in life. This question proved to be strongly related to the two indicators we have been discussing. Of those who said they were very happy, fully 92 percent said they were doing pretty well getting the things they want, a figure that declined to 74 percent of the pretty happy and only 34 percent of the not too happy. The results are virtually identical on the second indicator. Of those who wanted their lives to continue in the same way, 93 percent said they were doing a good job of getting what they want in life, compared to 79 percent of those who want to change some parts of their life and only 35 percent of those who want to change many parts. Another question asked the respondents how much they worried, and the

[†]Hornell Hart, *Chart for Happiness*, New York: Macmillan, 1940.

Table 9.15. **Happiness by Desire to Change Life**

Assessment of Happiness	Attitude toward Present Life		
	Want It to Continue in Same Way	Want to Change Some Parts	Want to Change Many Parts
Very happy	477	373	32
Pretty happy	372	1,033	157
Not too happy	22	160	163
	871	1,566	352

percent who worried a lot climbed from 23 percent to 52 percent as happiness declined. As for changing parts of one's life, worry increased from 25 to 50 percent as the amount of desired change increased. The two indicators also related the same way to several background questions. For example, as income increased, the percentage who said they were very happy climbed from 19 to 41 percent and the percentage who wanted their lives to continue in the same way rose from 22 to 37 percent. On education, the results were also much the same. Of those who had not been graduated from high school the percentage very happy was 40, a figure climbing to 48 percent of the high school graduates and 62 percent of those who went to college. The percentage wanting their lives to continue in the same way rose from 43 to 63 percent as education increased.

Thus far we have seen that in some four tests, the two indicators of happiness behave in the same way, in keeping with the theory of interchangeability. But we found one background variable where the theory broke down: age. It turns out that these two indicators of happiness relate to age in very different ways, as can be seen from Table 9.16. Age turns out to be negatively related to the question "How happy are you?," whereas it is positively related to the question about wanting to continue life in the same way. These seemingly paradoxical results suggest that the two indicators may not be tapping the same concept after all. An explanation of the paradox is not hard to come by. Upon further consideration, the "change your life" question turns out to be somewhat ambiguous. For many people, it proba-

Table 9.16. **A Comparison of the Relationship between the Two Happiness Indicators and Age**

Age	Percentage Very Happy	Percentage Wanting to Continue Life in Same Way
21–29	38%	27%
30–39	30%	26%
40–49	29%	35%
50–59	29%	39%

bly has the meaning that we intended, satisfaction or dissatisfaction with the way one's life is going. But Table 9.16 suggests another meaning. For those in the early stages of the life cycle, the response, "continue in much the same way" can mean a rejection of an anticipated future of greater gratification. The question as now worded has a time focus ambiguity. It confuses satisfaction with the way one's life has gone with endorsement of the status quo. Older people who want their lives to continue in the same way presumably are satisfied with what they have achieved and therefore are happy. But equally happy younger people may not give this response because they have not yet obtained what they set out to achieve. Clearly the starving graduate student has no desire to have life continue in the same way it is now.

It is important to stress that this breakdown of the doctrine of interchangeability has come about from an examination of two *indicators* of the same concept, not two indices each composed of several indicators. It is very likely that the idiosyncracies of particular indicators are washed out when they are combined with other indicators into an index.

TYPOLOGIES

The thrust of this chapter has been to come to grips with the problem of classifying the units under study in terms of the concepts under analysis. The goal has been to classify each unit in terms of the degree to which it possesses the concept under study. We have reviewed the process of index formation, a process of classifying the objects under study along a single dimension, the concept under study viewed as a continuum ranging from low to high. But sometimes the researcher wants to develop a different system of classification of the objects under study, one that results not in a single dimensional continuum but rather a series of different types that bear on some underlying conceptual scheme.

Typologies frequently are encountered in sociological theory and research and it is important to note their differences from indices. An index reduces multiple dimensions to a single dimension; a typology, in contrast, retains two or more of the original dimensions. The resulting types are based on two or more of the dimensions of the underlying property space. We have already reviewed the dimensions underlying some of the more famous typologies in sociology in our discussion of specifying the dimensions of a concept. What remains to be considered in this section is the nature of typologies and their functions for social research.

The typologies that one encounters in sociology and social research fall into two categories, those that are derived from theory and those that are derived from social research. The well-known typologies are those developed by a theorist to explain and understand some phenomenon. A classic case of such a typology is Durkheim's types of suicide. Concerned with such fundamental sociological issues as social order and social cohesion, Durkheim developed a theory of suicide based on three types, egoistic suicide, altruistic suicide, and anomic suicide. The dimensions, as we have noted, are whether the social norms emphasize the individual or the group and whether such norms are in fact present or absent. Another famous typology is the one developed by Riesman to characterize character structure. Riesman, too, developed three types of character, the inner directed, the other directed, and the tradition directed. Typologies such as Durkheim's and Riesman's constitute advances in social theory. They do not grow out of research; rather they emerge as the theorist confronts a problem.

If theoretically derived typologies emerge from the heads of theorists, empirically derived typologies emerge from tables generated by research. Empirically derived typologies can be further subdivided into two types according to whether the dimensions that go into them are empirically related. Sometimes a researcher will be interested in the deviant cases in a table that shows a fairly strong relationship between two variables. To study these deviant cases, the researcher constructs a typology out of the cells of the table. I had occasion to do this recently in a study of the impact of inflation and recession on American families.* In that study, two measures of the impact of inflation were developed. One, objective inflation crunch, dealt with the extent to which family income had fallen behind rising prices. The respondents were asked whether, compared with a few years ago, they were better off financially, had kept even, were a little worse off financially, or were a lot worse off. The other measure, subjective inflation crunch, was concerned with how much the family was hurting because of rising prices. Some nine indicators were used to measure subjective inflation crunch. There was clearly a very strong relationship between objective and subjective inflation crunch. Of those who were low on objective crunch only 29 percent were high on subjective crunch, whereas among those high on objective crunch fully 69 percent were high on subjective crunch. Nonetheless, we were interested in the deviant cases, those who were high on one dimension but low on the other, and so we constructed the following typology:

Inflation Crunch

Objective	Subjective	N	%	Type
Low	Low	565	29%	Untouched
High	Low	361	18	Stoics
Low	High	236	12	Complainers
High	High	794	41	Suffering victims
		1,956	100%	

*David Caplovitz, *Making Ends Meet: How Families Cope with Inflation and Recession*, Beverly Hills, California: Sage Publications, 1979.

We became curious about the two deviant groups, the stoics and the complainers, and the analysis showed that the stoics tended to be retired people, who, though falling behind rising prices, were taking it in stride, probably because their consumer needs were greatly diminished by their age. The complainers, in contrast, tended to be larger families, blue-collar families, and younger families. As this example illustrates, one important function of typologies is to permit the analysis of deviant cases when the two dimensions of the typology are correlated.

A second reason for developing a typology based on empirical data is almost the reverse of deviant case analysis. This occurs when an expected relationship is not found. In spite of good reasons for expecting variable X to be related to variable Y, no relationship at all exists between the two. At this point the researcher may well want to develop a typology from the table in order to specify the null relationship.

A good example of this is provided by one of my students' papers dealing with the NORC data. Three of the questions in the NORC survey dealt with financial satisfaction, and the student developed an index of this concept and proceeded to analyze its causes and consequences. The three questions read as follows:

1. We are interested in how people are getting along financially these days. So far as your family is concerned would you say you are pretty well satisfied with your present financial situation, more or less satisfied or not satisfied at all?

Pretty well satisfied	34%
More or less satisfied	42
Not satisfied at all	24
	100%

2. During the last few years, has your financial situation been getting better, getting worse or has it stayed the same?

Getting better	41%
Stayed the same	40
Getting worse	19
	100%

3. Compared with American families in general, would you say your family income is below average, average or above above?

Below average	20%
Average	53
Above average	27
	100%

The index based on these three questions classified 43 percent of the sample as well satisfied with their financial situation, 29 percent as moderately satisfied, and 28 percent as dissatisfied with their financial situation.

Of all the hypotheses about the determinants of satisfaction with one's financial resources, certainly the most obvious one is income. The higher one's income, presumably the more satisfied one is with one's financial position. Were the data to show a strong correlation between satisfaction and income, the critics of sociology would point to this finding as another instance of sociology documenting the obvious. However plausible the hypothesis, however, the data did not support it, as can be seen from Table 9.17. Not only is there no relationship between income and being well satisfied with one's financial situation, but from the bottom row we see that in fact there is a negative relationship: the higher one's income, the more likely one is to be dissatisfied with one's financial situation. Clearly there is a world of difference between the objective facts of income and the subjective feelings of satisfaction. The strange patterns of Table 9.17 might possibly be explained by reference group theory, with the more well-to-do comparing themselves with even more well-to-do people while the poor compare themselves with other relatively poor people.

This startling relationship between income and satisfaction led the student to pursue the matter further by constructing a typology from income and satisfaction. Each of these variables was dichotomized. Those earning below $15,000 were considered "poor" and those earning over $15,000, "rich." The distribution on the satisfaction variable was dichotomized close to the midpoint into the satisfied and the dissatisfied. The following typology resulted:

	N	%
Satisfied poor	332	23%
Dissatisfied poor	462	33
Satisfied rich	276	19
Dissatisfied rich	350	25
	1,420	100%

Table 9.17.   *Financial Satisfaction by Income*

Satisfaction with Finances	Income			
	Under $6,000	$6,000– 14,999	$15,000– 19,999	$20,000 and Over
Well satisfied	42%	41%	45%	44%
Moderately satisfied	39	30	24	25
Dissatisfied	19	29	31	32
	100%	100%	100%	100%
	(286)	(508)	(221)	(405)

Table 9.18.   Satisfaction–Income Typology by Occupation

Occupation	Satisfied Poor	Dissatisfied Poor	Satisfied Rich	Dissatisfied Rich
Professionals	13%	13%	19%	23%
Managers and administrators	25	31	38	41
Crafts and kindred workers	44	35	36	25
Farm and farm managers	3	2	1	1
Service workers	15	20	6	11
	100%	100%	100%	100%
	(300)	(410)	(264)	(335)

Table 9.19.   Financial Satisfaction–Income Typology by Education

Education	Satisfied Poor	Dissatisfied Poor	Satisfied Rich	Dissatisfied Rich
Less than high school	42%	40%	19%	16%
High school graduate	36	36	39	34
Some college	22	25	42	49
	100%	100%	100%	100%
	(332)	(462)	(276)	(350)

Table 9.20.   Financial Satisfaction–Income Typology by Intelligence

Intelligence	Satisfied Poor	Dissatisfied Poor	Satisfied Rich	Dissatisfied Rich
Relatively low	66%	69%	56%	45%
Relatively high	34	31	44	55
	100%	100%	100%	100%
	(314)	(454)	(276)	(342)

Among both the poor and the rich, the dissatisfied outnumber the satisfied. Analysis of this typology shed little light on the anomalous findings of Table 9.17, but there is a hint that the dissatisfied on each income level were somewhat more privileged than the satisfied. This is suggested by data bearing on occupation, education, and intelligence. Table 9.18 shows the relationship between the typology and occupation. The Ns in Table 9.18 are smaller than the Ns in the typology because a number of people in the sample were retired or unemployed. Before examining the data of Table 9.18, note should be taken of the direction in which the data have been percentaged. The basic rule in tabular analysis is to percentage on the independent variable, but this rule is frequently violated in typological analysis. Although occupation is likely to influence financial satisfaction, in Table 9.18 we treated the typology as the independent variable and occupation as the dependent variable to facilitate comparisons between the various types. The data of Table 9.18 show that the dissatisfied among both the poor and the rich are more likely to have the higher occupational status of professionals, managers, and administrators than the satisfied poor and rich. Among both the poor and the rich, the satisfied are more likely than the dissatisfied to be craftsmen. In short, these data suggest that occupational status contributes to satisfaction with financial situation independent of income.

Table 9.19 shows the relationship between the typology and education. Although the differences are small, it would seem that the dissatisfied among both the poor and the rich were more likely to have college educations. Conceivably education contributes to the raising of aspirations to the point where less satisfaction is derived from accomplishments.

A final hint as to why the satisfied differ from the dissatisfied on each income level is provided by data on intelligence. The NORC surveys have developed a measure of intelligence based on word recognition. Table 9.20 shows the relationship between intelligence and the typology. Among the poor, there is little difference in intelligence between the satisfied and the dissatisfied, but among the rich, the dissatisfied are more likely to be high on intelligence than the satisfied. Conceivably the more intelligent, like the better educated, have higher levels of aspirations which they experience as frustrating.

Table 9.20 brings to a close our discussion of typologies. We have suggested that typologies are generated by theoretical work and empirical research. Empirically generated typologies serve two functions: to analyze deviant cases when the variables that comprise the typology are highly correlated and to help interpret a null relationship when a positive relationship was expected.

In this chapter we discussed the various processes of translating concepts into measuring tools for classifying the units under study, measuring tools called indices. We also discussed another system for classifying the units under study, typologies, and we saw how typologies differ from indices.

10

Bivariate Analysis

Once the researcher has developed appropriate measures of the critical variables, the data can be analyzed. Although sometimes the researcher is content to merely describe the phenomena under study, the causes and consequences of the topics of research are frequently of greater interest. In this and the next chapter, we examine the processes through which the researcher establishes causal connections between the variables of the study. We begin by considering the concept of causation.

THE MEANING OF CAUSE

For one variable to be a cause of another, two conditions must be met. First the presumed causal variable must precede the presumed effect variable in time. If X is to be a cause of Y, it must exist before Y exists, that is, it must come before Y in time. This is an obvious requirement and yet, as we shall see later, the researcher frequently has difficulty establishing the time order of the variables. Second, if X is a cause of Y, it must vary as Y varies, that is, there must be a statistical relationship between the two variables. If X varies independently of Y, then it cannot be a cause of Y. And so to establish causal connections between variables, the researcher must study the extent to which they are related.

There are three different ways in which X can be a cause of Y, that is, there are three different types of causation. If the presence of X always leads to the presence of *Y*, then we say that *X* is a *sufficient* condition for *Y*. In tabular form a sufficient condition might look as follows:

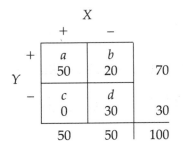

In this hypothetical table, 50 cases are *X* and 50 cases are not *X* and 70 cases are *Y* and 30 cases are not *Y*. The joint distribution of the cases, shown in the cells of the table, indicates that all cases that are *X* are also *Y* (cell *a*) and there are no cases that are *X* that are not *Y* (cell *c*). The zero in cell *c* indicates that whenever *X* is present, *Y* will be present, meaning that *X* is a sufficient condition for *Y*.

A second meaning of causation involves the idea of a *necessary* condition. If *Y* can not exist unless *X* is present, then *X* is a necessary condition for *Y*. This does not mean that *Y* will always exist when *X* is present, merely that it will never exist if *X* is absent. In tabular form, a necessary condition looks like this:

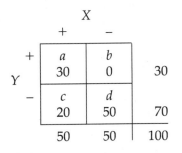

When *X* is a necessary condition for *Y*, *b* is the empty cell, because *Y* can never exist in the absence of *X*. But *Y* will not always occur when *X* occurs, as can be seen by the 20 cases in cell *c*, for these cases are positive on *X* and negative on *Y*. Since *Y* cannot exist in the absence of *X*, all the cases that are negative on *X* must also be negative on *Y*. This is shown by the 50 cases negative on *X* being located in cell *d*, which means negative on *Y* as well. Whereas the verbal expression of a sufficient condition is "If *X*, then *Y*," a necessary condition is expressed as "If not *X*, then not *Y*."

A third and final meaning of causation is the case in which *X* is a necessary and sufficient condition for *Y*. This means that whenever *X* occurs, *Y* will occur and whenever X is absent, Y will be absent. In tabular form, a necessary and sufficient condition looks like this:

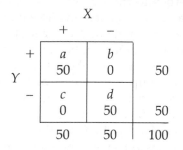

When X is a necessary and sufficient condition for Y we find that every time X is present, Y is present and every time X is absent, Y is absent. This outcome results in two empty cells, cells b and c. A necessary and sufficient condition is expressed as "If X and only X, then Y," meaning that Y will always occur when X occurs and will never occur when X does not occur.

RESEARCH DESIGN TO TEST CAUSALITY

The ideal research method for establishing causal connections among variables is the *experimental* method. The experimental method satisfies two conditions that are essential for establishing causality. First, it solves the problem of the time order of X and Y, for in an experiment, X always precedes Y in time. Second, the experimental method rules out other factors that might be causing Y apart from X. To borrow a phrase from Campbell and Stanley,* ruling out "plausible rival hypotheses" is a major task confronting the researcher, and the well-designed experiment performs this function. At the heart of an experiment is a comparison between two groups, one of which has been exposed to the critical stimulus, the presumed causal variable, and the other of which has not. The group that has been exposed to X is called the *experimental group* and the group that has not been exposed to X is called the *control group*. The time order problem between X and Y (the cause and the effect) is solved because the researcher controls the introduction of X and thus knows that it is introduced before Y occurs. Plausible rival hypotheses are eliminated by constructing the experimental and control groups in such a way that they are alike in all respects except that the experimental group is exposed to X and the control group is not.

*Donald T. Campbell and Julian C. Stanley, *Experimental and Quasi-Experimental Designs for Research*, Chicago: Rand McNally, 1966.

There are two ways of constructing the experimental and control groups so as to make them alike. One method, *matching*, involves assigning the same number of properties to the two groups. For example, the control group might have the same number of men and women as the experimental group, the same number of young and old people, the same number of white and black people, the same number of rich and poor people. The problem with matching is that the number of characteristics on which the control and experimental groups can be matched is limited, because when matching is attempted on more than a few variables, the researcher quickly runs out of cases. It is not sufficient to have the same number of men and women, the same number of old and young, the same number of white and black. Rather, the two groups must have the same number in each combination of these characteristics, for example, the same number of rich, young, white men, the same number of rich, young, white women, and so on. This requirement restricts the number of characteristics on which the groups can be matched and leaves open the possibility that Y is caused by some factor other than X which was not used in matching the two groups. In short, matching does not rule out all possible rival hypotheses.

A second method of making the experimental and control groups equivalent, the method that is used in all sophisticated experiments, is *random assignment*. By randomly assigning cases to the experimental and control group the researcher is assured that chance alone determines whether a case is assigned to the experimental group or the control group and that there is no underlying logic to the assignment. If the cases are randomly assigned to the two groups, then the two groups should have roughly the same assortment of characteristics.

A number of experimental research designs have been developed, but the essence of experimentation can be seen by considering two classic experimental designs. Schematically, these true experimental designs are as follows:

1. R O_1 X O_2
   R O_1 O_2

2. R X O
   R O

The top row in each design refers to the experimental group and the bottom row to the control group. R stands for random assignment, O stands for an observation of the group, that is, a measurement of the group with regard to the critical dependent variable, the effect variable, and X stands for the independent or causal variable. As can be seen by these designs, only the experimental group is exposed to the critical causal variable, X. Design 1 differs from design 2 in that it involves measurements of the dependent variable both before and after the introduction of X. In design 2, the dependent variable is measured only after the introduction of X in the experimental group. In design 1 the impact of X is measured by comparing the difference between O_2 and O_1 in the experimental group and in the control group. If there is a greater difference between O_2 and O_1 in the experimental group than in the control group, then that greater difference is attributed to the independent variable, X. In the second research design, the assumption is made that the experimental and control groups, as a result of random assignment, are so alike that their scores on the dependent variable would be the same prior to the introduction of the independent variable X and therefore it is not necessary to measure their prior scores. In the second design, the impact of X is measured by subtracting the control group's score on the dependent variable from the experimental group's score.

This can be made clearer by an example of a hypothetical experiment. Suppose a researcher wants to test the utility of a particular procedure for improving reading speed. He or she would randomly assign subjects to an experimental and a control group. The experimental group might then be given an hour or so to practice the procedure that is supposed to improve reading speed while the control group is not exposed to this procedure. In experimental design 1, the reading speed of the people in both the experimental and control groups would be measured before the experimental group is introduced to the new method for improving reading speed. Then after the experimental group has practiced the new method for an hour or so, the reading speed of the people in both groups is measured again. Suppose that on the pretest the people in the experimental group read an average of 310 words a minute while the people in the control group read an average of 315 words a minute. After the experimental group has had an opportunity to practice the new method of reading the two groups are retested and on the posttest it is found that the experimental group is reading, on the average, 425 words per minute, whereas the control group, on the average, is reading 320 words per minute. The experimental group's reading speed has improved 115 words a minute, whereas the control group's speed has improved by only 5 words. The difference between these two changes amounts to 110 words, and this improvement can be attributed to the new reading procedure, X. In the second research design the impact of X is arrived at simply by subtracting the control group's average reading score measured after the experimental group has been introduced to X from the experimental group's average reading score after it has been trained in X, which again gives 110 words as the impact of X. Since the experimental and control groups have been made equivalent by random assignment of cases, we can be assured that the improvement in reading speed is indeed a result of X.

True experimental research can be carried out only in a laboratory under artificial conditions. Experimental research is characteristic of psychology where the subjects typically are students who are randomly assigned to experimental and control groups. In contrast to research in psychology, research in sociology is largely carried out in natural settings, using methods of careful observation including interviews with subjects. Sociologists do empirical research rather than experimental research and they make use of preexperimental or quasi-experimental research designs. Campbell and Stanley identify three of these preexperimental designs. The first, the *one-shot case study*, consists of an independent variable, the stimulus, followed by an observation of the group that has been exposed to the stimulus. Schematically the one-shot case study is $X \quad O$. This is an extremely primitive design, one that is so full of flaws that its results are seldom reliable. This design has been used primarily in educational research where X is a new way of teaching a course. At the end of the course the students are tested on what they have learned, and in the absence of a control group the researcher will compare the group's test scores with national norms. If the group seems to be performing above the national norm, then the researcher assumes that the new method of teaching the course is the reason for the higher scores.

A second preexperimental design is what Campbell and Stanley call the *one-group pretest–posttest comparison*, which schematically is $O \quad X \quad O$. In this design the researcher measures the group on the dependent variable before it is exposed to X, the independent variable; after the exposure to X the group is retested, and if it does substantially better on the test, then the improvement is attributed to X. Like the one-shot case study, the one group pretest–posttest comparison is a flawed design, vulnerable to plausible rival hypotheses.

A third preexperimental design is what Campbell and Stanley call the *static group comparison*, which has this form:

$$X \quad O$$
$$O$$

In this design a sample of subjects is divided into two groups according to whether they possess X. The two groups are then measured on some other variable O and if they differ significantly on this other variable, the difference is attributed to X. The static group comparison is the classic research design in survey research. The survey researcher tries to establish causal connections among variables by dividing a sample according to how much of a presumed independent variable X they possess. The different groups on X are then compared on some other variable Y. If their scores on Y are different, then this difference is attributed to X, that is, X is considered a cause of Y. Of course, the survey researcher must always be concerned that some other variable apart from X is causing the variation on Y. In a later chapter we consider how the survey researcher tries to solve this problem.

PLAUSIBLE RIVAL HYPOTHESES

Campbell and Stanley list a series of plausible rival hypotheses that haunt the preexperimental research designs but that are ruled out by true experiments. The first of these is *history*. By history Campbell and Stanley mean all the events of the world that are occurring over the course of the research.

The critical causal variable might well be some event that occurs simultaneously with *X*, the presumed causal variable. For example, during a campaign to improve public opinion of the United Nations something might happen at the United Nations that reflects glory upon it and improves public opinion of it. The more favorable opinion might be the result of this event rather than the advertising campaign.

A second plausible rival hypothesis that might undermine experiments done on children is, according to Campbell and Stanley, *maturation*—the changes that occur in youngsters as they grow. The dependent variable *Y* might well be caused by these changes due to maturation rather than to the variable *X*. For example, an experiment designed to teach youngsters to walk earlier might be contaminated by the fact that over the course of the experiment the youngsters' legs mature enough to make it possible for them to walk.

A third plausible rival hypothesis is *testing*. In the one-group pretest–posttest comparison, the improved score on the posttest might result not from the presumed independent variable *X* but rather from the practice the subjects obtained by taking the pretest. The pretest itself might be the cause of the improvement on the posttest.

A fourth plausible rival hypothesis is *instrumentation*. The posttest score might be different from the pretest score because the measuring instrument has somehow changed between the pretest and the posttest. This possible error haunts research in which measurements are based on the judgments of judges. Where teams of judges are used to measure the dependent variable on the pretest and the posttest there is the danger that changes in the team of judges might result in changes in the measurements independent of the *X* factor. For example, judges might be used to assess the physical fitness of subjects at the beginning of a year-long program designed to improve physical fitness. At the end of the year, a different set of judges might be used to measure the fitness of the subjects and their standards might be higher or lower than the first set of judges, resulting in their giving the subjects different scores at the end of the course than they had at the beginning. This change would be due to the change in the judges rather than to the content of the training course. If different indicators are used in the pretest and posttest, different scores might result because one set is easier than the other. This is a common form of instrumentation.

The remaining three plausible rival hypotheses discussed by Campbell and Stanley are more germane to sociological research, especially survey research. These are *regression*, *selection* and *mortality*.

Regression refers to the statistical phenomenon of extreme scores tending to move toward the mean, that is, away from the extreme on the retest. The people who do poorly on a test are likely to do better on the retest by chance alone. After all, they cannot do much worse than they did before. All they can do is the same or better, and at least some of them do better, bringing up the group score on the retest, moving that score toward the mean of all group scores. Regression is the chief flaw of the pretest–posttest comparison design. The researcher using this design does not know whether the pretest score was unusual or whether the posttest score will be different simply because of regression toward the mean.

A classic example of this flaw played a significant role in ensuring one politician of a successful career. In the early 1950s, when Abraham Ribicoff was the governor of Connecticut, there was an unusually high death toll on the Connecticut highways. Ribicoff campaigned for very strict speeding laws and succeeded in having these laws adopted. Within a year of the adoption of new speeding laws, the death rate on Connecticut highways dropped significantly. Ribicoff was widely acclaimed for having lowered the highway death toll, and this publicity ensured him of victory when he ran for the Senate. Some years later, statisticians were able to show that the drop in the highway death rate was due to regression toward the mean rather than strict speeding laws. By chance alone, the year before the new laws were adopted saw a very high death rate, and the following year the death rate returned to a more nearly normal figure. Proving that regression was at work required taking into account the death rates for a number of years prior to and following adoption of the new laws. Ruling out the regression effect requires a series of pretests and posttests, not just the one of each that is characteristic of the pre-test-posttest comparison design.

Selection, more accurately self-selection, refers to the fact that without random assignment of people to control and experimental groups (as in true experiments), there is always the danger that people will self-select themselves in such a way as to produce the score on the dependent variable independent of their exposure to X. Much research on election campaigns has documented that expensive campaigns in which vast sums of money are spent on advertising actually have little effect on the vote for the simple reason that the people who tune into the messages of political parties are already sympathetic toward that political party. Through self-selection, the potential impact of campaigns is minimized.

Many years ago, when the movie *Gentleman's Agreement*, which was about antisemitism, appeared, a study was done to find out whether exposure to this movie lessened antisemitism. A large sample of people was interviewed and asked questions that allowed measuring how antisemitic they were. They were also asked whether they had seen the movie *Gentleman's Agreement*. The research found that those who had seen the movie were significantly less prejudiced against Jews than those who had not seen the movie. But this finding was largely discounted because it was felt that people who were less antisemitic would be more likely to see the movie.

The static group comparison frequently runs up against this problem of self-selection. Where self-selection is at work, the time order of X and Y is reversed; instead of X coming before Y in time, Y comes before X in time. In the *Gentleman's Agreement* study, it was low antisemitism that caused people to see the movie, not the movie that lowered antisemitism. And in political campaigns the people who were not more likely to agree with a message because they heard it, but rather they were more likely to hear it only because they already agreed with it. Again, the time order of X and Y is reversed.

Mortality is a plausible rival hypothesis that haunts longitudinal or panel studies. Since people invariably drop out of panel studies, the sample at the end of the research is smaller than the sample at the beginning, and it is always possible that the difference in the pretest and posttest is effected by the kinds of people who dropped out. This is a problem that frequently confronts educational research. For example, a new course might be judged to be highly effective in teaching reading because the reading scores at the end are significantly higher than they were at the beginning. But during the course of the year, some children move away, reducing class size. If it should turn out that the children who moved tended to be slow readers, then their absence at the end would result in a significantly higher class average. In many urban neighborhoods, the families that are apt to move a lot are the unstable families, families in which the children may well be poor readers. Thus mortality can very well be the critical factor accounting for the change in test scores, rather than X, the experimental course.

In striving to establish a causal connection between variables X and Y, the researcher must answer five questions or confront five problems.

1. Is the observed relationship between X and Y statistically significant or could it have happened by chance?
2. How strong is the relationship between X and Y? (This is the question of the size of the correlation between the two variables.)
3. Does X come before Y or is selection at work, meaning that Y comes before X? (This is the time order problem.)
4. Why does X cause Y? What is the critical intervening variable that explains why X causes Y? (This is the problem of interpretation: if the researcher is satisfied that the relationship is significant and that the correlation is of sufficient magnitude to pay attention to and that X does indeed precede Y in time, the relationship must be interpreted.)
5. Are there certain conditions under which X is especially likely to cause Y, that is, conditions that act as catalysts?

Only by answering these questions will the researcher have done a complete job of establishing causality.

THE PROBLEM OF SIGNIFICANCE

Once the analyst has connected an independent variable to a dependent variable, the first task is to determine whether there is a statistically significant relationship between the two variables. Thus a "test of significance"—a procedure for finding out whether the observed relationship between X and Y could have happened by chance—is carried out. If it could have happened by chance then it is not significant and the analyst must conclude that there is no relationship between the two variables. A test of significance tells the researcher the *probability* that the observed finding could have happened by chance. If the probability is high, say 50 out of 100 or 30 out of 100 or even 10 out of 100, the researcher rejects the possibility that there is a relationship between the variables and assumes that the observed relationship did indeed happen by chance. But if the test of significance shows that the probability of the relationship occurring by chance is low, say no more than 5 out of 100 times or 1 out of 100 times, then the researcher rejects the hypothesis that the relationship could have happened by chance (this is the *null hypothesis*) and accepts the relationship as *significant*, meaning that there is a relationship between the variables. In social science two levels of significance have come to be accepted as proof of a relationship, the .05 level and the .01 level, meaning that such a relationship could have happened by chance only 5 times out of 100 or only 1 time out of 100. The convention is that these odds are too low to justify the null hypothesis of no relationship.

In a test of significance the observed relationship between the variables is compared with what is called the *expected* relationship, that is, the relationship one would expect by chance alone. The more the observed relationship departs from the expected relationship, the more likely is the relationship to be significant. To calculate a test of significance one needs to know how to compute the expected or chance relationship between the two variables. This calculation, in turn, rests on the laws of probability. The probability of an event occurring is determined by the frequency of that event over all possible events. For example, if there are 40 black balls in a box containing 100 balls, the probability of selecting a black ball from the box is equal to 40 divided by 100, 40/100, or .4. (Probabilities are always expressed as decimals or fractions.) We need to make note of two of the many laws of probability, the law of addition and the law of multiplication. The law of addition applies to the case in which we are concerned with the probability that *either* one of two independent events will occur. To determine this, add the probabilities of each event occurring. For example, if in addition to the 40 black balls there are 10 red balls in the box, the probability of selecting either a black ball or a red ball is .4 plus .1, or .5.

The law of multiplication applies to the case in which we are concerned with the probability that two independent events will both occur. For example, let us suppose that in a sample of 100 people, 50 are men and 50 are women. And from a series of questions designed to measure political orientation, let us suppose that this sample has 60 conservative and 40 liberal people. This information would appear as follows in a table relating sex to political orientation:

	Sex		
Political Orientation	Men	Women	
Conservative	*a*	*b*	60
Liberal	*c*	*d*	40
	50	50	100

The numbers of men and women and conservatives and liberals appear in the margins of the table. The question that the law of multiplication answers is how many people have particular combinations of these two variables if the two variables are unrelated. By chance alone, how many women are conservative and how many are liberal and how many men are conservative and how many liberal? To find out, we must multiply the probabilities of each event. Since 50 percent of the sample is made up of men and 60 percent of the sample is conservative, the probability by chance of being a male conservative is $.5 \times .6 = .30$. Thus cell *a* of the table would contain $.3 \times 100$, or 30 conservative men. The number of liberal men would be $.5 \times .4 \times 100$, or 20. The multiplication law of probability would show us that there are also 30 conservative women and 20 liberal women, the same proportions as for the men. The table of expected or chance values for these variables would look like this:

	Sex		
Political Orientation	Men	Women	
Conservative	30	30	60
Liberal	20	20	40
	50	50	100

A simplified version of the formula for finding expected values is to multiply the two marginals that define the cell and divide by N; in this instance, the probability of being a conservative man is $60 \times 50/100 = 30$.

Once the expected values are computed, they must be compared with the observed values to determine the significance of the finding. Let us suppose that when sex is related to political orientation the following results are obtained:

	Sex		
Political Orientation	Men	Women	
Conservative	24	36	60
Liberal	26	14	40
	50	50	100

From the numbers in the table it is obvious that sex is related to political orientation, with the men tending to be liberals and the women, conservatives. But do these *observed* values differ sufficiently from the expected values to be significant, or could these observed values have happened by chance? To find out we must compute a test of significance. There are many tests of significance, but the most commonly used one in tabular analysis is also simple to calculate. It is known as chi square. The formula for chi square is

$$X^2 = \Sigma \frac{(O - E)^2}{E}$$

where O refers to the observed value in the cell, E refers to the expected value, and the symbol Σ means sum of. The formula calls for subtracting the expected from the observed value within each cell as a way of measuring how much the observed value differs from the expected value. The sum of these discrepancies would measure the degree to which the observed frequencies differ from the chance frequencies. But because half of the signs of these discrepancies are minus, summing them would result in zero. Thus to eliminate the minus signs, the formula calls for squaring the discrepancies. These squared discrepancies are then divided by the expected values. The reason for this is that any given discrepancy will be more significant the smaller the expected value. For example, if $O - E$ yields the number 10 and the expected value is 5, this discrepancy is more significant than if the expected value were 8. These discrepancies divided by the expected value are then summed to yield chi square, the measure of significance.

What is the chi square value for the hypothetical tables presented above? The observed and expected values were:

	Observed Values				Expected Values		
Political Orientation	Men	Women			Men	Women	
Conservative	24	36	60		30	30	60
Liberal	26	14	40		20	20	40
	50	50	100		50	50	100

The operations in computing chi square are as follows:

Cell	O	E	$(O - E)$	$(O - E)^2$	$(O - E)^2/E$	=
A	24	30	−6	36	36/30	1.2
B	36	30	6	36	36/30	1.2
C	26	20	6	36	36/20	1.8
D	14	20	−6	36	36/20	1.8
					$\chi^2 =$	6

The chi square for this table is 6. Determining whether a chi square of this magnitude is significant requires consulting a table of chi square values, which is found in the appendix of most statistics books. Such a table will tell you the probability of a chi square occurring by chance.

To use the table of chi square values one must not only calculate chi square but must also know the "degrees of freedom" for a table. The more cells the table contains, the more degrees of freedom it has. The idea of degrees of freedom refers to the number of cells of a table that must be filled in before all the other cells of the table can be derived given a particular set of marginals for the table. For example, in the table relating sex to political orientation, all we need do is fill in one cell, say cell *a*, and we would then know how many cases fell in the other three cells. Thus by subtracting 30 from 50 we would know that there must be 20 cases in cell *c*, the cell for liberal men, and by subtracting 30 from 60 we would know that there must be 30 people in cell *b*, the conservative women; by subtracting 30 from 50 or 20 from 40, we would know that there must be 20 liberal women. The fourfold table thus has 1 degree of freedom, meaning that we need fill in only one cell. A three-by-three table has 4 degrees of freedom, meaning that four of the nine cells must be filled in before we can derive the other five. The formula for calculating degrees of freedom for a table is to multiply the number of row categories minus one by the number of column categories minus one. Thus in the three-by-three table the formula is $(3 - 1) \times (3 - 1)$, or $(2 \times 2) = 4$. For a four-by-five table the number of degrees of freedom is 3×4, or 12.

The significance of a particular chi square will vary depending on the number of degrees of freedom. The more degrees of freedom, the larger the chi square must be to reach a particular level of significance. By consulting a chi square table, we see that for 1 degree of freedom, a chi square of 6 is significant at the .02 level, meaning that it could have happened by chance only 2 times out of 100, a probability so low that we can safely conclude that the finding is significant.

THE PROBLEM OF CORRELATION

Once the researcher is satisfied that the observed relationship is statistically significant, the question of how strong the relationship is between X and

Y must be considered. This is the question of the correlation between *X* and *Y*. Just as there are numerous tests of significance, so there are numerous measures of correlation. Some of them, like the product–moment correlation coefficient, or Pearson's *R*, named after the man who invented it, require variables that are at least interval scales. Others can be used on ordinal and nominal data. Which measure of correlation to use also depends on the number of cells in the table, that is, the number of categories on each variable. Measures commonly used on ordinal data where there are three or more categories on each variable are tau and gamma, and later we discuss these measures in more detail. But the idea of correlation can be most easily grasped by considering the simplest of all tables, the fourfold table in which there are two categories on each variable. The ingredients of the fourfold table are shown below:

$$
\begin{array}{c}
& & X & & \\
& + & & - & \\
Y \;\; + & a & \big| & b & \quad a+b \quad A \\
\;\;\; - & c & \big| & d & \quad c+d \quad B \\
& a+c & & b+d & \quad N \\
& C & & D &
\end{array}
$$

The cells of the table have been identified by the lowercase letters *a*, *b*, *c*, and *d*. The marginals are shown as the sums of the appropriate cells, but they are also known by the uppercase letters *A*, *B*, *C*, and *D*. The total number of cases appears in the lower right hand corner of the table and is signified by the letter *N*. The cells, the marginals, and the total *N* are the elements from which measures of correlation are to be constructed. The problem is to determine how to combine these elements to measure correlation. One commonsense approach would be to add the cases that support the hypothesis that *X* causes *Y*. These are the cases that fall into cells *a* and *d*. Cell *a* contains the cases that are plus on *X* and plus on *Y* and cell *d* contains the cases that are minus on *X* and *Y*. If *X* causes *Y*, then the cases that are *X* should be *Y* (cell *a*) and the cases that are not *X* should not be *Y* (cell *d*). If cells *a* and *d* support the causal hypothesis, cells *b* and *c* refute it, for these cells contain the cases where *X* and *Y* are out of harmony, that is, *X* exists but not *Y* or *Y* exists but not *X*. The sum of these negative cases could be subtracted from the sum of the positive cases. Then to standardize this result we would divide by *N*. The formula used to measure correlation is $[(a+d)-(b+c)]/N$. This measure would yield a value of 1.0 if all the cases fell into cells *a* and *d* and none fell into cells *b* and *c*, and it would yield a value of -1.0 if all the cases fell into cells *b* and *c*. This value of -1.0 would signify a perfect negative correlation, meaning that *X* causes *Y* not to happen. Finally, like any good measure of correlation, this formula yields a value of 0 if there is no correlation, meaning that the proportion of cases in cell *a* is the same as the proportion in cell *b*. In short, this additive index has many of the properties of an ideal measure of correlation. However, although it frequently yields the same value as other measures of correlation for the fourfold table, it sometimes does not and therefore it is held in low repute and is never used as a measure of correlation.

A very common, though crude, measure of correlation for the fourfold table is the percentage difference. The cell entries are converted into percentages and the percentage of cell b is subtracted from the percentage of cell a. The larger the difference, the stronger the correlation. By computing the formula for the percentage difference we can compare it with the formula for the additive index developed above. The percentage difference equals $a/(a + c) - b/(b + d)$. When the arithmetic of this subtraction is carried out we have:

$$\frac{a}{(a + c)} - \frac{b}{(b + d)} = \frac{ad - bc}{(a + c)(b + d)}$$

This formula for the percentage difference uses all four cells and two of the four marginals and it ignores the total N. The numerator in the additive index was based on adding the positive and negative cases. The numerator for the percentage difference is based on multiplying the positive and negative cases. This principle of multiplication, with the product of the negative cases subtracted from the product of the positive cases, is known as the *cross-product* and appears in other measures of correlation more reputable than the percentage difference.

The flaw of the percentage difference as a measure of correlation is that when the marginals are assymetrical the results will vary somewhat, depending on the direction in which the table is percentaged. For example, suppose that when X is related to Y, the observed values are as follows:

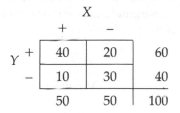

When this table is percentaged on the columns we get the results shown in Table A and when it is percentaged on the rows, we get the results in Table B.

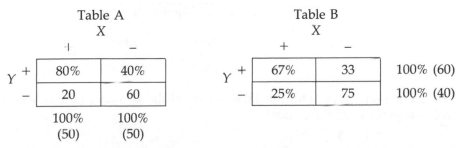

When the percentaging is done on the X variable (Table A) the percentage difference is 80% minus 40%, or 40 percentage points. But when the percentaging is done on the Y variable (Table B) the percentage difference is 67% minus 25%, or 42 percentage points. This instability of the percentage difference when the percentaging is done in different directions has undermined its reputation as a measure of association. This is especially the case when the analyst has no good reason for percentaging the table in one direction rather than the other. But the rule for percentaging tables, as noted in Chapter 6, is to percentage on the independent variable, and when it is clear which of the two variables is the independent variable, as when a social status is related to an attitude (the assumption is that the social status comes before the attitude in time), then the percentage difference has some merit as a measure of association.

To avoid this flaw of the percentage difference, phi, another measure of correlation for the fourfold table, was developed. Phi is a highly respected measure of correlation amounting to simply averaging the column percentage difference and the row percentage difference. In the example above we saw that the column percentage difference was 40 points, or .4, and the row percentage difference was 42 points, or .42. The phi value for this table would be .41, the average of the two percentage differences. The formula for phi has the same numerator as the percentage difference, the cross-product. But whereas the percentage difference was based on the product of only two marginals, phi takes into account all four marginals and requires that all four marginals be multiplied by each other in the denominator. But the product of four marginals is much larger than the product of two marginals used in the percentage difference and thus to make phi comparable to the percentage difference this large number in the denominator must be reduced. This is done by taking its square root. It is in this fashion that phi standardizes the marginals, creating two marginals that are the average of the original four marginals. The formula for phi is (ϕ) is

$$\phi = \frac{ad - bc}{\sqrt{ABCD}}$$

The phi value for the example presented above is

$$\phi = \frac{1200 - 200}{\sqrt{(50)(50)(60)(40)}}$$

$$\phi = \frac{1000}{\sqrt{6,000,000}} = \frac{1000}{2449.49} = .41$$

As can be seen, the phi for this table is indeed the average of the row and column percentage differences.

It is more accurate to view phi as an approximation of the average of the column and row percentage differences rather than the exact average of these percentages. This can be seen from another example.

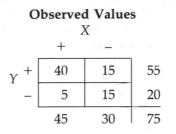

Observed Values

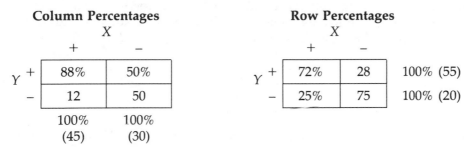

The percentage difference in the columns is 38 points and in the rows it is 47 points, averaging to 42.5. The phi for this table is

$$\phi = \frac{(40)(15) - (15)(5)}{\sqrt{(45)(30)(55)(20)}}$$

$$\phi = \frac{525}{1218.606} = .431$$

whereas the average of the two percentage differences is .425, phi is .431. These numbers are sufficiently close that phi can be safely thought of as the average of the two percentage differences.

Phi and the percentage difference have an important characteristic in common. They will yield a perfect correlation of 1.0 only when X is both a necessary and a sufficient condition for Y, that is, when both the *b* and *c* cells are empty. This is a more rigorous test of correlation than one that would yield a perfect correlation when X is either a necessary or a sufficient condition for Y, that is, when only one of the four cells is empty. Because phi holds to the more rigorous meaning of causation, researchers have invented a measure of correlation that does honor to a necessary or a sufficient condition by yielding a perfect correlation when only one cell is empty. This measure is known as Q. Like the percentage difference and phi, Q is based on the ingredients of the fourfold table. But whereas the percentage difference and phi were based on marginals as well as the values in the internal cells, Q has to ignore the marginals. The reason for this is that when X is both a necessary and a sufficient condition, the marginals of the fourfold table have to be symmetrical. If the cases are divided 60 and 40 in the columns they must be divided 60 and 40 in the rows. Only when the marginals are symmetrical is it possible to have two empty cells. But if X is a necessary *or* a sufficient condition for Y then only one cell will be empty and the marginals of the table will not be symmetrical. Because the marginals are not symmetrical, any measure of correlation that takes account of the marginals cannot reach the perfect value of 1.0. Q is thus a measure of correlation that is based entirely on the values of the cells a, b, c, and d. Its numerator is the same as that for the percentage difference and phi, the cross-product, and its denominator is very much like its numerator except for the change of sign from minus to plus. The formula for Q is

$$Q = \frac{ad - bc}{ad + bc}$$

If in the previous table X were a sufficient condition for Y, the observed values would be

	X +	X −	
Y +	45	10	55
−	0	20	20
	45	30	75

The Q value for this table is

$$\frac{(45 \times 20) - (10 \times 0)}{(45 \times 20) + (10 \times 0)} = \frac{900}{900} = 1.0$$

The zero cell reduces bc to zero and leaves ad to be divided by itself, yielding the perfect value of 1. Q always yields a higher correlation than does phi or the percentage difference, and researchers who like to think that their hypotheses have merit are likely to use Q for this reason. But the research pro is not fooled by this and is likely to employ the more rigorous test, phi.

As noted, the disreputable additive index that we developed will frequently yield the same value of correlation as more reputable measures. This is especially true when the marginals of the fourfold table are symmetrical as in the following examples:

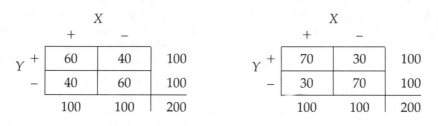

The additive index for the table on the left is (120 − 80)/200 = .20. The percentage difference is 60 percent minus 40 percent or .20, phi is (3600 − 1600)/√100 × 100 × 100 × 100 or 2000/10,000, which equals .20, and Q is (3600 − 1600)/(3600 + 1600), which equals .20. In short, all four measures yield the same value. And for the table on the right, all four measures yield the value of .40. However, when the marginals are not symmetrical, then Q will be significantly different from the other three and the percentage difference and phi will diverge somewhat. And there are some instances when the additive index will be totally different and clearly wrong. This can be seen from the following hypothetical table:

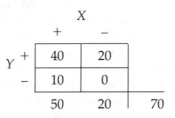

Upon close examination, it will be seen that this table shows a negative relationship between X and Y in that all the cases that are not X are Y while some of the cases that are X are not Y. The percentage difference reflects this negative correlation in that the percentage for cell *a* is 80 percent and cell *b* 100 percent for a percentage difference of −.20. But the additive index gives us (40 + 0) − (20 + 10)/70 = (40 − 30)/70 = 10/70 = +.14. Not only is the number wrong, but even the sign is wrong on the additive index. The correct principle is multiplication of the positive and negative cells, not their addition.

Measures of Correlation for Ordinal Data

More common than the fourfold table in research is the multicelled table, with three or more categories on each variable. Such tables are made possible by ordinal variables, which are very frequently encountered in social research. It will be recalled from Chapter 8 that the essence of an ordinal variable is making distinctions between more and less of a property and classifying objects into categories signifying more and less. The idea of an ordinal scale suggests a method of measuring correlation. If two ordinal scales X and Y, are correlated, then the unit that possesses more of X should possess more of Y. Moreover, if X and Y are correlated, then the unit that has more of X than another unit should also have more of Y than that other unit. For example, if person A has more of X than person B, he should also have more of Y than person B. A measure of correlation could thus be developed by counting the number of pairs in the sample where the order of the members of the pair is the same on each variable. The more pairs in the sample for which this is true, the higher the correlation.

Several distinguished measures of correlation are based on this idea of counting pairs in which the rank order on the two variables is the same and comparing that number with the number of pairs in which the rank order on the two variables is different. The greater the number of pairs in which the rank order is the same, the higher the correlation; the greater the number of pairs on which the rank order is different, the lower the correlation. To develop measures of correlation based on pairs within a sample, it is essential to calculate the number of pairs contained in a sample. For example, if there are only five people in the sample, then each person could be paired with four other people and five times four would equal the number of pairs in a sample of five people. Actually, this simple multiplication results in the same pair being counted twice, once when person A chooses person B as a partner and again when person B chooses person A as a partner. To correct for this, we must divide the product by two. The formula for the number of pairs in a sample of N size is $N(N - 1)/2$. In a sample of 100 people, the number of pairs is $100 \times 99/2$ or $9900/2 = 4950$.

There are five possible outcomes when two units are compared on two variables. Their scores on the two variables can be different and the unit that scores higher on the first variable can also score higher on the second variable, that is, the rank order on the two variables is the same. This is the outcome that signifies correlation. The second outcome is when the rank order is different on the two variables, with the first person scoring higher on X and the second person scoring higher on Y. The third outcome is when the members of the pair are tied on X and have different scores on Y. The fourth outcome is when the members of the pair are tied on Y and have different scores on X. The fifth outcome involves ties on both variable X and variable Y. Several measures of correlation for ordinal data have been developed and one way in which they differ is whether or not they take the ties into account. To work out these measures of correlation we need some data, which are provided in the following hypothetical table:

	Variable X		
Variable Y	High	Medium	Low
High	60	42	31
Medium	32	39	28
Low	8	19	41
	100	100	100	300

According to this table, 60 people scored high on variable X and high on variable Y. We now want to pair these people with people who scored lower than they did on both variables X and Y. These are the people in the cells that are below on variable Y and to the right on variable X. There are four such cells, the medium-medium cell with 39 people, the medium-low cell with 28 people, the low-medium cell with 19 people, and the low-low cell with 41 people. When the 60 people in the high-high cell are paired with the 127 people in these four cells we get 60×127 or 7620 pairs. These pairs are all indicative of a correlation between X and Y. To these pairs—where the rank order between the partners is the same—must be added the other pairs in the table with the same rank order on the two variables. As we move down from the high-high cell to the medium-high cell, the cells below and to the right of it also contain the cases that when paired with it will yield the same order pairs. These are the cases in the low-medium cell and the low-low cell. Another cell of the table which has cases below and to the right of it is the cell that is high on Y and medium on X. The cases in the medium-low cell and the low-low cell combine with the high-medium cell to generate same rank ordered pairs. Finally, the medium-medium cell has a cell below and to the right of it, the low-low cell. All the pairs with the same rank order in the table are

$$
\begin{aligned}
N_s &= 60\,(39 + 28 + 19 + 41) + 32\,(19 + 14) + 42\,(28 + 41) + 39\,(41) \\
&= 60\,(127) + 32\,(60) + 42\,(69) + 39\,(41) \\
&= 7620 + 1920 + 2898 + 1599 \\
&= 14{,}037
\end{aligned}
$$

The table turns out to contain 14,037 same-ordered pairs. We must now calculate the number of different-ordered pairs in the table. Starting in the lower left hand corner, the low-high cell with 8 cases, different-ordered pairs involve it and all the cells above and to the right of it, the medium-medium cell, the medium-low cell, the high-medium cell and the high-low cell. The other different-ordered pairs involve cells matched with those above and to the right of them, such as medium-high matched with high-medium and high-low and medium-medium matched with medium-low and high-low. The different-ordered pairs in the table are

$$
\begin{aligned}
N_d &= 8 \ (39 + 28 + 42 + 31) + 19 \ (28 + 31) + 32 \ (42 + 31) + 39 \ (31) \\
&= 8 \ (140) + 19 \ (59) + 32 \ (73) + 39 \ (31) \\
&= 1120 + 1121 + 2336 + 1209 \\
&= 5786
\end{aligned}
$$

We now see that the table contains 5786 differently ordered pairs. A very respectable measure of correlation known as tau (τ) has been developed based on the count of same-order and different-ordered pairs. The formula for tau is

$$
\tau = \frac{N_s - N_d}{\text{all possible pairs}}
$$

It should be noted that this formula for a respectable measure of correlation is the exact analogue to the additive measure of correlation for the fourfold table, the favorable cases minus the unfavorable cases divided by N. Here the different-ordered pairs are subtracted from the same-ordered pairs and the result is divided by the total number of pairs, which is analogous to N. The tau value for the preceding table is

$$
\begin{aligned}
\tau &= \frac{14{,}037 - 5786}{(300 \times 299)/2} \\
&= \frac{8251}{44{,}850} \\
&= .184
\end{aligned}
$$

It should be noted that tau ignores the pairs involving ties on either or both X and Y. Shortly we will consider a modification of tau that takes into account tied pairs. It should also be noted that tau yields a perfect correlation only when there are no different-ordered pairs, that is, when X is both a necessary and a sufficient condition for Y.

Just as researchers who found this restriction too stringent for the fourfold table invented Q,which would give a perfect correlation if X were only a necessary condition or a sufficient condition for Y, so a measure of correlation for ordinal data has been invented to serve the same function, and it is modeled after Q. This measure, known as gamma (γ), ignores total N and deals only with the internal cells. The formula for gamma is

$$
\gamma = \frac{N_s - N_d}{N_s + N_d}
$$

This formula is very much like Q, which had the cross-product with a minus sign in the numerator and a plus sign in the denominator. The gamma value for the preceding hypothetical table is

$$\gamma = \frac{14{,}037 - 5786}{14{,}037 + 5786}$$

$$= \frac{8251}{19{,}823}$$

$$= .416$$

The gamma coefficient is substantially larger than the tau value for this table, in keeping with Q being much larger than phi. It should be noted that gamma, like tau, ignores all the pairs that are tied on either X or Y. But the tied pairs have meaning that affects the idea of correlation. Cases that have the same value on X but different values on Y suggest that X is not a cause of Y and therefore the ties should count against the correlation between X and Y. To find the pairs that are tied on X but are not tied on Y, we multiply the frequences of the cells in the same column, for example, 60 times 32 and 60 times 8. The number of pairs tied on X in the hypothetical table is

$$T_x = 60 (32 + 8) + 32 (8) + 42 (39 + 19) + 39 (19) + 31 (28 + 41)$$
$$+ 28 (41)$$
$$= 60 (40) + 32 (8) + 42 (58) + 39 (19) + 31 (69) + 28 (41)$$
$$= 2400 + 256 + 2436 + 741 + 2139 + 1148$$
$$T_x = 9120$$

The pairs tied on Y but not on X can be found in a similar fashion:

$$T_y = 60 (42 + 31) + 42 (31) + 32 (39 + 28) + 39 (28) + 8 (19 + 41)$$
$$+ 19 (41)$$
$$= 60 (73) + 42 (31) + 32 (67) + 39 (28) + 8 (60) + 19 (41)$$
$$= 4380 + 1302 + 2144 + 1092 + 480 + 779$$
$$T_y = 10{,}177$$

A measure that is held in very high repute has been developed to take account of the ties. It is known as tau beta. The formula for tau beta is

$$T_b = \frac{(N_s - N_d)^2}{(N_s + N_d + T_X)(N_s + N_d + T_Y)}$$

This formula is the equivalent of the square of gamma corrected for the ties. Working this formula out for the data in the hypothetical table we get

$$T_b = \frac{(14{,}037 - 5786)^2}{(19{,}823 + 9120)(19{,}823 + 10{,}177)}$$

$$T_b = \frac{68{,}079{,}001}{868{,}290{,}000}$$

$$T_b = .078$$

We have seen that three different measures of correlation for ordinal data yield radically different results. The gamma for our hypothetical table is .416, the tau is .184, and tau beta is .078. The sophisticated researcher is likely to take correlation coefficients with a grain of salt.

THE TIME ORDER PROBLEM

The third problem that sometimes confronts the analyst attempting to establish causal connections among variables is the time order problem: does X come before Y in time or does Y come before X? In many instances the time order problem does not arise because convention has it that certain types of variables precede other types in time. For example, social statuses such as sex, age, race, social class, and religion are presumed to precede personality traits, values, and attitudes in time. If socioeconomic status is found to be related to anxiety or alienation or political conservatism, it is assumed that socioeconomic status causes these traits rather than that the traits cause socioeconomic status. But there are some instances where the time order of X and Y is by no means clear. Numerous studies have shown that the people who have been exposed to the political messages of a political party are more likely to support that party than the people who have not been exposed to the messages of the party. But it would be a mistake to conclude that the political messages have made converts to the party. Rather, the people who are predisposed to the political party are more likely to listen to its messages and the people opposed to the party tend to tune out its messages. As this example shows, underlying the time order problem is the plausible rival hypothesis of selection. People tend to self-select themselves to exposure to the independent variable with the result that their attitude determines whether they hear the message rather than the message changing their attitude. In short, Y causes X rather than X causing Y.

A number of studies have been haunted by the time order problem. As we noted earlier, a movie of the late forties, *Gentleman's Agreement*, dealt with antisemitism. The American Jewish Committee commissioned a study to find out if the movie had the effect of reducing antisemitism. A large survey was conducted and the respondents were asked a series of questions that permitted measurements to be made of their antisemitism. The respondents were also asked whether they had seen the movie. Analysis of the data disclosed that those who had seen the movie were less antisemitic than those who had not seen it. The American Jewish Committee was strongly tempted to conclude that the movie had reduced antisemitism, but they could not because they could not rule out the possibility that only those who did not dislike Jews would want to see the movie. In short, through the process of self-selection, antisemitism may have caused the movie to be seen or to be missed.

A classic study that was haunted by the time order problem dealt with the impact of racial segregation in public housing.* In the late 1940s, when the official U.S. government policy was to construct public housing projects that were racially segregated, a study was done comparing white house-wives who lived in segregated housing projects in Newark, New Jersey with white housewives who lived in integrated housing projects in New York City. The research found that the housewives in the integrated projects were much less prejudiced against blacks than the housewives in the segregated projects. If this finding could be attributed to the segregated housing projects, it had profound significance. For one thing, such a finding directly challenged the wisdom of one of the founding fathers of American sociology, William Sumner, who said, "Stateways cannot change folkways." What Sumner meant of course is that laws could not change sentiments and attitudes, the way people think. But if outlawing segregated public housing so that people of different races live together could eliminate prejudice from the minds of people, then stateways certainly can change folkways. But before this exalting finding could be believed the plausible rival hypothesis of selection had to be ruled out. Quite possibly, only less prejudiced people would want to live in an integrated project and only prejudiced people would move to a segregated project.

Deutsch and Collins tried to come to grips with this problem by mar-shalling evidence that suggested that the time order was housing pattern causes prejudice rather than that prejudice causes the housing pattern. They first noted that at the time the projects were built there was a severe housing shortage and people were considered very lucky to get accommodations whatever the housing pattern. In short, they argued that the housing shortage prevented people from indulging their prejudices when choosing a place to live. They then introduced a series of control variables which allowed them to compare the racial attitudes of people with similar back-grounds in the different projects. In short, if one's religion has some bearing on one's racial views, then by comparing people of the same religion from the different projects one could learn whether the differences in racial

---

*Morton Deutsch and Mary E. Collins, *Interracial Housing: A Psychological Evaluation of a Social Experiment*, New York: Russell and Russell, 1951.

attitudes between those living in segregated and integrated projects persist even when religion is taken into account. If Catholics who live in integrated projects are less prejudiced than Catholics who live in segregated projects, then it is more likely that the residency pattern is what is accounting for the difference. Deutsch and Collins matched their two samples on religion, socioeconomic status, and a host of other variables and in every instance they found more prejudice associated with segregated projects than with integrated projects. These findings lent some credence to the residency pattern–prejudice time order.

A third type of evidence that Deutsch and Collins used to support their hypothesis was based on retrospective questions. They asked their respondents how they felt toward blacks before they moved into the projects. These data indicated that the white housewives in integrated projects were more likely than the housewives in the segregated projects to have moved from prejudiced attitudes in the past to nonprejudiced attitudes in the present. A final datum that Deutsch and Collins used to argue for the stateways–folkways time order was the play patterns of children in the projects. They noticed that the play groups in the integrated projects were integrated with white children and black children playing together, whereas in the segregated projects the children's play groups were strictly segregated by race. They infer from this finding that the children in the segregated projects lived in an environment which taught them to play only with children of their own kind, whereas the children in the integrated projects were encouraged by their environment to play with children of a different race.

Although the evidence Deutsch and Collins assembled to support their hypothesis is persuasive, it is by no means conclusive. It is always possible that selection did play some role. The only way that selection can be safely ruled out in this research and the American Jewish Committee's study of antisemitism is to carry out before-and-after studies, that is, studies measuring the key dependent variable before exposure to the independent variable. This would have required measuring antisemitism before *Gentleman's Agreement* opened and then returning after the movie opened and reinterviewing the same people. And in the Deutsch and Collins study it would have meant measuring racial prejudice before the people moved into the projects.

Another well-known study that had a time order problem was the study of the impact of heredity versus environment on IQ designed by Otto Klineberg.* Klineberg focused on black children who had migrated from the South to the North. His control group consisted of black children who remained in the South. Measurements were obtained of the IQs of both groups of children and the results showed that the children who had migrated had decidedly higher IQs than the children who remained in the

---

*Otto Klineberg, *Negro Intelligence and Selective Migration*, New York: Columbia University Press, 1935.

South. Such a finding pointed to the superiority of the Northern environment where schools were integrated compared with the Southern environment for black children who had to attend segregated schools. (The research was done in the 1940s, before the Supreme Court ruled that schools must be desegregated.) But this finding too is vulnerable to the argument of self-selection. It is generally believed that migrants are more ambitious and probably more intelligent than their brethren who stay behind, and so the children of migrants may have inherited their intelligence from their parents. Without a longitudinal research design to provide measures of intelligence prior to migration to compare with the measures taken some years after migration, Klineberg could not definitively rule out the selection hypothesis. But with the static data on hand, Klineberg carried out a mode of analysis that greatly strengthened the environment hypothesis. He stratified his sample of migrant children according to the number of years that they had been in the North. If the Northern environment is the critical factor affecting IQ, then it should follow that the longer the child has been North the higher his IQ relative to the children who remained in the South. The data confirmed Klineberg's hypothesis. The longer the child had been in the North, the higher his IQ was likely to be. The method used by Klineberg is simply degree of exposure to the critical stimulus, and other researchers confronted with the time order problem have used this method as well.

Perhaps the most famous time order problem in social research is the one encountered by Emile Durkheim in his classic study of suicide. At first glance it would seem that if anyone should be free of the time order problem, it would be the student of suicide, for after all suicide is the final act of a person's life and everything else must come before it. But this neat assumption quickly breaks down when one considers a psychological predisposition toward suicide, which is the antecedent of the suicidal act. This personality trait, the psychological predisposition toward suicide, might well come before the social statuses that Durkheim considered crucial to suicide such as marital and military status.

To support his thesis about egoistic suicide, Durkheim presented data showing that single people were much more likely to commit suicide than married people and this pointed him toward the interpretation that single people are more on their own, suffering from egotism, whereas married people have group support to help them overcome crises that arise. Of course the selection hypothesis is relevant here as well. It might well be that people with a strong predisposition toward suicide are not interested in marriage, meaning that Y (suicide) is causing X (married status) rather than the other way around. Durkheim was in no position to measure a psychological predisposition toward suicide. After all, he had to content himself with official statistics on suicide. He therefore could not directly rule out this counter hypothesis. But he did find a way of further analyzing his data that greatly strengthened his case. His technique was to stratify his data on suicide rates by age groups. His reasoning was that most young people who were not yet married, say people in their twenties, would eventually be married. Their current singleness was therefore not the result of some predisposition to remain single, a predisposition that might lead them to suicide. But if young single people committed suicide more often than young married people, this would probably mean, Durkheim reasoned, that it was the marital status that was influencing suicide rather than the other way around. Durkheim presented the relevant data in a four-variable table that considered sex, marital status, age, and suicide rate (Table 10.1). Durkheim's table presents 18 comparisons of suicide rates for single and married people; in 16 of the 18 the single people have much higher suicide rates than the married people. A major exception occurs among the youngest men, those between 15 and 20. Here the married men are much more likely to commit suicide than the single men. Since marriage is so unusual for these very young men, they may be highly deviant to begin with. The other exception is a minor one and is found among 70- to 80-year-old women, where the married have a slightly higher suicide rate than the single. Like all multivariate tables, Durkheim's table has more than one set of findings. By reading down the columns, we learn that suicide strongly increases with age. But the critical finding for Durkheim's time order problem is that on every age level (with the two exceptions noted) the single people have higher rates of suicide than the married. This is true even among the young singles, most of whom will eventually marry.

In developing his arguments for altruistic suicide, Durkheim cited data showing that the suicide rate was much higher among army personnel than the civilian population. His thesis was that the army culture places a pre-

Table 10.1. France (1889–1891): Suicides Committed per 1,000,000 Inhabitants of Each Age and Marital Status Group, Average Year[a]

Age	Men		Women	
	Single	Married	Single	Married
15–20	113	500	79	33
20–25	237	97	106	53
25–30	394	122	151	68
30–40	627	226	126	82
40–50	975	340	171	106
50–60	1,434	520	204	151
60–70	1,768	635	189	158
70–80	1,983	704	206	209
Above 80	1,571	770	176	110

[a]Reprinted with permission of Macmillan Publishing Co., Inc., from *Suicide* by Emile Durkheim. Copyright 1951, renewed 1979 by The Free Press, a Division of Macmillan Publishing Co., Inc.

mium on the group and undermines individualism. In the army, Durkheim argued, the group is more highly valued than the individual, with the result that individuals place less value on their own lives and are ready to sacrifice their lives, if need be, for the sake of the group. But again the selection hypothesis challenges this interpretation. It might well be that people with a strong predisposition toward suicide are attracted to the army, a relatively high-risk environment. To support his thesis and rule out the selection hypothesis, Durkheim employed the same strategy that Klineberg did many years later, degree of exposure to the crucial stimulus. The transition from civilian life to army life, Durkheim argued, should be most stressful during the early months in the army, when the recruit is being subjected to the rigors of basic training and a way of life radically different from the one he had been accustomed to as a civilian. If these strains of transition are to blame for the higher rate of suicide among military personnel when compared with civilians, the suicide rate should be much higher during the first year or so of military service and steadily decline thereafter. But if the higher suicide rate in the army is to be explained by the culture of the army, then the longer the person is in the army, the more exposed he has been to this culture and the more likely he is to commit suicide. In short, if the rate of suicide increases with length of service, this would support Durkheim's hypothesis that military life is causing the suicide.

Durkheim presented data on both the French army and the English army to test this hypothesis. For the French army, he had direct information on length of service, but for the English army, he knew only the age group and assumed that the older the age group, the longer the military service. Durkheim's data are given in Table 10.2. The French data show that the suicide rate increases with length of service, and the English data show that both at home and abroad the suicide rate increases with the age of the

Table 10.2. Suicide Rates by Length of Military Service[a]

Length of Service (years)	French Army: Suicides per 100,000 Men	Age (years)	English Army: Suicides per 100,000 Men	
			Home	India
Less than 1	28	20–25	20	13
1– 3	27	25–30	39	39
3– 5	40	30–35	51	84
5– 7	48	35–40	71	103
7–10	76			

[a]Reprinted with permission of Macmillan Publishing Co., Inc., from *Suicide* by Emile Durkheim. Copyright 1951, renewed 1979 by The Free Press, a Division of Macmillan Publishing Co., Inc.

soldier. To Durkheim, this showed that the greater the exposure to the critical stimulus, the army culture, the more likely is suicide to occur. Clearly the suicide rate is not being caused by the strains of the transition from civilian to military life for the rate is lower among those who are experiencing the transition than it is among those who have long since adjusted to army life.

This review of the time order problem in Durkheim's work concludes our discussion of this problem. In this chapter we dealt with the questions confronting the analyst seeking to establish causal connections among variables that are handled in bivariate analysis. These are the problems of statistical significance, correlation, and the time order of X and Y. In the next chapter we consider the problems that are handled by multivariate analysis.

11

Multivariate Analysis

As noted in Chapter 10, the researcher concerned with establishing causal connections among variables must come to grips with five problems. Three of these were dealt with in the last chapter: significance, correlation, and the time order of X and Y. The fourth and fifth problems, interpretation and conditions affecting the causal relationship, are considered in this chapter.

The problems of interpretation and finding conditions affecting the correlation require the introduction of additional variables, that is, the elaboration of the two-variable relationship by introducing third variables.

A three-variable table is one in which the original relationship between X and Y is reexamined in the light of varying values of the third variable. If a two-variable table takes up only a single sheet of paper of computer output, a three-variable table takes up two or more sheets of paper depending on the number of categories on the third variable. A three-variable table in which there are three categories on the third variable would look like Table 11.1. As can be seen from the three-variable table, the relationship between X and Y is shown under each condition of the third variable, in this instance, three different times.

The correlation between X and Y in each part of the three-variable table is known as the *partial correlation* as distinct from the original correlation between X and Y shown in a two-variable table, which is also known as the zero-order correlation. Contained within every three-variable table are three two-variable tables. The first two-variable table is the relationship between X and Y which can be computed by adding the numbers in each part of the table, thereby collapsing the three fourfold tables of the three-variable table into one fourfold table. The second two variable table contained within the

Table 11.1.   Form of a Three-Variable Table, with Two Categories Each on the First and Second Variables and Three Categories on the Third Variable

three-variable table is the relationship between the third variable (the test factor) and the independent variable X, and the third two-variable table is the relationship between the test factor and the dependent variable Y. These two tables are constructed from the marginals of the three-variable table. The column marginals show the relationship between X and the test factor; the row marginals show the relationship between Y and the test factor. These two correlations, the test factor and X and the test factor and Y, are known as the *marginal correlations* (because they are based on the marginals).

INTERPRETATION

A common goal of the researcher is to find an *interpretation* of some presumably causal relationship uncovered by analysis. The researcher wants to know why X is causing Y; to answer this question, third variables that bear on the hypotheses must be introduced. An excellent example of interpretation is provided by Hans Zeisel in his book *Say It with Figures*. Zeisel presents data (Table 11.2) showing that men have more automobile accidents than

Table 11.2.   Automobile Accidents by Sex[a]

	Men	Women
Never had an auto accident	56%	68%
Had at least one accident	44	32
	100%	100%
	(7,080)	(6,950)

[a]From *Say It with Figures*, Fifth Edition, by Hans Zeisel. Copyright 1947, 1950, © 1957, 1968 by Harper & Row, Publishers, Inc. Reprinted by permission of Harper & Row, Publishers, Inc.

women. When I use this material in my course I ask my students for possible interpretations of this finding, and through the years a number of hypotheses have been offered, including the following:

1. Men are more likely to drink and be drunken drivers.
2. Men work harder and are more likely to be tired when they drive.
3. Men are more ready than women to take risks.
4. Women are smarter than men and do a better job of reading road signs.
5. Men drive more than women.

To test these hypotheses, it is necessary to classify the people in the study according to their position on the variable introduced by each hypothesis. For example, to test the first hypothesis we would have to know how much men and women drink before they drive, and to test the second we would need to develop some measure of fatigue and apply it to the people in the study. Of these various hypotheses, Zeisel has data that bear only on the last one, that men drive more than women.

Miles driven per year is introduced as the third variable. The sample first is divided into two groups, those who drove less than 10,000 miles per year and those who drove more than 10,000 miles a year, a classification of light and heavy drivers. Then within each group the relationship between sex and automobile accidents is reexamined. The data on the three variables are shown in Table 11.3. This table shows that when miles driven per year is taken into account the relationship between sex and automobile accidents disappears. Women are just as likely as men to have automobile accidents in the group that drove under 10,000 miles a year and the same is true in the group that drove more than 10,000 miles a year. In short, the *partial correlations* are zero. This reduction of the partial correlations toward zero is the statistical result of finding a variable that interprets the relationship between

Table 11.3. Automobile Accidents by Miles Driven per Year[a]

	Miles Driven Per Year			
	Under 10,000		Over 10,000	
	Men	Women	Men	Women
No accidents	75%	75%	48%	48%
At least one accident	25	25	52	52
	100%	100%	100%	100%
	(2,070)	(5,035)	(5,010)	(1,915)

[a]From *Say It with Figures*, Fifth Edition, by Hans Zeisel. Copyright 1947, 1950, © 1957, 1968 by Harper & Row, Publishers, Inc. Reprinted by permission of Harper & Row, Publishers, Inc.

X and Y. We now know that the reason why men have more automobile accidents than women is because they drive more than women do. The variable, miles driven, interprets the relationship between X and Y.

The second statistical property of interpretation is that the third variable, the test factor, is positively related to both the independent variable X and the dependent variable Y. These correlations are found in the marginals of the three-variable table. The base figures in the columns show that men are much more likely than women to drive more than 10,000 miles per year. The percentages are a clue to what the marginals in the rows would be. Since many more men and women have accidents if they drive over 10,000 miles a year, it is clear that the frequency of accidents is positively correlated with miles driven. In short, when the three-variable table interprets the relationship between X and Y, we will always find that the marginal correlations are positive and stronger than the original correlation between X and Y.

Explanation versus Interpretation

Sometimes a third variable will generate the results of interpretation in that the partial correlations will both be smaller than the original correlation and the marginal correlations will be positive but will not actually interpret the finding. Rather we may have found a third variable that "explains" in the sense of rationalizing the relationship between X and Y. The difference between interpretation and explanation hinges on the time order of the test factor and the independent variable X.

The test factor is an interpretive variable only if it intervenes in time between X and Y, that is, comes after X and before Y in time. In the example of interpretation used here, miles driven per year meets this requirement of being an intervening variable. It clearly comes after sex and before automobile accidents in time. But suppose the test factor is an antecedent variable, one that comes before X in time. In this instance we would have an example of explanation. Both the independent and dependent variables are being caused by the antecedent variable. In such an event, the relationship between X and Y is spurious, meaning that it does not indicate a causal relationship. One famous spurious relationship is the finding that countries with high populations of storks have higher birthrates than countries with small populations of storks. But it would be wrong to presume that the high stork population is causing the birthrate. Rather both characteristics are the result of the stage of economic development of the society. The stork population is largest in agrarian societies, which tend to have high birthrates. The state of the economy is the antecedent variable, causing both the stork population and the birthrate. Another well-known example is the strong relationship between the number of fire engines at the fire and the amount of damage done by the fire. It would be absurd to assume that the fire engines are causing the damage. Rather the amount of damage and the number of fire engines are caused by the size of the fire. The researcher who knows the time order of the variables will have no difficulty sorting out cases of interpretation from cases of explanation. Unfortunately, however, the time order of the variables is not always known and the researcher is not certain that the findings are interpreted accurately.

SPECIFICATION

The fifth problem confronting the researcher trying to establish causal connections among variables is finding conditions that strengthen the relationship between X and Y. This is known as *specification* of the correlation. A third variable is said to specify the correlation when one of the partial correlations is larger than the original correlation and the other partial correlation is smaller. This indicates that the third variable is operating as a condition affecting the correlation between X and Y. In *The Logic of Survey Analysis** Rosenberg provides a number of examples of specification, including one involving the concept of self-esteem, which he has studied in depth. Rosenberg found that self-esteem of adolescents was related to social class, with 50 percent of the youngsters from the upper class, 46 percent of those from the middle class, and 39 percent of those from the lower class having high self-esteem. The overall percentage difference in this two-variable table is 11 points. Rosenberg then introduced sex as a test factor with the results shown in Table 11.4. The table shows that the relationship between socioeconomic status and self-esteem is much stronger among boys than girls, the overall percentage difference among boys being 19 points but among girls only 6 points. Sex thus specifies the correlation between SES and self-esteem, with maleness enhancing the correlation and femaleness weakening it.

Table 11.4. Percentage High Self-Esteem by SES and Sex[a]

Socioeconomic Status	Boys		Girls	
Upper	55%	(89)	47%	(106)
Middle	47%	(1383)	46%	(1311)
Lower	36%	(168)	41%	(172)
% difference	19		6	

[a]From Morris Rosenberg, *Society and the Adolescent Self-Image*, Princeton, New Jersey: Princeton University Press, 1965, p. 41. (Cited in *The Logic of Survey Analysis*.)

*Morris Rosenberg, *The Logic of Survey Analysis*. New York: Basic Books, 1968.

Rosenberg provides another example of specification. He shows that blacks are more likely to score high on anomia than whites, 44 compared with 32 percent, for a percentage difference of 12 points. Place of residence was introduced as a test factor in this analysis, with people classified according to whether they grew up in a rural or urban environment. The results of this analysis are shown in Table 11.5. The difference between whites and blacks is much greater among those from rural areas than among those who grew up in urban areas. In the rural group the percentage difference is 25 points, but in the urban group it is only 6 points. Clearly place of residence specifies the correlation between race and anomia.

There are two statistical properties of three-variable tables that indicate specification. Like the properties indicative of interpretation, these involve the partial correlations and the marginal correlations. In specification one of the partial correlations is always larger than the original correlation and the other is smaller. As for the marginal correlations, the test factor is not related to either or both of the original variables X and Y. In Table 11.4 approximately 70 percent of the rural sample is white and in the urban sample whites also constitute about 70 percent. Nor is anomia related to place of residence. Some 39 percent of the rural residents and 41 percent of the urban residents are high on anomia, a difference too small to be statistically significant for this size sample.

Specification of a Zero Correlation

When researchers find that their hunches are not supported by the data, that contrary to their expectations there is no relationship between X and Y, they frequently end that line of analysis and turn to a different topic. But sometimes researchers are so convinced they will find a relationship that they do not stop at the zero correlation but rather introduce third variables in the hope that a third variable might be masking a relationship between X and Y which will become evident when that third variable is taken into account. This operation is known as specifying a zero correlation. An example is provided by the data of Table 11.5. As noted, there was no relationship between place of residence and anomia. But when race is taken into account as the test factor, we find that place of residence is related to anomia, as can be seen from Table. 11.6.

Among blacks place of residence is strongly related to anomia with blacks from urban environments much more anomic than those from rural environments. But among whites there is a slight negative correlation, with urban whites slightly less anomic than rural whites. When zero-order correlations are specified, it is typically found that the correlation changes direction from one group to the next on the third variable, and that the zero correlation is the result of averaging a positive and a negative correlation.

Zeisel provides another example of specification of a zero-order correlation using Gallup data from 1940 dealing with attitudes toward getting

Table 11.5. Anomia by Race and Place of Residence (Percentage High on Anomia)[a]

Anomia	Rural		Urban	
	White	Black	White	Black
High	21%	46%	37%	43%
Low	79	54	63	57
	100%	100%	100%	100%
N	(211)	(89)	(436)	(190)
% difference	25		6	

[a]From Lewis M. Killian and Charles M. Grigg, "Urbanism, Race and Anomia," *American Journal of Sociology* **46** (May 1962), p. 662. (Reprinted with permission of the University of Chicago Press.) (Cited in *The Logic of Survey Analysis*.)

Table 11.6. Percentage High on Anomia by Place of Residence and Race[a]

Anomia	Whites		Blacks	
	Rural	Urban	Rural	Urban
High	46%	43%	21%	37%
Low	54	57	79	63
	100%	100%	100%	100%
N	(211)	(436)	(89)	(190)
% difference	−3		16	

[a]From Lewis M. Killian and Charles M. Grigg, "Urbanism, Race and Anomia," *American Journal of Sociology* **46** (May 1962), p. 662. (Reprinted with permission of the University of Chicago Press.) (Cited in *The Logic of Survey Analysis*.)

involved in European affairs. Those who wanted the United States to stay out of the war in Europe were known as isolationists, and the Gallup poll showed there was no relationship, contrary to expectation, between age and isolationism. Socioeconomic status was then introduced as a test factor with the results shown in Table 11.7.

The figures in the total column show no relationship between age and isolationism, but when SES is introduced as a test factor we find that in the upper class isolationism decreases with age by 13 percentage points and that in the middle class there is also a tendency for isolationism to decrease with age with a 5 point difference. But among the lower class, the correlation is reversed. In this group isolationism increases with age. Socioeconomic status was thus masking complicated relationships between age and isolationism. Among the well-to-do the relationship is negative; among the underprivileged it is positive.

Table 11.7. Percentage Isolationists by Age and
Socioeconomic Status[a]

Age	Upper	Middle	Lower	Total
Under 30	30%	28%	22%	26%
30–49	21%	23%	26%	24%
50 and over	17%	23%	34%	26%
% difference	−13	−5	+12	

[a]From *Say It with Figures*, Fifth Edition, by Hans Zeisel. Copyright 1947, 1950, © 1957, 1968 by Harper & Row, Publishers, Inc. Reprinted by permission of Harper & Row, Publishers, Inc.

INDEPENDENT EFFECTS: MULTIPLE CAUSATION

A third outcome of three-variable analysis is the discovery that the third variable has an effect on the dependent variable Y independent of the original independent variable X. This outcome frequently occurs when the researchers identify a number of variables that influence the dependent variable. When they then examine the impact of two causal variables simultaneously in a three-variable table, they often find that both variables continue to be related to the dependent variable independent of each other. An example of this type of outcome is provided by a study I did some years ago of people who no longer identified with their religion of origin and considered themselves as having no religion, people who we called apostates.* In that study a number of personality characteristics were found to be related to apostasy; these included feelings about parents, political radicalism, intellectualism, personality strain, and commitment to idealism. When these traits were examined two at a time, we almost invariably found that each variable continued to be related to apostasy when the other was held constant. For example, in a two-variable table it was found that intellectualism had a fairly strong relationship with apostasy. Among those who scored low on an index of intellectualism only 8 percent were apostates, a figure that rose to 13 percent among those who were in the medium category and 28 percent among those who were high on intellectualism. The overall percentage difference is 20 points. The quality of parental relations was also related to apostasy, with 8 percent of the students who said their relations with their parents were good, 15 percent of those who said parental relations were fair, and 26 percent of those who said relations with their parents were poor apostatizing. Here the overall percentage difference is 18 points.

The joint impact of intellectualism and quality of parental relations is shown in Table 11.8. (These data refer only to the students who said they were raised as Protestants.) By reading across the rows and down the

*David Caplovitz and Fred Sherrow, *The Religious Dropouts*, Beverly Hills, California: Sage Publications, 1977.

Table 11.8. **Apostasy by Quality of Parental Relations and Intellectualism**[a]

Intellectualism	Quality of Parental Relations			% Difference
	Good	Fair	Poor	
Low	6% (4,323)	10% (1,808)	18% (529)	12
Medium	9% (1,832)	16% (933)	25% (319)	16
High	21% (706)	27% (438)	51% (196)	30
% difference	15	17	33	

[a]From David Caplovitz and Fred Sherrow, *The Religious Dropouts: Apostasy among College Graduates*, Beverly Hills, California: Sage Publications, 1977, p. 80.

columns we see that both parental relations and intellectualism have an effect on apostasy. The percentage differences in the rows and columns tell an additional story. Not only is each independent variable having an effect on the dependent variable, but each variable is acting as a condition affecting the degree of influence of the other variable. As quality of parental relations deteriorates, the influence of intellectualism on apostasy becomes stronger. And the more intellectual the respondent, the stronger the effect of parental relations on apostasy. In short, this table illustrates specification as well as independent effects. The initial relationship between intellectualism and apostasy yielded a percentage difference of 20 points. We now see that two of the partial correlations are smaller, but that one is larger than the original correlation. The same is true for quality of parental relations. In the two-variable table, it showed a percentage difference of 18 points. We now see that one of the partials is smaller, one about the same, and one larger than the original correlation, in keeping with the outcome of specification.

Although tables demonstrating independent effects frequently show specification as well, this need not be the case. In some instances one of the two independent variables might reduce somewhat the effect of the other, although by no means washing it out altogether, as in the case of interpretation. The reason for this is that the independent variables that are influencing the dependent variable tend to be related to each other. As a result, when the effect of only one of these variables is considered in a two-variable table, the effect of the independent variable is being assisted by its silent partner, the other variable that is not being held constant. When the partner is held constant in a three-variable table, each may have its effect reduced somewhat since it does not have the secret partner.

An example of such an outcome is found in a study dealing with the impact of inflation.* The respondents were asked a series of questions that measured their commitment to free enterprise. This attitude was found to be related to the four subsamples in the study, the poor, blue-collar workers, retired people, and white-collar workers. Only 33 percent of the poor were

*David Caplovitz, *Making Ends Meet*, Beverly Hills, Calif.: Sage Publications, 1979.

committed to free enterprise, compared with 58 percent of the working class, 66 percent of the retired, and 75 percent of the middle class. The overall percentage difference between the poor and the middle class is 42 points. On a measure of inflation crunch—that is, the extent to which the family was hurting because of inflation—some 77 percent of the respondents who were low were committed to free enterprise compared with 49 percent of those who were high, a percentage difference of 28 points. Table 11.9, which shows the results when these variables are considered in a three-variable table, indicates that both inflation crunch and type of sample are strongly related to commitment to free enterprise when the other variable is held constant. But the partial correlations are somewhat smaller than the original correlations. The overall difference between the poor and the white-collar samples was 42 points, and in Table 11.9 the partial correlations are 30 and 35 percentage points. In the two-variable table, inflation crunch showed a 28 percentage point difference in commitment to free enterprise between the groups low and high on inflation crunch. In Table 11.9 the percentage differences for inflation crunch range from 18 to 25 points, that is, the partials are somewhat smaller than the original correlation.

SUPPRESSION–DISTORTION EFFECT

A fourth outcome of three-variable analysis is what Rosenberg identifies and explicates as *suppression* or *distortion* in his book *The Logic of Survey Analysis*. An expected relationship either does not occur or is weaker than expected. Further analysis might indicate that some third variable is working at cross-purposes with the original independent variable. This third variable, which is influencing the dependent variable as well, turns out to be negatively related to X, the original independent variable.

An example of suppression–distortion is provided by the data in the annual NORC polls. These surveys contain three questions that measure faith in people. It turns out that an index of faith in people is positively

Table 11.9. Commitment to Free Enterprise by Subsample and Inflation Crunch[a]

Subsample	Inflation Crunch			% Difference
	Low		High	
Poor	52%	(54)	29% (269)	23
Blue collar	73%	(232)	48% (349)	25
Retired	75%	(169)	57% (140)	18
White collar	82%	(487)	64% (282)	18
% difference	30		35	

[a]From David Caplovitz, *Making Ends Meet: The Impact of Inflation and Recession on American Families*, Beverly Hills, California: Sage Publications, 1979, p. 198.

related to education and to age, but these relationships are weak. Among the poorly educated 28 percent are high on faith in people, among those in the middle on education 33 percent are high on faith in people, and among the highly educated 39 percent are, for a percentage difference of 11 points. For age, the figures range from 30 to 39 percent, a 9-point difference. Table 11.10, the three-variable table, shows that age is negatively related to education and hence these variables are working at cross-purposes. The hidden partner in the two-variable tables is lowering the correlation between X and Y (whether X be age or education). When the effect of one of these independent variables is examined while the other is held constant, we suddenly find strong correlations emerging. In interpretation, as we saw, the partial correlations reduced toward zero and the original correlation was due entirely to the marginal correlations. In specification, the marginal correlations tended to be zero and the original correlation was due entirely to the partials. We now find that in suppression–distortion both the partial correlations and the marginal correlations play a role. In this instance, all the partial correlations are *larger* than the original correlations, while one marginal correlation is positive and the other is negative. In this instance, both age and education are positively related to faith in people but age and education (one of the marginal correlations) are negatively related.

Rosenberg presents a hypothetical example in which the distorting variable leads to a reversal of the original correlation between X and Y. When attitude toward civil rights is related to social class, the data show, somewhat surprisingly, that the working class is more sympathetic to civil rights than is the middle class (Table 11.11). Rosenberg then introduces race as a test factor with the results shown in Table 11.12. Here we find that the middle class is now more pro-civil rights than the working class. This holds true among both blacks and whites. The test factor, race, is strongly related to civil rights as blacks, whatever their social class, are more in favor of civil rights then are whites. But race is negatively related to social class in that blacks, who are more likely to support civil rights, nonetheless are more likely to belong to the social class that opposes civil rights, the working class. This relationship can be seen from the base figures, as the great majority of the blacks belong to the working class while the great majority of the whites belong to the middle class. Race was not only reducing the relationship

Table 11.10. **High Faith in People by Age and Education**

Education	Age						% Difference
	Under 30		30–49		50 plus		
Low	25%	(85)	33%	(111)	45%	(211)	20
Medium	34%	(120)	43%	(194)	52%	(223)	18
High	44%	(191)	54%	(128)	63%	(119)	19
% difference	19		19		18		

Table 11.11.   Attitude Toward Civil Rights by Social Class[a]

Civil Rights Score	Middle Class	Working Class
High	37%	45%
Low	73	55
	100%	100%
N	(120)	(120)

[a]From Morris Rosenberg, *The Logic of Survey Analysis*, New York: Basic Books, 1968, p. 94.

Table 11.12.   Attitude Toward Civil Rights by Social Class and Race[a]

Civil Rights Score	Blacks		Whites	
	Middle Class	Working Class	Middle Class	Working Class
High	70%	50%	30%	20%
Low	30	50	70	80
	100%	100%	100%	100%
N	(20)	(100)	(100)	(20)

[a]From Morris Rosenberg, *The Logic of Survey Analysis*, New York: Basic Books, 1968, p. 95.

between social class and civil rights, but it actually was able to reverse the relationship giving the false impression that the working class was more in favor of civil rights than the middle class.

Lazarsfeld's Elaboration Formula

Paul Lazarsfeld invented a formula that shows the relationship of the original correlation between X and Y (xy) to the various correlations that are in the three-variable table.* The Lazarsfeld equation is

$$(xy) = (xy)^{t+} \oplus (xy)^{t-} + (xt)(ty)$$

On the left side is the original correlation, shown in a two-variable table, between x and y. On the right are the two partial correlations and the two marginal correlations. The plus sign with the circle around it signifies that the two partial correlations are to be averaged and that this average should be weighted by the proportion of cases in each of the partial tables. For example, if 60 percent of the cases were plus on T, then the partial correla-

*See Patricia Kendall and Paul F. Lazarsfeld, "The Problems of Survey Analysis," in Robert K. Merton and Paul F. Lazarsfeld (Eds.), *Continuities in the American Soldier*, Glencoe, Illinois: Free Press, 1950, pp. 133–196.

tion for T^+ should be given a weight of 60 and the partial correlation for T^- should be given a weight of 40 when the average is computed. According to the formula, the marginal correlations should be multiplied together. Three of the outcomes of three-variable analysis can now be located with the aid of this formula in the following scheme:

$$(xy) = (xy)^{t+} \oplus (xy)^{t-} + (xt)\,(ty)$$

Interpretation	0	0	Positive number
Specification	Larger	Smaller	0
Suppression–distortion	Larger	Larger	Negative number

In all his writings about the elaboration formula, Lazarsfeld focused on interpretation and specification and never saw that the outcomes indicating suppression–distortion also fit within his formula. Both partials can be larger than the original correlation because one of the marginal correlations is positive and the other one is negative, so that the product of the two is always a negative number.

As can be seen from the formula, the various outcomes of elaboration are dependent on the partial and marginal correlations. Another way of locating these outcomes is to construct a property space from the two dimensions, the partial correlations, and the marginal correlations. This is done in Table 11.13. At least four sectors of this property space are empty, for they involve logically impossible combinations of the marginal and partial correlations. For example, cell *b* refers to an outcome where both partials are smaller than

Table 11.13. Outcomes of Elaboration Based on Marginal and Partial Correlations

Relation of Partial Correlations to Original Correlation	Character of Marginal Correlations		
	T Positively Related to *X* and *Y*	*T* Not Related to *X* or *Y*	*T* Positively Related to *Y*, Negatively to *X*
Both partials smaller	*a* Interpretation, Independent effects	*b*	*c*
One smaller, one larger	*d* Independent effects	*e* Specification, Specifying O correlation	*f* Specifying O correlation
Both larger	*g*	*h*	*i* Suppression

the original correlation and the marginal correlations are zero in that the test factor is not related to X or Y. But according to the elaboration formula this is impossible because the average of the partial correlations will be smaller than the original correlation. Similarly, cell c is impossible for here the marginal correlations are negative, and since this negative number must be added to partial correlations that are smaller than the original correlation, the number on the right side of the equation will be still further reduced and much smaller than the number on the left side. For the same reasons, cells g and h refer to impossible combinations since the number on the right side of the equation will be much larger than the number on the left.

In addition to locating the three main outcomes of three-variable analysis—interpretation, specification, and suppression—this property space also allows us to locate independent effects and the specification of zero-order correlations. We have seen that independent effects always involve positive marginal correlations since the test factor is always related positively to both X and Y, but partial correlations can both be smaller or one can be smaller and the other larger than the original correlation. Hence we locate independent effects in both cells a and d. Specification of a zero-order correlation always involves partial correlations in which one is larger and the other smaller than the original correlation. But two outcomes of the marginal correlations apply. Either the test factor can be unrelated to X or Y or it can be positively related to one and negatively related to the other. Hence we have located specification of a zero-order correlation in both cells e and f of this table.

We have considered in this chapter several outcomes of three-variable analysis. In addition to the outcomes reviewed in which the researcher learns something, there is, of course, a very common outcome, where the researcher learns nothing because the test factor has no impact on the original correlation. The logic of these outcomes applies to more complicated tables as well, tables involving four, five, or even more variables. But the researcher who engages in tabular analysis as distinct from regression analysis seldom deals with more than three variables for the simple reason that additional variables reduce the base figures on which the percentaging is done to the point where the percentages become highly unstable.

12

Regression Analysis and Correlation

MARK GALLOPS

Social researchers seldom are concerned simply with the association between two variables. Rather, they are interested in causation. Investigations into social causation ask how changes in one variable at one point in time affect changes in another variable at a subsequent point in time. This chapter reviews two analytic techniques that enable the researcher to answer this question. In contrast to the earlier chapters in this section, this chapter presents more formal statistical techniques which allow for the development of more complex models of explanation.

In empirical social research, data on several variables usually are collected at one point in time for a number of individuals or other units of analysis. In reference to time this is known as "cross-sectional" data because it provides a picture of reality at one moment in time. Using these data, researchers want to say as much as possible about the causal relationships between variables of theoretical interest. Once information is collected the social researcher will want to establish that a relationship exists between the variables defined by the theory under study. A correlational analysis is one way to determine this. If the association is present, the researcher will then want to estimate the size and character of the causal effect proposed by his or her theoretical understanding of their relationship. Because cross-sectional data are collected at one point in time individual characteristics cannot be examined over time to see if changes in one produce changes in another. By testing whether characteristic *A* differs for different categories of characteristic *B* across the sample we can infer that individual changes in *B* over time will lead to shifts in *A*. Given this assumption linear regression analysis can be used to test for and measure the size of the directional association.

Chapter 10 reviewed several of the most elemental measures of association. These were measures of reciprocal association. They are used primarily to assess the relationship between two variables which are nominal or ordinal in character. This chapter reviews two techniques appropriate for interval scales, the Pearson product–moment correlational analysis and linear regression analysis. The Pearson product–moment correlation is also a measure of reciprocal association, but it is discussed at length in this chapter because it provides the foundation for carrying out and understanding linear regression analysis. One of the advantages of these methods is that they can examine the relationships of several variables simultaneously, and they provide standardized measures of the size of these relationships. They also introduce the possibility of controlling for the effects of other variables when looking at the association between any pair of variables. While these methods of analysis allow the researcher to say more about the relationships between variables, they also require more restrictive assumptions about the character of the variables which are analyzed. These assumptions will be discussed in detail later.

The first section of this chapter discusses the characteristics of variables, known as measures of central tendency and dispersion, whose use is essential in computing and understanding correlational and linear regression analysis. These characteristics are the mean, the variance, and the standard deviation. Second, the logical and statistical meanings of correlational analysis are presented. Further, the restrictions on the types of variables to which this method and linear regression analysis can be applied are reviewed. Methods to statistically control the effects of other variables are also discussed. Third, correlational analysis is extended to show how it provides the basis for linear regression analysis. In addition, a simple bivariate regression analysis is carried out. Next a brief description shows how the bivariate case in regression analysis can be extended to deal with cases of three or more variables and how the process of statistical control works in the regression technique. Finally, certain special topics in regression analysis, such as the use of "dummy variables," are discussed. The chapter closes with a review of several important considerations the researcher must keep in mind when using correlational and linear regression analysis.

THE CHARACTERISTICS OF A VARIABLE'S DISTRIBUTION

Every variable has a distribution, and each distribution has special characteristics. It is the characteristics of the distribution which are used to compute the level of association between two or more variables. The distribution of a variable simply refers to the number of cases that fall into each of its categories. For a variable such as sex the distribution refers to how many individuals are men and how many are women. For more complex variables such as education it refers to how many people have achieved a specific number of years of schooling.

Several statistics provide summary information on the character of a variable's distribution. First are the measures of central tendency. There are three of these; the mean, the median, and the mode. The *mode* is that category of a variable in which most individuals fall. For a variable such as sex, in a sample where there are 430 women and 470 men, the mode would be the value assigned to the category for men. In the case of the variable education, measured in years, the mode would be 12 as most people in the population stopped their education after completing high school and thus have 12 years of education.

The *median* is that value of a variable above which 50 percent of the cases fall and below which 50 percent of the cases fall. For the variable sex, with the distribution just described, the median would also be the value assigned to men because over half of the cases of the sample reside in that category. (It should be noted that the mode and the median have little meaning when applied to a dichotomous variable.) In the case of education, however, the median would not be the same value as the mode. Assume that a sample of 900 people was distributed on the variable education as shown in Table 12.1. In this case the median would be 13 years since summing the percentages cumulatively from either the high values or the low values will reach the 50-percent level when the proportion of those people with 13 years of education is added to the existing sum.

The last measure of central tendency, and the most important, is the *mean*. This statistic is the simple arithmetic average of all the values of the variable, summed across the cases and divided by the total number of cases. This procedure is represented by

$$\text{mean} = \bar{X} = \Sigma x_i / N \tag{12.1}$$

$\bar{X}$ represents the mean, N represents the number of cases in the sample, and X represents the value of each individual case where i has the range 1 through N. For the variable sex, where all women are assigned the value 0 and all men are assigned the value 1, the mean is .522 (470/900). For

Table 12.1. *Hypothetical Distribution of Education Completed*

Years of Education	11	12	13	14	15	16	17	Total
Number in category	40	400	100	60	30	210	60	900
Percent in category	4.4%	44.4	11.1	16.6	3.3	23.3	6.6	100%

education the mean is 13.57 years of education. What do these values represent? It is obvious that no one has a value for sex of .522, or any value other than 0 are 1. Moreover, no one has a value for education other than a whole number representing a year. It is substantively meaningless to say someone has 13.6 years of education. Unlike the median and the mode, the mean does not necessarily have a value which is a category of the variable. Rather it represents that point on the value continuum which is the shortest average distance from the distribution of cases on that continuum. For the variable sex, which is a nominal one, it represents the percentage of cases in the category assigned the highest value. Thus the mean of .522 indicates that 52.2 percent of the sample are men, since the category for men was coded 1. If the coding had been reversed—if women were assigned the value 1 and men 0—the mean would have been .478, indicating 47.8 percent of the sample are women. Such a change in coding is legitimate when dealing with nominal variables because no information is lost in making the conversion.

The case of education is different in this regard. Here the mean is computed on an interval-level variable. The mean of 13.57 signifies that on average the sample has more than a high school degree (12 years) but less than an associate of arts of degree (14 years). Rearranging the order of the categories is not possible with a variable such as education because their rank order contains important information: the categories are not only ranked but are separated by constant intervals (one year of schooling). It is consequently possible to give a substantive interpretation to the value of the mean even though it does not correspond to a category of the variable. In the case of an interval-level variable the mean can be discussed in terms of distances from existing categories, whereas this is not meaningful in the case of nominal or ordinal variables.

The mean of a variable has two other characteristics that play an important role in the discussion of correlational and linear regression analysis:

$$\Sigma(X_i - \bar{X}) = 0 \tag{12.2}$$

and

$$\Sigma(X_i - \bar{X})^2 = \text{a minimum} \tag{12.3}$$

Equation 12.2 indicates that the sum of the differences between each individual value and the mean of those values will equal zero. Equation 12.3 indicates that for any value chosen on the value continuum of a variable, the mean is the unique value that will produce the lowest value when the deviations of each observed value from it is squared and then summed.

Knowing the mean allows two other characteristics of the distribution of a variable to be computed, the variance and the standard deviation. The *variance* is the average of the squared distance of the observed values of a variable from its mean:

$$\text{variance} = s^2 = \Sigma(X_i - \bar{X})^2/N \tag{12.4}$$

The symbols here are defined in the same terms as they were in computing the mean. The variance of a variable is based on the sum of the squared differences of each observation from the mean. The distances from the mean are squared in order to give them all positive values, and their sum is then divided by the number of cases to obtain the average "squared" distance. The numerator of this equation is known as the *total variation* in the dispersion of the variable.

The *standard deviation* is a nonlinear function of the variance; it is its square root. The standard deviation, *s*, inverts the function that was used to make all the deviations from the mean positive. (In this chapter it is always assumed that when the square root of a value is taken only the positive value is used.)

$$\text{standard deviation} = \sqrt{s^2} = s \tag{12.5}$$

In Table 12.2 the distribution characteristics of education for a sample of 20 men are computed. (The following sample, which will be analyzed throughout this chapter, is a subset of a larger data set. Although the data set from which it is taken is a random sample, the one analyzed here is not, as it was, selectively chosen to generate results which would allow certain issues to be discussed.)

Table 12.2. Measures of Dispersion for Education

Years of Education	Number in Category	$\bar{X}$ Mean of Sample	$(X_i - \bar{X})$	$(X_i - \bar{X})^2$	Total Variation in Category
9	2	12.75	−3.75	14.063	28.126
10	1	12.75	−2.75	7.563	7.563
11	2	12.75	−1.75	3.063	6.126
12	7	12.75	−0.75	.563	3.941
13	2	12.75	0.25	.063	.126
14	2	12.75	1.25	1.563	3.126
15	1	12.75	2.25	5.063	5.063
16	1	12.75	3.25	10.563	10.563
18	2	12.75	5.25	27.563	55.126

$\bar{X}$ = Mean = 12.75   Variance = s^2 = 5.988   Standard deviation = s = 2.447

THE LOGIC OF SAMPLING AND THE NORMAL DISTRIBUTION

In every episode of social research the investigator has two basic concerns: Does a relationship exist between the variables under examination in the form which the researcher expected? And how reliable is the relationship found among the sample of cases examined? The first is a concern with the adequacy of the theory which led the researcher to examine the pattern of associations among a particular set of variables. The second is a concern with the comparability of the relationships found in the sample to those in the population from which it is drawn. The first issue, which was discussed in Chapter 10, is reconsidered later in this chapter. The second issue is discussed at some length here as it is essential to understanding the meaning of the Pearson correlation and linear regression and how significance tests are made of the estimates of associations between the variables.

Two basic problems exist in considering the reliability of a set of data, measurement error and sampling bias. Measurement error refers to systematic differences between objective reality and the information collected due to the character of the topic investigated or to problems in the research instrument. The first type of measurement error can take the form of underreporting by respondents due to the sensitivity of the research topic. Researchers in areas such as criminal activity, marital problems, and homosexuality often find that people are not willing to talk about these aspects of their lives. On the other side of the coin, overreporting may occur: people may inflate their estimates of annual income and other measures of "social success" to impress the researcher, thus creating systematic upward bias.

The research instrument, in many cases a survey interview, can create systematic errors by providing response categories for questions that are emotionally or ideologically charged. For instance, in looking at the class identification of individuals several studies found that the respondents refused to label themselves members of the "poor" or "lower" classes regardless of their financial situation. They preferred to place themselves among the working class because it was a less negative label.

In social research the investigator attempts to minimize systematic errors. The goal is to eliminate all but purely random measurement error, which is not specific to any category of a variable being measured but is randomly and evenly distributed across all categories of the variables analyzed.

The second limitation on the reliability of social research and its findings is sampling bias: How closely does the distribution of characteristics within the sample approximate the distribution among the population? The measures of the distribution of a variable can be used to determine the likelihood that the mean of the sample, and its variance or standard deviation, equals or is close to those characteristics in the population. The characteristics of the population are commonly referred to as *parameters* and characteristics of the sample as *statistics*.

Empirical social research attempts to ensure that measurement errors are random and that sampling from the population is random. If these conditions are obtained, and it is generally assumed they are, researchers can test the reliability of their findings by computing significance tests. The logic of significance tests is based on the logic of hypothetical repeated random sampling. A researcher will usually draw only one random sample from a population. By building upon inductive statistical theory it is possible to define the probability with which the statistic will fall within a specific distance of the parameter. Statistical theory holds that any given population has a fixed set of parameters. These parameters can be approximated by repeated random sampling from that population. If a large number of samples were drawn, it would be possible to construct a distribution of the sample statistics called a *sampling distribution*. The distribution of sample means, for example, will be a normal distribution with the population parameter as its mean. This is true regardless of whether the distribution of the variable in the population is normal.

The normal distribution is commonly known as the *bell-shaped curve* and one of its most popularly recognized forms is the IQ distribution. Based on repeated samplings and nationally administered tests the IQ distribution is known to have the shape seen in Figure 12.1. The normal curve shows the proportion of people falling into each IQ category in the population. The normal curve has several standard characteristics. First, it is symmetrical about the mean; as shown here, the distribution to the right of the value 100, the mean, is the mirror image of the distribution to the left of it. In the case of the normal curve, the mean = the median = the mode. In addition, the exact proportion of the population that exists at specific distances from the mean is known (distances as measured in units of the standard deviation). Assume that the total area under the curve is represented by the value 1, or 100 percent, meaning the distribution contains all the cases in the population. Under a normal curve exactly 34.13 percent of the population lies within the first standard deviation on either side of the mean. In terms of the IQ distribution, 34.13 percent of the population has an IQ greater than 100 and less than 115. The same is true for the range of IQs from 85 to 10. Further, 47.73 percent of the population lies within 2 standard deviations distance on each side of the mean. This means 47.73 percent of the population has an IQ between 100 and 130. By using simple addition it is possible to determine the probability of having any IQ given the knowledge of the mean

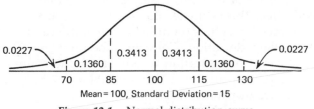

Mean = 100, Standard Deviation = 15

Figure 12.1. Normal distribution curve.

and standard deviation of the distribution. For instance, since the mean is the median we know that 50 percent of the population has an IQ greater than 100, half has an IQ lower than 100. Adding this to the proportion falling within 2 standard deviations of the mean we know that only 2.27 percent of the population has an IQ greater than 130 and 2.27 percent has an IQ less than 70.

This logic translates back directly to a consideration of the relationship between population parameters and sample statistics. Repeated samplings from the population would create, theoretically, distributions of statistics which would be normal with the parameter as the mean. Using this information we can make probability statements about the distance between the observed statistic of the sample and the unobserved parameters of the population. Because this is a feature of all sample statistics, such as the mean and the standard deviation, we can apply this process to measures of association such as correlations and regression coefficients which are computed on the basis of these statistics.

The general use of statistical tests deals with the problem of accepting or rejecting the null hypothesis, H_0. The null hypothesis, in the case of measures of association, states that there is no relationship between the variables in the population. Given the statistics of a sample, such as the estimate of an association and its standard error, which is equivalent to its standard deviation, we can state how likely it is that the corresponding relationship in the population is zero. This logic, discussed here in abstract terms, is applied to specific examples later in the chapter.

One characteristic of the sample that affects its ability to approximate the character of the population is its size. In the case of education the range of the variable "years of education" in the population is potentially 0 to 20. If a sample is drawn from the population that contains fewer than 20 individuals, then it is not possible for the sample to match the distribution of the population. In general, the smaller the sample size the less efficient it will be in approximating the parameters of the population. In dealing with this problem it is a common procedure to adjust the computation of the estimate of the variance to correct for sample size. This adjustment has the form

$$s^2 = \Sigma(X_i - \bar{X})^2/(N - 1) \tag{12.6}$$

This equation adjusts the estimate of the variance upward by decreasing the denominator slightly. For very small samples, such as one with 20 cases, the correction will affect the estimate. But as the sample size increases the adjustment has very little effect on the estimate of the variance and, consequently, the standard deviation. Correcting the previous estimates of the distribution statistics for education to adjust for the sample size yields variance = 6.303 (5.988) and standard deviation = 2.5106 (2.447). (The former estimates are in parentheses.)

We now turn to the characteristics of Pearson's correlation and linear regression analysis and their importance as tools for the social researcher.*

THE PEARSON PRODUCT–MOMENT CORRELATION

The Pearson product–moment correlation is a linear and symmetrical measure of association between two variables. The Pearson correlation is linear because it estimates the patterned variation of two variables around their means and is symmetric because for any pair of variables the measure of the correlation is constant, looking at variable A's association with variable B or looking at B's association with A. Both of these features are reflected in the manner in which the correlation is computed and in the substantive interpretation of the correlation.

The method of computing the Pearson correlation builds directly on the information about the distribution of the variables discussed above. The computational definition of the correlation between two variables, X and Y, is given by

$$r_{xy} = r_{yx} = \frac{\Sigma(X_i - \bar{X})(Y_i - \bar{Y})}{\sqrt{\Sigma(x_i - \bar{X})^2 \Sigma(Y_i - \bar{Y})^2}} \qquad (12.7)$$

If $x_i = (X_i - \bar{X})$ and $y_i = (Y_i - \bar{Y})$, this equation can be rewritten as

$$r_{xy} = r_{yx} = \frac{\Sigma x_i y_i}{\sqrt{(\Sigma x_i^2)(\Sigma y_i^2)}} \qquad (12.8)$$

The elements in these equations are familiar when compared to those used in computing the variance of a single variable. The numerator represents the joint variation of the variables about their respective means. The behavior of each case on the two variables is computed, the two elements are multiplied, and the products are summed across all cases in the sample. The value of the numerator is commonly referred to as the *covariance* of the two variables.

The denominator contains two components, the total variation of each variable. Σx_i^2 and Σy_i^2 are the numerators in the computation of the variances of these variables. The value of N, the number of cases in the sample, does not appear in the equation because it occurs once in the numerator and once in the denominator, thus canceling itself out of the computation. Verbally, the correlation between two variables can be defined as the covariation between two variables standardized by the amount of total variation present in each.

*A more extensive introductory discussion of these issues can be found in Hubert M. Blalock, *Social Statistics* (2nd Edition), New York: McGraw-Hill, 1972, Chapters 7 and 8.

Three features of the Pearson correlation are important to note. First, the fact that $r_{xy} = r_{yx}$ shows that the relationship is symmetric. Once again this means the correlation is constant regardless of the order or sequence in which the variables are examined. Second, the values of the measure of correlation are bounded and must exist within the range of -1 to $+1$. A value of -1 represents perfect negative correlation and a value of $+1$ represents perfect positive correlation. The closer the correlation is to 0 the weaker the correlation is between the two variables. Since the denominator has the total variation of both variables as its components, the numerator can never exceed the denominator in size, it can only approach the size of the denominator as the portions of covariance generated by each case have a constant sign and do not cancel one another out in the process of summing. If the values of X are always below its mean when the values of Y are above its mean, and the values of X are above its mean when the values of Y are below its mean, the value of the numerator will have a negative sign and approach the value of the denominator. In the opposite but parallel case the size of the numerator will approach the size of the denominator with a positive sign. In the former case the limit for the value of the correlation would be -1; in the latter case, $+1$. The third feature is that the correlation is in standard units, which means its size is not dependent on the type of units in which the two variables are measured. In the numerator of the correlation equation the units in which each variable is measured are multiplied by one another, making the covariance a function of two types of measurement unit. The denominator adjusts for this by dividing the covariance by both of these units, making the correlation a standardized measure. This allows the researcher to make direct comparisons of the strength of association between different variables based on their correlation.

It is useful to examine graphically what the limits of the correlation are as a measure of association. The four graphs seen in Figure 12.2 are the scatterplots of the patterns of covariation between two interval-level variables A and B. Figure 12.2a is an example of negative correlation: when B is high A is low, when A is high B is low, the values of A and B move in opposite directions, Figure 12.2b presents a case of positive correlation: both A and B move in the same direction, they increase or decrease together. Figure 12.2c is an instance of a zero correlation: when A is high B may be either high or low; the values of A and B vary independently of one another. Figure 12.2d is special because there is an association between A and B, but it is nonlinear. In this case A and B are positively related up to a point, after which they are negatively related. As in Figure 12.2c, the correlation here would be zero even though a relationship exists; it is zero because the relationship is nonlinear. The linear assumption is that the pattern of covariation between two variables is constant across the range of values within each. In cases where this assumption is false, as in the last case, the positive covariation over one range of values will tend to cancel out the negative covariation for anther range.

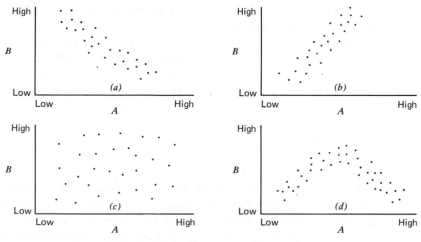

Figure 12.2. Four types of scatterplot.

Let's proceed to the problem of actually computing the correlation between two variables. Taking the sample of 20 men previously examined we can now measure the association between their level of education and their other characteristics. One sociologically interesting relationship is that between education and income. Table 12.3 presents the computation of the distribution characteristics of income for our sample. Income is presented here in 10 discrete categories in units of thousands of dollars. Information on income could be collected in units accurate to the penny. However, in most social research, variables with a broad range of values are often measured in a set of bounded categories. In such cases the researcher can assume that the cases which fall within this category are best represented by the midpoint of

Table 12.3. Measures of Dispersion for Income

Income in Thousands	Number in Category	$\bar{Y}$ Mean of Sample	$(Y_i - \bar{Y})$	$(Y_i - \bar{Y})^2$	Total Variation in Category
3.5	1	13.175	−9.675	93.606	93.606
6.5	1	13.175	−6.675	44.556	44.556
7.5	1	13.175	−5.675	32.206	32.206
8.5	1	13.175	−4.675	21.856	21.856
9.5	4	13.175	−3.675	13.506	54.024
10.5	1	13.175	−2.675	7.156	7.156
13.0	4	13.175	−.175	.031	.124
15.5	4	13.175	2.325	5.406	21.624
22.5	2	13.175	9.325	86.956	173.912
30.0	1	13.175	16.825	283.080	283.080
$\bar{Y}$ = Mean = 13.175		Variance = s^2 = 38.534		Standard deviation = s = 6.208	

the category. In this sample one individual had an income in the $3000 to $3999 range. His score for income was coded 3.5. This procedure was carried out for every respondent in the sample. Unless the researcher has extra knowledge of the distribution of cases within a category, the midpoint is the best estimate. Since the variable must be measured at least as an interval scale, using bounded categories simplifies the computation without excessively limiting the researcher's information on the variable. Of course, the manner of constructing categories should not be arbitrary and should not be so restrictive as to make the new variable meaningless. Such a situation would occur, for example, if income were coded into two categories, $0 to $14,999 and $15,000 to $30,000. The analysis could still proceed by assigning all cases in the first category the value of $7500 and all cases in the second $22,500, but so much information on the dispersion of the variable is lost that analysis with it is meaningless. Categorizing multiple-level interval or ratio variables is a useful strategy but only when carried out in an informed way. As always, the researcher should be extremely sensitive to the characteristics of the data.

Using Eq. 12.7 we can now compute the correlation between education and income for our sample of 20 cases (see Table 12.4). The correlation in this sample between income and education proves to be large. The positive correlation indicates high levels of education are associated with high levels of income, and low levels of education are associated with low levels of income. The size of the correlation tells how closely matched changes in one variable are by changes in the other.

What does this mean in terms of the spatial configuration of the data? When examining the relationship between two variables it is useful to examine a scatterplot of their behavior in a two-dimensional graph such as Figure 12.3. The positive correlation between the variables is marked by their common movement from the lower left sector of the graph to the upper right portion. The graph shows that many individuals stopped their education after completing high school (12 years) and there is a wide range of incomes for this group ($7,500–15,500). For those who finished college (16 years or more) there is a large jump in income level. The graph also shows that the relationship between the two variables is approximately linear. There appear to be roughly constant incremental increases in the values of both variables.

INTRODUCING CONTROLS: THE PARTIAL CORRELATION

Once a researcher has established that a relationship exists between two variables the next stage of research often involves the introduction of a set of control variables to see whether the association is the result of both variables having a common relationship with a third, previously unexamined variable. Correlational analysis provides a means of testing this possibility by

Table 12.4.   Computation of Correlation between Education and Income

Education X_i	Income Y_i	$(X_i - \bar{X})$ x_i	$(Y_i - \bar{Y})$ y_i	$x_i * y_i$	$(X_i - \bar{X})^2$ x_i^2	$(Y_i - \bar{Y})^2$ y_i^2
9	9.5	−3.75	−3.675	13.781	14.063	13.506
9	13.0	−3.75	−.175	.656	14.063	.031
10	3.5	−2.75	−9.675	26.606	7.563	93.606
11	6.5	−1.75	−6.675	11.681	3.063	44.556
11	13.0	−1.75	−.175	.306	3.063	.031
12	7.5	−.75	−5.675	4.256	.563	32.206
12	8.5	−.75	−4.675	3.506	.563	21.856
12	9.5	−.75	−3.675	2.756	.563	13.506
12	9.5	−.75	−3.675	2.756	.563	13.506
12	13.0	−.75	−.175	.131	.563	.031
12	13.0	−.75	−.175	.131	.563	.031
12	15.5	−.75	2.325	−1.744	.563	5.406
13	9.5	.25	−3.675	−.919	.126	13.506
13	15.5	.25	2.325	.581	.126	5.406
14	10.5	1.25	−2.675	−3.344	1.563	7.156
14	15.5	1.25	2.325	2.906	1.563	5.406
15	15.5	2.25	2.325	5.231	5.063	5.406
16	22.5	3.25	9.325	30.306	10.563	86.956
18	22.5	5.25	9.325	48.956	27.563	86.956
18	30.0	5.25	16.825	88.331	27.563	283.080

$$\Sigma(x_i * y_i) = 236.880 \qquad \Sigma(x_i)^2 = 119.76 \qquad \Sigma(y_i)^2 = 732.14$$

$$r_{xy} = r_{yx} = \frac{236.880}{\sqrt{(119.76)(732.14)}} = \frac{236.880}{87{,}681.086} = \frac{236.880}{296.110}$$

$$r_{xy} = r_{yx} = .7999$$

computing the correlations between two variables while controlling for their common association with one or more other variables. This type of correlation is called a partial correlation.

Take the case of a researcher who wants to examine the relationships among three variables, X, Y, and Z. The researcher is interested primarily in the relationship between X and Y but believes Z may be related to both. He computes the correlations between Z and X and those between Z and Y and finds that both are nonzero. Now he wants to know what the correlation between X and Y is once the association with Z is extracted from it. Knowing the correlations between each pair of variables, r_{xy}, r_{xz}, and r_{yz}, he can compute the partial correlation $r_{xy.z}$. The variable(s) to the right of the period in this designation are always those whose association has been controlled. The equation for estimating the partial correlation is

$$r_{xy.z} = \frac{r_{xy} - (r_{xz})*(r_{yz})}{\sqrt{1 - r_{xz}^2}\ \sqrt{1 - r_{yz}^2}} \qquad (12.9)$$

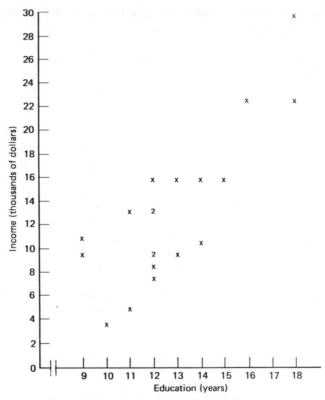

Figure 12.3. Scatterplot of education by income.

In order to take the relationship to variable Z out of the correlation between X and Y two steps are performed in Eq. 12.9. In the numerator the simple correlation between X and Y, r_{xy}, is reduced by the degree of association which exists between Y and Z, r_{yz}, and between X and Z, r_{xz}. The denominator then adjusts this value by the level of variance in X and Y which is not related to Z. $(1 - r_{yz}^2)$ represents the proportion of variance in variable Y which is not related to Z; correspondingly, $(1 - r_{xz}^2)$ is the proportion of variance in variable X which is not associated with Z. The denominator shows that in order to take the influence of Z out of the correlation it is necessary to take away the portion of variance in both X and Y which is associated with Z. Since the denominator will always be less than zero, unless $r_{xz} = r_{yz} = 0$, it serves to adjust the numerator upward.

We can apply the concept of partial correlation to the analysis of the relationship between income and education. Let the variable Z represent the age of the respondent in years. Our concern is how much of the correlation between income and education can be attributed to the fact that older individuals have higher levels of education and income. Suppose the observed correlation between age and education, r_{xz}, was .20, and the correlation between age and income, r_{yz}, was .35. What would the correlation be between education and income after controlling for age? The equation for the partial correlation gives

$$r_{xy.z} = \frac{.80 - (.20){*}(.35)}{\sqrt{1 - (.20)^2} \ \sqrt{1 - (.35)^2}} = \frac{.80 - .07}{.96 * .88} = \frac{.73}{.92} = .793$$

Even given the modest size of the correlations between age and the primary variables, controlling for age only reduced the correlation from .799 to .793. By computing the partial correlation we found that almost none of the association between education and income in the sample is due to the effects of age.

Controlling for one variable is known as *computing a first-order partial*. It is possible using the same general procedure to compute partials controlling for two or more variables. The procedure becomes fairly complex because in order to compute a second order partial correlation the elements in the equation are first-order partial correlations. For computing the nth-order partial correlation the elements must be $(n - 1)$th order partial correlations. Although such an analysis is difficult to carry out by hand, these statistics are generated easily by high-speed computers and are available in basic statistical packages such as SPSS and SAS. (The same is true for complex regression analyses discussed below.)*

The social researcher can answer three questions by using the Pearson correlation.

1. Does a linear relationship exist between the two variables?
2. Is this relationship positive or negative?
3. How strong is this relationship?

Yet there are several questions this type of analysis cannot answer. Because the Pearson correlation is symmetric it gives no information about the causal direction or causal effect of one variable on another. Logically a social researcher would consider the education of an individual to be a characteristic that existed prior in time to the person's income level. Although the correlation computed here indicates there is a strong association between the two variables, it does not provide an estimate of the causal weight of one variable on the other. To estimate this effect an assumption must be added to the analysis which defines the time order of the variables and specifies which variable is the "mover" and which variable the "moved." Building on the elements of correlational analysis linear regression analysis provides such an analytic technique.

*For a discussion of the procedure for computing higher order partial correlations, see Robert M. Thorndike, *Correlational Procedures for Research*, New York: Gardner Press, 1978, Chapter 5, and Fred W. Kerlinger and Elazar J. Pedhazur, *Multiple Regression in Behavioral Research*, New York: Holt, Rinehart and Winston, 1973, Chapter 5.

Before turning to the character of linear regression analysis it is best to make explicit the requirements placed on variables in these two types of analysis. In correlational and in regression analysis it is assumed the variables have a great deal of internal structure. It is assumed that the categories of the variables have some natural rank order. It is also assumed that the intervals between adjacent values of a variable over its entire range are equal. The first is an ordinal assumption; the second is an interval one.

These two assumptions are crucial for both techniques, since both are computed by measuring the distances across intervals, implicitly assuming the distances are in constant units. Both measures are based essentially on deviations from the mean so the units in which these distances are measured must be constant and meaningful. These techniques consequently require that the variables to which they are applied be at least interval in form. Correlational analysis also assumes that the variables on which it is used are normally distributed in the population. In some cases it is possible to relax these assumptions, but for the student who is becoming acquainted with these techniques it is best to learn the general rules before exploring the exceptional cases.

REGRESSION ANALYSIS

Regression analysis, like correlational analysis, builds on the assumption that there exists a linear relationship between two or more variables. It differs from correlational analysis in that it posits a direction of the effects between the variables. It assumes that a set of causal relations exists among the variables. Whereas the inherent character of a correlation coefficient is its symmetry, an inherent feature of a regression coefficient is its asymmetry. While $r_{xy} = r_{yx}$, $b_{yx} \neq b_{xy}$, where b represents an unstandardized regression coefficient.

The key to understanding linear regression analysis is to be aware that it is a means for estimating the line which best fits the relationship within a set of variables. Where only two variables are examined the line can be drawn in two-dimensional space. Where more than two variables are involved the line runs through n-dimensional space, n representing the number of variables analyzed. We will apply linear regression analysis to the two-variable case of education and income which we have already examined. Building on the techniques in linear regression analysis applied to the relationship between two variables, known as a *bivariate analysis*, a researcher can develop a body of information which can be readily generalized to the n-variable case.

The relationship between any two variables can be more or less adequately described by a line. This line will always run through one point established by the means of the two variables. When one point of a line is known it is necessary only to determine one other point to uniquely define this line. The general equation for a line defined in terms of two variables is

$$Y = A + bX \qquad (12.10)$$

A and b are constants, and X and Y vary. A is known as the Y intercept since it represents the value of Y when the variable X equals 0. b is the regression coefficient or the slope of the line. b defines how many unit changes in Y occur with each unit change in X.

An infinite number of lines can be drawn through the point $(\bar{X},\bar{Y})$. The task of linear regression analysis is to choose that one line which runs through the points $(0,A)$ and $(\bar{X},\bar{Y})$ such that the sum of the squared distances between every observed point (X_i, Y_i) and the line is smaller than the sum would be for any other line which is drawn. The element linear regression analysis estimates to establish this best-fitting line is the slope of the line, or the coefficient b. The regression coefficient is the logical element to base our attention on because it determines how the information given in the causal variable X is translated into information about the caused variable Y. Linear regression analysis is an analytic strategy for developing a best guess for the values of Y_i given information about a set of values X_i.

Linear regression analysis is explicitly concerned with estimating the causal weight of one variable on another, but it cannot provide a test of the causal assumption itself. Regression analysis can test whether the effect of one variable on another is likely to be zero in the population, but if it establishes the effect does in fact exist, it cannot tell the researcher in which direction the effect runs. The burden of establishing the validity of the causal assumption rests on the researcher's theoretical understanding of the variables being examined, past research on their relationship, the manner in which they are measured, and the time order of their existence.

How are the coefficients of the regression line estimated? First the researcher specifies the causal order of the variables. Y is commonly used to denote the dependent variable and X is used to denote the independent variable. For theoretical and substantive reasons the researcher will choose variables to analyze on the basis of expectations that a change in one variable will lead to changes in another one. In the example being used here the researcher would develop the argument that the individual's level of education causes or produces a level of income. First the researcher must clearly establish that the educational process precedes in time the process of earning income. Second the researcher must develop a conceptual argument that links the process of education with that of earning income. The research could develop any of several conceptual links between the variables, building on different theoretical traditions and considerations. Different theories can lead to the same expectations about an empirical relationship. Finding a significant relationship between two variables tells the researcher only that the effect exists, it does not define the relationship. The social researcher must always be cognizant that the significance test is meaningful only within the context of the theoretical test. The researcher is obliged to show that the relationship has such a character that it could not be explained by an equally plausible theoretical argument. The researcher must clearly establish the theoretical reasons for the empirical analysis. These reasons will determine the character of the model which is estimated and should provide a unique set of expectations which can be compared to the observed effects.

The causal model used here has the following form:

$$\text{income} = A + b * \text{education}$$

This model proposes that an individual's income level will be a function of a constant, A summed with a constant coefficient b multiplied by the level of the respondent's education. We expect b to be positive since more education should produce more income for the individual. The manner of computing the regression coefficient b is very similar to that of computing the Pearson correlation. Using the conventions we employed previously, let X represent the variable education, Y represent the variable income, x_i represent the difference between the ith individual's education and the mean for the sample, and y_i represent the difference between the ith individual's income and the mean for the sample. The equation for computing the regression coefficient is

$$b_{yx} = \frac{\Sigma(x_i * y_i)}{\Sigma x_i^2} \tag{12.11}$$

The sequence of subscripts of the coefficient b is important here because the relationship, as we have emphasized, is asymmetric. The convention is to place the dependent variable as the first subscript and the independent variable, or causal factor, as the second subscript. The numerator of this equation is the same as the numerator for the correlation coefficient—it is the covariance of the two variables. For the regression coefficient, however, the denominator is the total variation of the independent variable. If the model were reversed and we were interested in the effect of Y on X, then the regression coefficient b would have the same numerator but a denominator composed of Σy_i^2. This shows why the regression coefficients are asymmetric and why $b_{yx} \neq b_{xy}$. The units involved in computing b_{yx} here are

(years of education) * (thousands of dollars)/(years of education)^2

Simplifying this yields (thousands of dollars)/(years of education). This indicates that the coefficient b_{yx} will substantively mean the number of thousands of dollars which the individual earns for each year of education attained.

Using the information on our sample which we derived for computing the correlation between education and income we can compute the regression coefficient:

$$b_{yx} = \frac{236.880}{119.76} = 1.978$$

In this sample, each year of education is associated with an increase in income of $1978. Completing the estimation of the elements of the regression equation, the constant A can be determined by substituting the mean values of education and income into the equation:

$$13.175 = A + (1.978)*(12.75)$$
$$A = -12.045$$

It is obvious that no individual will have an income of $-$\$12,000. The Y intercept represents the hypothetical value for income which, given the observed pattern in the sample, would correspond to 0 years of schooling. Since the size of this sample is small, no one in the sample has an education of less than 9 years, and the coefficient portrays a very steep relationship between education and income, the peculiar estimate of A is understandable. Reversing the logic to see what level of education is associated with 0 income we find the value is 6.1 years. We know that small elements of the population from which the sample is drawn have levels of education of 6 years or less, and that these individuals do earn income, so we would conclude the line estimated here is limited in its utility to predicting the incomes of those with relatively high levels of education (> 8 years). As a rule it is important to examine the character of the estimates of the regression equation closely to see if they violate the logical limits within which they should fall. If they do, the researcher should discover why this is so and interpret the findings appropriately.

Once the researcher has estimated the elements of the regression equation, she is in a position to ask how well the model fits the data. Is the explanation provided by the causal variable(s) adequate in explaining the dependent variable or could the effect found be the product of random effects allowing her to conclude there is no causal relationship between the variables in the population from which the sample was drawn?

Figure 12.4 presents the information which the regression model provides about the relationship between education and income. The line in Figure 12.4 is the best fitting line estimated from the observed association of education and income. The line represents a set of predicted values of income, commonly signified as $\hat{Y}_i$ which are associated with each value of education. Given the predicted value defined by the regression line each observed value for income can be seen as having two components. One is the vertical distance between the observed value and the predicted one,

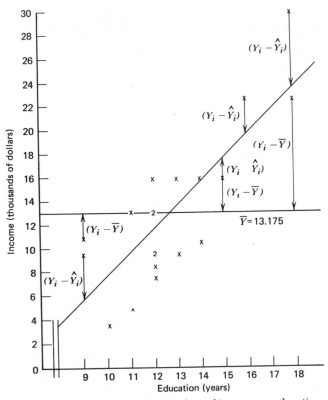

Figure 12.4. Plot of the regression line of income on education:
$$\hat{Y}_i = -12.045 + (1.978 * X_i)$$

$(Y_i - \hat{Y}_i)$, and the other is the vertical distance between the predicted value and the sample mean of income, $(\hat{Y}_i - \overline{Y})$. By using this information these two distances can be compared. Algebraically the total distance of the dependent variable from its mean can be written as

$$(Y_i - \overline{Y}) = (Y_i - \hat{Y}_i) + (\hat{Y}_i - \overline{Y}) \tag{12.12}$$

By redefining $(Y_i - \hat{Y}_i)$ as e_i and adding $\overline{Y}$ to both sides, Eq. 12.11 can be rewritten as

$$Y_i = \hat{Y}_i + e_i \tag{12.13}$$

This means that each observed value of income equals a predicted value $\hat{Y}_i$ based on the explanatory power of the model, plus an error term e_i which is that part of income that the regression model could not explain. In the model $\hat{Y}_i$ is defined in terms of education so Eq. 12.12 can be rewritten as

$$Y_i = A + b X_i + e_i \tag{12.14}$$

The goal of the regression model is to generate a line such that the errors are as small as possible. Formally, the criterion in regression analysis that allows it to derive the estimate of a unique line which best fits the data is that it minimizes the value Σe_i^2 or $\Sigma(Y_i - \hat{Y}_i)^2$.

A standard measure used to describe how well the model fits is the proportion

$$R^2 = \frac{\Sigma(\hat{Y}_i - \bar{Y})^2}{\Sigma(Y_i - \bar{Y})^2} \qquad (12.15)$$

The numerator of this equation, the *regression sum of squares*, represents the amount of variation in the dependent variable accounted for by the regression model. The denominator, the *total sum of squares*, is the total variation in the dependent variable that the model could conceivably account for.

The upper bound of the statistic R^2 is 1. If the model fits the data perfectly, $\hat{Y}_i = Y_i$ and $(\hat{Y}_i - \bar{Y}) = (Y_i - \bar{Y})$. The lower bound of $R^2 = 0$. If $\hat{Y}_i = \bar{Y}$, then the numerator will be zero and $R^2 = 0$. In every case $R^2 \geq 0$ since both elements of the proportion are squared and are consequently positive. The logic of this proportion as the appropriate measure of fit can be stated in this way. The mean of a variable is the one best guess of all the values of that variable. If a model is to improve on our power to guess the values of the dependent variable, it must improve on the predictive power of the mean. The information added to this process by another variable, a predictor variable, should allow a guess of the values of the dependent variables other than its mean, and these values should be, on the average, closer to the observed values than the mean. Consequently, a proportion—the predicted values distance from the mean/the true values distance from the mean—tells how much the information provided by the causal factor improves the prediction power over the previous best guess. Table 12.5 presents the partitioning of the variance in the dependent variable income between that which is explained by the model and that which is unique or independent, commonly called the *residual sum of squares*. The value R^2 is known as the *coefficient of determination* or the *level of explained variance*. The variance of the dependent variable about its mean is partitioned in this way:

total sum of squares = regression sum of squares
+ residual sum of squares

The total variance is divided into two components, the explained variance, which is represented by R^2, and the unexplained variance, which is $(1 - R^2)$. If each term in this equation is divided by the total sum of squares, it can be written in standardized form:

$$1 = R^2 + (1 - R^2) = \frac{\text{regression sum of squares}}{\text{total sum of squares}} + \frac{\text{residual sum of squares}}{\text{total sum of squares}}$$
$$(12.16)$$

Table 12.5. Computation of Sums of Squares

X_i	Y_i	$\hat{Y}_i$	$(\hat{Y}_i - \bar{Y})$	$(\hat{Y}_i - \bar{Y})^2$	$(Y_i - \hat{Y}_i)$	$(Y_i - \hat{Y}_i)^2$
10	3.5	7.734	−5.441	29.604	−4.234	17.927
11	6.5	9.713	−3.642	11.985	−3.213	10.323
12	7.5	11.691	−1.484	2.202	−4.191	17.564
12	8.5	11.691	−1.484	2.202	−3.191	10.182
9	9.5	5.757	−7.418	55.027	3.743	14.010
12	9.5	11.691	−1.484	2.202	−2.191	4.800
12	9.5	11.691	−1.484	2.202	−2.191	4.800
13	9.5	13.669	.494	.244	−4.169	17.381
14	10.5	15.647	2.472	6.111	−5.147	26.492
9	13.0	5.757	−7.418	55.027	7.243	52.461
11	13.0	9.713	−3.642	11.985	3.287	10.804
12	13.0	11.691	−1.484	2.202	1.309	1.713
12	13.0	11.691	−1.484	2.202	1.309	1.713
12	15.5	11.691	−1.484	2.202	3.809	14.508
13	15.5	13.669	.494	.244	1.831	3.353
14	15.5	15.647	2.472	6.111	1.147	.022
15	15.5	17.675	4.45	19.803	−2.125	4.516
16	22.5	19.603	6.428	41.319	2.897	8.393
18	22.5	23.559	10.384	107.827	−1.059	1.121
18	30.0	23,559	10.384	107.827	6.441	41.486

$$\bar{Y} = 13.175 \quad \Sigma(\hat{Y}_i - \bar{Y})^2 = 468.528 \quad \Sigma(Y_i - \hat{Y}_i)^2 = 263.569$$

$$R^2 = \frac{468.528}{732.140} = .639$$

In the bivariate case a basic identity holds:

$$R^2 = r_{xy}^2 = (.7999)^2 = .639$$

In the bivariate case the coefficient of determination is the square of the simple correlation between the two variables in the model. This is true only in the bivariate case for reasons discussed later.

Once the coefficient of determination has been computed it is possible to test whether the causal effect estimated by the model is likely to be present in the population. The formula for computing the significance test is

$$F = \frac{R^2/k}{(1 - R^2)/(N - k - 1)} \tag{12.17}$$

where R^2 is the coefficient of determination, N is the sample size, and k is the number of causal factors included in the model. Besides serving as the significance test for regression models this equation is also used to determine the significance of simple correlations, in which case $k = 1$.

In this case, $F = .639/(.361/18) = 31.95$. Examining a table of the critical values of the F statistic, which can be found in any statistics text, we find that where the degrees of freedom are 1, 18, corresponding to $(k/N - k - 1)$, the critical value of F at the .001 level is 15.4. The value here of 31.95 well exceeds this critical limit. Based on this test and the assumptions in the regression model we can conclude that the causal effect of education on income exists in the population and is not due to chance. The F statistic indicates that an effect of the size found would occur in a sample of 20, in a model with just one predictor variable, less than once by chance if 1000 such samples were randomly drawn from a fixed population.

While this significance test was computed directly from the size of the coefficient of determination, it is also a significance test of the regression coefficient b. The F-test of the level of explained variance is closely related to the t-test of the regression coefficient. The relationship* is defined by

$$F = t^2 \qquad\qquad (12.18)$$

For this regression model the t statistic for b is 5.652, which is also significant at the .001 level with 1, 18 degrees of freedom. (If the F statistic is significant, then the t statistic will also be significant at the same level.) Both of these statistics provide a means for rejecting the null hypothesis, H_0, that no relationship exists between income and education. If the size of the effect is sufficiently large, as it is in this case, then the researcher can reject the null hypothesis and safely conclude that the relationship between the two variables in the population from which the sample is drawn is not zero.

It may be useful to approach the procedure of the significance test from the opposite direction: Does education affect income? Since we are dealing with a sample from the population we must be reasonably sure that any effect we find will not be due to the chance effects of taking a small sample from a large population. If there were no effect, $R^2 = 0$ and $b_{yx} = 0$ in the population. To ensure that we do not make the mistake of rejecting the null hypothesis when it is true, we set up critical levels of R and b_{yx} which the observed values must exceed if we are to reject H_0 with any degree of confidence; here we set this level at 95 percent. This means if the observed value exceeds the critical level and we reject H_0, we will do so wrongly in only 5 cases out of every 100 that occur. By referring to an F table, we can determine what the value of R^2 must be to satisfy our criteria given the sample size. The critical value of F at the .05 level, when the degrees of freedom are 1, 18, is 4.41. Using this information in Eq. 12.17,

$$4.41 = \frac{R^2/1}{(1 - R^2)/(20 - 1 - 1)}$$
$$R^2 = .191$$

*This relationship applies only when there is one degree of freedom in the numerator.

For a sample of size 20 in which a regression model has only one explanatory variable the coefficient of determination must be .191 or greater to allow us to reject H_0 for the population with 95 percent confidence, or at a 5 percent risk of error.

This brief discussion of significance tests points to another advantage of linear regression analysis. In this type of analysis the researcher does not lose degrees of freedom as rapidly as he would if using cross-tabular analysis, nor is he faced with the problem of empty cells created when small samples are analyzed. In linear regression analysis 1 degree of freedom is lost because the researcher begins knowing the sum of the values over the dependent variable. This means the last case of the dependent variable will always have a known value if the sum of all N values and the sum of $(N - 1)$ values are known. The researcher loses 1 degree of freedom for every explanatory variable, or predictor, included in the regression model. Even with a sample as small as 20 it is possible to construct a model with several predictors and still maintain a reasonable number of degrees of freedom, allowing for an estimate of the coefficients of the regression equation.

When the researcher is limited to cross-tabular analysis by the character of the data, either nominal or ordinal, the number of degrees of freedom in the analysis is limited by the number of cell frequencies that are undetermined, not by the number of cases whose values are undetermined. The number of degrees of freedom in regression analysis has an upper bound of $(N - 1)$ but in cross-tabular analysis the upper bound is contingent on the number of categories in each variable included in the analysis. As a rule the researcher desires to maintain as many degrees of freedom as possible. Since the addition of each explanatory variable results in the loss of only 1 degree of freedom, the researcher can develop and test more complex explanatory models using regression analysis than cross-tabular analysis.

Another related strength of linear regression analysis lies in its capacity to test models with relatively small samples. The relationship between education and income could not be examined usefully in cross-tabular form because the table would be dimensioned 9×10, 9 categories of education by 10 categories of income, producing 90 cells, most of which would be empty for any small sample. Any situation such as this could not be summarized effectively by any of the measures discussed in Chapter 10. Estimates of the elements of a regression equation can be derived with fairly small samples as long as the number of explanatory factors is reasonably limited. This strength of regression analysis is based on the greater information contained in interval-level variables and the more assumptions the researcher can make as to their characteristics.

MULTIPLE REGRESSION: THE ESTIMATION OF CONTROLLED EFFECTS

As was the case with the Pearson correlation, the procedures used to analyze the simple bivariate case can be generalized easily to analyses involving three or more variables. Like the Pearson correlation, regression analysis can examine the relationship between two variables controlling for one or more others. By introducing one or more new predictors into a bivariate regression model, multiple regression analysis is carried out. All effects in the multiple regression model are estimated in such a way that their coefficients reflect their impact on the dependent variable independent of, or controlling for, all other predictors included in the model. The basis of multiple regression is the partialing out of the effects which combinations of the independent variables jointly have on the dependent variable. This directly corresponds to the logic and the method of partial correlations. However, the coefficients estimated by the multiple regression provide more information than partial correlations because they represent the simultaneous independent effects of all of the predictor variables. In a regression model where income Y is regressed on education X and age Z, and where x_i, y_i, and z_i represent the distance of the observations on each variable from their means, the coefficients for the two independent variables would be computed by

$$b_{yx.z} = \frac{(\Sigma z_i^2)(\Sigma x_i y_i) - (\Sigma x_i z_i)(\Sigma y_i z_i)}{(\Sigma x_i^2)(\Sigma z_i^2) - (\Sigma x_i z_i)} \tag{12.19}$$

$$b_{yz.x} = \frac{(\Sigma x_i^2)(\Sigma y_i z_i) - (\Sigma x_i z_i)(\Sigma x_i y_i)}{(\Sigma x_i^2)(\Sigma z_i^2) - (\Sigma x_i z_i)} \tag{12.20}$$

Despite the large number of elements in these equations the logic in their computations is clear. First note the denominators of both are the same; the product of the total variation in the two independent variables is adjusted by the portion of it which is caused by their joint variation, their covariance, which is the numerator in the equation estimating their correlation. The numerators of these equations contain the covariance of the dependent variable with the independent one, multiplied by the total variation in the other independent variable in the model, and adjusted by the other covariation in the model. The element in the numerator to the right of the minus sign matches that element in the same location in the partial correlation equation, there represented as correlations instead of covariances.

The partial correlation coefficients present the unit changes in the dependent variable associated with one unit change in the independent variable. The partial regression coefficient reinforces the researcher's control, since the effect of one predictor exists independent of the other variables in the model. It also gives an estimate of the size of the effect and allows a significance test to be made to determine how likely it is that this effect exists in the population.

As more predictor variables are introduced into the regression model the method for estimating the partial regression coefficient becomes successively more complex since it involves controlling for $(k - 1)$ correlations among the k independent variables. The logic for increasingly complex explanatory models is fortunately the same and understanding the meaning of the partial regression coefficient in models with two independent variables is the same as that for models with more than two.

THE STANDARDIZED REGRESSION COEFFICIENT

To this point the discussion of regression analysis has focused on deriving and understanding the coefficients as they pertain to unit changes in values of the variables in the model. Coefficients in this form allow the researcher to make substantive statements about the effects of the independent variables in meaningful terms, such as the importance of each year of education for the number of dollars it adds to the individual's income. In some cases the researcher may be interested in making statements about the relative strength of the independent variables as predictors in the regression model. One way to do this is to compare the amount of explained variance, the portion of the regression sum of squares, that is due to the effect of each independent variable. Another way to approach this problem is to reestimate each regression coefficient in a standard form, in common units, so that a direct comparison of their size may be made. Each unstandardized regression coefficient is written in terms of units of the dependent variable divided by units of the independent variable. The method for standardizing the coefficients is to multiply them by the standard deviation of the independent variable divided by standard deviation of the dependent variable.

Returning to the regression model for predicting income we add information about the age of the respondents. Assume the equation estimated for this new model is

$$\text{predicted income} = -9.327 + 1.83 * \text{education} + .235 * \text{age}$$

It appears from this equation that education has a much stronger effect on the individual's level of income than does age. According to the equation each year of education produces a predicted value $1830 dollars higher while each year of age only leads to a prediction $235 greater. But the researcher cannot take comparisons of standardized regression coefficients at their face value. There are far more units of age then there are of education. In this sample, education has a range from 9 to 18 years; age has a range from 20 to 55 years. Thus it is possible for individuals to have greater differences on the variable age than on the variable education. We calculated earlier that $s_y = 6.208$ and $s_x = 2.511$. Assume that the standard deviation for age, s_z, is 12.495. The standardized regression coefficients, β, for this equation are

$$\beta_{yx.z} = 1.83 * (2.511/6.208) = .740$$
$$\beta_{yz.x} = .235 * (12.495/6.208) = .473$$

These coefficients show what proportion of change in the dependent variable, measured in standard deviations, is associated with a 1-standard deviation change in the independent variable. They are now in constant units, which allows for a direct comparison of the effects of the independent variables if certain assumptions are made. These assumptions are that the distributions of these two independent variables are roughly the same and, optimally, normal. If this is true, then the standardized regression coefficients can be directly compared. In this example we see that the effect of education on income is greater than that of age but it is not as great as an uninformed reading of the unstandardized coefficients would suggest.

The following general guide for the use of standardized and unstandardized coefficients should prove useful: when the researcher wants to compare the effects of different variables in one population standardized coefficients should be used; when the researcher wants to look at the effect of one variable across different subpopulations, as in comparing the effect of education on income for men and for women, unstandardized coefficients should be used.

USING DUMMY VARIABLES IN REGRESSION ANALYSIS

Earlier in this chapter we stressed the restrictive assumptions on the character of variables necessary to carry out either Pearson's correlation or linear regression analysis. It was argued that these analytic strategies were appropriate only when the researcher had at least interval-level data on both dependent and independent variables. Many variables in social research do not meet this restriction, so a great deal of attention had been paid to developing methods that allow other types of variable, especially nominal ones, to be included in regression models. One useful and common strategy employed in empirical research is the dummy coding of nominal variables. Dummy coding refers to the procedure of taking a variable whose categories represent qualitative states and creating $(C - 1)$ dichotomous variables from it, where C is the number of categories in the variable. These new dummy variables are coded 1 for those respondents who have a particular quality and 0 for those respondents who do not. In this form a nominal, or an ordinal, variable can be included as a predictor in the regression model. Except in special circumstances nominal variables cannot be used as dependent variables. It is generally required that the dependent variable always be at at least the interval level.*

---

*For a discussion of methods for circumventing this restriction, see Eric A. Hanusek and John E. Jackson, *Statistical Methods for Social Scientists*, New York: Academic Press, 1977, Chapter 7.

Before proceeding to the discussion of how dummy variables are used in regression analysis it is first necessary to look at what the Pearson correlation between an interval and a dichotomous variable means. It was pointed out earlier that the mean of a dichotomous variable coded 0 and 1 represents the percentage of those cases which fall into the category coded 1. In the expression computing deviations from the mean there will be only two values, the percentage of times the characteristic does exist $(0 - \bar{X})$, and the percentage of times the quality does not exist $(1 - \bar{X})$. In our sample of 20 there are 8 blacks and 14 whites. If blacks are coded 1 and whites 0 on the variable race, the mean is .4. In computing the deviations from the mean the value $(1 - .4)$ occurs 8 times and the value $(0 - .4)$ occurs 12 times. The total deviations from the mean, squared, is 4.8, the variance is .252, and the standard deviation is .492. The formula for computing the variance of a dichotomous variable is

$$s^2 = N * \bar{X} * (1 - \bar{X})/(N - 1) \tag{12.21}$$

Computing the correlation between a dummy variable and an interval variable, such as the one between race (R) and income (Y), produces a measure of how much the means of the two groups differ. The numerator of the correlation coefficient, $\Sigma r_i y_i$, weights the deviations from the mean differently from the two groups. In the case where one variable is a dummy variable the equation for computing the correlation can be rewritten as

$$r_{yR} = \frac{N * \bar{R} * (1 - \bar{R}) * (\bar{y}_{i1} - \bar{y}_{i0})}{\sqrt{N * \bar{R} * (1 - \bar{R})} \ \sqrt{\Sigma(y_i^2)}} \tag{12.22}$$

The new elements introduced in this equation, $\bar{y}_{i1}$ and $\bar{y}_{i0}$, represent the means of the deviations in income in the cases where race equals 1 and race equals 0, respectively. Although this equation is somewhat more complex than the one for the general case it straightforwardly indicates how the correlation is a measure of the difference of means between the two groups. If the correlation r_{yR} is less than 0, it means the average black income is lower than the average white income; if it is greater than 0, then the opposite is true; if close to or at 0, it means the difference between the groups is small.

The introduction of a dummy variable into a linear regression model is based on this logic. Initially the researcher can predict the values of the dependent variable only on the basis of its mean. The explanatory power of a dummy variable is that it allows the researcher to derive two means from making the prediction, one for the cases in the 0 category, one for the cases in the 1 category. Does knowing the mean of the dependent variable in each subgroup then improve our ability to predict the values of the dependent variable over knowing only the mean for the full sample?

The following equations present the information needed to compute the correlation between race and income in our sample and estimate the regression equation of income on race.

$$N * \bar{R} * (1 - \bar{R}) = 4.8 \qquad \sqrt{N * \bar{R} * (1 - \bar{R})} = 2.19$$

$$\Sigma(y_i)^2 = 732.146 \qquad \sqrt{\Sigma(y_i)^2} = 27.058$$

$$\bar{y}_{i1} = -3.488 \qquad \bar{y}_{i0} = 2.325$$

$$r_{yR} = \frac{20(.4)(1 - .4)(-3.488 - 2.325)}{\sqrt{20(.4)(1 - .4)} \sqrt{732.146}} = \frac{4.8(-5.813)}{2.191(27.057)} = \frac{-27.902}{59.282}$$

$$r_{yR} = -.471$$

$$b_{yR} = \frac{(4.8) * (-5.813)}{4.8} = -5.813$$

Race is strongly and negatively correlated with income, indicating that blacks in the sample have lower incomes than whites. The unstandardized regression coefficient b_{yR} shows that blacks have a mean income $5813 less than the mean for whites. Unlike the variable education where individuals could have scores within the range of 9 to 18 years, on the variable race there is only one possible unit change. The regression coefficient of a dummy variable always represents the difference in means between the two groups.

By using the information on the means of the variables in the sample it is possible to compute the missing term of the regression equation, the Y intercept:

$$13.175 = A - 5.813 * .4$$
$$A = 15.50$$

The complete regression equation thus is

$$\text{income} = 15.5 - 5.813 \text{ race}$$

Since the regression coefficient represents the difference between group means, only by knowing the mean of one group is it possible to compute the mean of the other. In regression equations containing a single dummy variable, A, the Y intercept, always represents the mean of the group coded 0 on the dummy variable. This can be seen if the possible values for race are introduced into the equation. When the respondent is white:

$$\text{predicted income} = 15.5 - (5.813 * 0) = \$15,500$$

When the respondent is black:

$$\text{predicted income} = 15.5 - (5.813 * 1) = \$9187$$

Does using the means of income within racial groups sufficiently improve the predictive power over the mean of the full sample to enable us to conclude that such a difference exists in the population? Knowing $R = r_{yB}$ we can compute the F statistic for the fit of the model:

$$F = \frac{(.471^2)/1}{(1 - .471^2)/(20 - 1 - 1)} = \frac{.222}{(.778/18)} = \frac{.222}{.043} = 5.16$$

The critical value of F with 1, 18 degrees of freedom is 4.41 so the effect of race is significant at the .05 level. This allows us to reject the null hypothesis that there is no difference between the mean levels of income for blacks and whites in the population.

The use of a dummy variable in linear regression analysis is not limited to subinterval variables which have only two categories. Nominal- and ordinal-level variables may have three or more categories, and the researcher will want to include as much information as possible in building explanatory models using multiple regression analysis. There is no limit on the number of dummy variables that can be included in a regression model other than the limits that apply to all variables as they pertain to the degrees of freedom available. The one limit that does apply to the use of dummy variables is that when a multiple-category nominal variable is converted into a set of dummy variables the number of these is the number of categories in the original variable minus one. Consider the case where the variable race/ethnic group has four categories: (1) white, (2) black, (3) Asian, (4) Hispanic. In developing a regression model only three of these categories would be assigned a variable:

$$\text{income} = A + b_1 * (\text{black}) + b_2 * (\text{Asian}) + b_3 * (\text{Hispanic})$$

The omitted category becomes the reference group. The mean value for this reference group on the dependent variable will always be represented by the Y intercept (A); the coefficients of the constructed dummy variables will represent the degree to which the mean for each group on the dependent variable differs from the mean of the reference group (A). In our example, assuming that every respondent in the sample belongs to one and only one of the categories of race/ethnic group, and stipulating that the variables black, Asian, and Hispanic each be coded 1 if the individual belongs to that group or 0 if not, the equation for the mean income of each group reduced as follows:

$$\text{White mean income} = A + (b_1 * 0) + (b_2 * 0) + (b_3 * 0)$$
$$\text{Black mean income} = A + (b_1 * 1) + (b_2 * 0) + (b_3 * 0)$$
$$\text{Asian mean income} = A + (b_1 * 0) + (b_2 * 1) + (b_3 * 0)$$
$$\text{Hispanic mean income} = A + (b_1 * 0) + (b_2 * 0) + (b_3 * 1)$$

BUILDING COMPLEX REGRESSION MODELS

In the examination of our sample thus far we have found two predictor variables that have significant effects on the individual's income, education, and race. The significant effects of each were found in examining bivariate models. Knowing this, the researcher would proceed to develop a model containing the effects of both to find out if their effects persist when the effects of the other is controlled. By adding only the information on the covariance of race and education to the earlier analysis we can estimate the elements of the model as follows:

$$\text{income} = A + b_1 * \text{education} + b_2 * \text{race}$$

$$\text{income} = Y \qquad \text{education} = X \qquad \text{race} = R$$

$$\Sigma y_i^2 = 732.14 \qquad \Sigma x_i^2 = 119.74 \qquad \Sigma r_i^2 = 4.8$$

$$\Sigma y_i x_i = 236.88 \qquad \Sigma x_i r_i = -9.0 \qquad \Sigma r_i y_i = -27.9$$

$$b_1 = b_{yx.R} = \frac{(4.8)(236.88) - (-9.0)(-27.9)}{(119.74)(4.8) - (-9.0)} = \frac{885.924}{493.752} = 1.794$$

$$b_2 = b_{yR.x} = \frac{(119.74)(-27.9) - (-9.0)(236.88)}{(119.74)(4.8) - (-9.0)} = \frac{-1208.826}{493.752} = -2.448$$

$$Y = A + 1.794 * \bar{X} + (-2.448 * R)$$

$$13.175 = A + (1.794 * 12.75) + (-2.448 * .4)$$

$$A = -8.719$$

$$\text{income} = -8.719 + 1.794 * \text{education} - 2.448 * \text{race}$$

By including both independent variables in one model the coefficients of both are reduced as would be expected, given their correlation of .375 with one another. The effect of each unit change in education has dropped from $1978 to $1794. The effect of being black has dropped even more markedly, from a negative increment of $5813 to one of $2448. The results of this joint regression show that a large part of the effect of race is found in the fact that whites in the sample have higher educations on average than blacks. The A constant in this equation no longer represents the mean income of whites; it once again specifies the point on the income axis through which the regression line passes.

One way of understanding how this equation models the relations between education and income is to see it as specifying two parallel regression lines. For whites the regression line has the form

$$\text{income} = -8.719 + 1.794 * \text{education}$$

For blacks the regression line has the form

$$\text{income} = -11.167 + 1.794 * \text{education}$$

When the respondent is white the last element in the equation becomes $-2.448 * 0 = 0$. When the respondent is black the last element becomes $-2.448 * 1 = -2.448$, which is combined with A to specify a different, and lower, Y intercept of the line for blacks. These equations indicate that blacks in the sample start the process of income attainment at a $2448 disadvantage with respect to whites, and for equal levels of education they always face this disadvantage. The fact that the regression coefficient for education is the same for blacks and whites indicates that despite their initial disadvantage blacks can expect the same income returns per added year of education as whites.

The substantive features of the estimates of this regression model have been reviewed to make clear how the coefficients derived should be interpreted. With the construction and estimation of each new regression model the researcher should be aware of the substantive meaning of each coefficient as well as the A constant. Given the portrait these estimates present of the complex relationship between race, education, and income we must ask if the estimated effects of race and education are large enough to be considered significant. Computing the F statistics for the increment in explanatory power added by introducing another independent variable into the model has a form different from the one used above. Once it has been determined that a particular variable has a significant effect the researcher wants to use a conservative test in judging the relevance of additions to the explanatory model. A conservative test gives priority to the form of the model that exists and requires the new factors to improve significantly upon it to justify their inclusion within it. This process follows the logic of maintaining the most parsimonious model possible. The goal is to maximize explanatory power while minimizing the number of predictors.

In the present case the two bivariate regressions, income with education and income with race, provide the baseline models against which the new elements are tested. The general equation for testing the significance of added effects is

$$F = \frac{R^2_{y.2} - R^2_{y.1}/(k_2 - k_1)}{(1 - R^2_{y.2})/(N - k_2 - 1)} \tag{12.23}$$

$R^2_{y.2}$ is the level of variance in variable Y explained by Model 2. $R^2_{y.1}$ is the level of variance in variable Y explained by Model 1. (Model 2 must contain all of the predictors found in Model 1.) k_2 is the number of independent variables in Model 2. k_1 is the number of independent variables in Model 1.

For the preceding regression model two F statistics need to be computed, one for the added effect of race controlling for education, the other for the added effect of education controlling for race:

$$F_R = \frac{R^2_{y.xR} - R^2_{y.x}/(k_2 - k_1)}{(1 - R^2_{y.xR})/(N - k_2 - 1)} = \frac{(.673 - .640)/(2 - 1)}{(1 - .673)/(20 - 2 - 1)} = 1.74$$

$$F_E = \frac{R^2_{y.xR} - R^2_{y.R}/(k_2 - k_1)}{(1 - R^2_{y.xR})/(N - k_2 - 1)} = \frac{(.673 - .222)/(2 - 1)}{(1 - .673)/(20 - 2 - 1)} = 23.74$$

These tests show that race does not significantly add to the model once the explanatory power of education is controlled. The F statistic for race, 1.74, is not significant at the minimum probability level of .05 (the tabulated F value for 1, 17 degrees of freedom at the .05 level is 4.45). The effect of education still contributes greatly to the explanatory model once the effect of race is controlled. The F statistic for education is well beyond the criterion value used to establish significance at the .001 level. (Tabulated F value for 1, 17 degrees of freedom at the .01 level is 15.75.)

The discussion of this regression model has shown how the estimates of the coefficients can be substantively interpreted and how significance tests of the estimated effects are to be made. Explanatory regression models can be made increasingly complex but the interpretive and statistical logic remains the same. Multiple regression analysis is among the most powerful analytic tools used in empirical social research. Many strategies have been developed for using linear regression methods in analyzing nonlinear features of relationships between variables. These will not be reviewed here but further readings will be recommended at the end of this chapter for readers who wish to investigate this further. The next and last section will review several general issues which the social researcher must keep in mind when using correlational and multiple regression analysis.

CONCLUSION

This chapter has quickly sketched some of the features of correlational and regression analysis. In such a brief space it is not possible to pursue the many statistical and conceptual intricacies involved in each technique. This chapter has been directed toward the more limited goal of making the researcher familiar with the basic elements and logic of these techniques.

In concluding this chapter the limiting assumptions of these techniques will be reviewed. Some of these were mentioned earlier in the text but, at the risk of redundancy, they will be recapitulated here, for it is crucial that the researcher be aware when these analytic techniques can appropriately be used, and what assumptions their inferential power is based on.

Both techniques assume the existence of a linear relationship. The efficiency of their estimates of association require this condition. In modeling relationships between social variables it is reasonable to begin with this assumption. In many areas of social research important relationships have been found to be linear, for instance between income and education. In addition, the social researcher seldom is equipped with a theory suggesting that a particular relationship will have a nonlinear form. Since a linear model is the most parsimonious form it has a great deal of appeal to researchers. Still in cases where a limited number of variables are to be analyzed the scatterplots of all bivariate relationships should be examined. This is an important aspect of the investigation because it allows the researcher to check the assumption of linearity and look for irregularities or patterns of nonlinearity in the relationships.

Second, both techniques assume that variables analyzed are at the interval level. At minimum at least one must be and the other should have the form of a dummy variable. If the latter is the case, then the correlation should be interpreted as a measure of the difference of means between the two groups and not as a measure of linear association. In any case the researcher should always be extremely rigorous in defining the character of variables and in interpreting the measures of association appropriately.

The next set of assumptions applies only to linear regression analysis. Because this technique develops explanatory models whose characteristics it seeks to generalize to the population, several conditions must exist to ensure the reliability of its inferences. First it is assumed there is no specification error in the form of the model. This means that all the relevant predictor variables are included in the model and no irrelevant ones are. Second it is assumed there is no measurement error in the values of the independent variables. It is acceptable to have measurement error in the values of the dependent variable as long as they are random because these can be absorbed by the error component, e_i, between the observed values and the predicted values of the dependent variable.

The last set of assumptions all deal with characteristics of the error term generated by the explanatory weakness of the regression model. The variance of the error term must be constant across categories of the dependent variable. This characteristic is known as "homoskedasticity." There should be no correlation among the error terms. There should also be no correlation between the error terms and the independent variable(s). Finally, the dependent variable and the errors generated by the model should have the same distribution form, differing only in their means.

These restrictions are placed on the behavior of e_i because if they do not hold, the ability to make significance tests and to infer from the sample to the population is undermined. The statistical basis for these constraints is complex and cannot be presented here. For the social researcher who is coming to use these techniques for the first time it is enough to know that the use of the full powers of linear regression analysis are possible only within the narrow set of conditions just outlined. [These issues are considered extensively in advanced statistical (Hanushek and Jackson, 1977, Chapter 3) or econometric textbooks (Wonnacott and Wonnacott, 1979, Chapters 3 and 4).]

Correlational and linear regression analysis are the most powerful analytic techniques currently available to the social researcher. This chapter has attempted to outline both their conceptual and statistical strengths. For any social researcher the full appreciation of these methods will come only through their use in applied investigations in conjunction with advanced readings on their properties.

RECOMMENDED SOURCES

Blalock, Hubert M. (1972), *Social Statistics* (2nd edition). New York: McGraw-Hill. This text is among the best general reviews of statistical methods available. It is useful for students at the introductory and intermediate levels of statistical training.

Hanushek, Eric A., and John E. Jackson (1977), *Statistical Methods for Social Scientists*. New York: Academic Press. This is an advanced text frequently used by graduate students in the social sciences. It reviews a number of strategies for circumventing problems in cases where the assumptions of regression analysis are not met.

Kerlinger, Fred W., and Elazar J. Pedhazur (1973), *Multiple Regression in Behavioral Research*. New York: Holt, Rinehart and Winston. Provides a good exhaustive treatment of simple and multiple regression in a number of applications. Also contains the best and most extensive treatment of the use of dummy variables in regression analysis.

Lewis-Beck, Michael S. (1980), *Applied Regression: An Introduction*. Beverly Hills: Sage Publications. This is the best short treatment (74 pp.) of the character of regression analysis. It contains brief discussions of most of the major problems which will be encountered by the researcher when using regression analysis.

Thorndike, Robert M. (1978), *Correlational Procedures for Research*. New York: Gardner Press. Beginning with Pearson's product–moment correlation this text discusses the major analytic techniques built upon it, including simple and multiple regression, discriminant function analysis, cluster analysis, and factor analysis. It is well written, oriented to problems faced by researchers, and concerned to communicate the substantive meaning as well as the statistical character of the techniques reviewed.

Wonnacott, Ronald J., and Thomas H. Wonnacott (1979), *Econometrics* (2nd edition). New York: John Wiley and Sons. One of the leading econometric textbooks used by graduate students. A good summary text for the advanced student and a reference work for the social researcher. Provides extensive treatment of technical problems encountered in using linear regression in the analysis of econometric data.

13

Longitudinal Studies

Sociologists, especially survey researchers, frequently are criticized for doing research at a single point in time. Static research makes it impossible to study social change and extremely difficult to carry out definitive causal analyses. The researcher is not always sure that the variable he or she thinks is a cause really precedes the effect variable in time, and so there is usually an element of uncertainty hovering over causal analyses of static data. To overcome these shortcomings, sociologists have devised ways of studying changes over time. Three types of research design for carrying out longitudinal studies have evolved, the trend study, cohort analysis, and panel studies. Each is discussed in this chapter.

A trend study measures the same variables at different points in time, and the researcher is able to document trends in these variables over time. A cohort study focuses on groups whose members share the same time frame and follows these groups over time. A typical cohort is a birth cohort, that is, people born in the same period of time, and the research documents changes that occur in these groups at different stages in the life cycle. Although birth cohorts are especially common in cohort analysis, the cohorts can share any time frame, for example, they may start college at the same time, or they may enter a hospital on the same day, or they may be people married in the same year. A panel study is one in which the same people are interviewed at different points in time. The word "panel" refers to a panel of people, that is, "a list or group of persons selected for a specific purpose." The critical difference between a trend study and a panel study is that in the trend study different sets of people are sampled from the same population at different points in time, whereas in the panel study the same people are reinterviewed at different points in time. A cohort study is comparable to a trend study of a particular cohort or age group. As in a trend study, the people sampled from the cohort may vary from one time period to the next.

TREND STUDIES

Trend studies are routinely carried out by governmental agencies as a way of documenting changes that are occurring in society. Considerable energies are spent by governments on social bookkeeping: keeping track of employment, unemployment, marriages, births, divorces, deaths, diseases, crime rates, the cost of living, the gross national product, and hundreds of other social indicators of the health and well-being of the nation. The cumulation of such data over time provides both government officials and social scientists with extremely valuable information on trends and changes within the society as a whole and various subgroups within the society.

In addition to the official records kept by governmental agencies, trend data are also generated by the public opinion polls carried out by the national polling agencies such as Gallup, Harris, and Roper. These firms frequently repeat the same questions from one year to the next. Using such poll data, Herbert Hyman and Paul Sheatsley have been able to document trends in racial prejudice in American society over a 20-year period. Table 13.1 shows trends in racial prejudice on three questions that were included in national polls carried out by the National Opinion Research Center in 1942, 1956, and 1963.* The trends on these three questions show a dramatic decline in racial prejudice over the 20-year period. It should be noted that the trend analyst not only can show the overall trend but can break the sample down into relevant subgroups and show the trends in these subgroups. In this instance, Hyman and Sheatsley break out Northerners and Southerners and show the trends in these subgroups. As would be expected, the data show the Northerners to be much less prejudiced than the Southerners, but more significantly, the Southerners as well as the Northerners show the trend toward greater tolerance.

A gold mine of information on trends in American society is the annual publication *Social Indicators*, produced by the U.S. Department of Commerce. This enormous tome contains trend data on population by sex, age, race, population distribution, fertility rates, public perceptions of ideal number of children, the percentage in favor of legal abortions, international comparisons in population growth, and movers and migrants as a percentage of the population, to mention only some of the topics covered in the first chapter of this book, entitled "Population." Other chapters deal with the family, social security and welfare, and health and nutrition, public safety, education and training, work, income, and culture.

---

*These data are from Herbert H. Hyman and Paul B. Sheatsley, "Attitudes Toward Desegregation," *Scientific American*, July 1964, pp. 2–9.

Table 13.1.   **Trends in Attitudes Toward Desegregation**

A. *School Integration*: Question: "Do you think white students and Negro students should go to the same schools or to separate schools?" (Percent "Yes")

Year	Total	North	South
1942	30	40	2
1956	49	61	14
1963	63	73	34

B. *Transportation*: Question: "Generally speaking, do you think there should be separate sections for Negroes on streetcars and buses?" (Percent "Yes")

Year	Total	North	South
1942	44	57	4
1956	60	73	27
1963	79	89	52

C. *Neighborhoods*: Question: "If a Negro with the same income and education as you moved into your block, would it make any difference to you?" (Percent "No")

Year	Total	North	South
1942	35	42	12
1956	51	58	38
1963	64	70	51

From the wealth of data in this annual volume, we focus on the data on labor force participation, which is provided by age, sex and race, to illustrate trend analysis.

Table 13.2 shows labor force participation over a period of 28 years, from 1948 to 1976. The data are broken down according to race and sex and one age group, men 65 and over. To simplify the presentation, we present data on the even-numbered years in this period. Table 13.2 contains a number of findings of considerable interest to the student of labor force participation. From the first two columns we learn that there has been a steady decline in labor force participation among both white and black males over a period of almost three decades. But this decline is much more pronounced among black males than white males. Among the whites, labor force participation declines by about 8 percentage points, from 86.5 to 78.4 percent. But among blacks, the decline is almost 17 percentage points, from 87.3 to 70.7. From 1948 to 1964, black men keep pace with white men in labor force participation, with participation declining about 6 percentage points in each group. But from 1966 through 1976, the black rate decreases much more sharply than the white rate, dropping 8.3 points in this period compared with a drop of only 2.2 points among the whites. What took place over this decade that drove more black men out of the labor force than white men? Was finding work so difficult for blacks in this period that they gave up and left the labor

Table 13.2.   Civilian Labor Force Participation of Persons 16 Years Old and Over by Race, Sex and Age, 1948 to 1976[a]

Year	White Males	Black Males	White Females	Black Females	White Males 65 Plus	Black Males 65 Plus
1948	86.5	87.3	31.3	45.6	46.5	50.3
1950	86.4	85.9	32.6	46.9	45.8	45.5
1952	86.2	86.8	33.6	45.5	42.5	43.3
1954	85.6	85.2	33.3	46.1	40.4	41.2
1956	85.6	85.1	35.7	47.3	40.0	39.8
1958	84.3	84.0	35.8	48.0	35.7	34.5
1960	83.4	83.0	36.5	48.2	33.3	31.2
1962	82.1	80.8	36.7	48.0	30.6	27.2
1964	80.8	80.0	37.5	48.5	27.9	29.6
1966	80.6	79.0	39.2	49.3	27.2	25.6
1968	80.4	77.6	40.7	49.3	27.3	26.6
1970	80.0	76.5	42.6	49.5	26.7	27.4
1972	79.6	73.7	43.2	48.7	24.4	23.6
1974	79.4	73.3	45.2	49.1	22.5	21.7
1976	78.4	70.7	46.9	50.2	20.3	19.7

[a]From U.S. Department of Commerce, Bureau of the Census, *Social Indicators, 1976*, Washington, D.C.: U.S. Government Printing Office, December 1977, pp. 372–373.

force? One major reason for the decline in male participation in the labor force over this period is the growth in retirement among the elderly, those men over 65. From the last two columns we see that male participation in the labor force declined sharply among both white and black men over 65 years of age. For the white men the decline among the elderly is 26 percentage points and among the black men it is 30 percentage points. But this trend among the elderly does not explain the sharp difference between black and white men in labor force participation in the later years. Whereas at the beginning of this period, black men were just as likely as white men to be in the labor force, toward the end of the period, the white male rate is substantially higher than the black male rate.

The women also show interesting patterns. The movement into the labor force on the part of women, which is well known, turns out to be mainly a phenomenon of white women. The data show a steady increase in labor force participation among white women over this period, from 31.3 percent in 1948 to 46.9 percent in 1976, for an overall increase of 15.5 percentage points. But black women do not show this trend. Their participation rate increased only 4.5 points over this period, and during the last decade the participation rate of black women did not increase at all. Black women were always more likely than white women to be in the labor force, but by the end of this 28-year period, the white women had almost caught up with the black women.

A table such as this contains a number of oddities. For example, there was a sharp decline in the rate of participation among the elderly of both races between 1956 and 1958. Why? Why did the black male rate decline sharply after 1966? The war on poverty was flourishing during this period and one goal of that war was to put the unemployed back to work, yet substantial numbers of black men left the labor force; they were neither working nor looking for work.

As can be seen from Table 13.2, trend data are highly informative and provide a picture of what is happening in society, the changes that occur, over time.

COHORT ANALYSIS

A cohort is any group of people who share the same time frame. Typically, research has been done on birth cohorts, that is, people born in the same period of time, usually 5- or 10-year periods, and hence people of comparable age. But cohorts can be located by any other time frame, for example, all those entering college in the same year, or graduating from college in the same year, might be treated as a cohort and followed through subsequent years. For example, one might study successive classes of entering graduate students at particular universities and note how long it takes each member of each cohort to get a Ph.D. Such research might show that the length of time for the Ph.D. is decreasing over time, as in the hypothetical Table 13.3. The data show that over a 30-year period the length of time of doctoral study declined markedly.

Cohorts can consist of any group of people who share the same experience at the same point in time, for example, all people who got married or divorced in a particular year, or all people who were admitted to a hospital on the same day. But as noted, most research has been done on birth cohorts. The example of a birth cohort shown in Table 13.4 is taken from Norval Glenn's monograph on cohort analysis.*

A cohort table based on birth cohorts shows the effects of three variables on the dependent variable: age, period, and cohort. The age variable is seen by reading down the columns of the table, the period variable is seen by reading across the rows, and the cohort variable is shown by the diagonals of the table. For example, the 21–28-year-old cohort in 1952 is the 29–36-year-old group in 1960 and the 37–44-year-old group in 1968. In 1952, 19 percent of this cohort had a high interest in politics, a figure that climbed to 22 percent in 1960 and declined to 17 percent in 1968. Inspection of the columns of Table 13.4 show that interest in politics increases with age, especially in 1952 and 1960. By 1968 the impact of age on interest in politics is sharply attenuated. The rows of Table 13.4 show that over time, interest in politics

*Norval D. Glenn, *Cohort Analysis*, Beverly Hills, California: Sage Publications, 1977. This section is heavily indebted to Glenn's work.

Table 13.3. Year of Award of Ph.D. by Year of Entry into Graduate School

| | Year of Award of Ph.D. | | | | | | | |
Year of Entry	1950	1955	1960	1965	1970	1975	1980	N
1945	10	30	7	3				50
1950		12	35	2	1			50
1955			14	33	3			50
1960				15	33	2		50
1965					17	32	1	50
1970						19	30	49
1975							21	21

Table 13.4. Percentage of Respondents Who Reported a "Great Deal" of Interest in Politics, United States

| | Year | | | | | |
Age	1952		1960		1968	
21–28	19%	(1,555)	18%	(447)	19%	(498)
29–36	22	(1,756)	22	(619)	17	(482)
37–44	24	(1,527)	25	(655)	17	(501)
45–52	29	(1,281)	22	(498)	20	(496)
53–60	31	(1,035)	29	(451)	19	(407)
61–68	34	(779)	28	(450)	19	(300)
69–76	37	(431)	30	(240)	23	(202)
Average	25%		24%		19%	
N		(8,364)		(3,360)		(2,886)

Source: Table 13.4 is reprinted from Glenn, Norval D. 1977. *Cohort Analysis.* Sage University Paper series on Quantitative Applications in the Social Sciences, 07-005. Beverly Hills and London: Sage Publications.

has declined somewhat. From the data on the total samples we see that interest declined from 26 percent in 1954 to 19 percent in 1968. Finally, the cohort data, shown by the diagonals of the table, indicate that as the cohorts aged, they tended to become less interested in politics (an effect of age) and that the older cohorts were somewhat more interested in politics than the younger cohorts, suggesting a difference in their socialization, that is, that they grew up at a time when interest in politics was greater.

The problem with age cohort tables is that the three independent variables—age, period, and cohort—are so intertwined that their separate effects cannot be isolated easily. For example, the columns of Table 13.4 reflect both age and cohort. The greater interest in politics with age in 1952 might well mean that people become more interested in politics as they get older. But it could also mean that older cohorts grew up in a period when interest in politics was greater. Similarly, the rows show a slight decline in interest in politics over time, suggesting that forces at work in society were causing a trend away from politics. But this row pattern could also be the result of changing cohorts over time. The 29–36-year-olds in 1968 show an interest in politics rate of only 17 percent compared with the 22 percent rate in the 29–36-year cohort in 1952. This could be caused by historical changes in society *or* differences in the earlier and later cohort. Finally, the cohort patterns shown in the diagonals, the trend toward declining interest within each cohort, could have resulted from period effects, the societal trend away from politics, or aging, the fact that the cohort is getting older over time.

Although these contaminating effects are in principle present in every age cohort table, the role of each independent variable usually can be sorted out on commonsense grounds. For example, the cohort patterns shown in the diagonals could indeed stem from aging rather than from period, but if so, the aging effect in the diagonals is the direct opposite of the aging effects in the columns. The columns show that older people are more interested in politics than younger people, suggesting that events in the aging process lead to interest in politics. But from the diagonals we see that as each cohort gets older, its interest in politics tends to decline. It is absurd to assume that aging has one effect when different age groups are compared and a different effect when the same group becomes older. The safest interpretation of the diagonal pattern is that it stems from the effect of period, the societal trend away from politics. A direct cohort effect is seen from comparing the different cohorts over time, that is, comparing the different diagonals in the table. It would appear that the older cohorts, presumably because of their socialization, are more interested in politics at any given time than the younger cohorts. Finally, the age pattern shown by the columns could indeed be the result of different cohorts rather than aging, but the fact that this age pattern appears in each time period strongly suggests that age rather than cohort is the critical variable. Older people are more interested in politics, even though the period effect is turning people away from politics over time, so that as people get older they are likely to lose interest in politics because of the period effect.

In his monograph, Glenn presents hypothetical data that tend to separate the three independent variables of age, period, and cohort. Table 13.5 is Glenn's hypothetical table showing that age is the cause of the variation in the data. The percentages are the same in each row of Table 13.5, showing that there is no period effect. Within each age group the same percentage of people manifest the dependent variable. But the columns show a steady increase in the dependent variable as the age of the group increases. The aging effect is also shown by the diagonal lines. As each cohort increases in age it is more likely to have the dependent variable. The older cohorts show more of the dependent variable than the younger cohorts, another sign of the aging effect.

Table 13.6 is Glenn's hypothetical table showing that the data patterns are

Table 13.5.   Cohort Table Showing Hypothetical Data (Percentages) in Which All Variation Is Caused by Age Effects[a]

	Year			
Age	1940	1950	1960	1970
20–29	40%	40%	40%	40%
30–39	45	45	45	45
40–49	50	50	50	50
50–59	55	55	55	55
60–69	60	60	60	60
70–79	65	65	65	65
Average	52.5%	52.5%	52.5%	52.5%

[a]Table 13.5 is reprinted from Glenn, Norval D. 1977. *Cohort Analysis.* Sage University Paper series on Quantitative Applications in the Social Sciences, 07-005. Beverly Hills and London: Sage Publications.

Table 13.6.   Cohort Table Showing Hypothetical Data (Percentages) in Which All Variation Is Caused by Period Effects[a]

	Year			
Age	1940	1950	1960	1970
20–29	70%	60%	50%	40%
30–39	70	60	50	40
40–49	70	60	50	40
50–59	70	60	50	40
60–69	70	60	50	40
70–79	70	60	50	40
Average	70%	60%	50%	40%

[a]Table 13.6 is reprinted from Glenn, Norval D. 1977. *Cohort Analysis.* Sage University Paper series on Quantitative Applications in the Social Sciences, 07-005. Beverly Hills and London: Sage Publications.

caused by period effects. The data do not vary at all with age, only with period. Over the 30-year period there is a steady decline in the percentage of people exhibiting the dependent variable. The cohort patterns in the diagonal also show the period effect as the percentages decrease as the cohort ages.

Table 13.7 is Glenn's presentation of the pure cohort effect. As we move from the youngest cohort in the upper right of the table to the oldest cohort in the lower left, we find a steady increase in the percentage on the dependent variable. Each cohort shows the same percentage of the dependent

Table 13.7. Cohort Table Showing Hypothetical Data (Percentages) in Which All Variation Is Caused by Cohort Effects[a]

Age	Year			
	1940	1950	1960	1970
20–29	50%	40%	30%	20%
30–39	60	50	40	30
40–49	70	60	50	40
50–59	80	70	60	50
60–69	90	80	70	60
70–79	100	90	80	70
Average	75%	65%	55%	45%

[a]Table 13.7 is reprinted from Glenn, Norval D. 1977. *Cohort Analysis*. Sage University Paper series on Quantitative Applications in the Social Sciences, 07-005. Beverly Hills and London: Sage Publications.

variable, whatever the time period. The cohorts thus show that there is no period effect, even though the percentages decline over time, a decline reflecting cohort effects rather than historical events at different periods. Real life tables based on empirical data will never show these pure effects, but by comparing real tables with these hypothetical tables one might get some clue as to which variables are important for the observed patterns.

A rich source of cohort data are the polls carried out by the major polling firms such as Gallup, Louis Harris Associates, and Elmo Roper. These firms frequently repeat questions in their surveys from year to year, and by sorting their respondents by age one could study changes in the views of cohorts.

In the cohort tables presented thus far, the age cohorts were listed down the left-hand side and the year across the top. This is the conventional way of presenting age cohort tables, but other formats are also used. Table 13.8 shows labor force participation for age cohorts born from 1900 to 1940 for the years 1950 to 1975. Whereas in the previous format the life cycle of a cohort was read along the diagonal, in Table 13.8 it appears in the rows of the table. To compare different cohorts at the same age in Table 13.8, one must read along the diagonal. The data of this cohort table confirm the pattern of the trend table shown earlier (Table 13.2), that there was a decline in labor force participation for men from 1950 to 1975.

Still another format for a cohort table is seen in Table 13.9. These data show survivorship rates for white male cohorts from birth to age 70. The cohorts are listed along the top and their age down the side. The data show that the life span of successive cohorts steadily increases. For example, whereas only two thirds of the oldest cohort, those born in 1899–1903, reach

Table 13.8. Labor Force Participation of Selected Cohorts by Sex 1950–1975[a]

Year of Birth of Cohort and Sex	Year of Labor Force Participation					
	1950	1955	1960	1965	1970	1975
1901–05						
Age at specified year	45–49	50–54	55–59	60–64	65–69	70–74
Male	NA	95.7	91.6	78.0	41.6	15.1
Female	NA	41.5	42.2	34.0	17.3	4.9
1906–10						
Age at specified year	40–44	45–49	50–54	55–59	60–64	65–69
Male	NA	97.1	94.8	90.2	75.0	31.7
Female	NA	45.9	48.7	47.1	36.1	14.5
1911–15						
Age at specified year	35–39	40–44	45–49	50–54	55–59	60–64
Male	NA	98.0	96.6	95.0	89.5	65.7
Female	NA	44.1	50.7	50.1	49.0	33.3
1916–20						
Age at specified year	30–34	35–39	40–44	45–49	50–54	55–59
Male	NA	98.2	97.5	96.1	93.1	84.4
Female	NA	39.2	46.3	51.7	53.8	47.9
1921–25						
Age at specified year	25–29	30–34	35–39	40–44	45–49	50–54
Male	NA	98.3	97.9	97.0	95.4	90.1
Female	NA	34.7	40.8	48.5	55.0	53.3
1926–30						
Age at specified year	20–24	25–29	30–34	35–39	40–44	45–49
Male	89.1	97.2	98.3	97.9	96.5	94.1
Female	46.1	35.3	36.3	43.6	52.9	55.9
1931–35						
Age at specified year	15–19	20–24	25–29	30–34	35–39	40–44
Male	65.9	90.8	97.0	98.0	97.5	95.2
Female	41.0	46.0	35.7	38.2	49.2	56.8
1936–40						
Age at specified year	X	15–19	20–24	25–29	30–34	35–40
Male	X	63.0	90.2	96.9	97.5	96.3
Female	X	40.7	46.2	38.9	44.7	54.9

[a]From U.S. Department of Commerce, Bureau of the Census, *Social Indicators, 1976*, Washington, D.C.: U.S. Government Printing Office, December 1977, p. 366.

Table 13.9. Cohort Survivorship for White Males from Birth to Age 70[a]

Age	Born 1899–1903	Born 1908–1912	Born 1918–1922	Born 1928–1932
0	100.0	100.0	100.0	100.0
1	86.7	89.7	92.3	93.9
5	81.2	85.6	89.4	92.0
10	79.8	84.2	88.4	91.3
15	79.0	83.3	87.8	90.8
20	77.3	82.2	86.9	90.1
25	75.8	80.9	84.6	89.1
30	74.3	79.7	83.2	88.1
35	72.9	78.4	82.3	87.5
40	71.2	77.0	81.3	86.4
45	69.2	75.3	79.6	(X)
50	66.5	72.7	76.9	(X)
55	62.6	68.6	(X)	(X)
60	57.3	62.6	(X)	(X)
65	50.0	(X)	(X)	(X)
70	40.7	(X)	(X)	(X)

[a]From U.S. Department of Commerce, Bureau of the Census, *Social Indicators, 1976*, Washington, D.C.: U.S. Government Printing Office, December 1977, p. 191.

the age of 50, more than three quarters of the cohort born 20 years later, in 1918–1922, reach age 50. In short, cohort data may be presented in a variety of ways.

PANEL STUDIES

The most sophisticated research design for studying change over time is the panel study, in which the same people are reinterviewed at different points in time. Each series of interviews is known as a wave and panel studies vary according to the number of waves. Many panel studies are based on the minimum of two waves but many others are based on three, four, five, or more waves. The first major panel study in sociology was conducted in 1940 by Paul F. Lazarsfeld, who originated panel studies. In that year, Lazarsfeld did a panel study of voters in the presidential election. That study involved six waves in which a sample of potential voters were asked questions about their voting intentions and interest in politics every month from May through October. In the 1950s Merton launched a five-year study of medical education and each year medical students filled out questionnaires. That study was eventually extended into the internship period and ultimately consisted of seven waves of interviews. In the 1960s NORC did a major study of the graduates of the college class of 1961, following up each year over a period of four years. In the early 1970s the Department of Labor launched the largest labor force participation panel study of all. Four samples of 5000 respondents each—young men, middle-aged men, young women, middle-aged women—have been reinterviewed each year over a period of 10 years, and that study is still continuing. Another long-range panel study of this stature has been carried out by the Survey Research Center of the University of Michigan. In a study of income dynamics, some 5000 families have been followed over a period of 14 years. In none of these long-range panel studies have all the waves of data been analyzed simultaneously, but in the shorter range panel studies, those of two or three waves, the heart of the analysis consists of studying the changes that take place from wave to wave.

The great advantage of panel studies over trend studies is that they make it possible to determine absolute or gross change and not merely net change from one time period to the next. This can be illustrated by a study of youth employment by the Bureau of Labor Statistics from 1963 to 1965. In each of these years a nationwide sample of men between the ages of 16 and 21 were interviewed.* Table 13.10 shows the trend in employment for this sample over the two-year period. The trend table shows a sharp increase in employment among male youth from 1963 to 1965. The unemployment rate was cut in half, from 18.7 to 9.4 percent. When confronted with such trend data, we are likely to think that 9.3 percent of the sample moved from unemployment to employment, that is, that the change is only in the direction of the trend, as indicated by Table 13.11. This is a *turnover table*, which shows a categorical variable at time 1 cross-tabulated with itself at time 2. The time 1 reading on the variable appears in the left column of the turnover table and the time 2 along the top. This turnover table is very much like any fourfold table showing the relationship between two variables, except in this table we are looking at the same variable measured at two points in time. A turnover table such as this shows not only net change but gross change as well. Of the two possible change cells, Table 13.11 shows that all the change occurred in only one cell, those who changed from unemployed to employed. None of the sample moved from employment in the earlier time period to unemployment in the later. In this example, the gross change equals the net change.

It is possible to get the same amount of net change with a much greater degree of gross change. Table 13.12 shows the extreme where gross change is three times the amount of net change. Here the trend remains the same, but the amount of turnover (gross change) has tripled to 28.1 percent. Unlike Table 13.11, this table shows change in both directions. Not only did many unemployed people find jobs, but some of the originally employed people

---

*This example and the others in this section are based on data from Bernard Levenson, "Panel Studies," in David L. Sills (Ed.), *International Encyclopedia of the Social Sciences*, Vol. 11, New York: Macmillan and Free Press, 1968, pp. 371–379.

Table 13.10.   Trend Data on Employment Status of Male Youth in 1963 and 1965

Status	1963	1965
Employed	81.3%	90.6%
Unemployed	18.7	9.4
	100%	100%
N	(2,126,000)	(2,126,000)

Table 13.11.   Panel Data on Employment Status of Male Youth in 1963 and 1965

1963	1965		
	Employed	Unemployed	
Employed	81.3%	0%	81.3%
Unemployed	9.2%	9.4%	18.7%
	90.6%	9.4%	100%
			(2,126,000)

Table 13.12.   Panel Data on Employment Status of Male Youth in 1963 and 1965

1963	1965		
	Employed	Unemployed	
Employed	71.9%	9.4%	81.3%
Unemployed	18.7%	0%	18.7%
	90.6%	9.4%	100%
			(2,126,000)

lost their jobs. In fact, no one in the sample was unemployed at both time periods. Tables 13.11 and 13.12 show the extreme gross changes that could have occurred with the same amount of net change. In the real world, the amount of turnover that is actually found is almost always somewhere between these two extremes. For example, the Bureau of Labor Statistics study actually found the amount of turnover shown in Table 13.13. Although the trend showed a net increase of employment of 9.4 percent, the gross change was twice as large, 18.7 percent. Although many of the originally unemployed found work, some remained unemployed two years later and some who were initially employed lost their jobs two years later.

The percentages in Table 13.13 are calculated on the total sample. They

Table 13.13. Panel Data on Employment Status of Male Youth in 1963 and 1965

| | 1965 | | |
1963	Employed	Unemployed	
Employed	76.6%	4.7%	81.3%
Unemployed	14.0%	4.7%	18.7%
	90.6%	9.4%	100%
			(2,126,000)

Table 13.14. The Transitional Probabilities for Employment Status of Male Youth, 1963–1965

| | 1965 | | |
1963	Employed	Unemployed	Total
Employed	94.2%	5.8%	100% (1,729,000)
Unemployed	75.1%	24.9%	100% (397,000)

tell us the number of people who have each combination of employment status based on the two time periods. But many times percentages in turnover tables are calculated on the time 1 marginals, which appear in the rows. When percentaged in this fashion, the transitional probabilities, that is, the likelihood of the initial states changing by time 2, become apparent. These transitional probabilities are seen in Table 13.14. The employed were much more likely to be stable between the two time periods, as only 5.8 percent of them changed position to unemployed by time 2. But the unemployed in 1963 were highly unstable, as most of them changed their position to employment by 1965. Fully 75 percent of the initially unemployed changed to employed over the two-year period.

Measuring Turnover

The panel researcher wants to measure the amount of turnover in panel tables, for turnover means change and the researcher wants to know the amount of change and the causes of the change. The researcher may wish to compare groups or different properties of the people in the same group. Do certain groups change more over time than other groups and do certain attitudes, values, and behaviors change more than other attitudes, values, and behaviors? To answer such questions the researcher must develop measures of turnover. Measuring change is the reverse of measuring correlation. Two variables are more closely related the larger the number of cases along the main diagonal in the plus-plus and the minus-minus cells. But change from time 1 to time 2 shows up in the cells along the minor diagonal, the plus-minus and the minus-plus cells. One way of measuring turnover would be to calculate the correlation coefficient for the turnover table and subtract it from 1. But there is no simple solution to the problem of measuring turnover, and a number of different indices of turnover have been proposed and are used, each resting on a somewhat different theory of change.

Compounding the problem of measuring turnover is measurement error. Measurement error invariably creeps into the research process and some of the turnover is simply a result of measurement error. It has been shown that when the same population is remeasured at a later time shifts occur on just about any item of information, even those characteristics that are presumed to be fixed such as age, sex, religion, and race. Some of this error stems from the respondent being inconsistent and some stems from the researchers' errors in recording and processing the information. For example, the interviewer may check the wrong box, or the coder may make a mistake, or the key puncher may punch the wrong hole. In developing measures of turnover the researcher may have to make some corrections in the measure of turnover to take measurement error into account. One way of measuring error is to carry out a three-wave panel, with a very short time period between the first and second wave and a fairly long time period between the second and third waves. If the gap between the first and second waves was a few days or a week, then the turnover that occurs in that brief period of time could be attributed to measurement error. If the gap between the second and third waves is six months or a year, then the amount of turnover in that period exceeding the amount of turnover in the short period can be attributed to real changes in the lives and experiences of the respondents.

One measure of turnover is the sum of the cases in the turnover cells of the table divided by the total N. For example, in Table 13.13 we saw that 14 percent of the sample consisted of people who were unemployed in 1963 but had found jobs by 1965 and 4.7 percent were employed in 1963 but had lost jobs by 1965, for a total of 18.7 percent who had changed in the two-year period. This measure of turnover ignores the marginals in the turnover table.

Another way of calculating turnover is to assume that the marginals are fixed and compare the actual amount of turnover with the total possible turnover that could have occurred given the marginals. This can be shown from hypothetical turnover tables. The marginals in Table 13.15 are highly skewed, whereas in Table 13.16 they are split 50–50. Using the total turnover index discussed above, we find that in Table 13.15 100 people changed position from time 1 to time 2, and since the total sample consisted of 1000, the changers amount to 10 percent for a turnover index value of .10. In Table 13.16, 200 people changed positions for an index value of .20. In short, according to the first measure of turnover, there is twice as much turnover in Table 13.16 as in Table 13.15. But a turnover index that treats the marginals

Table 13.15. Hypothetical Turnover Table

First Interview	Second Interview		
	Yes	No	
Yes	50	50	100
No	50	850	900
	100	900	1000

Table 13.16. Hypothetical Turnover Table

First Interview	Second Interview		
	Yes	No	
Yes	400	100	500
No	100	400	500
	500	500	1000

as fixed and compares the actual turnover with the maximum amount possible given the marginals shows quite a different story. Given the marginals in Table 13.15, the maximum amount of turnover possible is 200 cases, and since 100 cases actually changed, the actual change divided by maximum change yields a value of .50. In Table 13.16, where the marginals are completely symmetrical and split 50–50, every single case could have changed from time 1 to time 2, for a maximum of 1000. Since 200 cases in fact did change, the actual change divided by maximum change is 200/1000, or .20. In short, this second index shows that Table 13.15 had more turnover than Table 13.16.

The matter of measuring turnover is more complicated than this simple index of the number of turnover cases divided by N implies. Several measures of turnover have been proposed, some of which were developed by Paul Lazarsfeld. In an article in *Continuities in the Language of Social Research*, Lazarsfeld develops three measures of turnover, each based on a different theory of change.* The first index, which Lazarsfeld calls the *oscillation* or *psychological index*, is based on the assumption that the characteristics measured over the course of the panel study are more or less stable traits that do not really change much over time. The changes that do occur in these

*Paul F. Lazarsfeld, "The Problem of Measuring Turnover," in Paul F. Lazarsfeld, Ann Pasanella, and Morris Rosenberg (Eds.), *Continuities in the Language of Social Research*, New York: Free Press, 1972.

characteristics probably stem from chance events. As a result of these events some people stray from their position and move to another position. But these changers are likely to revert back to their previous, "true" position on a subsequent wave, their places taken by others who stray from their basic position. This model assumes that the marginals in a turnover table are constant and do not change from wave to wave. Lazarsfeld illustrates this model by referring to the readers and nonreaders of a magazine. Because of psychological quirks, some of the true readers will not buy the magazine in a given week while some of the nonreaders, perhaps because of a special article, will buy it. Lazarsfeld presents these facts in the following format:

	Proportion in Each Position	Proportions in Each "True" Group Who Bought Magazine M in Successive Weeks	
		Week 1	Week 2
True readers	p_r	$1 - x$	$1 - x$
True nonreaders	$p_{\bar{r}}$	x	x
	$p_r + p_{\bar{r}} = 1$		

Not all the true readers will buy the magazine in a particular week; x percent will not. As a result, the number of true readers who do buy the magazine equals $1 - x$ in each week. By the same token, some of the true nonreaders will buy the magazine in a particular week for any of a number of unusual or accidental reasons. Lazarsfeld assumes that the number of true readers who do not buy the magazine is equal to the number of nonreaders who do buy it. Hence the percentage of nonreaders who buy is symbolized by x. Since the nonreaders balance the readers, the marginals of readers and nonreaders do not change from week to week. The index of turnover in this oscillation model is x, and solving for x is rather complicated. Assuming that 30 percent of the sample bought magazine M in the first week and 30 percent bought it in the second week, the equation for solving x is

$$.3 = p_r(1 - x) + p_{\bar{r}}x$$

That is, the percentage of readers equals the proportion of true readers who bought the magazine $(1 - x)$ plus the proportion of true nonreaders who bought the magazine (x). This equation has two unknowns, p_r and x, and hence requires another equation for its solution. Lazarsfeld assumes that the turnover table would look like Table 13.17. The probability of buying one week and not the other is the product of the two independent probabilities, $(1 - x)(x)$. The proportion who fall into the change cells is given by Lazarsfeld as

$$p_{1\bar{2}} = p_{\bar{1}2} = x(1 - x)(p_r + p_{\bar{r}}) = x(1 - x) = .1$$

Table 13.17.   Assumed Turnover Table[a]

| | Second Week | | |
	Reader	Nonreader	
First Week Reader	.2	.1	.3
Nonreader	.1	.6	.7
	.3	.7	

[a]Reprinted with permission of Macmillan Publishing Co., Inc. from *Continuities in the Language of Social Research*, P.F. Lazarsfeld, A.F. Pasanella and M. Rosenberg (Eds.). Copyright © 1972 by The Free Press, a Division of Macmillan Publishing Co., Inc.

This works out to $x^2 - x + .10 = 0$, a quadratic equation for which Lazarsfeld gives the following solution (Formula 2, page 359):

$$x = 1 - \frac{\sqrt{1 - 4(.1)}}{2} = .12$$

For Table 13.17 x thus has a value of .12, which is the measure of turnover in this psychological model of turnover.

Lazarsfeld developed a second model of turnover, one that he calls a *sociological model*. Here he assumes that the distribution of attitudes in the group has an influence on the stability of the attitudes of individual members. For example, if a substantial majority of the group has attitude A, then the people with attitude A will be more stable and change less than people who are in the minority with attitude nonA. In this sociological model, the likelihood of changing, x in the preceding case, is weighted by the marginals, with the people in the majority being weighted (multiplied) by the minority marginal and the people in the minority being weighted (multiplied) by the majority marginal. Instead of the number of nonreaders who buy the magazine equaling the number of readers who do not buy it in any week, the proportion of nonreaders who buy will be less than the proportion of readers who do not buy because they are in the majority and will change less than the readers in the minority.

A third theory of turnover is based on the *Markov chain model*. This index is based on the transition probabilities. Whereas both the psychological and sociological models assume constant marginals, the Markov chain model assumes changing marginals. A second difference is that the subjects in the psychological and sociological models are assumed to have memories, that is, they remember their true position and tend to return to it in subsequent waves. In the Markov chain model, the subjects do not have memories. Once they leave their original position, they assume the transition probability of their new position. They are treated like all the other subjects in their new class. The Markov chain model assumes that the transition probabilities are fixed and remain the same from wave to wave. This index is equal to the sum of the transitional probabilities, and it tells us the speed with which the Markov chain achieves equilibrium, that is, the marginals achieve stability and stop changing. This can be seen in Tables 13.18 and 13.19. Table 13.18 is a hypothetical turnover table showing transition probabilities. Of the 700 cases that were plus at time 1, 200 shifted to minus at time 2, for a transition probability of .29. Of the 300 cases that were minus at time 1, 100 shifted to plus at time 2, for a transition probability of .33. The turnover index is the sum of these two transition probabilities, .62. Since this number is fairly large, it will take several waves before equilibrium is reached and the marginals are stable. This progression is seen in Table 13.19, in which the cell entries in each successive turnover table are calculated by applying the transition probabilities to the row marginals of the previous table. As can be seen from the data in Table 13.19, by the seventh wave the marginals have become stabilized. Although the marginals stop changing, the amount of turnover is just as great on the seventh wave as on the second wave. In every one of these turnover tables about 300 cases change position from one wave to the next.

The three indices of turnover reviewed here are explained in more detail in the Lazarsfeld article cited. The point to keep in mind is that the different indices will not always yield the same results. In some cases one index will show one table showing more turnover than a second table whereas another index will show the second table as having more turnover than the first. Which index is more appropriate in any given case depends on the theory of change that the researcher is working with.

Qualified Turnover

A major task of the researcher is uncovering the causes of the changes revealed by turnover tables. Just as efforts to interpret the correlations

Table 13.18. *Hypothetical Turnover Table*

		Raw Ns					Transition Probabilities		
		Time 2					Time 2		
		+	−				+	−	
Time 1	+	500	200	700	Time 1	+	71	29	100%
	−	100	200	300		−	33	67	100%
		600	400	1000					

Table 13.19.   A Succession of Turnover Tables in a Seven-Wave Panel Study

		Time 2 +	Time 2 −				Time 3 +	Time 3 −	
Time 1	+	500	200	700	Time 2	+	426	174	600
	−	100	200	300		−	132	268	400
		600	400	1000			558	442	1000

		Time 4 +	Time 4 −				Time 5 +	Time 5 −	
Time 3	+	396	162	558	Time 4	+	385	157	542
	−	146	296	442		−	151	307	458
		542	458	1000			536	464	1000

		Time 6 +	Time 6 −				Time 7 +	Time 7 −	
Time 5	+	381	155	536	Time 6	+	379	155	534
	−	153	311	464		−	154	312	466
		534	466	1000			533	467	1000

shown by two variable tables require introducing additional variables into the analysis, so the panel analyst elaborates turnover tables by introducing additional variables. To determine the kinds of people more likely to change from time 1 to time 2 the researcher subdivides the sample on the basis of some property and then studies turnover within each subgroup. The variable used to find out which subgroup has more turnover and which has less is called a *qualifier*.

The Bureau of Labor Statistics, which carried out the study of employment among male youth, introduced education as a qualifying variable in the analysis of employment turnover. The results are seen in Table 13.20. When employment turnover is qualified by education, we learn that unemployment is a much greater problem for high school dropouts than high school graduates. Of those who were employed in 1963, the graduates were much more likely to remain employed in 1965 than the dropouts, 98.4 compared with 88.8 percent. And the graduates who were initially unemployed were much more likely to find work two years later than the dropouts who were initially unemployed, 88.6 compared with 68.3 percent. Table 13.20 shows that among the originally employed, the graduates were much more stable and showed much less turnover than the dropouts, but the reverse is true for the initially unemployed. For this group, the graduates

Table 13.20. *Employment Status of Male Youth in 1963 and 1965 by Education*[a]

	High School Graduates				High School Dropouts			
	1965				1965			
1963	Employed	Unemployed		N	Employed	Unemployed		N
Employed	98.4%	1.6%	100%	(963,000)	88.8%	11.2%	100%	(766,000)
Unemployed	88.6%	11.4%	100%	(132,000)	68.3%	31.7%	100%	(265,000)
N	(1,065,000)	(30,000)		(1,095,000)	(861,000)	(170,000)		(1,031,000)

[a]Adapted from Bernard Levenson, "Panel Studies," in David L. Sills (Ed.), *International Encyclopedia of the Social Sciences*, Vol. 11, New York: Macmillan and Free Press,1968, pp. 374, 375.

347

showed much more turnover than dropouts (88.6 compared with 68.3 percent). The qualified turnover table tells us that education contributes to employment.

In the 1960s a study was done of the employment status of white and black graduates of vocational high schools in Baltimore at successive quarters following graduation. Table 13.21 shows the turnover between the first and second quarter for the male graduates of vocational schools in Baltimore. From the first to the second quarter the trend was toward employment as more of the male graduates were employed at the end of the second quarter than at the end of the first. Most of the unemployed at time 1 had found jobs at time 2, but a few of the originally employed were unemployed by time 2. Table 13.22 shows the results when this turnover table is qualified by race. The trend toward employment is shown by both whites and blacks, but blacks who were employed at time 1 were much more likely than whites to lose their jobs by time 2 (13 compared with 4 percent).

Tables 13.21 and 13.22 show the transitional probabilities. When turnover is calculated as a percentage of the total number of cases we find that 17 percent of the cases turned over between time 1 and time 2 with 11 percent moving from unemployment to employment and 6 percent moving from employment to unemployment. Among the white males, total turnover is only 12 percent, with 8 percent moving toward employment and 4 percent toward unemployment. Among the blacks, turnover was much greater, as fully 25 percent of the sample changed position from time 1 to time 2. Some 15 percent of the blacks left the ranks of the unemployed and found work by time 2 but almost as many, 10 percent, lost their jobs between time 1 and time 2. The qualified turnover table makes clear that employment is much more unstable for blacks than for whites.

Mutual Effects

In much of the data analysis presented in this book we assume that causation occurs in a linear process, with X causing Y, without Y feeding back and causing X. In reality, however, many social processes involve such feedback loops. Panel analysis makes it possible to study such feedback. This is

Table 13.21. Turnover in Employment Status of Male Graduates of Vocational Schools in Baltimore, First To Second Quarter[a]

First Quarter	Second Quarter		
	Employed	Unemployed	
Employed	92%	8%	100%
Unemployed	56%	44%	100%

[a]From Bernard Levenson, personal communication.

Table 13.22. *Turnover in Employment Status of Male Graduates of Vocational Schools Qualified by Race[a]*

	Whites Second Quarter			Blacks Second Quarter		
First Quarter	Employed	Unemployed		Employed	Unemployed	
Employed	96%	4%	100%	87%	13%	100%
Unemployed	58%	42%	100%	54%	46%	100%

[a]From Bernard Levenson, personal communication.

accomplished when data are obtained on two interacting variables over time. In the simplest case, the two variables are dichotomous attributes, such as "yes" or "no," or "favor" or "opposed." The turnover table showing the interaction of two such variables contains 16 cells. This 16-fold table is the basic "mutual effects" table.

Levenson provides a good example of a mutual effects table in an encyclopedia article on panel analysis. He provides data on how husbands and wives might vote on a controversial issue like fluoridating a community's water supply. In a panel study both spouses are asked whether they would support or oppose such a plan if they had to vote on it. The interviews take place several months apart. The data that Levenson presents appear in Table 13.23. At time 1, 518 (77 percent) of the 671 couples were in agreement on the fluoridation issue. By time 2 the number of couples in agreement had increased to 548 or 85 percent, indicating that the trend was toward agreement. But changes occurred in the other direction as well. Some of the couples who were initially in agreement ended up in disagreement. Altogether, these were the cases in cells b, c, n, and o, a total of 15 cases. In 12 of these changes, it was the husband who changed away from the wife, while in only 3 cases did the wife "defect." Thus as far as undermining agreement is concerned, the husband is four times more influential than the wife.

When we examine the couples who were initially in disagreement but ended in agreement because one spouse changed opinion, we find, in cells e, i, h, and l, a total of 65 such cases. Of the 65 cases, 50 agreements were generated by the wife changing her opinion to her husband's, and in only 15 cases did the husband change his opinion to his wife's. The husband turns out to be three times as influential as the wife in generating agreement.

Just as a number of indices have been proposed for turnover, so a number of mutual effects indices have been developed. One such index calculates the number of conversions divided by the total possible number of conversions, correcting this for the number of defections divided by the total possible number of defections. For example, in Table 13.23, 153 couples were in disagreement at the end of wave 1. By wave 2, 65 of these cases had moved to agreement and in 50 of these cases the wife had moved to the husband's position. Thus 50/153 represents the percentage of conversions engineered by the husband. There were 518 couples who were initially in agreement but by time 2, the wives in cell b and cell o had deserted their husbands, a total of only 3 cases. A measure of the husband's influence is thus $(50/153) - 3/518)$, or $.346 - .005 = .341$. This is a measure of the husband's influence but from this should be subtracted the wife's influence for an overall measure of the relative strength of the husband's influence. Of the original 153 cases of disagreement, 15 involved the husband switching to the wife's position. Of the original 518 couples in agreement, the husband deserted the wife in 12 cases (cells c and n). The measure of the wife's influence is thus $(15/153) - (12/518)$ or $.098 - .023 = .075$. When this is

Table 13.23. Opinion of Spouses at Successive Interviews on Fluoridation Issue[a]

Husband / Wife	Time 2 Husband Wife Favor		Oppose		Time 1 totals
Husband Wife	Favor	Oppose	Favor	Oppose	
Time 1					
Favor — Favor	a 300	b 1	c 4	d 3	308
Favor — Oppose	e 25	f 40	g 1	h 10	76
Oppose — Favor	i 5	j 2	k 45	l 25	77
Oppose — Oppose	m 3	n 8	o 2	p 197	210
Time 2 totals	333	51	52	235	671

[a]"Panel Studies" by Bernard Levenson. Reprinted with permission of the publisher from *International Encyclopedia of the Social Sciences*, David L. Sills, Editor. Volume II, Page 377. Copyright © 1968 by Crowell Collier and Macmillan, Inc.

subtracted from the husband's influence, .341, we arrive at the value of .266 as a measure of the relative strength of the husband's influence.

Another index of mutual effects is based on a principle opposite to that of the preceding index. The index just calculated is based on the conversion of one characteristic to agreement with the other. A second index is based on the preservation principle, the likelihood that each property will persist at time 2. The data of Table 13.23 show that of the 384 husbands who were in favor at time 1, 366, or 96 percent, remained in favor at time 2. Of the 287 husbands who were initially opposed, 94 percent continued to be opposed at time 2, for an average preservation effect for husbands of 95 percent. For wives, 92 percent of the 385 initially in favor remained in favor at time 2 and 89 percent of those opposed remained opposed at time 2, for an average of 91 percent. Husbands were thus more likely to persevere in their opinions than wives, suggesting that they were more influential.

A third index of mutual effects is based on the ability of one spouse to predict the position of the other spouse at time 2. In this index the husband's position at time 1 is correlated with the wife's position at time 2 and the wife's position at time 1 is correlated with the husband's position at time 2, as in Table 13.24. As the phi values for these tables show, the husband's position at time 1 is more strongly correlated with the wife's position at time 2 than is the wife's position at time 1 correlated with the husband's position at time 2, indicating that the husband's influence over the wife is stronger than the wife's influence over the husband.

Lazarsfeld developed yet another index of mutual effects based on the change cells in the 16-fold tables and ignoring the marginals.* Unlike the indices of turnover, these various indices of mutual effects are not based on different theories and they are likely to yield similar results regardless of the marginals of the table.

Another example of a mutual effects 16-fold table is provided by Morris Rosenberg. In a panel study of occupational choice and occupational values, he was able to classify both the choices and the values according to whether they were people-oriented or non–people-oriented. Table 13.25 is his panel table. A comparison of the marginals for 1950 and those for 1952 shows that there is a trend toward consistency as the number of people whose values and choices were consistent increased between 1950 and 1952. This increase was entirely due to people changing their choices and values from people-oriented to non–people-oriented, as the number in this category increased from 231 to 266 cases, whereas those with people-oriented choices and values remained constant at 266. Initially, there were 255 people who were inconsistent in 1950 (89 POOCC-NPO values and 166 NPOOCC and PO

---

*See Paul F. Lazarsfeld, "Mutual Effects of Statistical Variables," in Paul F. Lazarsfeld, Ann Pasanella, and Morris Rosenberg (Eds.), *Continuities in the Language of Social Research*, New York: The Free Press, 1972. Using the letters of the cells in Table 13.23, the Lazarsfeld index is $I = [e/(e + b) - o/(o + 1)] - [i/(i + c) - n/(n + h)]$.

Table 13.24.   The Correlation Between Husband's Position at Time 1 and Wife's Position at Time 2 and Between Wife's Position at Time 1 and Husband's Position at Time 2, Respectively

Husband Time 1	Wife Time 2 Favor	Oppose		Wife Time 1	Husband Time 2 Favor	Oppose	
Favor	330	54	384	Favor	308	77	385
Oppose	55	232	287	Oppose	76	210	286
	385	286	671		384	287	671
	φ = .67				φ = .53		

Table 13.25.   "People-Oriented" Occupational Choices and Occupational Values in 1950 and 1952

Occupational Choices and Values, 1950[a]	Occupational Choices and Values, 1952[a]				
	POOCC-PO Values	POOCC-NPO Values	NPOOCC-PO Values	NPOOCC-NPO Values	Total
POOCC-PO values	163	15	30	18	226
POOCC-NPO values	21	29	8	31	89
NPOOCC-PO values	36	8	73	49	166
NPOOCC-NPO values	6	14	43	168	231
Total	226	66	154	266	712

[a]Reprinted with permission of Macmillan Publishing Co., Inc. from *The Language of Social Research*, P.F. Lazarsfeld and M. Rosenberg (Eds.). Copyright 1955 by The Free Press, a Corporation.

values). Of these initial inconsistents, 137, or 54 percent, became consistent in 1952, 102, or 40 percent, remained inconsistent, and a tiny fraction, 16 cases, or 6 percent, remained inconsistent but changed both their values and choices over the two-year period. As to whether consistency was achieved by values changing more than occupation or vice versa an answer is provided by examination of the cells showing movement from inconsistency to consistency, seen in Table 13.26. The cases in the upper-left-hand cell and the lower-right-hand cell changed their values to conform to their occupational choice, and the cases on the minor diagonal changed their choices to conform to their values. In the former category are 70 cases and in the latter, 67 cases, indicating that changes were almost as likely to occur in either direction, with choices being no more stable than values.

The discussion of panel analysis in the preceding pages has been based on research on individuals at two points in time. But panel analysis can be done on units more complicated than individuals such as organizations or pairs such as friends or couples. (In fact, the units in Table 13.23 were married couples rather than individuals.) And panel studies can be done at several

**Table 13.26.   Inconsistent People in 1950
Who Became Consistent in 1952**

	1952	
1950	POOCC- PO Values	NPOOCC- NP Values
POOCC-NPO values	21	31
NPOOCC-PO values	36	49

points in time, not just two. Three- and four-wave panels open up new lines of analysis such as looking at the people who flipflop and return to their original position and the early and late changers. In spite of the value of three- and four-wave panels, hardly any three-wave panel analyses have made their way into the literature. Panel studies of organizations are also rare, but some work has been done on panel studies of sociometric data where the units are pairs. Levenson has shown that unilateral choices, where A chooses B as a friend but B does not reciprocate, tend to be either reciprocated or withdrawn at time 2.* In static studies these unilateral choices were puzzling and the tendency was to assume that these people were faulty in their social perceptions. But Levenson's panel data showed that these unilateral choices at time 1 can be interpreted as "overture making," a normal process.

In this chapter we reviewed the various ways in which social researchers have studied change over time, through the methods of trend studies, cohort analysis, and panel studies. Panel studies in particular show considerable promise for the study of causation and change.

*Bernard Levenson, "Sociometric Panels," in Paul F. Lazarsfeld, Ann Pasanella, and Morris Rosenberg (Eds.), *Continuities in the Language of Social Research*, New York: Free Press, 1972, p. 423.

14

The Analysis of Group Properties: Contextual Analysis

Survey research frequently has been criticized by sociologists as being more appropriate to social psychology than to sociology. According to this view, survey research taps opinions, values, and attitudes of individuals, which are then related to the statuses of the individuals. What it does not do is permit the study of social groups, which is a central concern of sociologists. For much of the history of survey research this criticism was well taken, but since the early 1950s surveys have been conducted which do permit the study of social groups as well as individuals. These surveys have employed the technique of multistage sampling for drawing the samples of people to be studied. For example, in the early 1950s Lipset, Trow, and Coleman carried out a study of printers who belonged to the International Typographical Union.* Instead of randomly sampling printers from membership lists of the union local, Lipset et al. first sampled printing shops and then within printing shops they sampled printers. This technique ensured that sufficient numbers of printers would be sampled from the same shops so that the shops as well as the individual printers could be units of analysis. In the mid 1950s Paul Lazarsfeld carried out a study of the impact of McCarthyism on college professors. Like Lipset, he developed his sample in

*Seymour Martin Lipset, Martin A. Trow, and James S. Coleman, *Union Democracy*, New York: Free Press, 1956.

two stages, first sampling some 165 colleges from the population of colleges and then sampling social science professors at these colleges. As a result, Lazarsfeld had data not only on 2451 professors but on 165 colleges as well.*

Since the pioneering work of Lipset and Lazarsfeld, many researchers have drawn their samples in such a manner as to permit the study of groups as well as individuals. In the late 1950s James Coleman studied high school students sampled from 10 high schools, and James Davis surveyed the participants of Great Books study groups, analyzing the study groups as well as the participants. In the 1960s Sewell and Armer studied the career plans of high school seniors who were classified according to the economic status of the neighborhoods in which they lived. In a similar study John Michael related plans to enter college to the climate of the high school attended, defined by the socioeconomic status of the students. In a more recent study of religious apostasy, college students and the colleges they attended were the units of analysis.[†]

The two-stage sampling procedure permits three kinds of data analysis. The groups can be analyzed with group characteristics being related to each other. The individuals can be analyzed as in traditional survey research. And finally, the groups and the individuals can be analyzed simultaneously in what is known as contextual analysis. Contextual analysis attempts to show how individuals are influenced by the groups to which they belong. A contextual table contains both individual and group variables, typically two individual variables and one group variable known as the contextual variable.

GROUP OR CONTEXTUAL VARIABLES

Group variables fall into two broad types depending on whether they are based on the properties of the individuals who comprise the group. Group variables that have no counterpart on the individual level are known as *primary* or *global characteristics*. For example, if the groups are colleges, then such variables as type of control, that is, public or private, denominational or nondenominational, coed or single sex, size of library, school quality, and location are global characteristics that do not depend on the properties of the individuals who comprise the school. In contrast are the group variables that derive from some mathematical manipulation of the properties of the ele-

*Paul F. Lazarsfeld and Wagner Thielens, Jr., *The Academic Mind*, New York: Free Press, 1958.
[†]James S. Coleman, *The Adolescent Society: The Social Life of the Teenager and Its Impact on Education*, New York: Free Press, 1961. James Davis, *Great Books and Small Groups*, Chicago: Aldine, 1961. William H. Sewell and J. Michael Armer, "Neighborhood Context and College Plans," *American Sociological Review* **31**, No. 2, 159–168 (April 1966). John Michael, "High School Climate and Plans for Entering College," *The Public Opinion Quarterly* **25**, 585–595 (1961). David Caplovitz and Fred Sherrow, *The Religious Dropouts: Apostasy among College Graduates*, Beverly Hills, California: Sage Publications, 1977.

ments (individuals) that comprise the group. These variables are known as *analytic* or *aggregate variables*. The rates of various individual properties within the group are such properties, as are averages. For example, groups can be characterized by the average income or average age of their members, or by the percentage of women or Protestants or liberals in the group. In addition to rates and averages are analytical properties based on measures of dispersion such as standard deviations, relational data such as friendship choices, frequently used to measure group cohesion, and levels of authority relations used to measure stratification and bureaucracy.

Apart from the two basic types of group property, primary and analytic, is a hybrid third type which formally is analytic in nature but substantively is more like a primary or global group property. This hybrid type is based on individuals' perceptions of the collectivity to which they belong. *The Academic Mind* by Lazarsfeld and Thielens uses a number of group properties of this kind. The faculty members were asked whether they felt their administration would come to their support if they were attacked on political grounds. On the individual level this is merely one person's perception of the administration, but when the responses of a number of faculty members are aggregated the resulting group variable comes close to being an objective statement of the supportiveness of the administration. Where most faculty members agree the administration would be supportive the chances are that the administration is indeed supportive; conversely, where most faculty members think the administration is not supportive the chances are that it is not. The faculty members also were asked to describe any academic freedom incidents they knew about on their campus, and these reports were aggregated to assign an academic freedom incident score to the college. Inasmuch as these group variables are based on aggregating individual data, they correspond to analytic characteristics, but inasmuch as the issue applies to the college rather than to the individual professor, the resulting group variable is much like a primary or global property.

THE ANALYSIS OF GROUPS AND THE ECOLOGICAL FALLACY

Multistage sampling, as noted, makes it possible for the survey researcher to study groups in a quantitative fashion. Correlations involving group properties have come to be known as ecological correlations from the days when the groups most frequently studied were geographical units such as cities or states. When the analysis is concerned with the behavior of groups, ecological correlations are justified, but ecological correlations came into disrepute when they were used to make inferences about the behavior of individuals. Before sample surveys became commonplace in the late 1930s and early 1940s, social scientists often tried to make inferences about individual behavior by analyzing group properties, which were readily available in official statistics. For example, analysis of voting behavior was carried out by

.analyzing data on election districts. The percentage of Republican or Democratic vote in the district was related to other characteristics of the district such as the median rent of the dwelling units in the district. The units under analysis were the districts, and from the ecological correlations inferences were made about the behavior of individuals. For example, if the Republican vote increased as the median rent of the district increased, the researcher would have assumed that rich people tended to vote Republican and poor people tended to vote Democratic. In a classic article, William S. Robinson pointed out the fallacy of inferring individual correlations from ecological correlations.* The assumption that individual properties will always behave as do the corresponding group properties, however plausible, is incorrect, as Robinson documents.

The fallacy of the ecological correlation can be shown by working through an example of voting behavior and median rent for election districts. The ecological correlation would emerge from such data as the following:

Election District	Percentage Republican Vote	Median Rent
1	15	$100
2	25	130
3	35	160
4	40	190
5	50	220
6	55	250
7	65	280
8	75	300

As the percentage of Republican voters increases, so does the median rent. In fact, in this sample there is a perfect correlation between the two properties.

The important thing to keep in mind about the group variables here is that they are based on mathematical manipulations of data on the members who comprise the group. The percentage Republican in the group is a statistic derived from the vote counts for the Republican candidate divided by the number of people who voted. And the variable median rent is based on the rent of the middle case in the distribution of cases on the rent variable.

The ecological fallacy becomes clear when we cross-classify the people who make up the groups in terms of the properties on which the group characteristics are based. In the case at hand, this means classifying the people in each election district according to their rent and their vote. Their vote is a dichotomous attribute, either Democratic or Republican. We can convert rent into a dichotomous attribute by determining the median rent in all the election districts and characterizing people as paying above or below

---

*William S. Robinson, "Ecological Correlations and Behavior of Individuals," *American Sociological Review* **15**, No. 3, 351–357 (June 1950).

the median rent. In the hypothetical example presented above, the median rent in all the election districts is $200. The results of such a hypothetical survey, in which a sample of 100 persons were interviewed in each of the eight election districts, appear in Table 14.1.

Table 14.1 presents only the marginals of the table relating rent and vote in each election district. In district 1, 15 percent of the sample voted Republican and 15 percent paid rent above the median. As we move from one election district to the next, we find that the percentage voting Republican steadily increases, as does the percentage paying above the median rent. It turns out that these marginals are the data that are needed to compute the ecological correlation. But the individual correlation depends on the distribution of the cases within the cells of each part of the table. This internal distribution is by no means determined by the marginals. Each of these four-celled tables has 1 degree of freedom, meaning that the internal distribution of the cases cannot be determined until we know the number of cases in at least one cell. The inference to the individual correlation from the ecological correlation is that the cases will be distributed in the cells in such a way as to show a strong positive relationship between voting Republican and paying above median rent. Almost instinctively we assume that in district 1, the 15 people who paid above the median in rent are the same 15 people who voted Republican and that the 85 people paying below median rent are the same 85 who voted Democratic. In short, the plausible expectation from the ecological correlation and the marginals of Table 14.1 is that the individual data will look something like those in Table 14.2.

Just as the ecological correlation was perfect so we find in Table 14.2 a perfect correlation between median rent and vote in each election district, with those paying above the median rent always voting Republican and those paying below the median rent always voting Democratic. These results are in keeping with the commonsense assumption that the well-to-do tend to support the Republican party. But as already noted, there is nothing about the marginals that required the cases to be distributed in this manner within the cells. In fact, instead of the cases being distributed in this way showing a positive relationship between rent and Republican vote, they could have been distributed in such a way as to show a negative relationship between rent and Republican vote given the same set of marginals. This can be seen in Table 14.3.

Examination of Table 14.3 shows that within each election district the people paying above median rent tend to vote Democratic and the people paying below median rent are likely to vote Republican. For example, in election district 1, all 15 people paying relatively high rent voted Democratic while 15 of those paying relatively low rent voted Republican. As the number of high-rent payers increases, the number of them voting Democratic also increases, reaching a peak in district 5 which is split 50–50 on rent paid. In districts 6, 7, and 8 the number of Democrats declines sharply, but even so, in these districts, those paying above median rent are more likely to

Table 14.1. Vote by Rent and Election District

Election District

District 1	Above Median	Below Median
Rep.	15	15
Dem.	85	85

District 2	Above Median	Below Median
Rep.	25	25
Dem.	75	75

District 3	Above Median	Below Median
Rep.	35	35
Dem.	65	65

District 4	Above Median	Below Median
Rep.	40	40
Dem.	60	60

District 5	Above Median	Below Median
Rep.	50	50
Dem.	50	50

District 6	Above Median	Below Median
Rep.	55	55
Dem.	45	45

District 7	Above Median	Below Median
Rep.	65	65
Dem.	35	35

District 8	Above Median	Below Median
Rep.	75	75
Dem.	25	25

Rent:
Vote

Table 14.2. Vote by Rent and Election District

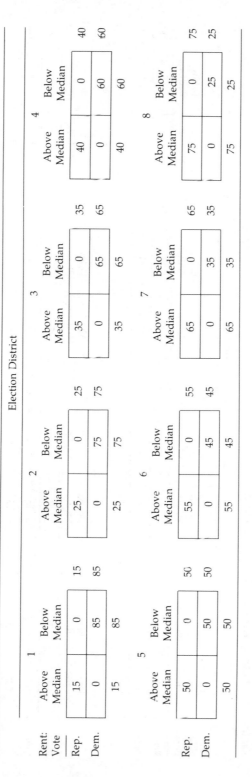

Election District

1

Rent: Vote	Above Median	Below Median	
Rep.	15	0	15
Dem.	0	85	85
	15	85	

2

Rent: Vote	Above Median	Below Median	
Rep.	25	0	25
Dem.	0	75	75
	25	75	

3

Rent: Vote	Above Median	Below Median	
Rep.	35	0	35
Dem.	0	65	65
	35	65	

4

Rent: Vote	Above Median	Below Median	
Rep.	40	0	40
Dem.	0	60	60
	40	60	

5

Rent: Vote	Above Median	Below Median	
Rep.	50	0	50
Dem.	0	50	50
	50	50	

6

Rent: Vote	Above Median	Below Median	
Rep.	55	0	55
Dem.	0	45	45
	55	45	

7

Rent: Vote	Above Median	Below Median	
Rep.	65	0	65
Dem.	0	35	35
	65	35	

8

Rent: Vote	Above Median	Below Median	
Rep.	75	0	75
Dem.	0	25	25
	75	25	

Table 14.3. Vote by Rent and Election District

Election District

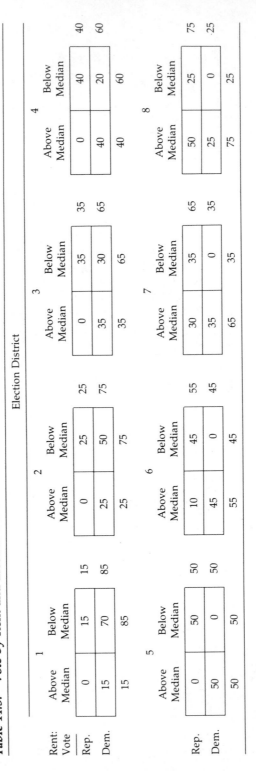

Rent: Vote	1 Above Median	Below Median		2 Above Median	Below Median		3 Above Median	Below Median		4 Above Median	Below Median	
Rep.	0	15	15	0	25	25	0	35	35	0	40	40
Dem.	15	70	85	25	50	75	35	30	65	40	20	60
	15	85		25	75		35	65		40	60	

Rent: Vote	5 Above Median	Below Median		6 Above Median	Below Median		7 Above Median	Below Median		8 Above Median	Below Median	
Rep.	0	50	50	10	45	55	30	35	65	50	25	75
Dem.	50	0	50	45	0	45	35	0	35	25	0	25
	50	50		55	45		65	35		75	25	

vote Democratic than those paying below median rent. Although logically feasible, the results of Table 14.3 are so bizarre that it would seem impossible for anything like this to happen in the real world. What could possibly explain such results? Even rather far out theories break down in light of all the data of the table. For example, one theory might be that people who are in the district minority fail to follow their own interests and adopt instead the interests of the majority. This would explain why those paying above median rent in districts 1 and 2 vote Democratic rather than Republican and why those paying below median rent in districts 7 and 8, the high-rental districts, vote Republican. But this interpretation fails to explain the voting behavior in districts 4, 5, and 6 where the split between above and below median rent is close to even and there is no distinct minority. Why in these districts should the above median renters continue to vote Democratic and the below median renters continue to vote Republican?

Although the results of Table 14.3 make no sense at all, it would be a mistake to conclude that it is impossible for the individual correlation to be in the opposite direction of the group correlation. Such seemingly anomalous results do happen and give validity to Robinson's thesis of the ecological fallacy. Robinson himself provides one example. He shows that on an individual level nativity is related to literacy. The native born are more likely to be literate than the foreign born, not surprisingly, although the correlation is only .118. However, when this relationship is examined on an ecological basis the results are very different. When states are characterized by the percentage of foreign born living in them and the percentage of illiterates within them, the ecological correlation of these two variables turns out to be $-.526$. In short, the relationship is positive on the individual level and strongly negative on the ecological level. Nor is it difficult to figure out why this is so. The foreign born probably were not as well educated as the native born, and in any event English is not their native tongue and hence they are not as likely as native born to be able to read English, thus the positive correlation between foreign born and illiteracy on the individual level. But states that attract the foreign born tend to be the large industrial states with greater per capita wealth and greater expenditures on education. These large industrial states have lower rates of illiteracy than small nonindustrial states such as those in the rural South.

A more classic example of the ecological fallacy was found in studies of military personnel during World War II, published under the title *The American Soldier*.* Stouffer and his associates at one point investigated satisfaction with chances for promotion on the part of army personnel. The question they used in their surveys read as follows: "Do you think a soldier with ability has a good chance for promotion?" Not surprisingly, those soldiers who had themselves been promoted in the past 12 months were much more likely to respond affirmatively than those who had not been

*Samuel A. Stouffer et al., *The American Soldier*, 2 vols., Princeton: Princeton University Press, 1949.

promoted. But a very different picture emerged when army units with differing rates of promotion were compared. The GIs in units with low rates of promotion had more favorable opinions about promotion opportunity than the GIs in units with high rates of promotion. For example, air force units had much higher rates of promotion than military police units, and yet the level of satisfaction with promotion opportunities was greater in the military police than in the air force units. Stouffer et al. use reference group theory to explain this apparent anomaly. They argue that in units where the promotion rate is low, the few who are promoted are especially grateful and the many who are not promoted are not ungrateful because so many of their peers are in the same boat they are in. But in units where many people get promoted, those who are promoted appreciate it less and those who are not promoted resent it more because they compare themselves with the many who were advanced.

ECOLOGICAL TABLES

Most ecological analyses in the social sciences are based on data about ecological units generated from official records. For example, studies of juvenile delinquency have been done with delinquency data characterizing census tracts or neighborhoods. Voting studies have been done based on election districts and suicide has been studied on the basis of ecological data. In all these instances information on the relevant variables came from official statistics kept by governing units—cities or states or the federal government. But some ecological analyses have been done with survey data generated by multistage sampling. One such study in which I was involved was Lazarsfeld's study of college professors during the McCarthy era (*The Academic Mind*). The 2451 social science professors sampled in that research came from 165 colleges. Of these colleges, 106 were represented by 10 or more faculty members, the arbitrary limit that was set for calculating rates among the faculty at the schools. These 106 colleges served as the units for the ecological analysis.

Ecological correlations were carried out in the *Academic Mind* study for several reasons. One important reason was to check on the reliability of an individual correlation. The key concept in that study was anxiety induced in faculty members by the climate of the McCarthy era. An index developed that measured this anxiety, the *apprehension index*, was based on questions about whether the professor was worried about being criticized for views expressed in class, whether writings had been toned down, whether certain political topics were avoided, and other questions quoted in Chapter 7.

One concern of the reseachers was with the role of the college administration in protecting faculty members from the abuse of McCarthyism. The respondents were asked whether their administration was supportive of faculty members who might come under political attack, and the researchers found that faculty members who felt the administration was supportive were much less anxious than faculty members who felt their administrations were not supportive. The researchers were inclined to interpret this finding as meaning that the behavior of the administration had much to do with whether faculty members suffered from McCarthyism. But they were worried that the correlation might well go in the other direction. Faculty members who, for whatever reasons, were anxious, might be more ready to perceive their administration as not supportive. To help unravel this time order problem for the variables anxiety and administration support, the relationship between them was reexamined on an ecological basis. The 106 colleges were characterized by the percentage of faculty members who were anxious and by the percentage who viewed their administration as supportive. The assumption the researchers made was that the college rate of administration support, based on the testimony of a number of faculty members, was closer to reality and a more accurate measure than the testimony of a single faculty member. If the ecological correlation were in the same direction and of the same magnitude as the individual correlation, then one could be much more sure that administration support or lack of it was a cause of anxiety rather than an effect of anxiety. Table 14.4 shows the results of this ecological analysis.* The units in Table 14.4 are colleges and the data show that schools high on administration support were much less likely to be anxious schools than those with low administration support. On the strength of this ecological correlation, the researchers felt more confident in concluding that administration support contributed to lessening individual anxiety.

Another reason for generating ecological correlations was to analyze the behavior of colleges in their own right independent of the faculty members

Table 14.4.   College Anxiety by Rate of Administration Support

	Administration Support	
Anxiety	Low	High
Low	30%	61%
High	70	39
	100%	100%
N	(47)	(59)

---

*This and Table 14.5 and 14.13 are from David Caplovitz, "Mode of Analysis of College Data," mimeograph, Bureau of Applied Social Research, Columbia University, May 22, 1956.

who helped make up the college. A number of the questions asked of the respondents dealt with their perception of the college and its environment; when aggregated these perception variables became the equivalent of primary characteristics of the college that have no equivalent on the individual level. One such variable is administration support, a trait of the college, not of the individual teachers. Another is whether the college has been under pressure from legislative bodies and a third is the type of control of the college, public or private. The researchers assumed that colleges that had come under attack by legislative bodies would be less likely to shield their faculty members from political criticism. The product–moment correlation showed a slight correlation in the expected direction of −.16. It then occurred to the researchers that private and public schools might react differently to political pressure since only the latter are subject to political control. The three-variable Table 14.5 shows the results. When we compare the marginals of the two fourfold tables we see that a much greater proportion of public schools report high pressure and low support than private schools. But—and this is the point of the table—of eight private schools that do report high pressure, all but one also report *high* administration support. In contrast, the great majority of the public schools under strong political pressure report low administration support (15 out of 19). The Pearson correlation between political pressure and administration support based on an expanded form of the three-variable table is −.294 for public schools; for the private schools it is just the opposite, +.285.

As these examples show, the analysis of groups and group behavior becomes possible with survey research data derived from multistage sampling.

CONTEXTUAL TABLES

Contextual tables present simultaneously individual and group properties. The most common form of contextual table consists of one group property

Table 14.5. *The Amount of Administration Support in Public and Private Schools by the Amount of Political Pressure on the Administration*[a]

Administration Support	Public Schools Pressure			Private Schools Pressure		
	Low	High		Low	High	
Low	10	15	25	11	1	12
High	7	4	11	20	7	27
	17	19		31	8	

[a]Table 14.5 reports raw numbers rather than percentages.

and two individual properties. The group property acts as a test factor elaborating the relationship between the two individual properties. In a paper published in 1961, James Davis developed a typology of outcomes of such contextual tables and much of the following discussion is based on Davis's work.*

Although the contextual (group) variable can be either a primary or analytic characteristic, and if analytic, it can be either the group counterpart of one of the individual variables or it can be different from the individual variables, Davis develops his typology with an analytic contextual variable which is the group counterpart of the independent individual variable. He presents these tables in graphic form in which the X axis is the group variable, the percentage of people in the group who have characteristic A. The Y axis represents the dependent variable, the percentage of people who have characteristic B. The graph then plots the percentage of the people who have characteristic A who also have characteristic B and the percentage of people who do not have characteristic A who have characteristic B. Figures 14.1, 14.2, and 14.3 present six different outcomes of contextual tables, ranging from the simple to the complex.

The contextual or group variable in Figure 14.1 is shown along the X axis. In Figure 14.1a the data show that only the individual variable A is influencing the dependent variable B. Whether the group contains a small or a large percentage of people with characterstic A has no effect on B. In short, in Figure 14.1a the contextual variable has no bearing on the dependent variable B. Figure 14.1b shows just the opposite results. The individual variable A has no effect on B, whereas the group variable, the percent of A in the group, has a pronounced effect on B. As the number of people in the groups with trait A increases, so does the number of people manifesting trait B. The individual outcome, B, is entirely dependent on the makeup of the group rather than on whether people in the group possess trait A or not. The logic of the outcomes seen in the figure might be made clearer by a hypothetical example. Suppose that A stands for supporting the Democratic party and non-A for supporting the Republican party, the group variable refers to the percentage of Democrats in the group, and B stands for liberalism. Figure 14.1a shows that Democrats are more liberal than Republicans regardless of the number of Democrats in the group. Liberalism is entirely a result of the individual characteristic and there is no group effect on this variable. In Figure 14.1b, however, a person's liberalism is caused entirely by the type of group to which he or she belongs. People express liberalism only when they are surrounded by liberal people. If the majority are Democrats, who are likely to be liberal, then not only do the Democrats in the group express their liberalism but the minority of Republicans in the group prove to be liberal as well. Conversely, when the majority of the group is Republican, not only do

*James A. Davis, Joe L. Spaeth, and Carolyn Huson, "Analyzing Effects of Group Composition," *American Sociological Review* **26**, No. 2, 215–225 (April 1961).

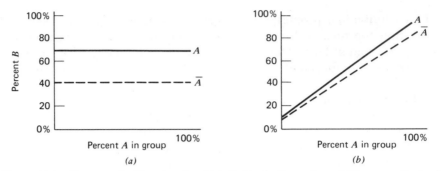

Figure 14.1. Contextual tables showing *(a)* individual effect only and *(b)* group effect only. From James A. Davis, Joe L. Spaeth, and Carolyn Huson, "Analyzing Effects of Group Composition," *American Sociological Review* **26**, No. 2, 219 (April 1961).

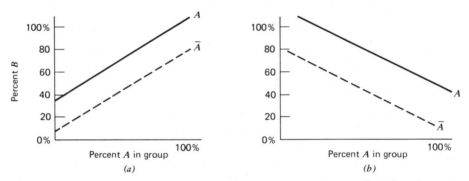

Figure 14.2. Contextual tables showing both an individual and a group effect. From James A. Davis, Joe L. Spaeth, and Carolyn Huson, "Analyzing Effects of Group Composition," *American Sociological Review* **26**, No. 2, 219 (April 1961).

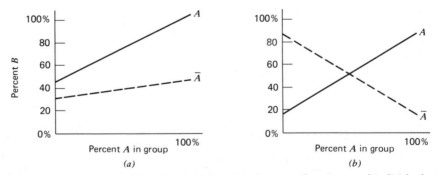

Figure 14.3. Contextual tables showing interaction between the group and individual variables. From James A. Davis, Joe L. Spaeth, and Carolyn Huson, "Analyzing Effects of Group Composition," *American Sociological Review* **26**, No. 2, 219 (April 1961).

the Republicans express conservatism, but even the minority of Democrats in these Republican groups tend to be conservative. The individual characteristic of being Democratic or Republican has no effect by itself on liberalism–conservatism.

Figure 14.2 shows the outcomes when both the individual variable and the contextual variable are influencing B. The gap between the As and the non-As in Figures 14.2a and 14.2b calls attention to the effect of the individual variable A on the dependent variable B. And the fact that both lines slope downward as the group variable increases indicates the effect of the contextual variable on the dependent variable B. In Figure 14.2a the direction of the individual correlation is the same as the correlation between the contextual variable and the individual variable B. Just as the As are more likely to be Bs than the non-As, so the more A the group, the more likely is the group to be B. In short, in Figure 14.2a the individual correlation and the ecological correlation are similar. In Figure 14.2b the individual correlation is the opposite of the group correlation, as was true in the *American Soldier* studies of satisfaction with individual and group promotion rates. In Figure 14.2b A stands for promotion and $\overline{A}$ is nonpromotion and the contextual variable reports the rate of promotion. As the graph shows, as promotion increases in the group the level of satisfaction decreases, but on the individual level the promoted are more likely to be satisfied than the nonpromoted.

Figure 14.3 shows the interaction between individual and group variables in their effects on the dependent variable. In both Figures 14.3a and b the contextual variable interacts with the individual variable. In Figure 14.3a the correlation between A and B is very low when groups are low on A. But as the rate of A increases in the groups, the correlation between A and B increases, as measured by the gap between the A and the non-A lines. In Figure 14.3b the correlation between A and B actually changes direction as the contextual variable changes. In groups that are low on A, the relationship between A and B is negative, but as A increases in the groups the correlation turns around and becomes positive. This is the ultimate in the way of specification of a two-variable relationship by introducing a third variable, in this instance, a contextual variable. In Figure 14.3b position on the dependent variable B is extremely sensitive to minority–majority status in the group. People who are in the majority tend to be high on B, whereas people in the minority are low on B. Thus in the groups that have low rates of A, the non-As are in the majority and they tend to have B, whereas in the groups that have high rates of A, the As are in the majority and they tend to have trait B. In the real world a number of characteristics might behave this way, for example, feelings of security, loneliness, being well-liked all would seem to be affected by whether one was in the majority or in the minority.

THE CONTEXTUAL FALLACY

In the ecological fallacy described previously, individual correlations were inferred from ecological or group correlations. The reverse fallacy sometimes arises in contextual analysis. A contextual effect is sometimes inferred from what is essentially an individual correlation. In the contextual graphs presented above, the contextual variable was an analytic variable that was the group counterpart of the individual independent variable. But what if the analytic group variable is different from the two individual variables? In this case, what appears to be a contextual effect might well be the result of individual variables, the individual independent variable, and the individual variable that is the counterpart of the contextual variable.

This can be demonstrated by the following hypothetical example. The contextual variable is the proportion of Democrats in the group which is some ecological unit such as an election district, city, county, or state. The individual independent variable consists of a liberal–conservative scale and the individual dependent variable consists of support for the SALT II treaty. Since the SALT II treaty was promulgated by a Democratic administration, Democrats are more likely to support it than Republicans. At the same time, political liberals tend to be more supportive of disarmament treaties than political conservatives, who are more concerned with maintaining the military strength of the United States. Contextual results can be presented not only in graphic form as above, but in tabular form as well. Table 14.6 shows the contextual table involving the three variables that have been identified.

Table 14.6 shows four group contexts, each consisting of 1000 people. The first group context is made up of groups that have an average of 20 percent Democrats and 80 percent Republicans. The second group context averages 30 percent Democrats and 70 percent Republican, the third is split 50–50 between Democrats and Republicans, and the fourth is strongly Democratic with an average of 80 percent Democratic and 20 percent Republican. Within each of these contexts, people are divided according to whether they are political liberals or conservatives. From the base figures we see that the percentage of liberals steadily increases as the context becomes more Democratic since Democrats are more likely than Republicans to be liberal.

The first finding in Table 14.6 is shown by the columns. Within each context, the liberals are much more likely than the conservatives to support

Table 14.6.   Percentage Supporting SALT II by Liberal–Conservative Orientation in Differing Democratic Contexts

Political Orientation	Average Democrats in the Group							
	20 Percent		30 Percent		50 Percent		80 Percent	
Liberal	40%	(300)	41%	(400)	48%	(500)	55%	(650)
Conservative	7%	(700)	8%	(600)	11%	(500)	16%	(350)

SALT II. The second finding is shown by the rows. Not only is there an individual effect as shown by the columns, but there also seems to be a contextual effect as the percentage supporting SALT II steadily increases as the groups become more Democratic. The contextual effect is somewhat more pronounced for the liberals than the conservatives (an aggregate percentage difference of 15 points compared with 9 points) but even the conservatives seem to be sensitive to the contextual effect. The difference between the liberals and conservatives shown in the columns is unambiguous. But the apparent contextual effect shown by the rows is suspicious for it might be a manifestation not of the contextual variable, the percentage of Democrats in the group, but merely the combination of the two individual variables that contribute to support of SALT II, liberalism and being Democratic. If the pattern shown in the rows is the result of political orientation and party affiliation, then the percentage supporting SALT II should be the same for each combination of political orientation and political party regardless of the group context. In short, the liberal Democrats should behave the same way in each group context as should the conservative Democrats, the liberal Republicans, and the conservative Republicans. Table 14.7 presents data that correspond to this requirement.

In Table 14.7 the liberal Democrats support SALT II to the same extent regardless of the group context of the percentage of Democrats in the group. The same is true of the liberal Republicans, the conservative Democrats, and the conservative Republicans. The data show an additive effect of the two individual properties, party affiliation and political orientation. Those who possess both of the predisposing traits, liberalism and Democratic affiliation, are most supportive of SALT II, those who possess neither of these

Table 14.7. Percentage Supporting SALT II by Liberal–Conservative Orientation and Party Affiliation in Each Group Context

Percentage Democratic in Group	Political Orientation			
	Liberal		Conservative	
20 Percent				
Democratic	60%	(100)	20%	(100)
Republican	30	(200)	5	(600)
30 Percent				
Democratic	60	(150)	20	(100)
Republican	30	(250)	5	(500)
50 Percent				
Democratic	60	(300)	20	(200)
Republican	30	(200)	5	(300)
80 Percent				
Democratic	60	(550)	20	(250)
Republican	30	(100)	5	(100)

traits are least supportive, and those who possess one of the traits fall in between, with liberalism counting more than Democratic party affiliation. The critical point in Table 14.7 is that the contextual variable, the percentage of Democrats in the group, has no bearing whatsoever on the likelihood of supporting SALT II. Collapsing Table 14.7 by combining the Democrats and the Republicans in each group context would reproduce Table 14.6, which shows an apparent contextual effect.

The way to test for the possible contextual fallacy when the contextual variable is an analytic property that does not correspond to the individual variables is to construct a four-variable table like Table 14.7 in which the contextual variable is controlled for on the individual level.

SAMPLES OF CONTEXTUAL TABLES FROM EMPIRICAL STUDIES

Since the early 1950s a number of studies that have been based on multistage sampling have employed contextual analysis. In this section we provide a sampling of these studies drawing on the work of Blau, Lipset, Trow, and Coleman *(Union Democracy)*, Selvin, Lazarsfeld and Thielens *(The Academic Mind)*, and Caplovitz and Sherrow *(The Religious Dropouts)*.[*]

Peter Blau studied a social welfare agency in a large city in which the social workers were organized into units of five or six under a supervisor. These units were the groups in which Blau related individual variables to group variables. One group variable Blau constructed based on sociometric or relational data was cohesiveness. The individual counterpart of this group variable was what Blau called the individual's attractiveness: whether he received friendship choices from his work peers. Blau related individual attractiveness to respect for the supervisor in groups of varying cohesiveness. The results of this analysis, presented in Table 14.8, show an additive effect between the individual and group variables. Reading down the col-

Table 14.8. Percentage Respecting Supervisor by Individual Attractiveness in Groups of High and Low Cohesion[a]

Individual Attractiveness	Group Cohesiveness	
	High	Low
High	76% (17)	50% (14)
Low	58% (12)	41% (17)

[a]From Peter Blau, "Structural Effects," *American Sociological Review* **25**, No. 2 (April 1960), p. 187.

[*]Peter Blau, "Structural Effects," *American Sociological Review* **25**, No. 2 (April 1960). Hanan Selvin, *The Effects of Leadership*, New York: The Free Press, 1960.

umns we see that individual attractiveness, the individual variable, contributes to respect for supervisors, and group cohesiveness is also a cause of respect for supervisors when individual attractiveness is held constant.

Another example of an additive effect is provided by a contextual table from *Union Democracy*. Lipset et al. were concerned with the determinants of activeness in union politics on the part of individual printers and they were able to show that printers who spent a lot of time with other printers in social situations were more likely to be active in union politics. They also found that printers who worked in large shops were more likely to be active than printers working in small shops. They then raised the question of which was more important, the group variable size of shop or the individual variable of social relations with printers. The results of their analysis are shown in Table 14.9. Again we see an additive effect, the individual variable (social relations) and the group variable (size of shop) both contributing to the individual dependent variable, activity in union politics.

In *Union Democracy* a number of interesting contextual analyses were carried out including an effort to examine the effect of two contextual variables on different levels on the behavior of individual variables. In union-wide elections in two successive years, 1951 and 1952, the New York local, which was the site of the research, voted for the conservative Independent party in 1951 and for the liberal Progressive party in 1952. In both of these elections, Lipset et al. were able to characterize the printing shop according to whether a majority voted for the Independent or Progressive party. On the individual level they were able to measure whether the printer was liberal or conservative in his political orientation and what party he voted for. They then constructed an individual variable based on these two individual data, whether the printer voted according to his predisposition or not (i.e., voting for the Progressive party if he were liberal and for the Independent party if he were conservative). These four variables were presented in a contextual table (Table 14.10). Table 14.10 shows that both group contexts, the climate of the union local and the climate of the shop within the local, had an impact on individual voting. In 1951, when the

Table 14.9. Activity in Union Politics by Social Relations with Other Printers and Size of Shop[a]

Relations with Other Printers	Size of Shop			
	Small		Large	
Low	18%	(74)	33%	(100)
High	22%	(82)	51%	(151)

[a]Reprinted with permission of Macmillan Publishing Co., Inc. from *Union Democracy* by Seymour Martin Lipset, Martin A. Trow, and James S. Coleman. Copyright 1956 by The Free Press, a Corporation.

Table 14.10.   *Percentage Voting in Accord with Political Predisposition by Union Climate and Shop Climate*[a]

	Union Climate			
Shop Climate	Independent (1951)		Progressive (1952)	
Independent				
Conservatives	87%	(55)	67%	(42)
Liberals	38	(34)	43	(23)
Progressive				
Conservatives	55	(33)	29	(76)
Liberals	68	(38)	90	(112)

[a]Reprinted with permission of Macmillan Publishing Co., Inc. from *Union Democracy* by Seymour Martin Lipset, Martin A. Trow, and James S. Coleman. Copyright 1956 by The Free Press, a Corporation.

union climate was conservative, conservative printers who worked in conservative shops were most likely to vote in accordance with their predisposition (87 percent). Conservative printers in that year who worked in progressive shops were not nearly as likely to vote in accordance with their predisposition (55 percent). Liberals in progressive shops, while having the support of their shop, still lacked the support of the broader union and hence 68 percent of them voted according to their predisposition. But a year later, when the union climate now conformed to their shop climate, fully 90 percent of these liberals voted in accordance with their predisposition. In both 1951 and 1952, the printers least likely to vote in accordance with their predisposition were those who were out of step with both their shop climate and the broader union climate. In 1951 these were the liberals working in independent shops in a year when the union climate favored the Independent party; in1952 these were the conservatives working in progressive shops in a year when the union favored the Progressive party. Only 38 percent of the former and 29 percent of the latter voted according to their predisposition.

Most contextual tables, as noted, involve three variables, one group variable and two individual variables. But contextual tables can be simpler than this, involving one group and one individual variable. The *Academic Mind* provides an example of such a two-variable contextual table. Faculty members were classified according to a liberal or permissiveness index, and this variable was used to construct a group rate of permissiveness. This group rate was then related to an individual variable, satisfaction with faculty relations. Table 14.11 shows this two-variable relationship. As the table shows, satisfaction with faculty relations is greater in the two more homogeneous environments, when the faculties are either predominantly permissive or predominantly conservative. When the faculties are divided on this dimension, satisfaction with faculty relations is lower.

Table 14.11.   Satisfaction with Faculty Relations in Various Permissiveness Contexts[a]

College Permissiveness	Number of Colleges	Percentage Highly Satisfied with Faculty Relations	
Mainly permissive	(21)	43%	(631)
Divided: majority permissive	(27)	32%	(664)
Divided: majority conservative	(18)	31%	(362)
Mainly conservative	(11)	48%	(197)

[a]Reprinted with permission of Macmillan Publishing Co., Inc. from *The Academic Mind* by Paul F. Lazarsfeld and Wagner Thielens, Jr. Copyright © 1958 by The Free Press, a Corporation.

Another contextual table from *The Academic Mind* shows the contextual variable acting as a condition, specifying the individual correlation (Table 14.12). The contextual variable, in this instance, is a "pseudo" global characteristic, the faculty's estimate of how protective the administration would be in case of a political attack. The individual independent variable is the permissiveness of the professor and the dependent variable is level of apprehension or anxiety. The permissive college professors take little comfort in administration support as their level of anxiety remains fairly constant as administrations become more supportive, but the nonpermissive professors clearly do benefit from administration support. As administrations become more supportive, they become less anxious, increasing the individual correlation.

Table 14.13, also from *The Academic Mind*, which shows the contextual variable specifying an individual correlation, is a multitable combining two separate contextual tables into one. In one of these subtables personal apprehension is related to belief in colleague support; in the other personal apprehension is related to belief in administration support. The contextual variable is another pseudo global characteristic, the frequency of reported academic freedom incidents, based on the reports of the individual faculty members. Rather than percentages, the data are phi correlation coefficients.

Table 14.12.   Anxiety by Permissiveness in Differing Contexts of Administration Protectiveness[a]

Individual Permissiveness	Protectiveness of Administration			
	Low (below 39%)	Medium Low (40–59%)	Medium High (60–79%)	High (80% plus)
Permissive	55% (117)	55% (268)	56% (366)	52% (151)
Not permissive	50% (143)	43% (315)	38% (336)	33% (158)
% difference	5	12	16	19

[a]Reprinted with permission of Macmillan Publishing Co., Inc. from *The Academic Mind* by Paul F. Lazarsfeld and Wagner Thielens, Jr. Copyright © 1958 by The Free Press, a Corporation.

Table 14.13.   Anxiety by Colleague Support and Administration Support According to Frequency of Academic Freedom Incidents at the College (Phi Coefficients)

Frequency of Incidents	Number of Colleges	Anxiety and Colleague Support	Anxiety and Administration Support
Very low	(49)	−.148	−.203
Low	(30)	−.117	−.151
High	(17)	−.079	−.148
Very high	(10)	−.005	−.105

In every instance the correlation is negative: the more support anticipated, the less the anxiety. From the rows we see that these correlations are always higher for administrative than for colleague support. Presumably, being able to count on administrative support is more relevant for how anxious one feels than is colleague support. But the key finding of the table is seen by reading down the columns. As the contextual variable, frequency of academic freedom incidents, increases, the correlations between anxiety and support from whatever source decreases. At campuses where academic freedom incidents are frequent, neither colleague support nor administration support allays anxiety.

Even more extreme examples of the contextual variable specifying an individual correlation are to be found in Hanan Selvin's *The Effects of Leadership*. The "group" property that Selvin constructs in this study is the leadership style of the leaders of army companies. These leadership styles are based on a series of assessments of their leader made by the members of the companies. Leadership style is thus an analytic group property in terms of how it is constructed, but it refers to a primary characteristic of the group rather than a characteristic that has a counterpart on the individual level. The contextual variable, leadership style, consists of three types, Persuasive, Arbitrary, and Weak. At one point the enlisted men were asked "How many times during your basic training did you blow your top, both on and off duty?" Table 14.14 shows the percentage blowing their top frequently

Table 14.14.   Percentage Blowing One's Top Frequently by Age and Leadership Climate[a]

Age	Leadership Climate					
	Persuasive		Weak		Arbitrary	
17–21	33%	(161)	34%	(105)	31%	(103)
22 and over	13%	(95)	20%	(46)	43%	(53)
% difference	+20		+14		−12	

[a]Reprinted with permission of Macmillan Publishing Co., Inc. from *The Effects of Leadership* by Hanan Selvin. Copyright © 1960 by The Free Press, a Corporation.

according to the age of the recruit and leadership climate. In the persuasive leadership climate the younger soldiers are much more likely to blow their tops than are the older soldiers. In the weak leadership climate the younger soldiers still lead the older ones but the percentage difference is reduced. In the arbitrary leadership climate the relationship is reversed; the older soldiers in this climate are more likely to blow their tops than are the younger ones. From the rows of the table, we learn that the younger soldiers are insensitive to the leadership climate. Whatever the climate, roughly the same percentage of young soldiers blow their top. In contrast, the older soldiers are very much affected by the leadership climate. As it shifts from persuasive to weak to arbitrary, the frequency of older soldiers blowing their tops sharply increases. Table 14.14 corresponds to the outcome of contextual analysis identified in Figure 14.3b, the case where the correlation changes direction under the influence of the contextual variable.

Selvin presents another contextual table showing this extreme form of specification. The dependent variable is going AWOL for a short period of time, the independent variable is again age, and the contextual variable is again leadership climate. The results are presented in Table 14.15. What turns out to be a positive relationship between youth and going AWOL in groups with persuasive leadership turns out to be a negative relationship in groups with weak and arbitrary leadership climates. And again it is the older soldiers who are most sensitive to the leadership climate.

CONTEXTUAL ANALYSIS AND THE UNRAVELING OF COMPETING PROCESSES

We have reviewed several functions of contextual analysis including the role of the contextual variable as an independent variable contributing to the individual effect along with the individual independent variable and the contextual variable serving as a condition specifying the individual correlation. Another important function of contextual analysis is to help unravel the contributions of competing processes in explaining some phenomenon.

An unusual example of this function of contextual analysis is provided by

Table 14.15. *Percentage Going AWOL by Age and Leadership Climate*[a]

	Leadership Climate					
Age	Persuasive		Weak		Arbitrary	
17–21	35%	(171)	46%	(117)	47%	(108)
22 and over	30%	(105)	49%	(49)	58%	(59)
% difference	+ 5		– 3		–11	

[a]Reprinted with permission of Macmillan Publishing Co., Inc. from *The Effects of Leadership* by Hanan Selvin. Copyright © 1960 by *The Free Press*, a Corporation.

Lazarsfeld's *Academic Mind* study. The major dependent variable in that study was a measure of apprehension or anxiety induced in professors by the climate of McCarthyism. In addition to queries about their own anxiety, the professors were asked a series of questions about how anxious or apprehensive their colleagues were. Not surprisingly, there was a strong relationship between one's own anxiety and perceived colleague anxiety. The following question arose: Did this relationship reflect projection, whereby anxious professors assumed others felt the way they did, or did the relationship reflect accurate perception in that anxious professors were at schools where the level of anxiety was high and most of their colleagues were indeed anxious? To unravel these processes, the researchers constructed a contextual table in which the group variable was the rate of apprehension at the college. Within these contexts, professors were divided according to their own level of apprehension and the dependent variable was perceived colleague apprehension or anxiety. If the original correlation was caused by projection, then anxious professors should report anxious colleagues regardless of the level of anxiety at the school. If, on the other hand, the perceptions were based on reality, then reports of colleague anxiety should increase as the level of apprehension at the college increases. The results of this contextual table are seen in Table 14.16.

The colleges in Table 14.16 were sorted into six contexts according to their rates of anxiety. Within each context, professors were sorted into three groups according to their level of anxiety. The percentages refer to perceived anxiety in colleagues. By reading across the rows we see that within each context, perception of colleague anxiety steadily increases with the anxiety level of the professors, an argument for projection. But by reading down the columns we see that on each level of anxiety, reports of colleague anxiety increase as the rate of anxiety at the college increases. This capacity to see reality correctly is most evident in the group with some anxiety, the middle column. Those who experienced no anxiety also showed a tendency to

Table 14.16.   Perceived Colleague Anxiety by Respondents' Anxiety in Different College Contexts of Anxiety[a]

Anxiety Levels of Colleges (%)	Number of Colleges	Respondents' State of Anxiety		
		None	Some	Great Deal
0–29%	12	5% (67)	18% (82)	— (15)
30–39%	20	9% (150)	26% (179)	55% (72)
40–49%	18	15% (144)	36% (184)	64% (131)
50–59%	25	19% (110)	39% (213)	68% (176)
60–69%	20	18% (72)	40% (171)	73% (190)
70–89%	11	31% (26)	49% (65)	68% (88)

[a]Reprinted with permission of Macmillan Publishing Co., Inc. from *The Academic Mind* by Paul F. Lazarsfeld and Wagner Thielens, Jr. Copyright © 1958 by The Free Press, a Corporation.

respond to the facts; their reports of colleague anxiety increase as the college rate of anxiety increases.

Other examples of the use of contextual analysis to unravel competing social processes are found in the Caplovitz and Sherrow study of religious apostasy among college graduates.* In that study it was found that some colleges, especially the high-quality colleges, had higher rates of apostasy than other colleges. The question this finding raised was whether there was something about the culture of the high-quality colleges that led the students to relinquish their religion of origin (a socialization process), or whether the high-quality colleges recruit the kinds of students who were likely to relinquish their religion (a selection process). The analysis identified a number of traits of students that contributed to their apostasy, including their commitment to radicalism, their lack of religiosity, their intellectualism, and poor parental relations. The analysis assumed that these apostasy traits were pretty much in place before the students came to college and hence the high rate of apostasy at certain types of college might be explained by their recruiting students with these traits. The contextual tables that were set up to unravel the selection and socialization processes had the college apostasy rate as the contextual variable. These contextual tables were highly unusual in that the group variable corresponded to the dependent variable (individual apostasy) rather than the individual independent variable as is more common. The individual independent variables in these tables were the apostasy-provoking traits. These tables were set up in three parts, one for each of the three major religious groups. The patterns held in each group, so we present the results for the Protestants only. Table 14.17 considers the impact of radicalism on apostasy in different college apostasy contexts.

If selection were the critical process making some colleges high on apostasy, we should find the radical students concentrated in the high-apostasy colleges, although they would be likely to apostatize at any type of college. In short, the mechanism of selection would lead us to expect that those high

Table 14.17. *Apostasy by Radicalism According to College Rates of Apostasy (Protestants Only)*[a]

| College Apostasy | Radicalism | | |
	Low	Medium	High
Low-apostasy schools	2% (3803)	9% (1332)	31% (131)
Medium-apostasy schools	6% (6192)	21% (5491)	42% (323)
High-apostasy schools	14% (615)	37% (1281)	59% (196)

[a]From David Caplovitz and Fred Sherrow, *The Religious Dropouts: Apostasy among College Students*, Beverly Hills, California: Sage Publications, 1977, p. 120.

*David Caplovitz and Fred Sherrow, *The Religious Dropouts: Apostasy among College Students*, Beverly Hills, California: Sage Publications, 1977.

on radicalism would apostatize to the same extent regardless of the level of apostasy at their school and that those low on radicalism would not apostatize whatever the level of apostasy at their school. The selection hypothesis thus would predict that the percentages in each column would be the same even though the school apostasy rate changes. The socialization hypothesis predicts the opposite outcome. According to this view, the apostasy of students should increase as their school rate of apostasy increases regardless of their position on radicalism. The data lend some support to the socialization hypothesis. As school apostasy increases so does the frequency of apostasy among students on each level of radicalism. Even the students low on radicalism are more likely to apostatize when college apostasy increases. The same is true of those who are in the medium and high categories on radicalism. Selection is also part of the story as is shown by the rows of the table, but clearly socialization is at work as well.

Table 14.18 presents the results of another of these contextual tables bearing on the influence of the college on apostasy. In this table, the apostasy-provoking trait is poor parental relations. Again we find that regardless of position on the apostasy-provoking trait, apostasy increases as the college level of apostasy increases. This holds true for those who had good relations with parents as well as those who had bad relations with parents, a finding that supports the socialization hypothesis. Inasmuch as the school rate increases, one might suppose that the increase on each level of parental relations is a tautology that must follow from the increase in the school rate. But these findings are not tautological. A college could score high on apostasy simply because most of its students have the apostasy-provoking trait. An analysis of the base figures in Tables 14.17 and 14.18 shows that there is a correlation between school apostasy and the apostasy traits. In spite of this correlation, the patterns in the columns clearly show that students are being influenced by their college climate independent of their relationship with their parents. The rows of Table 14.18 show yet another finding. It turns out that the contextual variable specifies the individual correlation between quality of parental relations and apostasy. At the low-apostasy schools there is no relationship; at the medium-apostasy schools there is a modest rela-

Table 14.18.   Apostasy by Quality of Parental Relation in Colleges of Varying Rates of Apostasy (Protestants Only)[a]

	Quality of Parental Relations		
College Apostasy	Good	Fair	Poor
Low-apostasy schools	4% (2079)	7% (870)	5% (484)
Medium-apostasy schools	8% (3701)	15% (1799)	16% (867)
High-apostasy schools	17% (1498)	27% (879)	33% (382)

[a]From David Caplovitz and Fred Sherrow, *The Religious Dropouts: Apostasy among College Students*, Beverly Hills, California: Sage Publications, 1977, p. 123.

tionship; only in the high-apostasy schools is the relationship fairly strong.

This discussion of the role of contextual analysis in sorting out competing processes in explaining some phenomenon brings to a close our review of the analysis of group properties and contextual analysis. We have seen how multistage sampling makes it possible to study groups within the framework of survey research. We examined the ecological fallacy, the error of inferring individual correlations from group correlations. We distinguished several types of group variables, global or primary properties that have no counterpart on the individual level, analytic or aggregate properties that result from some mathematical manipulation of individual data, and finally pseudo global properties that are constructed in the same way as aggregate properties but which refer to global properties of the group. We looked at samples of ecological tables based on survey research and then took up contextual analysis, the joint analysis of group and individual properties. We presented a formal typology of the outcomes of contextual analysis and then considered examples of contextual analysis from empirical studies. The contextual fallacy was identified and discussed and the various functions of contextual analysis were illustrated. I hope this chapter conveys some of the richness of data analysis that becomes possible when groups as well as individuals are sampled.

PART FOUR

How to Write a
Research Report

Part 4 deals with a topic never covered in research texts: how to write the research report. We begin with the critical topic of organizing the final report, that is, generating its table of contents. Chapter 15 is about how to construct the table of contents. The theme of the chapter is that the researcher is in the dark until the table of contents has been set. Until this is done, the data cannot even be analyzed. A researcher who analyzes data before generating a table of contents is guilty of the cardinal sin of research—what the chapter identifies as "crass empiricism." This chapter introduces a new typology of research projects and suggests that each type of study has its own table of organization.

Chapter 16 is about the art of writing. Its mission is to teach readers how to improve their writing. It carries out this difficult task in a unique way. After the editor is identified as the guardian of good writing, the work of the editor is described. Copy editing is distinguished from rough editing, then the tasks of the copy editor and the rough editor are discussed. Rough editing is broken down into exposition and substance, and the various ways in which the editor improves the exposition and substance of the manuscript are noted. This chapter has a hero—a sociological editor of the first rank whose work illustrates every theme in the chapter. His name is Robert K. Merton.

15

How to Organize a Research Report

As noted before, this book is organized according to the stages of a major research project, beginning with raising the research funds, moving on to collecting the data, analyzing the data, and then writing a research report. Most researchers who are successful in getting grants have little difficulty with the first three stages. Where they all too frequently have serious problems is in the fourth stage, writing the research report. An untold number of major research projects, some of which are now famous, stumbled in this stage. The final research reports never appeared or else appeared only after many months or years of delinquency.

The struggling research director who is unable to write the research report tends to behave in characteristic ways that quickly identify him to the experts as one who is having difficulty. A classic symptom of the foundering researcher is the ordering of a plethora of tables from the computer. The researcher seems to believe that buried somewhere in the pile of computer output is some magic finding that will generate a research report. Time is wasted poring over the pounds of computer output, checking the tests of significance that have been computed for each table and pulling out all the tables that are statistically significant. The computer output is generated by instructing the computer to tabulate every variable in the study by every other variable in the study. The number of study directors, even relatively sophisticated ones with scholarly reputations, who behave in this manner, running everything against everything, is shocking. I am convinced that there is no bigger sin in social research than this strategy of running everything against everything. So that we can banish this sin, we must give it a name. For years I have been calling it *crass empiricism*. My research course has a slogan, which is drilled into the students: "Avoid crass empiricism, avoid crass empiricism." The repetition is for emphasis.

The way to avoid crass empiricism is simple: never run a table unless you have a reason for running it. I find the world "hypothesis" stuffy and I tell my students that they do not have to have hypotheses, only reasons. Having a reason for running a table means that the researcher has an expectation that variable X will be related to variable Y in a certain way. Unfortunately, many researchers slightly more advanced than the crass empiricists register great disappointment when their expectations are not borne out by the data. I once had a colleague who was so angry when the data failed to support his expectation that he banged his fist against the wall so hard that he broke his hand.

Once the researcher has a reason for running a table, he or she should not care at all what the data show, for whatever the result it is of value. There are only three possible outcomes of the table. The finding can support an expectation of a relationship, which should give the researcher pleasure. Or the finding can be that there is no relationship between X and Y, contrary to expectations. Given the expectation, this null finding is news that deserves to be reported. The third and final outcome of the table is that there is a relationship between X and Y but it is in the opposite direction of the one predicted by the researcher. If the null finding is news, then this discovery of a reverse relationship is even bigger news that deserves reporting. In short, once you have a reason for running the table, the results of the table, whatever they are, are grist for your mill.

I have invented a formula that measures the degree to which the researcher is a crass empiricist or, conversely, a pro:

$$D_{\text{ratio}} = \frac{\text{number of tables in final report}}{\text{pounds of computer output}}$$

I tell my students that a D ratio that is greater than 1 is the sign of a pro who has avoided crass empiricism. Unfortunately, there are all too many researchers who have more pounds of computer output than tables in their reports, meaning that they got less than one usable table from each pound of output, a pound representing perhaps as many as 20 or 30 tables.

GENERATING A TABLE OF CONTENTS

If having a reason for a table is the way to avoid crass empiricism we must ask where these reasons come from. The answer is that the tables we run are determined by the table of contents that we have evolved for our report. All too many researchers think that the starting point for report writing is to run tables. This is not true. The correct starting point is generating the table of contents for the final report. Until the researcher has made up a table of contents he does not know what he is doing, and until he knows what he is doing he cannot run tables (unless he is a crass empiricist). A table of contents for the final report is in no way dependent on the tables generated.

The table of contents flows from the nature of the problem being researched. The chapters are organized in terms of descriptions of the phenomenon under study and the causes and consequences of the the phenomenon or problem. The table of contents for the final report can be generated long before the data are even collected, much less analyzed. I can illustrate this from my own work. In 1967 I began a study of debtors in default, people who were being sued for not paying their consumer debts. Although this was a 3-year project, I had to submit a progress report each year as part of the renewal application. In March 1968, while the questionnaires were being coded, I wrote a progress report for this study; on page 9 of this report I presented a table of contents for the final report, which looked like this:

Although it is premature to predict the precise character of the final report for this study, we can indicate a tentative outline of its major sections and themes as follows:

Chapter 1   Introduction
            (a) Installment credit in America
            (b) Consumer law in the four cities
            (c) Sampling procedures and response rate
Chapter 2   The Creditor-Plaintiffs and the Defendants: A Social Portrait of the Parties to the Dispute
            (a) Types of businesses that are plaintiffs
            (b) Social characteristics of the defendants
Chapter 3   The Nature of the Transaction
            (a) Loans vs. purchases
            (b) Merchandise bought
            (c) Where bought
            (d) Role of door-to-door selling
            (e) Satisfaction with transaction: role of fraud
Chapter 4   The Breakdown of the Transaction: Reasons for Not Paying
            (a) Overextension on part of consumer
            (b) Unexpected emergencies: illness and loss of job
            (c) Reaction to consumer fraud
Chapter 5   Creditors' Remedies I: Harassment
            (a) Forms of harassment
            (b) Types of creditors who employ harassment
            (c) Types of debtors subjected to harassment
Chapter 6   Creditors' Remedies II: The Role of the Courts
            (a) Service of process (who gets served and who does not; kinds of plaintiffs with good and poor records of service)
            (b) Judgment (percent in favor of plaintiff; percent of default judgments)

The chapters in this table of contents are organized following a very common principle: chronology. The opening chapter, the Introduction, is a statement of the problem and a review of the research design (sampling in four cities, how debtors were sampled, etc.). The opening chapter generally ends with an outline of the chapters to follow. Chapter 2 describes the parties to the dispute. Here a detailed statistical portrait of the default debtors is provided, describing the types of people who are prone to this kind of problem. The third chapter begins the chronology of the process, dealing with the nature of the transaction that resulted in default. The fourth chapter takes up the next stage, the breakdown in the transaction, the reasons why the debtor did not maintain payments. Once the transaction breaks down, the creditor exerts the remedies described in Chapters 5 and 6. Chapter 7 deals with how the debtor-defendants respond to the actions taken by the creditor-plaintiffs. Chapter 8 takes up the special legal circumstances in one of the sampled cities. Chapters 9 and 10 look at the consequences of the debt problem, its impact on the debtors' lives.

Much of this story is descriptive. Thus the parties to the dispute are described, the nature of the transaction that gave rise to the dispute is described, the reasons for the default are described, as are the actions taken by the creditors to collect the debt. The debtors' responses are then described, and finally two chapters are devoted to consequences of the debt problem. The important thing to keep in mind is that this table of contents is in no way dependent on the findings. Whatever the tables show, this is the story that has to be told. Developing a table of contents simply means organizing the story, and the story that has to be told becomes evident from consideration of the problem under study. Once a table of contents has been developed, the researcher immediately knows what has to be included in the final report. The data needed for each chapter must then be generated.

In this instance, the researcher starts by going to work on Chapter 2, the description of the creditor-plaintiffs and the debtor-defendants, by ordering the tables needed to write this chapter. The chapter, at least in rough form, can be written in a few days, certainly no longer than a week. It is not until the researcher has written this chapter that he proceeds to the next one. This is how research reports should be written. The researcher should order only the tables needed for the chapter that he will next be working on. A report based on this table of contents could be written in 11 weeks, allotting one week per chapter. This may come as a surprise to many researchers who have labored months or even years over their reports. But the chances are that the researcher who requires more than one week to write each chapter is the researcher who does not know what he is doing.

A mark of the virtues of knowing what you are doing is that your first draft can easily be your final draft. This happens to be the case in my own work. I have discussed this with numerous colleagues and they tell me that their work frequently goes through three or four drafts. When I tell them that I do only one draft they are amazed. I then tell them that I never start writing until I work out the organization of the chapter or paper; it turns out that they often do not follow this procedure. They start writing before they know what they want to say and it is only when they have produced several drafts that they come to know what they want to say. For many years I have kept a record of the time I spend at the typewriter writing my reports and papers. On a three by five card, I enter the date, the hours at the typewriter, and the number of pages produced. I can report that each chapter of this book took me from 6 to 18 hours to produce. I am convinced that I can do this simply because I have worked out the organization beforehand. Of course, all chapters had to be edited, but none had to be rewritten.

The table of contents for the default-debtor study was developed two years before the report was written and six years before the book based on the report appeared. It is of some interest to compare it with the final table of contents of the book:

1968 Progress Report Table of Contents	Table of Contents of *Consumers in Trouble*, 1974
1 Introduction	1 Introduction
2 The Creditor-Plaintiffs and the Debtor-Defendants: A Social Portrait of the Parties to the Dispute	**I The Parties to the Dispute: The Debtors and Their Creditors**
	2 Portrait of the Default-Debtors
3 The Nature of the Transaction	3 Portrait of the Creditors: The Initial Transaction
4 The Breakdown of the Transaction: Reasons for Not Paying	**II Reasons for Default**
	4 Classifying the Reasons

(Continued)

<table>
<tr><td colspan="2">1968 Progress Report
Table of Contents</td><td colspan="2">Table of Contents of
Consumers in Trouble, 1974</td></tr>
</table>

	1968 Progress Report Table of Contents		Table of Contents of *Consumers in Trouble*, 1974
5	Creditor's Remedies, I: Harassment	5	Debtor's Mishaps and Shortcomings
6	Creditor's Remedies, II: The Role of the Courts	6	Allegations of Wrongdoing by the Seller
7	The Debtor's Response to the Legal Action	7	Payment Misunderstandings
8	The Philadelphia Story	8	Partial Payments and Other Reasons for Default
9	The Impact of the Debt on the Defendant's Job	9	A Quantitative Analysis of Reasons for Default
10	Impact of the Debt on Health and Marriage	**III**	**Creditor's Remedies and the Role of the Courts**
11	Conclusions and Recommendations	10	Harassment and Repossession
		11	Seeking a Judgment: The Role of the Courts in the Collection Process
		12	Execution upon Judgment: The Garnishment Cities
		13	Execution upon Judgment: The Philadelphia Story
		IV	**Consequences of the Debt Problem**
		14	Impact on the Debtor's Life
		15	Conclusions

A major difference between the initial table of contents and the final one is that the latter is organized into four sections. These major parts were all present in the initial table of contents but they were not seen as such. The first chapter is the same in the two tables of contents, The Introduction. Chapters 2 and 3 in the final version are very similar to Chapters 2 and 3 in the original version, with one difference. Instead of Chapter 2 dealing with both creditors and debtors, the final Chapter 2 deals with the default debtors only. The creditors are dealt with along with the original transaction in the third chapter of the final version. The most significant difference between the initial table of contents and the final one has to do with the theme of the original Chapter 4, the reasons for default. In the final version, this chapter was expanded into six, because the reasons for not paying turned out to be much more complicated than originally anticipated. As a result, the book has four more chapters than the original table of contents. The section on creditor's remedies and the courts is similar in both the original and final versions. Chapter 5 in 1968 became Chapter 10 in 1974. The story in the original Chapters 6 through 8, dealing with the legal process, became

Chapters 11 through 13 of the book. Initially we envisioned two conse-quences chapters, one dealing with the job and the other with health and marriage, but in both the report and the book these were combined into one chapter. Except for the serious misjudgment of the complexity of the rea-sons, the two tables of contents are similar. They are both organized in the same chronology from the parties involved, through the nature of the transaction, the reasons for default, creditors' remedies including debtors' responses, to consequences for the debtors' lives.

How the Reasons for Default section evolved from one chapter to six is an interesting story. As can be seen from the 1968 table of contents, I initially saw three major reasons for default: overextension on the part of the con-sumer, that is, taking on more debt obligations than he could handle; unexpected emergencies that result in a loss of income, such as illness or job loss; and fraud on the part of the seller, which undermines the debtor's willingness to pay. These three reasons plus an "other" category constituted the code that I had developed for this item. I had an associate who super-vised the work of some four or five coders and I was not at all involved in the coding process. I was not aware of the results of the coding until I received a copy of the code book that had the marginals for all the questions. When I got to the question about reasons for not paying I discovered to my aston-ishment that fully 35 percent of the cases were classified as "other." Almost always, the "other" category contains no more than 4 or 5 percent of the cases, and this unusually large percentage was a clear sign that something was wrong. And so many months after the coding had been completed, two assistants and I went back and recoded all the questionnaires on the reason for default. As a result, the new classification included 12 major headings and within each were subcategories of reasons. In all we coded more than 50 reasons for default. And from the recoding came the six chapters dealing with this theme in the book.

The moral of this case study is that it is possible well in advance of the data analysis to generate the table of contents of the final report. And the table of contents developed early on will bear a close resemblance to the final one.

A TYPOLOGY OF RESEARCH PROJECTS

In developing a table of contents it is helpful to know what type of study one is doing, for the table of contents will vary with the type. I am convinced that all empirical studies in sociology fall into one of three basic types: the major dependent variable study, the major independent variable study and the special population study.

The Major Dependent Variable Study

The major dependent variable study is very popular in social research. It is a study devoted to uncovering the causes of some phenomenon which is the dependent variable. Voting studies fall into this category, as do studies of various social-psychological traits such as anxiety, alienation, authoritarianism, anomia, religiosity, Machiavellianism, faith in people, morale.

The major dependent variable study has a characteristic table of organization. The opening chapter, one that passes for theory, provides the justification for studying the phenomenon. The question of why cheating, apostasy, anxiety, alienation, and so on, is being studied is answered here. The second chapter usually deals with the problem of measurement, the classification of the people in the sample according to the dependent variable. If the dependent variable is measured by some index, then the construction and testing of that index is described in Chapter 2. The subsequent chapters are organized by the independent variables, which are related to the major dependent variable. The dependent variable remains the same throughout, but the independent variables change from chapter to chapter. A chronological sequence is a fairly common organizational principle in major dependent variable studies. This can be illustrated by the table of contents for the book based on my study of apostasy.[*]

Chapter	Title
1	Introduction
2	Social Origins and Apostasy
3	Self-Images, Value Orientations, and Apostasy
4	Intellectualism and Apostasy
5	Religiosity and Apostasy
6	The College and Apostasy
7	The Dynamics of Apostasy
8	Updating Apostasy
9	Summary and Conclusions

This work was a secondary analysis of a major panel study carried out by NORC of the graduates of the class of 1961 who were reinterviewed each year through 1964. NORC is the organization that pioneered in asking two questions about religion: the religion in which the respondent was raised, and the respondent's current religion. By cross-tabulating these questions it is possible to identify people who say they were raised in one of the major religions but today have no religious affiliation (the apostates) in contrast with the identifiers, the people who continue to identify with the religion in which they were raised. The analysis for such a study consists of comparing the two groups. The first analytical chapter dealt with independent variables that referred to the social origins of the graduates, for example, region of the country, hometown size, father's occupation and education, family socioeconomic status, sex. Chapter 3 dealt with personality variables, self-images

[*]David Caplovitz and Fred Sherrow, *The Religious Drop Outs: Apostasy among College Graduates*, Beverly Hills, California: Sage Publications, 1977.

and value orientations as they bear on apostasy. Chapters 4 and 5 dealt with important personality traits, commitment to intellectualism and religiosity. Chapter 6 introduces the social context, the type of college the student was attending. To what extent was apostasy more likely to occur in certain types of colleges than in others and to what extent did the contextual variable (type of college) influence the relationship between the independent variables dealt with in the previous chapters and apostasy? For example, was intellectualism especially likely to lead to apostasy at high-quality colleges? Since the NORC study was a panel study, Chapter 7 examines the panel data and shows how apostasy changed over time, that is, the extent to which early apostates returned to the fold and new apostates emerged. NORC reinterviewed the members of the original sample some four years after the last wave in 1968, and these data and data from other studies were used to update the apostasy story in Chapter 8.

In carrying out this analysis, it was necessary to construct indices of the various independent variables introduced in the chapters. And the analysis became progressively more complex as in each subsequent chapter the new independent variable was examined in the context of the earlier independent variables. For example, in Chapter 3 we not only showed how self-images and value orientations were related to apostasy, but we examined these relationships in light of the main variables of the previous chapter, family socioeconomic status, using three-variable table formats.

Given any major dependent variable, it is fairly easy to make up a table of contents for the report. This can be shown by taking some dependent variable that I have never done research on. For example, a voting study would involve comparing those who say they are Democrats with those who say they are Republicans. One obvious chapter might deal with the social origins of the respondents, say region and hometown size, plus variables that measure the socioeconomic status of the family of origin, for example, father's occupation and education or how well off the family was when the respondent was growing up. This chapter might then be followed with one dealing with the current social statuses of the respondent, his or her education, occupation, income, religion, age, and marital status. By using variables of the previous chapter on parental social status, it would be possible to identify upwardly and downwardly mobile people and see how this affects their party affiliation. The next several chapters would deal with values and attitudes presumably related to party affiliation, for example, liberalism versus conservatism, attitudes about the economy, and attitudes on various social issues such as abortion, pornography, the death penalty. If the data are available, indices could be developed of various personality traits—authoritarianism, anomia, alienation, and so on—and these could be related to party affiliation.

A study of drug use among high school students would have a similar table of organization. The first chapter would explain how the students were being classified as drug users or nonusers. The next chapter might deal with family-of-origin variables. A third chapter might deal with personality measures; a fourth chapter might deal with behavioral correlates of drug use: Are the drug users more likely to engage in other deviant activities like theft, truancy, and so on? A fifth chapter might deal with the respondent's peer group: Does he have many friends? Does he belong to a gang? Do his friends use drugs? A sixth chapter might deal with respondents' relationships with parents: Are they permissive or strict? Is the family complete or broken? Is the family close or distant? A seventh chapter might deal with school: How well is the student doing in school? To what extent does he conform to the rules, playing hookey, showing up late, and so on?

A study of attitudes toward abortion could easily be organized in a similar way. The first chapter would deal with the measurement of attitude toward abortion and the classification of people according to the index that is developed of this attitude. The next several chapters could deal with social statuses of family of origin and those currently occupied by the respondents. The next chapters could deal with personality traits and value orientations.

Common to all these studies is a research report that will provide a very detailed picture of the phenomenon under study and its causes: how Democrats differ from Republicans, how drug users differ from nonusers, and how those who support abortion differ from those who are opposed to abortion. As training in developing tables of contents, the reader might well invent a major dependent variable study and try generating the table of contents for such a report.

The Major Independent Variable Study

The major independent variable study is the reverse of the major dependent variable study. The independent variable remains the same throughout the report and the dependent variables shift from chapter to chapter. Instead of being organized in terms of the causes of the phenomenon, the chapters are now organized in terms of the consequences of the phenomenon. All evaluation research falls into the major independent variable type. In evaluation research the researcher must answer these questions: What difference does the program being evaluated make? Does it in fact have the desired consequences?

This type of study can be illustrated by research evaluating the Head Start Program that came into being with the war on poverty in the mid-1960s. The design of such a study requires comparing youngsters who were exposed to Head Start with a control group of youngsters who were not exposed to Head Start. The chapters would then be organized in terms of the presumed consequences of Head Start. One chapter could compare the two groups on reading ability, another could deal with mathematical ability. A third chapter could deal with social skills, and subsequent chapters could deal with the longevity of the Head Start effect: Do the differences between those who were exposed to Head Start and those who were not persist one year later, two years later, three years later? In carrying out the analysis it will be necessary to hold constant the other variables apart from exposure to a Head Start program that might be affecting these outcomes, such as intelligence or the socioeconomic status of the family of origin.

A major independent variable study that has been carried out over the past decade or so dealt with the impact of income maintenance. In elaborate studies that were initially sponsored by the Office of Economic Opportunity poor families in certain communities were given a guaranteed income slightly above the poverty line and they were compared with families that did not receive this subsidy. The chapters of these reports investigated the impact of the subsidy on employment, familial stability, and other major facets of life.

The Special Population Study

The major dependent variable study and the major independent variable study are familiar to researchers. Less well known is the third type of study, which I call the special population study. In this type of study, one is focusing on a special group, which tends to be a deviant group, and the objective of the research is to describe in detail all the facets of this special, deviant group. I have done a good deal of research of this type. My study of poor consumers *(The Poor Pay More)* falls into this category as does my study of debtors in default *(Consumers in Trouble)* and my study of addicts who were employed while addicted *(The Working Addict)*. What distinguishes the special population study from the other two types is that it does not involve any control group to compare with the group exhibiting the critical characteristic. In the major dependent variable study the analysis is based on comparisons of two groups, those who have the dependent variable and those who do not. In the major independent variable study, the same logic applies: the two groups are those who were exposed to the critical stimulus (e.g., Head Start) and those who were not. But in the special population study, the researcher must work with only one group. Thus I did not have a sample of middle-class consumers to compare with my sample of low-income consumers; I did not have a sample of debtors who were not in default to compare with my default debtors nor did I have a sample of addicts who did not work (or a sample of workers who were not addicts) to compare with my working addicts. What are the implications of not having a control group? How does the researcher tell his or her story?

Without the control group, the researcher is not in a good position to investigate causes and consequences, which can be done readily in the other two types of studies. But shedding light on causes and consequences is one of the goals of the researcher doing a special population study and this is achieved by approximating causal analysis. The researcher will infer from the characteristics that the special population has what might be causes of the condition and consequences of it. But the primary task is to describe the special population in great detail and provide a rich picture of what it means to be a member of that special population. I have referred to these special populations as deviant groups, for that is what they tend to be. For example, in my research, most poor people are not supposed to be consumers of expensive durables; if they are, then we need to understand how this is possible. Similarly, default debtors are a distinct minority. Most debtors pay their bills and do not end in default. And most addicts do not have full-time jobs. Those that do are an exception.

The purpose of studying these special populations is to find out how these deviant groups came into existence and what their experiences are like. Sometimes we can learn from studying deviant groups how larger social systems have broken down. This is the case in my study of default debtors. By studying them we can learn how the credit system can break down. By studying working addicts we can learn how adjustments can be made to addiction that permit a relatively normal life.

There are many special populations or deviant groups that could be fruitfully studied and this type of research is fairly common, although its characteristics are not as well understood as those of the major dependent and independent variable studies. For example, a study of never marrieds over 40 would be such a deviant group since most people over 40 are married. Studies of juvenile delinquents, of raped women, of prisoners, of people with rare diseases or the mentally ill would all fall into this category since these are deviant groups.

We have seen that in the major dependent variable study, the dependent variable remains the same in each chapter while the independent variables shift from chapter to chapter. The reverse is true of the major independent variable study. The independent variable remains the same in each chapter while the dependent variables shift from chapter to chapter. In the special population study, both the independent and dependent variables shift from chapter to chapter, or, perhaps more accurately, the dependent variable definitely shifts from chapter to chapter, whereas the independent variables may be more or less the same in each chapter. The critical difference from the major independent variable study is that whereas the dependent variable shifts from chapter to chapter, there is a cluster of independent variables in the special population study, whereas in the major independent variable study there is but one independent variable, the critical stimulus that is being investigated.

The chapters in a special population study report take up various facets of the deviant group under study, and each facet becomes a dependent variable that is analyzed in the chapter, that is, it is related to a bundle of independent variables in order to learn what the causes of that facet might be. This can be illustrated by the table of contents for *The Poor Pay More*. The book is organized into 13 chapters as follows:

1. Introduction
2. The Merchant and the Low Income Consumer
3. Buying Patterns: Purchases of Major Durables
4. Shopping Patterns I: Scope of Shopping
5. Shopping Patterns II: The Peddler Economy
6. Price Patterns: The Cost of Major Durables
7. Credit Patterns: Sources and Users of Credit
8. Family Finances: Debts and Assets
9. The Marginal Families: Consumption and Insolvency
10. Consumer Problems I: Shady Sales Practices
11. Consumer Problems II: Consequences of Missed Payments
12. Coping Patterns: Apathy, Ignorance and Ineffectiveness
13. Conclusions: Theoretical Observations and Practical Recommendations

The opening chapter, the introduction, provides a statistical portrait of the low-income consumers under study. The second chapter is based on depth interviews with approximately 25 merchants in the low-income community and it is entirely qualitative. (Chapters 4 through 12 are based on the survey of approximately 450 low-income households.) Chapter 3, "Buying Patterns," introduces a key variable, consumer activity, based on the number of major appliances owned. This variable is measured by an index of the number of appliances. This dependent variable is then analyzed in terms of the characteristics of the families, for example, family size, ethnicity, education of the family head, family income, and occupation. This bundle of social characteristics serves as the independent variables used to analyze the various facets of consumer behavior.

Chapters 4 and 5 take up another aspect of consumer behavior, where the consumers buy their goods. Chapter 4 constructs a new dependent variable, shopping scope, based on the number of appliances that were purchased outside the immediate neighborhood. This variable is analyzed in terms of the same independent variables used in the previous chapter. Chapter 5 takes up a phenomenon common in low-income areas, buying from door-to-door peddlers, whose traditional slogan is "a dollar down, a dollar a week," although given inflation, it is no doubt now several dollars down and several dollars a week. Again an index was made of this new dependent variable, the frequency of purchasing major durables from door-to-door peddlers and again this dependent variable is analyzed in terms of the same cluster of independent variables.

Chapter 6 takes up another facet of consumer behavior: price. Consumers who spent a lot of money on their television sets are contrasted with those who paid relatively little. The same independent variables are used to examine the correlates of price. Chapter 7 takes up yet another facet of consumer behavior, method of payment. A new dependent variable is constructed: those who never use credit, those who use it occasionally, and those who use it frequently; the same patterns of analysis are followed. Chapter 8 deals with family finances and reviews the assets of the family, such as savings and insurance, and its debts. This information is used to construct an index of family insolvency. Chapter 9 relates the family insolvency index both to the social characteristics used as independent variables in the preceding chapters and to the various indices of consumer behavior developed in the preceding chapters. Chapters 10 and 11 deal with the consumer problems the families have, including their being victims of fraud. The final data chapter deals with how the families cope with their problems.

The organization of *The Poor Pay More* is typical of a special population study. Each chapter takes up another facet of the phenomenon under study, the consumer behavior of low-income families. How active are they as consumers, where do they shop, how much do they pay, and what method of payment do they use? What is their financial situation, what consumer problems do they have, and finally how do they cope or not cope with their problems?

The Working Addict, another special population study, follows a similar format. The book has eight chapters and, as is true of the others, the opening chapter provides a statistical portrait of the social characteristics of the people being studied. Chapter 2 then describes the drug history of the working addicts, what drugs they use, how much they use, how long they have been using drugs, and so on. Chapter 3 describes their work history, what jobs they have had, what job they most recently had, how long they had held their job, their income from work, and so on. Chapter 4, "Labor Force Participation and the Drug Habit," pulls together the themes of Chapters 2 and 3. Here we examine the age of addiction and whether addiction preceded or followed labor force participation. The cost of drugs and method of payment for drugs are dealt with here, and whether the addicts used drugs while on the job is considered as well. "The Impact of Drugs on the Job," Chapter 5, deals with the impact of drugs on job performance. This is followed by "The Drug Culture and the Work Place," which examines the extent to which co-workers use drugs, whether drugs are purchased at the work place, and time spent with co-workers using drugs. The final data chapter, Chapter 7, examines the extent to which these working addicts are involved in the broader drug culture, that is, whether they hang out with other addicts and engage in criminal activities to support their drug habit.

A Note on Typology

The assumption in this discussion has been that the three types of study are mutually exclusive. In fact, this need not be the case. Some studies can combine the logic of a major independent variable study and a major dependent variable study, with half of the analysis treating the critical phenomenon as an independent variable and the other half treating it as a dependent variable. A case in point is provided by a student of mine who is currently writing her dissertation on unmarried, teen-age mothers. She has a sample of more than 400 such girls. If this were all she had, she would have a special population study. But in addition, she has a sample of teen-age girls from the same culture who are not mothers who serve as the control group. In the first part of her dissertation, she will treat teen-age motherhood as a dependent variable. She will have chapters examining the social characteristics of teen-age mothers in contrast with the nonmother teen-agers and she will compare the sexual activities of the two groups of girls. These chapters will help answer the question of why some teen-agers become pregnant and have children. The second part of the dissertation will treat teen-age motherhood as the independent variable. Here the student will be examining the consequences of teen-age motherhood. How do the teen-age mothers compare with the nonmothers with respect to schooling? Do they remain in school or do they drop out? And what about their work histories? And what about their social and psychological adjustment? Such a study is a mixture of the first two types.

What if this student did not have the control group of teen-agers who are not mothers? How could she tell her story if she had data only on the special population of teen-age mothers? An obvious organizational principle for such a report would be a chronological reconstruction of the process. The first chapter might describe the social characteristics of these girls, and census data on the population social characteristics might be used for comparison. The subsequent chapters might take up each phase of becoming a teen-age mother, beginning with sexual experiences. How sexually active were these teen-age mothers? At what age did they first have intercourse and how often and with how many different boys? Did they use birth control devices and did they become pregnant because they did not use these devices? The next chapter might deal with the decision to have the child rather than an abortion. To what extent was abortion a realistic alternative for these girls? Did they know about abortions? Could they have afforded abortions? Did they want abortions? Did they discover they were pregnant only when it was too late to have an abortion? The third chapter in this reconstruction of the saga might deal with each girl's relationship with the baby's father. Does she wish she could marry the father and if so, why can't she? Does she even know who the father is? The fourth chapter might deal with prenatal care. Did the girl receive any medical assistance prior to the birth of her child, and if so, where? A fifth chapter might deal with the birth itself. Where was the child born, at home or in a hospital? What were the arrangements for the birth? To what extent did the girl receive support and encouragement from her family? A sixth chapter might deal with the arrangements for caring for the baby. Which teen-age girls take care of their babies themselves, and which have their babies cared for by relatives, and which teen-age mothers put their babies up for adoption? Subsequent chapters might deal with the adjustments of the teen-age mothers. How many of them go back to school and graduate from high school? How many go to work and if so, what kinds of jobs do they get? And what is the mental health of these teen-age mothers? Are they happy? Depressed? What kinds of social adjustments have they made? Although I know nothing about teen-age mothers, even this nonexpert had no difficulty developing a valid table of contents for a study of the subject.

The reader might invent a research topic and try developing the table of contents for such a report. For example, what would the table of contents for a study of women architects look like? How would it appear if there were control groups of women in different occupations or nonworking women and what would it look like if the sample consisted of only women architects? Suppose it were a study of the morale of assemblyline workers or a study of fear of crime or a study of sterilization as a method of birth control? The key message of this chapter is that a table of contents for any of these studies can be developed without ever looking at the data or running a single table. If I have succeeded in convincing the reader that this is possible, then I will have made a major contribution to the research process. The number of successful authors should increase dramatically.

16

The Principles of Sociological Writing

Social scientists, especially sociologists, have been sharply criticized in the lay press for their writing style. The consensus is that most sociologists don't know how to write. Their prose is obtuse, obscure, even close to illiterate. This is a serious indictment, for there is a close connection between writing and thought. Fuzzy writing is the product of fuzzy thinking. Clear writing stems from clear thinking, and those who cannot write well probably cannot think well. To be a good writer one must understand what one wants to say. It is no accident that seminal thinkers like Freud and Marx wrote extremely well. Since it is very difficult if not impossible to teach people to think clearly, one might suppose that any discussion of the art of writing is a hopeless task. But the central thesis of this chapter is that there are certain principles of good writing, which, if adhered to, can improve significantly the writer's prose style.

Society's guardian of good writing is the editor. It is the editor who improves the prose of the author, and many successful authors are deeply indebted to their editors. The task of this chapter is to describe what the good editor does. By reviewing the work of the editor, principles of good writing are likely to emerge. As the dedication of this book shows, my training in methodology was at the hands of Paul F. Lazarsfeld. Part 3 of this text is based on what I learned from Lazarsfeld. My mentor for editing is the other famous teacher I had at Columbia, Robert K. Merton. As many sociologists know from their own experience and what I tried to show in a

1977 essay,* Robert Merton is a great editor and much of what I say in this chapter is based on his editorial work.

There are two types of editing, *copy* editing and *rough* editing, and editors generally specialize in only one. Copy editing deals with the style of the prose and is carried out by blue penciling the manuscript, making corrections, additions, and deletions. Copy editors help authors write the sentences and paragraphs that express their ideas. Rough editors, in contrast, are concerned with the substance of the story and how it is being told. If copy editors correct words and sentences, rough editors take on the organization of chapters and entire books. Rough editors may conclude that a chapter should be omitted or added or is out of place. Their task is to help the author tell the story correctly and to make sure that the story itself is correct and true. The rough editor is like a silent partner in the enterprise, a hidden author. Although rough editing comes before copy editing, this chapter takes up copy editing first because it is less complicated than rough editing.

COPY EDITING

Copy editors perform a number of important functions. At the very least, they correct the punctuation, spelling, and grammar of the text. But good copy editors do much more. They banish offensive words, exorcise awkward phrases, spot redundancies, eliminate hyperbole, substitute better words for the words in the manuscript, and occasionally contribute substantively to the story by adding new clauses, sentences, and even paragraphs that clarify the thought.

Both my dissertation and first book, *The Poor Pay More*, were copy edited by Robert K. Merton, and I illustrate these functions of the copy editor by drawing upon these materials.

Banishing Offensive Words

Sociologists are notorious for using offensive words that never should appear in print. Sociologists are fond of neologisms and are even prone to inventing these words themselves. There may be nothing more offensive than adding the suffix "wise" to a noun to connote "regarding" or "pertaining to" as in such monstrosities as "healthwise," "statuswise," or "classwise." But perhaps equally offensive are verbs made out of nouns or adjectives by adding "ize" as in "finalize," "bureaucratize," or "operationalize." Converting nouns into verbs in this fashion is a disease of government bureaucrats as well as social scientists; not only should such words be banished from the profession, but I would be in favor of banishing their

---

*David Caplovitz, "The Other Mertons," *Contemporary Sociology* 6, No. 2, 142–150 (March 1977).

users as well. Also offensive are the pretentious words that become fashionable on their way to being cliches: "exponential," "parameter," "quintessential," and "interface," for example. A good copy editor expunges such pretentious words.

The computer has given rise to a new rash of neologisms, and unless this emerging practice can be nipped in the bud, we run the risk of destroying the English language. Since the computer is capable of labeling tables by printing out the names of variables, short code names are developed for variables. These names have great value in table running, but a new breed of researchers has come to treat these code names as real words, using them in reports. I have seen dissertations that use these code names in the text. For example, in a study of faculty members, the code name "ressup" was assigned to the variable "received research support." Incredibly enough, the student refers to "ressup" in his text, and these code names are even showing up in journal articles. Unless we are prepared to live with "librad" (liberal–radical), "aborthealth" (abortion because of danger to mother's health), "seccar" (second career), and "hideg" (highest degree)—and preside over the death of the English language—we teachers of methodology must drill into our students the message that they can never use the code names for their variables in their texts.

Omitting Needless Words

As E. B. White tells us, that guardian of the language, William Strunk, Jr., would admonish his students to "omit needless words"; he was so enamored of this rule, in fact, that he would repeat it over and over again.* Even good writers will find that their prose frequently carries excess baggage. Avoiding needless words is not only economical, but it sharpens the prose. This can be illustrated by samples of Merton's copy editing of my book *The Poor Pay More*.

Rarely are words simply deleted by the copy editor. Reducing the number of words frequently involves substituting words, inserting new words, and rearranging words. One of the rare instances in which Merton simply eliminated words without adding anything is the following sentence:

DC: Short of persuading these families not to consume, the most desirable change that could be brought about in their shopping patterns would be to get them to buy for cash instead of credit.

RKM: Short of persuading these families not to consume, the most desirable change in their shopping patterns would be to get them to buy for cash instead of credit.

Here Merton slashed the phrase "that could be brought about," saving five words, without in any way changing the meaning of the sentence.

*William Strunk, Jr. and E. B. White, *The Elements of Style*, New York: Macmillan, 1959.

More typically, the process of omitting needless words involves rearranging the words, adding words, and substituting words as in the following examples:

DC: In this section, we consider the economic and social costs of insolvency. (12 words)

RKM: Insolvency presumably has its economic and social costs. (8 words)

DC: At several points in the interview families were asked whether they were having difficulty financing certain necessities of life. (19 words)

RKM: Families were variously asked about possible difficulties in meeting certain necessities of life. (13 words)

DC: Such incidents are particularly pathetic because of the kind of double jeopardy in which the consumer is placed. (18 words)

RKM: In these cases, the consumer is subjected to a kind of double jeopardy. (13 words)

DC: Our society, more than any other, has witnessed the development of institutions through which expert knowledge and skill are applied to the solution of human problems. (26 words)

RKM: More than ever before, American society has developed institutions for applying expert knowledge and skill to the solution of human problems. (21 words)

DC: Of course, it is the consumer's traditionalism that also underlies the dysfunctions of the system. (15 words)

RKM: The consumer's traditionalism also makes for the dysfunctions of the system. (11 words)

DC: Put in raw numbers, we tried at one time or another to interview 555 families and of this number, viable interviews were obtained from 464. (26 words)

RKM: Put in raw numbers, some 555 families were selected for interviewing and of this number usable interviews were obtained from 464. (21 words)

In each of these examples, Merton rearranges words, substitutes words, and adds as well as deletes words; in so doing he sharpens the prose. In some instances a copy editor might delete an entire sentence, as Merton deleted "It is to these questions that we now turn." Beside the deletion Merton wrote: "I've eliminated a score or so of these needless pointers to each act of the play, the stagehands and the winch operating the backdrop." Somewhat insecure writers rely on rhetoric to keep track of their story, and Merton's point is that these flags are not necessary.

The savings are more substantial in longer passages, as the following examples show:

DC: More than half of those currently in debt to peddlers have been dealing with the same man for more than a year. About a third have been buying from him for more than two years and 11 families have dealt with the same peddler for over five years. (48 words)

RKM: More than half of those in debt to peddlers had been dealing with the same man for more than a year; about a third, for more than two years and 11 families, for over five years. (36 words)

DC: By reading across each row of the table, it can be seen that in every instance it is the families with large consumer debts relative to assets, who are most likely to have experienced difficulty in coping with the necessities of life. (42 words)

RKM: In every instance, it is the relatively insolvent families (those with large consumer debts relative to assets) who most often report difficulty in coping with the necessities of life. (29 words)

In the first of these examples a series of expressions referring to time was sharply reduced; in the second Merton eliminates rhetorical phrases and sharpens the sentence by giving it an active voice.

An even longer passage, consisting of four sentences, resulted in the saving of many words through the labors of the copy editor:

DC: In the remainder of this section we shall be alerted to possible interpretations of this finding. As we proceed to specify the characteristics of the marginal families, we shall consider whether any of them help explain the racial pattern. In the course of this analysis we shall come to learn more about the three racial groups. The first thing to be considered is the possibility that the racial pattern is merely an artifact of differences in age of household head and family size. (83 words)

RKM: The rest of this section will deal with possible interpretations of this finding. Identifying the characteristics of the marginal families may help explain the racial pattern as well as telling us more about the three racial groups. The racial pattern might merely be an artifact of differences in age of household head and family size. (55 words)

All of these examples of omitting needless words came from *The Poor Pay More*. A final example is provided by Merton's commentary on an introductory sociology textbook he was editing:

Au:*   While there are differences among sociologists as in other disci-

---

*"Au" is the traditional copy editor's abbreviation for "Author."

plines, it is in connection with the notion of interaction that it is possible to find the largest single area of consensus.

RKM: This sentence contains a choice selection of "idle words," words that do not work and should therefore not be kept at your expense: "while" as other than a temporal term; "it is in connection with" here wholly superfluous; "it is possible to find," which adds nothing; "area of consensus" as a sad equivalent for "agreement." What you mean to say, I believe, is something like this:

"From this comparison of sociology and the other social sciences we learn that the concept of social interaction is central to sociology. Although not all sociologists agree with this view, more of them accept it than any competing one."

In spite of identifying 14 needless words in this author's sentence, Merton's rewrite contains almost as many words as the original, 39 versus 43.

Exorcising Awkward Phrases and Sentences

Merton found in my work several awkward phrases that he expunged; for example, "durable goods market," which appears in several of the examples in two later sections. But his commentaries to other authors are frequently marked by his identification of awkward phrases and sentences. One of his clients was guilty of the following phrases:

gaining in relative commonness
a public is any group
a sought after state
justice is whatever men agree to enforce
they provide hooks
emotion oriented character of family interaction
a resultant degree of regularized behavior, norms and rules

The last comment led Merton to query the author: "resultant of what?" Other awkward phrases by this author invited the following questions:

Au: Two reputable scientists
RKM: This seems odd usage, implying that there are disreputable scientists. Do you mean scientists of repute?

Au: People have needs—or think they do.
RKM: This may come as something of a shock phrase to students who have been assured throughout the book that people do have needs.

Au: The divorce rate is disturbingly high.

RKM: What would be an appropriate rate of divorce? By what sociological and psychological criteria?*

Sloppy language is conveyed in this commentary by Merton:

> When you write that "the final piece is an AUTHENTIC account of the daily life" . . ., don't you come close to the innuendo that the preceding accounts may not be authentic?

One paragraph in this author's text was shot through with awkward phrases, as Merton notes:

> "A very purposive club"—this seems rather strange phrasing; so, too, "an extremely irrational crowd" and for that matter "a collection of deviants." I question the statement that these are meaningful descriptions. On the contrary, they seem rather odd and awkward phrases.

Another of Merton's authors provides additional examples of awkward phrases:

> "Whyte uses a research objective . . ." An awkward phrasing. Objectives are not ordinarily "used."
>
> "to do research on . . ." seems awkward. Why not: investigate.
>
> When I first read the phrase "to measure their concepts" I found it jarred a bit. When you go on to write of "concepts that are measured" I jump once more. Is it the case that concepts are measured? Or that the phenomena organized in terms of concepts are measured?
>
> "descriptive studies . . . their ability . . ." To my mind a bit awkward to speak of studies having an ability.
>
> "These procedures examine the data to see . . ." It is awkward to anthropomorphize the procedures.
>
> "Such as actually associating, wishing to associate and following as a leader." The last phrase, "following as a leader" is both obscure and awkward. Can you be a little more definite? As I read it this says that a leader follows and I somehow doubt that this is what you mean.
>
> "Performs the collecting after." This is a very awkward phrase. Somehow one does not perform a collecting. Could you say "collects these measures after the items are combined"?

---

*These and all subsequent commentaries from Robert K. Merton's work are his property and are used with his permission.

Redundancies

The good copy editor spots redundancies, which have a way of sneaking into the prose of even relatively good writers. Merton was forever calling his authors' attention to their redundancies. The following samples are from his commentaries on three textbooks that he edited:

> "relatively more specific" = redundancy; more = relatively
>
> "try to develop a method, a disciplined and systematic way of studying human behavior." Redundancy: "way" does not improve upon "method"; "disciplined" contains the idea of "regular and systematic." Why not "a disciplined method of studying human behavior" or "a method of studying human behavior systematically."
>
> "wants to account for and explain . . ." Why say it twice?
>
> "the most basic tool"—belongs in the same kit as "most unique," "very perfect," and "most ideal."
>
> "interactions . . . had with each other." The recurring redundancy. Why not "interactions in a group . . ."?
>
> "unreasoned prejudices." Can prejudices (a judgment formed before due examination, an unconsidered, premature judgment, etc.) be anything but "unreasoned"? Suggest eliminating the redundant "unreasoned."
>
> "The great majority of respondents agreed on and answered the question the same way." Suggest you eliminate "agreed on and," which seems redundant.
>
> "a degree of regularized behavior, norms and rules." Query: What is the student to understand by the implied distinction between "norms" and "rules"?

False Emphasis and Hyperbole

As the guardian of good exposition, Merton was leery of what he called "false emphasis" in the form of italics and exclamation points and the verbal equivalent of false emphasis, "hyperbole." These comments illustrate this view:

> Do eliminate the ! The point is a good one and so stands on its own merits.
>
> "The exciting idea that follows from this is that . . ." The term "exciting idea" is disproportionate to what is being said. In order for an idea to be suitably described as exciting one must, I think, build up to it as having some sort of intellectual excitement.
>
> "Totemism is one of the most important systems of belief." I question the use of that blur word "important." Why is T. important? Important for

what? How are systems of belief graded in importance as this sentence implies? Is totemism more important or less important than, say, belief in competitive sports?

I'd eliminate italics for "add" and "questions." Let the text convey your emphasis.

Substituting and Adding Better Words

As noted, the good copy editor improves the text by finding better words than the words the author has selected. The original words may be weak, ambiguous, or too colloquial or they may be close to cliches. The good copy editor spots these defective words and finds better ones. Again this can be illustrated by Merton's work on my book and dissertation.

DC: Every year, more and more Americans turn to installment credit in order to satisfy their consumer aspirations. Nor are low income families excluded from this path to better living.

RKM: Every year, more and more Americans turn to installment credit to satisfy their consumer aspirations. Nor are low income families excluded from this road to present purchases through future payments.

DC: He is then sold a smaller amount of more expensive goods.

RKM: He is then persuaded to buy a smaller amount of more expensive goods.

DC: To show the full extent of this activity in the durable goods market, we shall examine separately the purchases of furniture and household appliances.

RKM: To appreciate the full extent of this consumption of durable goods we must examine separately the purchases of furniture and household appliances.

DC: To characterize the families that are active in the durable goods market . . .

RKM: To characterize the families actively engaged in buying goods . . .

DC: At first glance it might seem that the peddler's customers must be the most underprivileged members of the low-income group.

RKM: It might seem self-evident that the peddler's customers are the most underprivileged members of the low-income group.

DC: If poverty itself is a major determinant of dealing with peddlers . . .

RKM: If poverty alone largely determines the resort to peddlers . . .

DC: There is considerably more variation in the prices paid for television sets and phonographs than for washing machines.

RKM: The variability of prices paid for television sets and phonographs is far greater than for washing machines.

A number of the changes that the copy editor made in these sentences shortened them, but the main function of the changes was to get rid of weak words, like "there is" as an opening to a sentence, awkward phrases like "durable goods market," and vague words like "areas" and to sharpen the prose, like "appreciated" for "show," "what they buy" for "merchandise," and "overriding all else" for "the main task."

The next two examples involve the same weak word, "factor," which is frequently used by social scientists in their writings:

DC: Even though non-white families are younger and larger in size than the white families, these factors do not account for the differences shown in Table 5.15.

RKM: It is true that non-white families are younger and larger in size than the white families, but this does not account for the differences shown in Table 5.15.

DC: Furthermore, a number of factors such as family income, where the goods were purchased, method of payment and significantly, race, are associated with cost.

RKM: And we shall find that such matters as family income, where the goods were purchased, method of payment and significantly, race, are associated with cost.

The phrase "a number of factors" is indeed weak. Since anything can be a factor, what is a factor?

The next sentence from my dissertation also involves a popular misuse of a word:

DC: The problem of the analysis is to uncover the images of competence held by students and faculty members as revealed by their assessments of each other.

RKM: The problem of the analysis is to uncover the images of competence held by students and faculty members as reflected in their assessments of each other.

The word "reveal" is used frequently when referring to findings, as in the expression "Table X reveals that . . ." But the word "reveals" is more appropriate to detective stories than to social science; it conjures up the surprise solution to a mystery.

The next example also calls attention to a common error in social science writing:

DC: When we distinguish between families who obtained credit at large

"bureaucratic" stores and those who turned to neighborhood
dealers or peddlers for credit, an interesting finding emerges.

RKM: For note how things stand when we distinguish between families
who obtained credit at large "bureaucratic" stores and those who
turned to neighborhood dealers or peddlers for credit.

The offensive phrase in this sentence is "an interesting finding emerges."
Merton circled this phrase and wrote, "this kind of verbiage is anticlimactic."
Another criticism is that it is an editorial. The author who calls something
"interesting" is making a value judgment and praising himself in the process. Unfortunately, social scientists all too often offer these editorials on
their findings, calling them "interesting," "important," or "fascinating."
    Sometimes the copy editor, to increase the clarity of the prose, adds
words to a sentence, but, as the following samples show, these additions are
not needless words. Rather they are very much needed to improve the
prose:

DC: Apart from adjustment to the city is the problem of adjustment to
public housing.

RKM: Apart from adusting to life in the city they must come to terms with
life in public housing.

DC: As the educational level of Negroes increases, trading with peddlers
decreases.

RKM: The higher the level of education among Negroes, the less often
they trade with peddlers.

DC: Among whites, education has no effect.

RKM: Among whites, education plays no part in this pattern of buying.

DC: They are apt to take on more middle class values, values which
frown upon heavy indebtedness and which encourage savings and
postponement of gratifications.

RKM: They are readier to take on the more middle class values, values
which though they are stretched to allow installment buying, frown
upon heavy indebtedness and encourage savings and postponement of gratifications.

The words the copy editor added to these sentences makes them easier to
read and understand.

Sharpening the Prose with New Material

Really good copy editors, like Robert Merton, not only manipulate words,
but they elaborate on the author's ideas by bringing in new material, adding
phrases, clauses, sentences, and even paragraphs. We have already seen

Merton doing this in the last example, adding the clause "though they are stretched to allow installment buying." But he did much more than add an occasional clause. In a chapter of *The Poor Pay More* dealing with insolvency (a classification of families according to how deeply in debt they were) I showed that insolvency was related to worry over financial affairs. To put a brave face on this hardly earth shattering finding, I wrote:

> Not surprisingly, financial worries are strongly related to family solvency . . . This is a rather important finding from the viewpoint of an action program, for it indicates that families will be receptive to efforts to help them cope with their financial problems.

I was so unimpressed with this section of the chapter that in the margin of the copy I sent to Merton I wrote, "Banal, no? Omit, no?" Merton wrote under my comments, "I vote for retaining this . . ." and then in blue ink between the lines of my text he wrote:

> Some of the previous findings may have left the impression that insolvent families go their way, almost as though they were totally unaware of their perilous financial state. This is, of course, possible. In more societies than one, people in chronically difficult circumstances come to take their problems for granted, and in a significant sense do not know that they are in trouble. Is this the case here? Are the insolvent families unconcerned in the sense that they take their condition as inevitable or irremediable? It is of no small interest, as we see from Table 21, that the more objectively difficult their financial state, the more often they worry about it. Evidently they are not resigned to their condition. And this expressed state of concern can provide a basis for organized remedial action among those who need it most.

It should be noted that Merton is building here on my "brave face" for the obvious finding that the insolvent families would be receptive to an action program. But he greatly enriches this thought and converts an obvious finding into an important one.

Elsewhere, Merton added an entirely new paragraph as a result of an idea that occurred to him while reading my text. In a chapter dealing with peddlers and impulse buying, I describe the demonstration party commonly known as a "Stanley Party" at which a housewife invites her friends to her home to meet a company representative who demonstrates various products, giving them the opportunity to purchase the items. Merton read this text and then added this paragraph:

> The entire affair is exotically like the "smallpox" parties before Jenner's discovery of the smallpox vaccine, in which people would be brought together with a victim of the dreaded disease so that after exposure to a mild case they could become immune. The "demonstration parties" are designed for contagion of another sort, in which, under the skilled guidance of a genial salesman, the itch to buy presumably spreads by example and mutual stimulation.

Good copy editors are a frequent source of embarrassment to authors. I was so pleased by this scholarly paragraph that I inserted it in my text and it appears in *The Poor Pay More*. The only problem is that I did not write it.

In this section I have tried to show what a good copy editor does. He, or more frequently she, banishes offensive words, omits needless words, exorcises awkward phrases, identifies redundancies, eliminates hyperbole, substitutes better words for those in the text, and occasionally makes substantive contributions by adding new material to the text.

ROUGH EDITING

The second type of editing is rough editing. The rough editor raises two critical kinds of questions: Is the story that the author is telling accurate? Is it complete? Does the argument make sense? The second is: Is the story being told in a logical way? Is the author communicating the message to the reader? The first question deals with substance and the second with exposition. The good rough editor makes substantial substantive and expositional contributions to the manuscripts. To elucidate the role of the rough editor, I will again draw upon Robert K. Merton, this time, his extensive commentaries to the authors he has edited.

Matters of Exposition

As noted, exposition concerns how the story is being told. Is the author conveying ideas clearly to the reader? Is the prose crisp or sloppy? Does the telling conform to time sequence or does it spill out randomly? After reading through Merton's critical commentaries to authors, I was able to classify his expositional criticisms into seven categories, although there are probably more expositional issues than the following seven:

1. Faulty openings.
2. Faulty endings.
3. Continuity bungling.
4. Need to define concepts.
5. Need for concrete examples.
6. Sloppy, fuzzy writing.
7. Basic structural flaws.

Faulty Openings

Of considerable importance in the effectiveness of the author's ability to communicate with the reader is the way the story begins. Faulty beginnings can confuse readers and turn them off to the point where they stop reading.

Merton often lectured authors on the faulty openings to their books and chapters. Here is a sample from his commentary on a textbook about organizations:

> If this is the first chapter, then you need a fairly detailed introduction, for this chapter now does not introduce the reader to the book: to its purposes, plan, place in "the field" e.g. relation to other books. What is the book designed to accomplish? Why should the student attend to the subject matter of organization at all, and how are you going to help guide him through the maze of materials on this subject? What problems are at the center of attention? . . . The intellectual core of a book is found in its introduction. This supplies the rules governing the construction of the book, the controlling objectives, the plan for getting to these objectives, the obstacles that stand in the way and the means for getting over or around these obstacles, the rationale for writing the book at all, etc.

Merton sets out here what he thinks any opening chapter should accomplish: make clear the objectives of the book, why the topic of the book is important, how the book is organized, and how it will achieve its objectives.

Faulty Endings

Just as the good rough editor zeros in on faulty openings, so he is sensitive to faulty endings. Merton criticizes the ending of one of the chapters of one of his authors as follows:

> This chapter closes rather abruptly and inconclusively with the extract from . . . Do consider adding a conclusion of your own; something that will round off your own discussion.

Merton is offended by the cliche reference to further research that one of his authors uses to end one of his chapters:

> "Further research . . . is certain to be interesting." A lame duck ending? Like other chapters, this one would profit from a conclusion that tells the essentials of the story.

Merton is telling his author that a good ending is one that summarizes the story that has been told.

A chapter of a methods textbook provoked this comment from Merton:

> The concluding paragraph in this chapter seems to me too swift. I think it will be extremely valuable if you were to indicate types of instances in which negative findings of a experiment have been instructive.

As an expert on exposition, Merton's key message to authors is that openings and endings must deal with the story that is being told. The opening should describe the story and its various facets and say what will be done in the book. The ending must tell the reader what has been done in the book, that is, it must summarize the story. In fact, a book is like a table. Before you present the story (the table), you tell the reader what it will be. Then you present the story (the table), and then you tell the reader what the story is (what the table shows) in your summary ending.

Continuity Bungling

A research report tells a story. A story is something that has a beginning, a middle, and an end, and stories are told in that sequence. But all too often authors deviate from this time sequence. They forget to refer to what they have already done, or they leap ahead to conclusions before they present the evidence. Frequently the proper time sequence can be managed by such phrases as "As we have seen," "As we shall show," "As noted before," and the omission of such phrases can make the text jarring.

One variant of continuity bungling is to make references to future discussions without developing those discussions. Merton calls one of his authors on this practice as follows:

> By this time I'm beginning to become a little concerned with the frequency of allusions to later discussions. You did it again here. Sometimes this is unavoidable but it seems to me that here you are just alluding to a subject which you are not discussing at present and it won't be discussed for another two chapters.

Our forgetful authors, as *The New Yorker* would say, are especially guilty of continuity bungling, for they forget that they have dealt with a topic in an earlier chapter. Merton reminds one author of this:

> The R&D studies are introduced here as though the reader were hearing, for the first time, about informal relations in organizations. But remember that the preceding chapter has dealt at length with this. A sentence or phrase should be inserted here to provide some sense of continuity.

And another author is given similar advice:

> This seems to overlap with the discussion in Chapter 6. Shouldn't a cross reference be used to remove the curse of repetitiveness?

Need to Define Concepts and Provide Concrete Examples

Merton was forever telling his authors to define their concepts and provide concrete examples of them. Inasmuch as these particular manuscripts were undergraduate textbooks, Merton would take the perspective of a college freshman and would often conclude that the freshman would get lost without adequate definitions and good concrete examples. The importance that Merton attached to this can be seen from this advice to one of his authors:

> This is a point that applies to the definitions of all the key concepts you introduce: these should be carefully examined to find out if they say exactly what you intend to say. Loosely constructed statements are inevitable in a book of this length. But the one place where looseness, redundancy, vagueness, incompleteness, etc. cannot occur without damaging the worth of the book is in the definition of concepts and the formulation of sociological propositions. As I've said before, and probably to the extent of eliciting nausea, key concepts should be formally defined when they are first introduced and the definitions should be scrutinized to see that they measure up to criteria of definiteness, exactness and adequacy.

And here is Merton reminding an author about the value of illustrative examples:

> This paragraph just cries out for a concrete example in order to insure communication with the reader.

> After the phrase "as a complex structure of roles," you need a parenthetical example that is concrete and can be graphic at once.

> I think you could insert a sentence or two here giving a concrete illustration of the rules for classifying husbands or wives in these categories. It would greatly improve the communication you are striving for in this paragraph.

Sloppy, Fuzzy, Loose Prose

The good rough editor quickly spots sloppy prose, prose that is fuzzy and loose, that obfuscates instead of clarifying. Merton had no tolerance for sloppy prose, as the samples that follow indicate:

> This paragraph does not have coherence or continuity. It seems, rather, to be a collection of notes on distinct matters which you propose to discuss at one point or another. I do not trace the shifts from subject to subject in the paragraph but do ask that you re-examine it from the standpoint of this remark.

Another author was also chastised for being imprecise with his terms:

> I pause here to collect a number of terms that appear to be used here interchangeably, although they are never defined and although sociological usage does not ordinarily treat them as synonymous. Since these various terms all refer to the key "independent variable" in this chapter, it would seem essential to have this cleared up. Here are some of these questionable quasi-synonyms:
>
> group pressures—p. 3
> group influences—p. 3, 7

social influences—p. 3, 4
influenced by social conditions—p. 4
learned and socially conditioned things—p. 4
social pressures—p. 4
particular social and cultural contexts—p. 5
social & cultural influences—p. 5
social differences—p. 5
a learned way of interpreting . . . interactions—p. 8
influenced by social & cultural pressures—p. 8

I don't continue beyond p. 8. It would be helpful to straighten out the key terms, define them in the appropriate place and decide, above all, whether you want to distinguish between social and cultural influences upon (a) attitudes, (b) overt behavior, (c) evaluations (judgments), (d) perceptions etc.

Basic Structural Flaws

The last category I have identified under faulty exposition is what I call basic structural flaws. This refers to lapses in the logic of the story line developed by the author. Has the author arranged pieces in the proper sequence? Do ideas flow in a smooth, orderly fashion? Has something important been left out? Basic structural flaws tend to be those that undermine the organization of the story. One of Merton's authors was criticized for what he left out of his story:

> A matter of general policy: Typically, you move from some materials on nonliterate societies, to contemporary complex societies. This gives your book a kind of polarized quality, with relatively little in between, dealing with complex societies of the past . . . Minor changes, here and there, can somewhat redress these emphases, particularly the relatively great amount of attention accorded nonliterate societies. For example, couldn't you easily adduce examples of diverse items of property from more complex societies, rather than mentioning some nonliterate societies alone and then shifting to a discussion of capitalism and socialism? Walter Hamilton's article on Property in the Ency. of the Social Sciences could alone supply you with enough examples.

Structural flaws involve errors regarding the location of ideas. This can happen in a variety of ways and some are illustrated by the next examples:

> On the question of the organization of the book: Is there any reason for postponing the notions of folkways and mores until the penultimate chapter? Surely, if you discuss these at all, they belong much earlier in the book. You've necessarily implied types of norms in chapter after chapter.

> The whole of this chapter invites the question whether it begins to do justice to the purpose and character of the book. To present the student with a ½ dozen classifications, some of them by your own account, archaic, incoherent and useless, and then to conclude that not much "progress has been made"; is to confront him with occasions for despair rather than to stimulate him to thought

or to educate him. Should you be using up your precious space this way? Perhaps the solution is to dispense with much of the detail of this chapter; refer to the existing classifications in a footnote, explaining briefly why you do not examine them in detail . . . and telescope this chapter with Ch. 2.

To make the drastic recommendation of merging chapters, as Merton does here, is at the heart of the task of the rough editor.

Matters of Substance

As noted, the second major concern of the rough editor is the validity of the author's story. Is it true or not? Is it complete or not? Are the concepts defined correctly or not? Does the author cite the relevant literature? Just as I catalogued different types of expositional criticism, so I have developed categories for Merton's substantive criticisms. I initially identified 17 sub-types, but many of them occurred so rarely that I merely mention them here: unwarranted assumption, faulty logic, false distinction, oversimplification, and self-evident commonplaces. What remained are the following seven categories:

1. Conceptual confusion.
2. False generalizations.
3. Empty assertions.
4. Extreme formulations.
5. Overstatements–understatements.
6. References to literature.
7. Tautologies and nonsequiturs.

Each of these categories is illustrated with excerpts from Merton's commentaries.

Conceptual Confusion

The most frequent type of substantive criticism that the rough editor makes deals with the errors that creep into the author's attempts to define concepts. More often than not, these definitions tend to be confused, ambiguous, murky, incomplete, or incorrect. The following examples of conceptual confusion are taken from Merton's commentaries on three textbooks.

> My point is that at present these key conceptual paragraphs tend to be loose and indefinite, grouping conceptually different matters under some rough heading as "social," "group," "cultural." It would take little to pin these down more definitely rather than allude to them informally. This would give particular point to each of the illustrative studies . . . You do in fact have the

beginnings of a list of "determinants." I suggest only that you highlight these at the outset of this section and so provide a framework for the reader.

SELF IMAGE: Is this simply a set of attitudes toward oneself? If so, what do you understand here by "attitudes"?; a readiness to act in a determinate way? I would suppose that self-image refers to a conception of oneself as having particular characteristics *and* an evaluation of these characteristics. And do consider this business on attitudes; the word is now being used so loosely as to lose almost all meaning.

This sentence seems to me somewhat questionable, if read strictly. A's role as a leader is not DISTINCT from his being an "object" as you suggest. For the role of leader INCLUDES both initiating action and responding to it. (Indeed, at the bottom of the page you imply as much: the dyadic relations are seen there as part of A's role, not as something different from it.

"Concrete indicants or manifestations." Do you really mean "concrete" or "empirical"? Concrete refers to phenomena in all their multitudinous fullness; empirical refers to that which can be perceived. And shouldn't you give the student some notion of the meaning of indicant? Does it include both indicators and "indexes"?

False Generalizations

The rough editor who also happens to be an expert on the subject matter of the book can spot statements that are not true. His keen eye protects the author from the embarrassment of making false statements. This function of the rough editor can be seen from the following excerpts from Merton's commentaries.

"The addition of a new member . . . tends by definition to affect the whole structure of the interdependent parts." This seems overstated to me. You apparently have in mind *small* social social systems where the addition of one member and one role could make a decisive difference. But participant-observers in a good sized community are not apt to "affect the whole structure."

Contrary-to-fact assertion: "It is *only* through communication that one person can influence another and change the direction of his behavior." This runs counter to all experiments and observations on changes of behavior in response to changes in the objective environment . . . Needs to be toned down.

"Since the cluster of elements is exactly the definition we gave to the ideal type." Do you really mean this? Are you saying now that any cluster of elements constitutes an ideal type? I think not.

The next three types of substantive rough editing are variations on false generalizations. Although the statements are not necessarily false, they are not quite true either. These categories are empty assertions, extreme formulations, and overstatements and understatements. These flaws are not as common as the preceding ones.

Empty Assertions

What Merton means by "empty assertion" is a statement that lacks empirical support so that there is no way of knowing whether it is true. Some examples follow:

> "The content of American education is remarkably similar everywhere." Statements of this general kind cannot easily be proved or disproved, since the degree of similarity can only be established by explicit criteria examined comparitively. They therefore tend to be rather empty assertions.

> Why do you even tentatively identify yourself with the vague and difficult to demonstrate thesis that "the nature of his unique genetic inheritance" is "probably most significant" for what the individual learns. Is this a sociological perspective? Will men of approximately the same genetic inheritance among the Bantu and among the British aristocracy learn the same sort of things?

> The emphasis of "education" is "on teaching RATHER THAN ON LEARNING." Will this stand inspection? What is the evidence for an unqualified statement of this kind?

Extreme Formulations

The validity of a proposition or generalization can be undermined not because the idea it contains is false but because it is stated in such an extreme way that its truth is questioned. Some examples follow:

> "Each society has its own basic personality type." Isn't this a rather extreme and unqualified statement? Do the Alorese [the society under discussion] speak for the French, British and Russians?

> The statement of the increasing concentration of ownership and control of the mass media "in the hands of a relatively few people" needs to be sharply qualified. It is far more complicated than this implies, and surely Siepmann does not demonstrate this to be so.

> "This pattern is based on the physical environment." Isn't this an excessive statement, unless you mean by "based" that it takes place in a physical environment, which scarcely needs to be said.

Overstatements and Understatements

Still another way in which the validity of generalizations can be undermined is by being overstated or understated. The author either inflates the statement, putting more into it than it can support, or underplays it, thus robbing it of its forcefulness. Merton would occasionally chastise authors for one or the other of these sins, as the following examples show:

> "mass media present on one-way traffic pattern"—isn't it somewhat overstated? From the standpoint of propagandists, potential recipients have considerable powers of resistance and (indirect) control. They can question and do; they can deny and do. And as you say, most of all, they can, and mostly do, refuse to pay attention. So far as I know, it would be obsolete to say that the potential audience "can only play the role of the passive receiver of messages."

> "The national state . . . as the respository of man's greatest loyalty." Do you really mean "greatest"? In what sense and on what grounds? As against the family?

> "A nuclear war might well destroy modern urbanism." I know what you intend to say here but this sentence seems such an understatement as to be self-defeating. The reader may find himself asking is "urbanism" the significant casualty in a nuclear war?

References to the Literature

Still another way in which the good rough editor improves the manuscript and fills gaps in the story is to refer the author to literature relevant to the points being made. Merton was forever calling his authors' attention to the literature, as the following examples indicate:

> Why not indicate the parable by source: Russell H. Conwell, Acres of Diamonds, is by far the best known version of it.

> The discussion of incest-taboo is so close to that of Kingsley Davis, Human Society, 401–4, that you might want to cite his discussion as well as Murdock.

> On Upward Mobility, why not cite pertinent items in Lipset-Bendix volume?

Tautologies and Nonsequiturs

The final categories of substantive rough editing are tautologies and nonsequiturs. There are so few of these criticisms in Merton's work that I have grouped them together. The following are examples of these criticisms:

> As Deutsch's experiment is briefly described, it sounds very much like a tautology: "cooperative groups" communicate more, accept more, are more friendly (i.e. are more cooperative). Don't you need to say a little more, perhaps in an additional sentence, to eliminate this unfounded sense of tautology?

> The last part of this paragraph approaches, if it does not actually achieve, a tautology. I refer to this: ". . . to the extent that people . . . do *not* act the way

others expect them to, there is greater readiness to change the patterns of social interaction AND LESS TENDENCY FOR THEM TO PERSIST." But if they do not conform to expectation, i.e. if they act in ways other than the previous patterns of interaction than by description the patterns do not persist. What are you gaining by this?

In two sentences you make "physical violence" the nub of the types of conflicts you don't like and then you follow this by reference to "emotional personal attacks (the meaning of this phrase is not clear), smear campaigns, lies," etc. This may not be a non-sequitur in the logical sense, but it is as a matter of exposition.

"For the biological differences among men are negligible in comparison with their similarities, yet the variations in beliefs, in social interaction, institutions and customs are enormous." The point you want to make is sound. But you do not make it with the result that this is close to being a non-sequitur.

The review of tautologies and nonsequiturs brings to a close our analysis of the role of the rough editor. In this chapter, the role of the editor has been described in some detail. The purpose of this exercise has been to impart principles of good writing by showing the broad range of writing flaws that the good editor corrects. The level of sociological writing will improve if authors avoid the kinds of pitfalls that have been enumerated in this chapter.

Afterword

As I noted in the preface, this textbook is the outgrowth of more than 30 years in the research business. As a research academic I have been surprised through the years at how few of my colleagues had truly mastered the skills of social research. Most of them had not been provided with the opportunities that I had, primarily my 12-year apprenticeship at Columbia's Bureau of Applied Social Research. This experience made clear to me that the only way in which people learn about research is by working on research projects and being exposed to all the various phases of the research process. I designed this book as an approximation of an apprenticeship on a large-scale research project.

As the reader now knows, this book is organized in terms of the major stages of a large study. The first section acknowledges a hard fact of research life, that research can be done only if the researcher can raise money. Having been a student and disciple of Paul F. Lazarsfeld, I have come to appreciate the virtues of the case method that he championed as the way of teaching research skills, and following his edict, this section is based almost entirely on the case method, presenting examples of winning and losing proposals. The case method was maintained through most of the book, from cases of questionnaires being developed (Chapter 6), cases of qualitative data being used in a quantitative study (Chapter 7), cases of multivariate analysis (Chapter 11), panel analysis (Chapter 13), and contextual analysis (Chapter 14), to cases of report organization (Chapter 15) and copy editing and rough editing (Chapter 16).

The research style that is at the heart of this book is survey research, that is, research that collects data by asking people questions. Part 2, Data Collection, was centered on the research instrument of surveys, the questionnaire.

Chapter 5 presented a portrait of the questionnaire and how it evolved over time. Chapter 6 presented histories of questionnaires as a way of learning how to construct questionnaires, and Chapter 7 dealt with the role of qualitative data in questionnaires.

Once the data are collected they must be analyzed, and Part 3 was concerned with data analysis. I could remember how insecure I felt as a graduate student when I had to confront tables, and I am convinced that many graduate students feel as uncomfortable with tables as I did. I thus devised as the first chapter of data analysis the presentation of tables. This chapter is intended to help students present their data in tabular form and acquaint them with the principles of reading tables. I then moved on to the topic of constructing variables, index formation, dealt with in Chapter 9. The next three chapters deal with the analysis of data. Chapter 10 is about the analysis of two variables and Chapter 11, the analysis of three variables. The exposition of tabular analysis in these chapters opens the book to the criticism of touting the methodology of the 1950s. To counteract this criticism, I commissioned a chapter on regression analysis (Chapter 12), the research tool that is dominant today. Part 3 then moved on to two topics of data analysis that are not given much currency in methods textbooks, longitudinal studies and contextual analysis.

Once the data are analyzed, the researcher must write a report, and the last section of this book tried to come to grips with this difficult task. Chapter 15 deals with the critical topic of organizing the research report. The theme of this chapter is that the researcher must first organize the table of contents before he or she can even analyze the data, much less write a report. The chapter is an attempt to explain how tables of contents can be organized. The final chapter, Chapter 16, is about the principles of good writing. Such principles are presented through an analysis of the role of the editor, the guardian of good writing.

By elucidating the tasks of the researcher, from fund raising, through data collection, data analysis, and report writing, this book, I hope, will make some contributions to research. A minimum goal has been to take the fear out of the research process, the fear of proposal writing and report writing and the fear of data analysis. If readers of this book come to feel a little more confident when they confront these research tasks, I will feel that I have succeeded.

As far as I know, no one has ever done research on why people write books. I suspect that one motive is to make money, for textbooks that are widely adopted do make considerable money for their authors. But apart from any other motives, an important reason for my writing this book has been pure enjoyment. I had considerable fun working on this project, setting out my pet ideas, from the sin of crass empiricism and the D ratio for measuring competence, to how to package proposals, the typology of tables, the empirical bases of typologies, my further elaboration of Lazarsfeld's elaboration scheme, the contextual fallacy, the types of research reports and the various kinds of rough editing and copy editing. When one's work becomes fun, one is truly living.

INDEX